THE JOSSEY-BASS
HIGHER AND ADULT EDUCATION SERIES

LEARNING COMMUNITIES

Reforming Undergraduate Education

Barbara Leigh Smith

Jean MacGregor

Roberta S. Matthews

Faith Gabelnick

JOSSEY-BASS
A Wiley Imprint
www.josseybass.com

Published by Jossey-Bass
A Wiley Imprint
989 Market Street, San Francisco, CA 94103-1741   www.josseybass.com

Jossey-Bass books and products are available through most bookstores. To contact Jossey-
Bass directly call our Customer Care Department within the U.S. at 800-956-7739, outside the U.S. at 317-572-3986 or fax 317-572-4002.

Jossey-Bass also publishes its books in a variety of electronic formats. Some content that
appears in print may not be available in electronic books.

For credits, see page 399.

Library of Congress Cataloging-in-Publication Data
Learning communities : reforming undergraduate education / Barbara L. Smith . . .
[et al.].— 1st ed.
     p. cm.
   Includes bibliographical references and index.
   ISBN 0-7879-1036-8 (alk. paper)
   1. College teaching—United States. 2. Group work in education—United States. 3.
Interdisciplinary approach in education—United States. 4. Education, Higher—
Curricula—United States. I. Smith, Barbara Leigh.
 LB2331.L392 2004
 378.1'2—dc22   2004008843

Printed in the United States of America
FIRST EDITION
HB Printing   10 9 8 7 6 5 4 3 2 1

CONTENTS

PART FIVE
Conclusion

INTRODUCTION

IN 1984, the Study Group on the Conditions of Excellence in American Higher Education wrote a report that would influence the next decades of educational theory and practice in the United States. *Involvement in Learning: Realizing the Potential of American Higher Education* declared that students would prosper intellectually and socially in academic environments that were supportive and challenging, in classes that included interdisciplinary perspectives, and in spaces where dynamic, engaged dialogues could occur. As part of their overall recommendations, the authors called on all institutions in higher education to create learning communities organized around specific intellectual themes or tasks (National Institute of Education, 1984). They believed that learning communities could be widely adapted in different institutional settings in order to create more engaging and effective learning environments and to address a variety of issues in undergraduate education. This important recommendation foreshadowed by almost ten years what would become a key component for reform in higher education.

Our first book, *Learning Communities: Making Connections Among Faculty, Students, and Disciplines,* was published in 1990. We had all been actively involved in establishing and leading learning communities for at least ten years. We believed passionately then, as we do today, that learning communities offer an effective and efficient strategy for deepening student and faculty involvement in learning and for supporting institutional transformation. Our intention in that first book was to set out a clear definition of learning communities, describe five models of learning communities that were then being used on many campuses, and provide various concrete examples of how to begin and implement learning communities. We gathered narratives from the learning community pioneers of the 1970s and 1980s who attested to their extraordinary and often unexpected insights into the teaching and learning process, and we reported on the then-current knowledge about how to build pedagogically active, engaged learning environments. To our surprise and great pleasure, we discovered that our little book found its way onto hundreds and hundreds of campuses, becoming a handbook for learning community development.

We always knew, however, that the book was a first attempt to describe learning communities and not a comprehensive text. If our vision was to show how learning communities could play a part in transforming higher education, then learning communities needed to be set in a much larger framework. In the late 1980s, as we prepared our manuscript, there were not yet enough assessment data available to support what we intuitively assumed: that learning communities could become a vital element of the educational landscape. In this book, we are able to provide literally hundreds of resources and references to illustrate the new knowledge gained about how people learn and in what arenas learning communities can flourish.

Now, at the beginning of the twenty-first century, learning communities are found in hundreds of colleges and universities, including two- and four-year institutions and public and private colleges and universities. We think they have become a national movement, purposefully engaging faculty, staff, administration, and students in creating active learning environments that prepare students for work and living in a complex world. The *National Survey of Student Engagement* (2002) found that participation in learning communities was positively correlated with all of its five benchmarks: diversity experiences, student gains in personal and social development, practical competence, general education, and overall satisfaction with the undergraduate college experience. On those campuses that have initiated and sustained learning communities, these and related outcomes have become predictable. This book attempts to illustrate how learning communities can be a versatile and effective approach in enhancing student learning and student success, promoting curricular coherence and faculty revitalization, and in some institutions, becoming a key element in institutional transformation.

Still, difficult questions remain: Through what visions, strategies, and resources will learning communities be able to endure? And in what ways will they have a deep and lasting impact on higher education? History tells us that educational reform efforts do not necessarily create large-scale institutional or cultural transformations. Many fail to live up to their original vision and potential and disappear with little enduring impact. Whether this will be true of the learning community movement remains to be seen. The reality is that although many learning community programs are just beginning to be created, quite a number have been in existence for more than ten years. And therefore, many of these more mature learning communities are now encountering the challenges of sustainability as their founders retire from higher education. We recognize that, like all broad movements, learning communities vary greatly in terms of goals, quality, and practice, and we recognize that continuing to ask hard questions about the congruence between our theory and our practice is one way to sustain the integrity of this movement.

In this new book, written almost fifteen years after the first, we report on the current state of learning community practice. We discuss some of the richest arenas for future learning community development and ask the types of hard questions about learning communities that are crucial if they are to realize their full potential. This book moves between theory and practice and incorporates the perspectives of key thinkers in higher education, linking those perspectives to learning community development and implementation. Yet even as this book goes to press, new information is being added, new learning communities are being launched, and older ones are being transformed because of changes in leadership and institutional strategy. This book, then, is at once a work in progress and a story of what we currently know. Like most stories, it has a point of view and a purpose. The particular programs and institutions that are mentioned are to be seen as exemplars for best practices. In a few years, other institutions might be used. Similarly, we recognize that named leaders of learning communities will change, but their reflections on their experiences will endure as guides for new adopters.

Throughout the book, we attempt to provide a broad view of relevant research and practice pertaining to each chapter's focus so that each chapter can stand on its own or be linked to other chapters. We encourage our readers to use this book as a resource and a guide, and we hope that the reference materials that are cited will encourage further investigations and linkages.

Scope of the Book

Chapter One lays out the contemporary forces shaping higher education and the major studies on undergraduate education reform. In a rapidly changing educational landscape, educational innovation is much needed but also hard to sustain. We assert in this chapter and throughout the book that learning communities can address many of these critical forces if an institution is strategic and intentional in its implementation.

Chapter Two provides a detailed history of learning communities, examining their growth as a national movement and describing some of the challenges facing contemporary learning communities. The history of learning communities is rich with many continuing themes about the relationship between education and democracy and how to cultivate effective educational communities that foster deep learning and social responsibility.

Chapter Three describes three primary learning community structures and the factors that influence choosing a specific curricular framework. We have intentionally avoided the word "model" in describing different types of learning communities because our experience has shown that those who have created learning communities inevitably adapt them to their particular institutional culture and resource base. We therefore focus here on major approaches-frameworks-structures to develop learning communities.

Chapter Four describes five core practices that we believe are key to vibrant and successful learning communities. These core practices reflect the research on teaching and learning from the past decade, and they support current and future thinking about creating effective learning environments for teachers and for students. Throughout this chapter, and indeed throughout book, we stress that there is no one learning community structure, and no one fixed list of pedagogical practices, appropriate for all settings or time frames. In fact, learning communities have been widely adopted precisely because they lend themselves to different institutional environments.

Chapters Five and Six focus on the use of learning communities in several important institutional contexts—the first year of college, general education, and developmental education. Although learning communities can be instituted in almost any area of the curriculum, we believe that *strategically* placing them in certain critical areas makes good sense, especially in a time of limited resources. In many institutions learning communities are situated in the freshman year as a means of building community and addressing the serious issue of student attrition. Some institutions have gone so far as to make learning communities a major part of their general education program. Chapter Five reviews the important scholarship and research on general education and on the first-year college experience while situating learning communities within this larger literature. Chapter Six focuses on learning communities in developmental education, an area of the curriculum where too many students are lost. In a time when nearly everyone goes to college, but access is far ahead of student success, this is a vitally important arena for educational improvement. The issues raised in this chapter go to the heart of our commitment to creating successful educational experiences for everyone, but as this chapter demonstrates, there is a large and enduring contradiction in our policies and practices in serving under-prepared students.

Chapter Seven provides a detailed discussion of assessment and learning communities, describing assessment approaches and results. The argument is made in this chapter that assessment is integral to all stages of learning community planning and development. Furthermore, assessment should be used to improve learning community programs and to demonstrate that they are effective. We view assessment as a pedagogy as well, and contend that assessment should be embedded in learning community classroom practices.

Chapter Eight focuses on the challenges of recruiting and supporting learning community teachers and ensuring successors for those who are or will soon be retiring from academia. A variety of approaches to faculty and staff development are described as well as crucial issues that need to be addressed in these domains. Colleges and universities are underinvesting in faculty development, which needs to be viewed as a collective enterprise linked to the ongoing viability of an institution. On some campuses, learning communities are forging new visions of what an academic community can be: a strong venue for doing good work, feeling the support and stimulation of kindred spirits, and continuous learning.

Chapter Nine discusses the process of implementing learning communities. The endurance of the learning community effort depends on the institution's strategic understanding of why learning communities are important and their ability to support this vision. Because they have been implemented in hundreds of different institutional environments, we now have a sense of the critical factors in making these change efforts successful. Moving from scattered small-scale innovations to more transformative efforts requires careful attention to sustainability issues. Many learning communities are now facing the issue of how to extend their reach beyond the early adopters and become institutionalized.

Chapter Ten concludes this book, presenting an overview of lessons from the contemporary learning community movement and our thoughts on challenges for the future.

Acknowledgments

It has been a privilege for the four of us to support the growth of learning communities over the past twenty-five years. We have been inspired by the creativity and commitment of our higher education colleagues across the nation as they have made this work their own. In writing this book we wish to acknowledge with respect and affection those hundreds of faculty, staff, and students who, through their incredible efforts, have offered us the content for our work. The voices of many of these people are anonymously quoted as colleagues in this book.

There are many, many other colleagues who have read and reacted to drafts of this text. We wish to thank Harold November, and the late

Emmanuel "Manny" Lerner and Robert Frase, alumni of the original Experimental College at the University of Wisconsin. These gentlemen are a testimony to the power of genuine learning communities.

We are deeply grateful to Mervyn Cadwallader, Rob Cole, K. Patricia Cross, Lynn Dunlap, Jerry Gaff, John Gardner, Larry Geri, Al Guskin, Jim Harnish, Jean Henscheid, Patrick Hill, Mary Marcy, Bob Schoenberg, Rita Smilkstein, and Pete Sinclair, who gave freely of their time and wisdom to read and comment on parts of this book.

Those who were interviewed for this book or who have generously shared valuable information on their learning community programs over many years include: Sharon Anthony, Cindy Avens, Gail Bakst-Jarrett, Carl Barrentine, Karen Barrett, Kerry Beckford, Jack Bennett, Glenn Blalock, Aaron Brower, Gary Brown, Corly Brooke, Jerry Cederblom, Marcos Cicerone, Chuck Colarulli, Grant Cornwell, Ken Cutright, Connie Della-Piana, Mary Donnelly, Skip Downing, Lynn Dunlap, Ann Dwyer, Jim Dybikowsky, Marie Eaton, Kimberly Eby, the late Becky Edgerton, Phyllis Endicott, Scott Evenbeck, Ben Flores, Julia Fogarty, Robert Fowler, William Fritz, Jeffrey Froyd, Joan Graham, Richard Guarasci, Doug Gruenewald, Maurice Hamington, Debora Hammond, Neal Harris, Julie Helling, Maria Hesse, Katherine Holman, Becky Hopkins, Mary Huba, Rosetta Hunter, Barbara Jackson, Robin Jeffers, Sue Jenson, Sherwood Johnson, Michaelann Jundt, Buzz Kellogg, Peter Kennedy, Bruce Koller, Will Koolsbergen, Jodi Levine Laufgraben, Gary Longstreet, Tom Lowe, Anne Mahoney, Marybeth Mason, Pam Meyer, Teresa Michals, Frankie Minor, Linda Mitchell, Linda Hamman Moore, Ed Morante, Jacque Mott, Sally Murphy, John O'Connor, Karen Oates, Jane Oitzinger, Judy Patton, Valerie Perotti, Steve Riter, Cheryl Roberts, Marian Rodriguez, David Schoem, Lisa Seale, Julianne Seeman, Frankie Shackelford, Rita Smilkstein, Bill Smith, Edith Sorell, Marilyn Spencer, Eve Stoddard, Edwina Stoll, Jayme Stone, Jan Swinton, Steve Teixeira, Ana Torres Bower, Joseph Tussman, Phyllis van Slyck, Alison Warriner, Roz Weedman, Audrey Wright, Terry Zawacki, and Richard Zelley.

We thank Alan Frantz, Pat Hutchings, Adam Nelson, Kerry O'Meara, Warren Olson, Gene Rice, Jack Schuster, Martha Stassen, John Tagg, and Vincent Tinto, who provided important and useful information, often on work not yet in print, that was very instrumental to our thinking.

We thank Mary Geraci and Sylys Knackstedt, who assisted us with the visuals in this book. Their expertise saved us countless hours.

And finally, we give loving acknowledgment and appreciation to our spouses: Rob Cole, John Howarth, David Paulsen, and Robert Matthews, all gifted teachers whose enduring interest has been deeply important.

In higher education, there has always been a grand vision to build communities of engagement and create teaching and learning environments that enable students to become competent citizens. However, reality has not always matched this vision. The learning community movement developed from a democratic belief that all students have the right to succeed. It has empowered educators to see their classrooms and their roles in new ways, and it continues to offer one of the most adaptive solutions to many of the critical issues facing higher education today and in the future. In writing this book, we affirm those principles of democracy, involvement, thoughtful dialogue, and civic engagement, and we salute the learning community pioneers and future leaders who will continue to improve the ways we learn and live.

We dedicate this book to our longtime friend and colleague Faith Gabelnick who inspired educational reform with "splendid audacity."

THE AUTHORS

Faith Gabelnick was president emerita of Pacific University, Forest Grove, Oregon, and president of Gabelnick Consulting Institute. Prior to her role as president of Pacific University, she served as provost of Mills College and as dean of the Lee Honors College at Western Michigan University. In her capacities as senior administrator and faculty member, she both initiated and supported the development of learning communities and designed and taught in learning communities. Gabelnick's professional focus was on institutional transformation, collaborative learning, and leadership. She led change initiatives throughout her career and embraced learning communities as a key strategy for effecting meaningful and lasting organizational and cultural shifts in how we live and learn together. A frequent writer about organizational leadership and change, Gabelnick's most recent books are *Dynamic Consultation in a Changing Workplace* and *The Psychodynamics of Leadership* (both with Edward Klein and Peter Herr). She passed away in June 2004.

Jean MacGregor, an adjunct faculty member in the Master's of Environmental Studies Program at The Evergreen State College, has both taught in and supported learning community development for the past twenty years. In 1985, she was one of the founding directors (with Barbara Leigh Smith) of the Washington Center for Improving the Quality of Undergraduate Education, a fifty-college grassroots partnership whose focus has been curricular reform and faculty and staff development in the state of Washington. In that capacity, she has supported campuses in Washington and across the nation in launching curricular learning community initiatives, most recently with grant support to the National Learning Communities Project from the Fund for the Improvement of Postsecondary Education (1996 to 1999) and The Pew Charitable Trusts (2000 to 2003). She sees herself as both a student and practitioner in the fields of collaborative learning and community organizing, and believes these foci are central to successful learning community programs. Her writing and consulting work have revolved around learning communities, collaborative learning, student intellectual development, assessment, and student self-evaluation.

Roberta S. Matthews is provost and vice president for academic affairs at Brooklyn College. She served as the first university director of the CUNY Honors College, and as interim president at LaGuardia Community College-CUNY, where she spent many years as an administrator and professor of English; she created and taught in the first learning community there in 1979. Matthews also served as vice president for academic affairs and dean of the faculty at Marymount College in Tarrytown, New York. Her experience in higher education spans public and private, small and large colleges. She has published widely and offered workshops on learning communities and active learning. Throughout her career, she has focused on curriculum and program development, career and institutional development, school-college collaboration, and international education. Through a series of wide-ranging, campus-based projects, she works with faculty, staff, and students to meet the challenges of higher education in the twenty-first century.

Barbara Leigh Smith is a member of the faculty and the former provost and vice president for academic affairs at The Evergreen State College. With Jean MacGregor, she founded the Washington Center for Improving the Quality of Undergraduate Education, a state-supported consortium that has disseminated learning community work throughout the nation. From 2000 to 2004 Smith and MacGregor codirected The Pew Charitable Trust's National Learning Communities Project. Smith believes that we can develop the collective capacity to change our institutions, but it takes persistence, organizational smarts, and rekindling people's sense of hope and personal empowerment. Partnerships between gifted teaching faculty and activist administrators are important in making this happen. Smith has numerous publications on learning communities and reform and experimentation in higher education, including *Against the Current: Reform and Experimentation in Higher Education* (which she edited with Richard Jones), *Reinventing Ourselves* (which she edited with John McCann), and the article, "The Challenge of Learning Communities as a Growing National Movement."

PART ONE

THE CONTEMPORARY AND HISTORICAL CONTEXT OF LEARNING COMMUNITIES

LEARNING COMMUNITIES AND UNDERGRADUATE EDUCATION REFORM

Vital and successful institutions stand out by their ability to maintain direction and a sense of meaning even amid significant shifts in the social landscape. . . . Now, however, as major economic and social change shakes American society, higher education is facing serious tests of its resourcefulness.

—William M. Sullivan

WE STAND AT AN IMPORTANT JUNCTURE in higher education, a time that calls for new levels of resourcefulness in thinking about undergraduate education and the relationships between the academy and its communities. We know more about what promotes student learning than ever before, but we still face considerable challenges in putting what we know into practice. Our students are increasingly diverse and the ways they attend college have changed dramatically in the last thirty years. The bucolic vision of students attending residential colleges has faded as more and more students commute, often attending two or three different institutions during the postsecondary experience. Many simultaneously hold full-time or part-time jobs and have family obligations. They step in and out of our institutions, combining a community college program with on-line courses and a residential experience. At the same time, a college education is becoming increasingly important, as our society's expectations for student performance rise and the emphasis grows on the new skills and abilities everyone needs to navigate and succeed in a changing, multicultural world.

Current faculty members, both those who led and those who resisted curricular change for the past twenty-five years, are retiring, offering an unprecedented opportunity to change the face and philosophy of the professoriate. Still, we know that new faculty are being educated in ways similar to their predecessors. Although there has been some progress in shifting the priorities and rewards to teaching, recent studies suggest that research remains a dominant force in the faculty culture. The nature of academic appointments is also changing, raising a host of questions about the implications for undergraduate education and the nature of community on our campuses. The issues of faculty succession and faculty work life thus become linked with educational reform.

We also find ourselves facing enormous political and financial challenges. Many of the publications cited in this chapter point to a financial crisis in higher education. Administrators spend too much time managing declining resources and trying to figure out ways to sustain their institutions. Our society is verging on an economy that requires nearly universal college attendance, while at the same time the prospective student population is the most diverse in our history. Jane Wellman's monograph *Weathering the Double Whammy* (2003) describes a broad fiscal crisis combined with a minority and immigrant student population that will require larger amounts of financial aid. Thus, access and affordability, hallmark challenges in the late twentieth century, continue to press higher education's social commitment to a better educated society in the twenty-first century. We are being asked to do more with less, to find more effective and less costly ways to improve student learning.

In response to these challenges, learning communities have arisen as one of many reform efforts in undergraduate education. Now offered at more than five hundred colleges and universities, learning communities have become a far-reaching and ambitious movement. Learning communities restructure the curriculum by linking or clustering two or more courses and enrolling a common cohort of students. We believe they are one of the most powerful interventions on the educational landscape because they provide a comprehensive, cost-effective framework for enhancing student learning that is applicable in many different types of institutions. Furthermore, a growing body of research demonstrates their effectiveness in addressing a variety of issues, from student retention to curricular coherence to faculty revitalization. Learning communities have much in common with many other reform efforts in their aspirations for and assumptions about what promotes student learning. Indeed, they provide a structural platform for integrating many of these other reform efforts, such as service learning, collaborative learning, and various inquiry-based approaches to learning.

In this chapter we explore the higher education landscape and the challenges that the academy now faces. This discussion is essential to understanding why higher education is at such an important juncture. We then turn to recent calls for reform that, as we shall see, make increasingly convergent recommendations. Taking on change in a time of limited resources is difficult but necessary. Clearly, we need ways to learn to do our work better and more effectively, to help students become better learners. The chapter concludes by explaining how reforming undergraduate education through learning communities has emerged as one way of accomplishing this.

Challenges to the Academy

New Colleges, New Students, New Challenges

In the last four decades higher education in the United States has been transformed through a dramatic increase in the number and types of colleges and universities and a corresponding increase in student enrollment. The expansion of the higher education system has created unprecedented opportunities for place-bound students. Enrollment in two-year colleges went from fewer than half a million in 1960 to four million in 1980 (Kerr, 1990). Half of all students in the United States today spend their freshman year in a community college. At the same time, institutions of all types have become more comprehensive and wide-ranging in their curricular offerings. Although state-supported colleges and universities educate a growing proportion of all students, new types of institutions have also appeared. Nontraditional progressive colleges, for-profit colleges and universities, and institutions that use technology as their primary mode of instruction have emerged. In addition, many existing colleges and universities have reexamined their missions. In America's research universities, where one-third of all undergraduates earn their baccalaureate degree, undergraduate education has clearly become a greater priority although the reach of the reform efforts falls well short of our aspirations (*Reinventing Undergraduate Education*, 2001; O'Connor and others, 2003). Many other four-year colleges and universities have crafted new mission statements. The result has been the identification of new sectors in higher education—from "the urban university" to "the new American college" to "the public liberal arts college" (Spear and others, 2003).

As higher education has expanded, the student body has become much larger and more diverse in terms of age, gender, ethnicity, and cultural background (Marcy, 2002; Newton, 2000). Now only 16 percent of the student population may be described as "traditional"—that is, ages eighteen to twenty-two, attending college full-time, and living on campus. Many now attend college part-time. More than 70 percent work, and 41 percent are over age twenty-five (Marcy, 2002). Many of these new students are the first generation in their family to attend college. The majority of the new students are women.

Patterns of college attendance have also changed. Largely commuter institutions have become a pervasive force in higher education, raising pressing issues about how to create a meaningful academic community in a nonresidential, transitory setting. Even more problematic when it comes to maintaining academic community and coherence is the precipitous decline in the number of students who attend only one college for all four years. Few students now graduate from the institution at which they began their college career.

The fates of the two-year and four-year colleges have become intertwined, and issues of transfer and interinstitutional articulation are increasingly important. To complicate matters further, recent studies show that students do not flow logically from high school to college or from two-year to four-year institutions (Ewell, 2002c; Adelman, 1999). In fact, there is substantial lateral movement across four-year institutions and considerable reverse transfer between two-year and four-year schools. Meanwhile, relationships between colleges and high schools have become increasingly complicated. Widespread reform efforts in primary and secondary education are aiming for higher levels of student achievement, and a number of "early college" efforts are demonstrating ways to integrate the high school and college experiences and increase college attainment rates (Hoffman, 2003). At the same time, expectations for students are rising as our society becomes increasingly dependent on the kinds of knowledge and skill that are gained through higher education. In fact, the Association of American Colleges and Universities asserts that we are verging on universal college attendance as a college degree becomes the equivalent of a high school education one hundred years ago (*Greater Expectations*, 2002).

The challenges of educating a new generation of learners become apparent when we tackle the issues of student preparation and achievement, the mismatch between student and faculty expectations, and the differences between what colleges think is important and what parents and employers want. Although American higher education is often said to be the envy of the world, the level of student achievement and preparation needs to improve. Many statistics indicate this to be the case:

Although high school graduates may have taken the correct number of courses to graduate, more often than not they are not the right courses for pursuing postsecondary education. "About 50 percent of all first-time community college students test as underprepared for the academic demands of college-level courses. . . . This percentage . . . has not changed significantly across the United States in at least two decades" (Roueche and Roueche, 1999, p. 5).

Students' academic preparedness is down on a variety of measures, but students' confidence in their abilities is higher than ever (Hansen, 1998).

"While participation rates in higher education have increased, the gaps between high and low income levels and college completion rates have not changed" (Roueche and Roueche, 1999, p. 3). In addition, "numerically, minority students are less equal now than they were thirty years ago on the criterion that really matters: college graduation" (Renner, 2003, p. 40).

As Karen and Karl Schilling point out, we need to look at expectations for effort and engagement if we are to improve student learning. Their research at seven institutions demonstrates a substantial mismatch between student and faculty expectations for academic work outside class, with faculty expecting three times more time on task than students report actually undertaking. Perhaps most significantly, the patterns of first-year student time investment seem to be durable across the four years, implying that the freshman year is an important place to set expectations and study habits (Schilling and Schilling, 1999). The 2002 Cooperative Institutional Research Program (CIRP) annual national survey of students corroborates these findings that students are studying less than ever, declining to an all-time low of 33 percent devoting six or more hours per week to studying (Higher Education Research Institute [HERI], 2003). This recent CIRP survey also indicates that trends among students show "grade inflation, increasing financial concerns, heightened stress, academic and political disengagement, declining social activism, and record-level volunteerism" (HERI, 2003, p. 16).

There is a growing demand from employers and parents and from inside the academy itself for a new kind of education that has higher expectations (*Greater Expectations*, 2002; Jones, 2003). Many are calling for a practical education that increases students' capacities for dealing with a rapidly changing world. They emphasize teamwork and collaboration and developing problem-solving skills rather than memorization and the accumulation of facts that will soon become obsolete. Often referred to as "lifelong learning" or "deep learning," these capacities have become imperatives in our rapidly changing society. In fact, the new research in cognitive science suggests that lifelong learning is also fundamental to our long-term health (Quartz and Sejnowski, 2002).

The Changing Face of the Faculty and Faculty Work Life

Over the past thirty years both the nation's faculty and faculty work life have undergone enormous change. After the large-scale expansion of the higher education system in the 1960s and 1970s, the academy is now in the midst of another shift as large numbers of faculty retire. In fact, more than one-third of the faculty turned over in the 1990s. In a significant study of the entering cohort, Finkelstein, Seal, and Schuster (1998) noted that this new generation is markedly different from the previous generation: these individuals are much more diverse, international, and female, and fewer are based in traditional liberal arts fields. An increasing number come to full-time positions after years of part-time work, and others come from outside the academy altogether.

Surprisingly, however, despite years of national attention on improving teaching and learning and rebalancing faculty roles and rewards, the new cohort is even more research-oriented than their predecessors (Finkelstein, Seal, and Schuster, 1998; O'Meara and Rice, 2004). In general, the new cohort does not differ markedly from their predecessors in relying on traditional lecture-based pedagogies, although women faculty have been found to spend more time with students and rely less on lecturing (Finkelstein, Seal, and Schuster, 1998). This information is corroborated by other recent studies of the freshman year that indicate a growing mismatch between students and faculty, with students reporting that most classes are lecture-based whereas they prefer more experiential approaches (Sax, 2000).

The structure of academic appointments is also changing. More faculty members are being hired to part-time and non-tenure-track appointments. This trend is expected to continue, raising concerns about equity, self-governance, and the ability to build strong local communities of faculty. "The faculty" is becoming a vast territory including different types of appointments with little systematic attention paid to supporting the needs of all. Few institutions, for example, match the University of Phoenix in the attention paid to part-time faculty although these faculty members constitute a majority of the teaching faculty at many institutions.

What we are also seeing is what Martin Finkelstein and Jack Schuster refer to as the "functional respecialization of the faculty, especially in research universities" (Schuster and Finkelstein, 2001). As Jack Schuster explains, "By this we mean that for 125 years or so the academy has focused on becoming more specialized (and subspecialized) by content area, for purposes of teaching and research. But now . . . a lot of faculty (the off-track, full-time) are being hired for teaching-exclusive or research-exclusive purposes. . . . This shift (it is hardly hyperbolic to call it revolutionary) entails a tangle of trade-offs for undergraduate education: promoting a much overdue reemphasis on teaching, but at the same time, in more subtle ways, undermining the long-term attractiveness of academic careers. In fact, the changes are progressing more rapidly than we can measure them, much less comprehend the downstream implications" (Jack Schuster, personal communication with the authors, October 2003).

Meanwhile, new conceptions are emerging of who can be a teacher and what being a teacher entails. The new universities that deliver education through technology have led the way in redesigning and disaggregating the four traditional faculty roles of curriculum design, curriculum delivery, assessment, and advising. By distinguishing these roles, it becomes obvious that other experts outside the traditional faculty can contribute to student learning and provide expertise that traditionally trained faculty may lack. Numerous reform efforts build on this insight, such as service learning initiatives that involve community members in instructional roles. Learning communities too are experimenting with new roles, building teaching teams that include librarians, student affairs professionals, and student peer leaders who bring new expertise to teaching in more traditional settings.

Calls for Reform in Undergraduate Education

A widespread national consensus is emerging about the issues we face. It is clear that we are on the edge of nearly universal higher education while we are still operating with an infrastructure built for a more selective, homogeneous student body and more generous financial resources. Furthermore, we know a great deal more about what promotes student learning: if widely adopted, these new practices could significantly raise levels of student achievement. Many of our policies, practices, and assumptions are no longer viable. Although there is no clear agreement either about what an undergraduate education should be at the beginning of the twenty-first century or about how to marshal the resources to achieve the vision when it is developed, there are numerous calls for reform and a growing research literature on student learning that offer guidance. With large-scale faculty retirements on the horizon, there is no better time to find ways of putting more effective practices into place.

Myriad recent studies recognize that higher education must restructure itself to meet the new challenges. They stress the rising stakes of under-performance in higher education and point toward concrete ways in which the academy can move ahead to improve undergraduate education and incorporate new information about student learning. Exhibit 1.1 summarizes recent significant reports on the different sectors in higher education. Although each speaks to the history and mission of its particular constituency, they have many similar themes and make similar recommendations. First and foremost, of course, is the need to provide access to a growing and diverse population and educate these students effectively. Some, especially those in the sciences, point to an alarming trend toward inequality in our higher education system, which endangers both our economy and our democracy. As one put it, "It is a fundamental responsibility of a modern nation to develop the talent of all of its citizens" (Project Kaleidoscope, 2002).

The reports also recognize that new approaches are needed to reach all students. Whether it is a commitment to a twenty-first century practical liberal arts education, as the Association of American Colleges and Universities (AAC&U) advocates, or the panoply of inquiry-based approaches to learning that the Boyer Commission urges all research universities to embrace, all recognize that both the form and the content of our curriculum must change. Many of the reports describe a variety of exemplary programs, demonstrating that we already have some excellent institutional models in all types of institutions. The challenge is to encourage wider adoption of these promising approaches.

A third important theme is the relationship between the academy and the larger society. All of these studies advocate for an engaged campus that is connected to the external community in meaningful ways. Like the community colleges, the state and land-grant universities have a long history of community-based education. Thus, it is not surprising that the title of the report compiled by the Kellogg Commission on the Future of State and Land-Grant Universities was *Returning to Our Roots* (2001). But this is not a call for a nostalgic return to the past; both the Association of American Colleges and Universities and the Kellogg Commission articulate a new vision for connecting the academy with the community that is squarely rooted in the twenty-first century and addresses local, regional, and increasingly global issues.

All of the recent reports recognize a need for institutions to rise above "business as usual" and put together a coherent response to the academy's challenges. This calls for difficult dialogues that are fundamental to exercising leadership and forging a renewed sense of purpose. It will also

Exhibit 1.1. Recent Major Reports on Undergraduate Education Reform

Greater Expectations: A New Vision for Learning as a Nation Goes to College (Association of American Colleges and Universities, 2002)

Analyzes the challenges facing higher education and makes the case for practical, learner-centered changes and a new notion of liberal learning. Describes many exemplary approaches already in place, including active and inquiry-based approaches and learning communities.

Returning to Our Roots (Kellogg Commission on the Future of State and Land-Grant Universities, 1999–2000)

These are six reports on the future of state and land-grant universities and the gap between the teaching and research missions. Report themes include the student experience, student access, the engaged institution, a learning society, a coherent campus culture, and renewing the covenant. Reports stress the need for reengagement and restructuring to become genuine learning communities.

Reinventing Undergraduate Education: A Blueprint for America's Research Universities (Boyer Commission on Educating Undergraduates in Research Universities, 1998)

Argues for the reinvention of undergraduate education in research universities with recommendations on areas to pursue, including undergraduate research, integrated first-year programs, collaborative learning, freshman seminars, capstone courses, inquiry-based teaching, faculty development, and others.

Reinventing Undergraduate Education: Three Years After the Boyer Report (Reinvention Center, Stony Brook, 2001)

Analyzes the extent to which research universities have responded to the Boyer Commission recommendations. Finds substantial responsiveness but also a need for reaching a wider spectrum of students and integration with faculty roles and rewards.

The Knowledge Net: Connecting Communities, Learners, and Colleges (American Association of Community Colleges, 2000)

Presents the case for community colleges to respond to massive societal changes and create learning-centered changes relevant to the twenty-first century.

Transforming Undergraduate Education in Science, Mathematics, Engineering, and Technology (National Research Council, 1999)

Argues that we are divided into a technologically knowledgeable elite and a disadvantaged majority. Calls for new approaches for all undergraduates to study science, math, technology, and engineering early in their undergraduate education.

Report on the Reports: Recommendations for Action in Support of Undergraduate Science, Technology, Engineering, and Mathematics (Project Kaleidoscope, 2002)

Summarizes the major reports in K–12 and postsecondary science education from 1986 to 2001 and concludes that the recommendations are largely congruent in terms of the case for reform. Stresses the need for new approaches that bring all undergraduates to an understanding of the role of science and technology.

require an unprecedented level of commitment, collaboration, and holistic thinking that in many ways goes against the grain of our habits and our structures. Despite this, there is a sense of optimism, not only that we must do this but that we can. This optimism is fueled in part by the growing recognition that we are increasing in our knowledge of what promotes student learning.

What Works in Enhancing Student Learning

Fundamental change requires transformational thinking. One of the main conceptual shifts that has been advocated is the need to move from a teaching to a learning paradigm. First put forward in Robert Barr and John Tagg's widely discussed 1995 article in *Change* magazine, this perspective was described in more detail in John Tagg's recent book *The Learning Paradigm College* (2003). This formulation of the issue resonates with much of the thinking about needing to put student learning at the center of our work. Putting learning first provides a lens through which we can view all of our policies, practices, and structures and helps define what is core and what is peripheral in our institutions. It points to the prevalent flaw of equating faculty effort with student learning and demands that we incorporate a growing body of new research on student learning into our practice. This conceptual shift is significant. The next step is to understand more clearly what promotes student learning and begin to incorporate that knowledge into our teaching practices.

The literature on student learning contains a number of common themes:

- o People construct new knowledge and understandings based on what they already know and believe. Students' prior knowledge affects how they respond to teaching; if we ignore it, it hinders our teaching.

- o Learners are not all the same. Our increasingly diverse students come to learning with a highly variable store of knowledge, experience, and competence and with diverse perspectives and preferred ways of learning.

- o Key to learning is activity, time on task, and social interaction with others, the active use and testing of information and ideas, and the active practicing of skills in a meaningful context.

- o Learning is best promoted by high expectations and clear learning outcomes, with frequent assessment of both students' starting points and progress and timely feedback from more expert peers and teachers.

○ Learning and understanding develop and are internalized over time, especially as learners engage in meaningful activities and reflect on what they know.

○ Learning cannot be kept separate from identity development.

○ Learning and understanding do not necessarily occur because one is taught.

○ No one type of teaching works all the time. Particular methods follow from the specific types of learning needed to achieve the desired results in a given course.

This research paints a much more complicated picture of learning than we had in the past (National Research Council, 1999; Zull, 2002; Gardiner, 1994; Pascarella and Terenzini, 1991; Brown, Collins, and Duguid, 1988). It also shows us that the challenge of improving student learning is not simply about introducing teachers to a few new "techniques." The relationship between pedagogy and content is complicated, and many of our ideas and practices are unexamined and based on misconceptions. Understanding how people learn, what effective learning environments look like, how modern technologies might have an impact on learning, and how all of this shapes the instructional role is a great challenge that requires rethinking how we train and support our teachers and construct our learning environments.

Disseminating the Research on Student Learning and Promising Practices

Over the past twenty years, there have been a variety of efforts to disseminate the research on student learning and promote promising practices at both the national level and on individual campuses. The major higher education associations have provided consistent and focused leadership to the effort to improve undergraduate education. The American Association for Higher Education, the League for Innovation in the Community College, and the American Association of Community Colleges have promoted national discussions about service learning, instructional uses of technology, and learning outcomes, while the Association of American Colleges and Universities has led the national conversations about diversity, liberal learning, and general education. Many other professional associations have also been active in the national effort to improve both undergraduate education and student learning.

One of the most important conceptual leadership efforts came from Ernest Boyer, Gene Rice, and Lee Shulman and their work on the scholarship of teaching, which called for a broader definition of faculty work and scholarship, a more empirically grounded sense of good practice, and more robust ways to describe and evaluate teaching. Since the early 1990s, The Carnegie Foundation for the Advancement of Teaching and the American Association for Higher Education (AAHE) have worked together to promote the scholarship of teaching approach as a concrete way to redefine and raise the status of teaching. Hundreds of campuses have been involved in this effort, which has led to a broader notion of faculty roles and rewards on many of them (O'Meara and Rice, 2004; Pat Hutchings, personal communication with the author, October 2003).

The assessment movement has also been important in undergraduate education reform. As Peter Ewell points out, the assessment movement started in the mid-1980s on the heels of the significant national report *Involvement in Learning* (Ewell, 2002a). Almost from the outset, assessment work developed a dual focus on improvement and accountability. At the same time, assessment reforms have focused on the classroom, giving teachers important tools for enhancing their practice. Tom Angelo and Pat Cross encouraged teachers to experiment with classroom assessment approaches, or "CATs," as they came to be called. Together they wrote an eminently practical handbook that provides dozens of examples that teachers can use in their classrooms to shed light on their assumptions about teaching and learning (Angelo and Cross, 1993). Also in the "ask-them" tradition, Richard Light's work at Harvard demonstrated that we all have a lot to learn from asking our students about their learning (Light, 1990, 2001).

Although many reform approaches have been cross-disciplinary, some have focused on the academic disciplines. Teaching journals have appeared in a number of disciplines, as have projects to encourage new pedagogical approaches. The AAHE was particularly important in collaborating with the disciplines on its twenty-three monographs on service learning in the disciplines, its work on teaching portfolios, and its work on the scholarship of teaching. Meanwhile, the Association of American Colleges reexamined study in the major, finding a widespread problem in terms of coherence (Association of American Colleges, 1990).

The National Science Foundation has given significant support to innovative approaches in the sciences, funding a variety of reforms in mathematics, the sciences, and engineering. Many of these efforts were designed to reverse the high attrition rates in these disciplines and address the shortage of graduates in mathematics, science, and engineering. Inquiry-based approaches to learning and an emphasis on undergraduate research are important ingredients in most of these reforms, as are efforts to change the chilly climate of many science classrooms and build a greater sense of community. Developing peer support systems among students has often been successful in building community and encouraging persistence in the sciences (Seymour and Hewitt, 1997).

Meanwhile, on individual campuses, one of the most promising trends has been the widespread establishment of teaching and learning centers and faculty development programs, providing a dissemination system for new information about student learning and a support system for growing numbers of new faculty members.

Old Structures and Practices

In spite of the calls for reform, exciting new research about student learning, and robust national dissemination efforts, much about higher education has changed but little in the last hundred years. Our academic structure remains a curriculum of social efficiency divided into three- or four-credit courses and fifty-minute classes. Grades, seat time, and credit hours remain the basic currency of higher education, even though they are increasingly recognized as inadequate measures of student learning. Although focusing on student learning outcomes is generally conceived as the best new alternative to credit hours and seat time, few institutions have adopted this approach in a deep and meaningful way (Ewell, 2002a). Those that have moved to student learning outcomes often find themselves caught between the new approach and perverse traditional policies, especially as they relate to funding and student financial aid.

Although it is true that large freshman lecture courses subsidize small upper-division courses, the attrition rate in that crucial first year makes this a dubious practice. Following the familiar pattern in higher education, many new reform efforts are add-on's and promising projects rather than true reforms. In fact, the emerging alternative practices (such as tutorials, seminars, learning portfolios, and so forth) are often viewed as labor-intensive and costly and face serious challenges in scaling up to reach large numbers of students.

Discipline-based academic departments continue as the mainstay of most college and university organizational structures. And although they have been important in delivering discipline-based courses, they pose a serious challenge to many functions and programs that are more institutionwide and cross-cutting, such as general education and interdisciplinary education, often creating role conflicts for faculty interested in these broader forms of teaching. As a result, general education programs often face staffing challenges because the faculty's primary loyalty is to their academic disciplines and their department.

Faculty culture remains rooted in a long tradition of autonomy and individualism. At research universities in particular, the faculty are increasingly specialized and national or international in their affiliations. Developing a sense of institutional community and overall faculty responsibility for it is a challenge, especially in larger institutions. According to William H. Sullivan in *The University as Citizen: Institutional Identity and Social Responsibility,* many faculty members have retreated to what he calls *instrumental individualism,* avoiding the more difficult and important alternative of coming to grips with a new institutional purpose appropriate to our times (Sullivan, n.d.). As a result, many institutions have found it very difficult to have meaningful discussions about the overall curriculum.

Peter Ewell has said that we are caught in a number of paradoxes, which he describes as "key dialectics"—seemingly opposing positions that must be accommodated (Ewell, 2002c). He suggests that the only way out of the apparent contradictions is a conceptual shift and new institutional structures and ways of doing things. Even in teaching and learning, for example, Ewell points out that we are faced with the paradox of increasing individualization and fragmentation of the curriculum *and* a need for coherence. As students become increasingly mobile, attending two, three, or four colleges, it is not easy to imagine a simple curricular fix to the coherence issue because the solution is beyond the purview of a single institution. In the organizational domain, Ewell says that we face the apparent contradiction that our existing modular forms of organization (academic departments) are not effective in certain areas—like general education, interdisciplinary education, and learning communities—that require more cross-cutting organizational structures. Here the challenge is to create meaningful hybrid structures that do not lead to turf wars and marginalization.

Promoting Change in a Time of Limited Resources

As the epigraph that began this chapter pointed out, higher education is now facing "serious tests of its resourcefulness with the significant shifts in the social landscape" (Sullivan, n.d., p. 1). Providing meaningful access to higher education for an increasing number of students is a clear priority, but this commitment comes on the heels of the recognition that resources for higher education will be constrained in the future, making "business as usual" impossible (Guskin, 1994a, 1994b, 1996; Guskin and Marcy, 2003; Massy and Wilger, 1996; Massy, 2003).

In comparison with other industrialized nations, the United States spends more per student on higher education and the gap widened between 1995 and 1998 (Sherman, 2003), but most observers contend that recent funding growth patterns for public higher education are not sustainable in the face of tax resistance and increased competition for resources. "In 1997, the Council on Aid to Education . . . analyzed ongoing trends in educational support and expenditures, and determined that if all sources of support continued to follow current trends, and higher education continued to model its expenditure pattern, higher education would face a funding shortfall of about $38 billion—nearly 25 percent of its needs—by 2015" (Council on Aid to Education, 1997, p. 3).

Already there are signs of increasing inequality in access to higher education (Educational Testing Service, 1998). Reports with such dramatic titles as *Losing Ground* (2002c) and *College Affordability in Jeopardy* (2002a), both from the National Center for Public Policy and Higher Education, and *Empty Promises* (2002) from the Advisory Committee on Student Financial Assistance, demonstrate that access is increasingly tied to income and that the American Dream is falling out of the reach of too many. Rather than face the challenge of setting new directions in the shifting landscape, many colleges and universities are facing the dilemma of containing costs and cutting budgets by a combination of hunkering down—hoping for a better day—and nibbling away at the budget base through across-the-board cuts, a strategy that will not work in the long run (Guskin and Marcy, 2003).

The Project on the Future of Higher Education is one effort aimed at exploring the future of higher education in the context of this increasing pressure on resources (see www.antioch.edu/pfhe). The project brought together sixteen leaders in higher education to explore future scenarios and suggest ways to enhance student learning, maintain quality in faculty work life, and cut costs simultaneously. They see using technology, creating new forms of instructional leadership, taking better advantage of approaches known to enhance student learning, and putting a sharper focus on student learning outcomes as key elements (Guskin and Marcy, 2001, 2003; Ewell, 2002c).

The kind of reforms that the Project on the Future of Higher Education and other national reports are recommending cannot come easily, in part because a variety of questionable assumptions shape our views of what is possible and desirable. As one higher education analyst, Ann Ferren, notes, we assume, for example, that quality means more expenditures per student and that class size is a primary measure of quality. There are many other questionable assumptions, such as the following: The more specialized courses a department offers, the better it is. Every faculty member ought to have the opportunity to teach one or more specialties. Enrollments are a measure of a department's success. Courses should be offered to satisfy all available markets and emerging interests (Ferren, 1997, p. 549).

After reviewing more than twenty-six hundred books, articles, and other writings about student learning, Patrick Terenzini and Ernest Pascarella (1994) reached similar conclusions about myths that get in the way of reform. Some of the widespread myths they cite are the following:

o Educational quality is a function of the institution's wealth, resources, and selectivity.

o The lecture is a proven, effective way of teaching undergraduate students.

o The only significant influences on student learning come through the faculty and in the classroom.

o Students' academic and nonacademic experiences are separate and unrelated influences on learning.

Questionable assumptions and myths close many doors to education reform, blinding us to resources and new ways of thinking about roles and responsibilities. They can also misdirect us toward simplistic solutions. Many reform efforts are narrowly conceived around a single factor, such as altering the lecture or reducing class size, without taking all the other factors into account that would make the effort more far-reaching and successful.

The Course Redesign Project

One significant recent project challenged some of these assumptions. It worked from the premise that we can improve student learning while simultaneously reducing the cost of instruction if technology plays an important role (Twigg, 2003). Supported by The Pew Charitable Trusts, the Course Redesign Project involved thirty colleges and universities that redesigned their large introductory-level courses, often called *gateway courses,* which enroll the great majority of students across the nation. The courses include algebra, American government, introductory psychology, and introductory chemistry (Twigg, 2003; see also www.center.rpi.edu/Pewgrant).

As project director Carol Twigg points out, most of the efforts involved substantial structural change: "Some eliminate some lectures; others eliminate all lectures. The premise is that faculty do not need to spend as much time presenting information. Lectures are replaced with a variety of learning resources, all of which involve more active learning or more individualized assistance. . . . The primary goal is to shift students from a passive, note-taking role to an active learning orientation. . . . As one math professor puts it, 'Students learn math by doing math, not by listening to someone talk about math'" (Twigg, n.d.).

This project demonstrated comprehensive innovation driven by learner-centered thinking that also reached a large number of students. It required a detailed examination of the real costs of instruction, something that has often been recommended but seldom implemented. As Twigg (n.d., p. 31) points out:

> Doing a careful analysis of the instructional tasks associated with the traditional course format allows one to gain an understanding of those that can be shifted from personnel to technology-based materials and those that cannot. After determining the pedagogical principles that need to be employed in the redesign and the kinds of instructional personnel who are essential to the specific tasks, one can experiment with a variety of designs and calculate their associated costs. Most academic problems can be addressed in a variety of ways; there is no one perfect redesign strategy. The principles are generic, however. Cost savings result from shifting the time spent by the instructional personnel to the technology.

A more learning-centered paradigm encourages us to make the crucial move to thinking about ways to enhance student learning that get beyond simply equating student learning with faculty time in the classroom. The Course Redesign Project demonstrates one way to rethink how large introductory classes can be taught by using technology, altering faculty time in the classroom, and creating new ways for students to work together. The project was successful in cutting costs, increasing student learning, and improving faculty satisfaction. Like learning communities, this project took structure, pedagogy, and roles and relationships as variables that could be altered.

Learning Communities and Undergraduate Education Reform

In this climate of rising challenges, growing calls for reform, broad-scale experimentation, and strong research on learning, learning communities have emerged as a compelling strategy to use in restructuring undergraduate education. Carefully designed and implemented learning communities can simultaneously address the issues of enhancing student learning and building the quality of our academic communities in a cost-effective manner. Because they can provide a holistic and coherent approach to reform, learning communities offer a potentially more sustainable approach than many more narrowly based reform initiatives.

A Definition

Although learning communities have a long and rich history, which is discussed in Chapter Two, the contemporary concept and implementation started to build into a national movement in the mid-1980s with substantial expansion in the mid-1990s. Now they have become so widespread that the term *learning community* is used to apply to many different educational strategies. More clearly defining learning communities and delineating their key features can help us understand these programs' intentions and also provide a standard against which to judge what they are attempting.

In this text, we use the term *learning communities* to refer to a variety of curricular approaches that intentionally link or cluster two or more courses, often around an interdisciplinary theme or problem, and enroll a common cohort of students. They represent an intentional restructuring of students' time, credit, and learning experiences to build community, enhance learning, and foster connections among students, faculty, and disciplines. At their best, learning communities practice pedagogies of active engagement and reflection. On residential campuses, many learning communities are also living-learning communities, restructuring the residential environment to build community and integrate academic work with out-of-class experiences.

The Social Construction of Knowledge

As reform efforts have evolved over the past eighty years, they carry a set of assumptions, summarized in Exhibit 1.2, about the nature of knowledge, student learning, the organization of the curriculum, and the role of the faculty. These assumptions are strongly associated with a view known as the *social construction of knowledge*. Citing the work of Kenneth Bruffee, K. Patricia Cross defines this view as follows: "We construct and maintain knowledge . . . by negotiating with one another in communities of knowledgeable peers. . . . Knowledge is actively built by learners as they shape and build mental frameworks to make sense of their environments. . . . Knowledge is not something that is transferred in an authoritarian structure from teacher to students but rather as something

Exhibit 1.2. Assumptions Underlying Traditional Approaches
to Education and Recent Reform Efforts

Traditional Assumptions About Higher Education	Assumptions Underlying Recent Reform Efforts
Discovery of knowledge is more important than practical applications.	Experiential learning and practice serve to deepen knowledge and understanding.
Meaning is seen as something that is individually constructed.	Meaning is seen as socially constructed, through collaborative learning.
Stresses objective nature of knowledge, rationalizes value of knowledge.	Admits subjective and value-laden nature of knowledge.
Emphasizes "procedural" and "separate" knowing.	Encourages connected, relational, and constructed knowing.
Student learning and development are seen as something occurring primarily in the classroom.	Student learning and development occur in and outside the classroom.
Focus more on the nature of the curriculum than on who is in the classroom.	Increasing focus is on who is in the classroom.
Curriculum is delivered through discrete courses, emphasizing seat time and credit hours.	Delivery system is organized around larger packages of time and credit; alternative ways of validating learning.
Curriculum is built around disciplines.	Curriculum is built around interdisciplinary foci, often around themes or problems or questions.
Emphasis is on didactic instruction, rather than connecting theory and practice.	Experiential learning and practice are used to deepen knowledge and understanding.
Teacher is seen as authoritative deliverer of content.	Teacher is seen as designer and manager of learning processes.
Reflection is considered an optional afterthought.	Reflection is seen as central to learning and meaning making.

that teachers and students work interdependently to develop. Thus it fosters active learning over passive learning, cooperation over competition, and community over isolation" (Cross, 1998, p. 5).

There is now a fairly strong consensus on these views of knowledge and student learning among most learning and student development theorists, cognitive scientists, and leaders and practitioners of reform efforts at both the K–12 and postsecondary levels. These perspectives have profound implications for how we think about curriculum, teaching practices, student assessment, and co-curricular activity, and especially for how we prepare faculty members for the professoriate. Although these assumptions are intriguing and hold great promise for strengthening student engagement and learning, they are also problematic because most faculty members were not taught in these ways and most have not been exposed to these theories and their implications for classroom practice.

Nonetheless, learning communities provide a significant arena for putting these theories into practice. The changed structure of learning communities brings together courses and disciplines, learners and teachers to provide a larger and more holistic platform for realizing the more recent assumptions described in Exhibit 1.2. The learning community structure is itself infinitely adaptable to different kinds of curricular and co-curricular settings. What has made it attractive and widespread is this adaptability; educators can shape and reshape the strategy around specific curricular or student needs. Central to learning community design and implementation are five core practices: community, integration, active learning, diversity, and reflection and assessment. Although these core practices, which are described in detail in Chapter Four, are important in any educational setting, they can be more fully developed in learning communities simply because learning communities provide more time and space by restructuring the curriculum. In this changed structure, new roles and relationships also become possible. Many different people can come together to teach in learning communities—faculty, student affairs professionals, librarians, graduate teaching assistants, student peer mentors. Learning community programs are often a team effort, setting up the conditions for interdependence and learning on the part of all the people who teach in them.

Learning Communities as a Reform Effort

At their best, learning communities embody an analysis of what is needed to reform higher education (curricular restructuring), a theory of learning (based on current research), a commitment to certain educational goals (putting student learning at the center of our work), and a commitment to the importance of community (a necessary condition for learning). They rest on the belief that we can improve student academic success if we design a more appropriate educational structure for addressing important intellectual and social issues, recognize learning as a shared responsibility, and encourage active learning and community building. They create venues for synergistic activity to occur among people and ideas.

The learning community approach offers a unique opportunity to be resourceful in a time of limited resources. Unlike many approaches to education reform, learning communities are not a simple response to one set of issues. They represent a holistic response, what Peter Senge has called a *high leverage point*. Because of this we believe learning communities have enormous potential in helping to achieve the larger aims of undergraduate education reform. They can be a convergence zone for many related reforms. At the same time, putting learning communities in place requires not only reforming the curriculum but also reforming many of our working relationships and the organizational systems on our campuses. This work of reform, of changing complex systems, is difficult because we tend to see the world and our education system in terms of separate, unrelated forces (Senge, 1990). We tend to underinvest in the kinds of ongoing dialogue, comprehensive planning, and staff development that are needed to bring about deep and enduring change (Ewell, 1997). As a result, educational reforms are usually additive rather than transformational, having little impact on our core values, structures, and practices. Some learning communities—though by no means most—seem to be reaching beyond this historic pattern of educational tinkering. In the next chapter we explore the history of learning communities and the lessons we can draw from this history. Time will tell whether learning communities will be remembered as a large but ultimately minimal reform movement or as an explosion of activity and energy whose leaders recognized their potential, harnessed their energy, and brought about the revolution they were able to create.

LEARNING COMMUNITY HISTORY

EDUCATION FOR WHAT? EDUCATION FOR WHOM?

Unless education has some frame of reference it is bound to be aimless, lacking a unifying objective. The necessity for a frame of reference must be admitted. There exists in this country such a unified frame. It is called democracy.

—John Dewey

The United States has ventured to unite both excellence and democracy; whether we can succeed or will break down under the fundamental conflict is not yet known. But we must make a good try at it. We must start by facing the fact that we do not yet have . . . the educational system required for this task.

—Alexander Meiklejohn

TODAY'S LEARNING COMMUNITIES draw on a rich intellectual heritage dating back to the beginning of the twentieth century. In this chapter we trace their history from their origins as small, isolated experiments struggling to survive to their current status as a widespread national education reform effort facing new challenges. There is both constancy and change in the history of learning communities, providing important lessons for today's reform efforts as well as raising questions about the future.

The philosophical, structural, and pedagogical roots of contemporary learning communities are found in the work of John Dewey and Alexander Meiklejohn in the 1920s, and in the early debates about democracy and the aims of general and liberal education. Many of the value conflicts that influence education reform efforts today can be traced back to these early debates. Contemporary learning communities face some of the same issues about "education for what" and "education for whom," but these questions of basic purpose arise in a radically changed educational, socioeconomic, and political environment. As we pointed out in Chapter One, many forces are dramatically reshaping the educational environment to produce a new climate and an unprecedented set of challenges. Nonetheless, the central questions that Meiklejohn raised about purpose many years ago are still with us: Why do we teach? What should we teach? For whom do we teach? What is our goal, and what is the source of its authority over us?

These are enduring questions.

The Influence of John Dewey

John Dewey spent most of his life as a university philosophy teacher, first at the University of Michigan, then at the University of Chicago, where he and his wife founded an experimental elementary school, and finally at Teachers College at Columbia University from 1904 to 1939. Dewey died in 1952. He wrote a great number of books and articles, most focusing on elementary and secondary education. His ideas were widely discussed around the world and continue to inspire educators. (See Louis Menand's prizewinning book *The Metaphysical Club: A Story of Ideas in America,* 2001, for a detailed account of the work of Dewey and his protégés.) Dewey is considered a major influence on contemporary work in learning communities because of his writings about the teaching and learning process, especially student-centered learning and active learning, and because of his educational and democratic values. His work put down the roots of experiential and cooperative learning.

Dewey stressed that students are *individuals* who come to any educational setting with diverse aspirations and prior experiences that must be taken into account. He distinguished between traditional and progressive education by saying that traditional education was "formation from without" while progressive education was "development from within" (Dewey, 1938, p. 17). A staunch developmentalist, Dewey believed that teaching must build on the individuality of each student. He thought education should be very purposeful about engaging the learner. The key, he believed, was to "consider the power and purposes of those being taught. It is not enough that certain materials or methods have proven effective with other individuals at other times. There must be a reason for thinking that they will function in generating an experience that has educative quality with particular individuals at a particular time" (Dewey, 1933, pp. 45–46). This required that teachers be experimental and intentional in their efforts, and closely attuned to their students.

While recognizing that schools are not the only place where learning takes place, Dewey regarded them as important for building the common culture. He found schools wanting in terms of furthering student development. Seeing education as "formation from without," many traditional teachers viewed the student's mind as a "cistern into which information is conducted" or "a piece of blotting paper that absorbs and retains automatically" (Dewey, 1933, pp. 261–262). Decades later, in his famous book *Pedagogy of the Oppressed* (1970), Paulo Freire called this the *banking* notion of education, which sees teachers as depositors of knowledge and students as depositories in an often impersonal teaching and learning environment with little or no attention to individuality or context. Like Freire, Dewey was convinced that these assumptions about learning were inaccurate in describing how people learn and led to educationally ineffective practices. The progressive school recognized that learning is an inherently social process. Dewey envisioned education as a more open-ended inquiry process rather than a teacher-dominated process of "handing down" knowledge as a finished product. This would require a close relation between students and teachers, and an authority relationship based on an attitude of "shared inquiry." Instead of being primarily a transmitter of knowledge, the teacher was now a partner in a collaborative relationship, less an external authority and more a leader of group activities (Dewey, 1933). Cooperative and collaborative approaches to education were one way of putting this theory into practice.

Dewey believed that citizens need to build the skills and habits of mind necessary for a democratic society. He thought this skill building should begin in local communities and day-to-day activities, and each generation would rediscover and rebuild these commitments in its own way (Halliburton, 1997). Schools were one of the crucial arenas for building citizenship skills, and educational processes could teach important lessons about social control and community life.

Dewey saw diversity as a central feature of any society and something to nurture and value. He believed that "progressive society counts individuals' variations as precious since it finds in them the means of its own growth. Hence a democratic society must, in consistency with its ideal, allow intellectual freedom and the play of diverse gifts and interests in educational matters" (Halliburton, 1997, p. 29).

Dewey's insights are clearly linked to contemporary thinking about effective educational environments and the purposes of education. Recent scholarship in a variety of fields reaffirms and builds on his work, reinforcing and deepening his observations about the social construction of knowledge, the importance of a developmental perspective, and the value of active and collaborative learning approaches to education (see for example, Menand, 2001; Halliburton, 1997; Gardiner, 1994; Pascarella and Terenzini, 1991; Belenky, Clinchy, Goldberger, and Tarule, 1986; Mentkowski and Associates, 2000; Bransford, Brown, and Cocking, 1999; Finkel, 2000; Finkel and Monk, 1983; Orrill, 1995, 1997). Today there is a renaissance of interest in Dewey's work in the higher education community. A number of scholars suggest that his work is central to a newly emerging concept of liberal education based on pragmatism (Orrill, 1995, 1997; Kimball, 1995a, 1995b). This is discussed further in Chapter Five in the context of learning communities and general education.

Meiklejohn's Experimental College

Alexander Meiklejohn is a central figure in the learning community history for his insights into the fundamental importance of structure, curricular coherence, and community.[1] A distinguished philosopher and educational theorist, Meiklejohn made wide-ranging contributions to higher education as a teacher, writer, and speaker.[2] He had a long and rich career as a dean at Brown, president of Amherst College, and later director of the Experimental College at the University of Wisconsin. After leaving Wisconsin, Meiklejohn moved to California and started the San Francisco School for Social Studies, an experiment in adult education that included Great Books for labor union locals (*Experimental College of the University of Wisconsin*, 1995). In the later years of his life he focused on defending civil liberties and the First Amendment.

A contemporary of John Dewey, Meiklejohn lived in a time of educational innovation and fervent debate about the direction of higher education. By the mid-1920s dozens of educational experiments were under way and others were being planned across the United States (Nelson, 2001).[3] Dewey and Meiklejohn shared a concern for education and democracy and both men felt that the current educational system and practices were inadequate, but in their lifetimes the two were often noted for their differences.[4] Meiklejohn was a philosophical idealist; Dewey was a pragmatist. Dewey became associated with an emphasis on the individual, whereas Meiklejohn focused on building the common interest, the tension between individual autonomy and institutional authority in democratic society, and the need to balance the two. Pragmatism, he believed, had failed to provide the intellectual synthesis that was needed. Various progressive institutions developed around these differing points of view—for example, St. John's around Meiklejohn's ideas and Goddard around Dewey's (Lane, 1984; Cadwallader, 1984b; Hill, 1984a). The contemporary learning community effort draws selectively from both philosophers, finding much common ground between them.

Meiklejohn spoke and wrote with great concern about the rising ascendancy of specialized academic majors and departments and the social and intellectual fragmentation in America's colleges and universities. His penetrating analysis of the dualisms in the modern university rings as true today as it did in the early twentieth century. He predicted that the uncritical acceptance of the Germanic model of the research university would inevitably lead to the neglect of general education and larger questions about the social purpose and social responsibility of higher education. In his time, many colleges had adopted the elective system, giving students great freedom to choose among a large number of courses and causing the demise of a more integrated notion of general education. A vigorous debate about the purpose of liberal education raged between the restorationists, who wanted to return to a classical core curriculum more typical of nineteenth-century America, and those arguing for a distinctively new American approach to liberal education. Both sides recognized that the elective curriculum failed to produce a coherent general education program, but there was no consensus on the solution (Orrill, 1995, 1997).

While at Amherst in the early 1920s Meiklejohn criticized these trends and described his vision of an ideal college.[5] Glenn Frank, the editor of *Century* magazine in New York, was drawn to Meiklejohn's ideas and published several of his articles on the need for radical changes in America's colleges and universities. Amherst did not take Meiklejohn up on his ideas, and he left in 1923 because of differences over his administrative approach and a growing discord with the senior faculty. After his departure, he tried unsuccessfully to raise funds to start an academy to implement his ideas.

Meanwhile, in 1925, Glenn Frank became president of the University of Wisconsin. He immediately began to talk about bringing Meiklejohn to Madison to put his ideas into practice. After considerable negotiations, Meiklejohn agreed to go there to establish the Experimental College.

Opened in 1927, the Experimental College is still regarded as one of the University of Wisconsin's most significant contributions to educational innovation (Cronon and Jenkins, 1994). It operated for five years, from 1927 to 1932, enrolling between 74 and 119 freshmen each year in a two-year, lower-division integrated program (Bureau of Guidance and Records, 1932). The students then did upper-division work in their major through regular university courses or transferred to another university. Meiklejohn had a clear concept of what he wanted to do under the broad guidelines established by Frank.

The Experimental College was to be a democratic project. Unlike many other reform efforts focusing on honors students, Meiklejohn wanted the school to attract a student body that was a cross section of the university. This, he thought, would be a genuine test of whether everyone could be liberally educated. The philosophy behind the Experimental College, which was clearly described in the first bulletin, explained the pedagogical approach and the ways it would differ from traditional courses and subjects. This bulletin also contained the first reference to the concept of *learning communities*. It spelled out how community would be fostered, how relationships between faculty and students would differ from traditional roles, and how the course of study would be organized. The new college was to be a complex innovation at many different levels. It was designed as a living-learning community, where the residential social experience would build solidarity between students and faculty. As he indicated in the bulletin, Meiklejohn was impressed with the insights of Woodrow Wilson, then president of Princeton, that residence arrangements had a profound impact on students' interests, "usually leading the imagination, the enthusiasm, the social attitudes of the student away from his studies and towards something else" (Meiklejohn, 1927, pp. 7–8). Meiklejohn's vision was that this community would support, rather than distract, the students from their common intellectual work.

The students would live in Adams Hall, a new men's dorm on the shores of Lake Mendota, and the faculty members would also have their offices there. Eventually Meiklejohn hoped to take over all of Adams Hall as the program expanded, but this dream was never realized. As a result, students who were not in the Experimental College lived in the same dorm but operated under dramatically different university rules and expectations, and this created a problematic situation in the long run. Larger meetings and lectures were held close by in a lecture hall of the College of Agriculture. Meals were provided in a refectory across the street.

The Experimental College attempted to intertwine the curricular with the co-curricular experience and cultivate both mind and body. Many of the students were active in establishing clubs, such as the Law Group, the Philosophy Club, and a popular theater group called the Experimental College Players. A number were also active in athletics. Meiklejohn believed the common residential experience provided a critical ground for building community among the students. Looking back on it many years later, the alumni described the residential experience as crucial and wondered how largely nonresidential colleges could create learning communities with a similar sense of community and engagement (Robert Frase and Harold November, personal communication, October 2001).

Various forms of active learning were used in the program, including tutorials and discussion-based seminars. Social relations were also innovative, with the formal designation of faculty as "advisers" rather than "professors." Faculty members were both generalists—team teaching and advising a common curriculum—and specialists in their fields. The role of adviser was important and sometimes difficult because faculty were asked to assume responsibilities for which they were not trained. In a later study of the Experimental College, the difficulties built into the advising role were described in detail (Meiklejohn, [1932] 2000). In addition to the one-on-one meetings with individual students, there were also group meetings of each faculty member's advisees. Grades were given for the two-year program as a whole at the end of the second year, but at the end of the first year each student's parents received a letter from Meiklejohn providing a general assessment of his progress. Grading was rigorous, as it turned out, but the lack of traditional grades immediately generated criticism from skeptics.

Meiklejohn rejected the then-prevalent elective system, which only exacerbated the fragmentation resulting from a course-based curriculum. He thought the elective system reflected "a lack of vision on the part of the faculty" and an abandonment of their responsibility for setting an appropriate curriculum (Miller, 1988, p. 44). Believing that lower-division education should prepare students for responsible citizenship, "Meiklejohn advocated an educational experience without the 'disease of departmentalism' that taught situations, not subjects" (*The Experimental College of the University of Wisconsin*, 1995, p. 42). Students would learn how to think, not what to think, and develop judgment and a "scheme of reference." They would do this through a common required curriculum, paradoxically combined with a dramatically redefined teaching and learning environment that encouraged their capacities for freedom and responsible self-direction. This new curriculum would sweep aside the common practice of organizing around courses and departments. Instead, students would enroll in an integrated, nearly full-time, two-year lower-division program. The curriculum was both historical and contemporary, focusing on democracy in fifth-century Athens and nineteenth- and twentieth-century America. Each civilization was studied holistically through a discussion-centered pedagogy based on significant books: Plato's *Republic* and *The Education of Henry Adams* figured prominently.

   Though he chose some classic texts because of their enduring value in addressing contemporary issues, Meiklejohn was not a traditionalist. Focusing on the contemporary world and the future was a new way of thinking about education, as was the notion of a lower-division education *program* that had the creation of an academic community as one of its primary goals. Meiklejohn's concern for the present was also evident in his challenging assignments that asked students to develop a personal point of view by extending their analysis to present-day problems (Miller, 1988; Brown, 1981; see also Meiklejohn, [1932] 2000, for a complete book list and list of assignments). Many of the alumni later remembered the writing assignments due every six weeks as particularly important experiences, giving structure and accountability to the learning process. A particularly powerful project required students to undertake research on their hometown during the summer between the freshman and sophomore years. Called the "Regional Study," it was to be patterned after the Lynds' *Middletown,* the popular sociological analysis of the time. This assignment was remarkable and eye-opening for college students, as both an exercise in experiential learning and an introduction to the way their hometowns functioned as local democracies; neither kind of assignment was common in college coursework of the day.

   As Miller points out in his landmark study of the roots of general and liberal education, Meiklejohn is a significant figure in the evolution of both (1988, p. 47):

> This was not simply a change in course content. Instead, the Experimental College program had made new assumptions about the objectives of education, about the relationship of education to the individual student and to contemporary society, and about the reasons for studying the past. However, Meiklejohn's attempt to integrate these assumptions with those of the classical curriculum resulted in tension between the intellectual and social ends of the program. While the primary goal of "making minds" was, to Meiklejohn, intellectual, there were also social and behavioral components to the goal.

   The tension that developed between the goal of building community through a common curriculum and the goal of fostering individual freedom by giving students responsibility for their own learning was never fully resolved in the endeavor. Nor was the attempt to create a unified and coherent living-learning community an unqualified success. As Miller (1998) points out in his account, the same tensions that tore at the community outside the college—a culture of individualism, fraternities, and competing outside interests—frustrated Meiklejohn's attempt to build a social community. In their 1932 analysis of the experience, the advisers concluded that a major "interference" with community building was the presence of what came to be competing communities and values in Adams Hall, with the Experimental College students living side by side with other university students (Meiklejohn, [1932] 2000). Similar tensions, inherent in any community-building endeavor, have challenged more recent learning communities as well.

As time went on, the Experimental College operated in increasingly rough waters, struggling against the current of the University of Wisconsin mainstream.[6] Sponsored by the enthusiastic new president Glenn Frank, who had no previous experience in higher education and had not yet established strong relationships inside the university, the program faced continuing challenges. Several early decisions exacerbated the problem of winning support from the university faculty. Meiklejohn's initial appointment and his salary, the highest of any professor in the university, became the first point of controversy. Then, after a promise to staff the program internally, many of the teaching faculty turned out to be Meiklejohn protégés brought in from Amherst or Brown. A number of other administrators also felt their authority had been undermined by the special rules and privileges in the Experimental College. Throughout the school's brief existence, both Frank and Meiklejohn had to negotiate compromises to win grudging approval for the program by the powerful College of Letters and Sciences.

The Experimental College students themselves were also controversial. Some of the issues were simply about being separate, special, and outside the usual rules and regulations. Conservatives among the Wisconsin faculty questioned not only the educational approach but also the apparent freedom the students enjoyed. The demographics of the student body drew criticism too. A number of the students were Jewish, nearly twice the proportion in the university as a whole. An increasingly large number were from out of state: 69 percent versus 31 percent in the university as a whole (Bureau of Guidance and Records, 1932). Some of the students had radical politics and quickly won a reputation as troublemakers. As a result, a rising tide of anti-Semitism and stereotyping was directed against the Experimental College students.

After several successive years of declining enrollment as the economic depression deepened, a decision was made in 1931 to close the school. Though the program had clearly been successful in terms of the performance of its graduates in the upper-division curriculum, it never met the initial enrollment expectations and it remained a continuing source of contention in the university.

As the Experimental College's life drew to an end, Meiklejohn and the advisers made a formal report to the University of Wisconsin faculty, analyzing their experiences and making recommendations for the future. Published under the title *The Experimental College* in 1932, the report provides a detailed retrospective and a remarkably insightful guide to future learning community change agents. The report pointed to a number of issues that proved to be substantial "interferences," as Meiklejohn called them, including the mixed dormitory plan, the dual appointment and allegiance of the faculty to the experimental program and their departments, and the problems that arose from inserting new arrangements into traditional administrative policies and processes. The Experimental College challenged all sorts of traditional procedures, from grading to required class attendance, thereby inevitably raising issues of substance as well as fairness and often breeding jealousy and suspicion (Meiklejohn, [1932] 2000).

As this retrospective points out, one of the original goals of the Experimental College had been to study and experiment with new approaches to undergraduate education. Much had been accomplished in exploring new student and faculty roles and relationships, community-building pedagogical approaches, and ways to integrate the curriculum. The advisers also noted that the experience was fragmented and incomplete. They had much more to learn.

Meiklejohn and his faculty concluded that the scale of the community was critical, as was the freedom the faculty enjoyed to use their best judgment to design an appropriate curriculum and learning community structure. He did not believe a community of learners could be mandated; it had to be built by small groups of dedicated students and faculty. To this end, he recommended that the experiment continue. He suggested that the University of Wisconsin set up a number of experimental units, some focused on the freshman and sophomore years, others on the junior and senior years. Some would be linked to the residence hall, others not. Some would be coeducational, others not. Each unit would be semiautonomous with great latitude to experiment. This would empower the faculty to take responsibility for the curriculum in a holistic way (Meiklejohn, [1932] 2000). None of these recommendations were acted upon.

Its life was short, but the program left a deep imprint on its graduates. Many alumni became leaders in various walks of life. Throughout their lives they remained keenly interested in the problems of democracy and had strong commitments to their local communities. Seventy years later, program alumni continued to gather for conferences and book seminars. Always looking forward, in the 1980s these alumni founded a project called "Voices of Youth" and sponsored conferences to bring high school and college teachers and students together. In the late 1990s, a dozen remaining alumni were delighted to attend the inauguration of the Bradley living-learning community at the University of Wisconsin, hoping that the new venture could re-create some of the spirit of the Experimental College. As they gathered, they frequently asked themselves what really had made the difference. Was it the learning community structure? The exceptional faculty? The curriculum? The fusion of the residential experience with the integrated curriculum? This remained a point of debate, but when asked what was most important about the Experimental College, many alumni pointed to Alexander Meiklejohn and the other faculty, the powerful program themes, and the coherence of the overall educational experience. This was clearly an education that mattered.

The legacy of learning communities at the University of Wisconsin was interrupted with the demise of the Experimental College, but it would later be resurrected through the integrated liberal studies program (ILS),[7] the Bradley living-learning community, the Chadbourne learning community program, an ambitious freshman interest group program, the Women in Science and Engineering (WISE) program, and other learning community initiatives. Ironically, seventy years after Meiklejohn's 1932 recommendation that the university establish multiple centers of innovation, it has come to pass.

Expanding Opportunities for Higher Education

The next important chapter in learning community history unfolded in the 1960s and 1970s, an era during which the higher education system nearly doubled in size and the community college system was broadly established. These decades brought widespread innovation, with various experiments in pedagogy, curriculum, structure, and faculty and student roles. Cluster colleges appeared as one major structural experiment aimed at humanizing the scale of higher education and promoting community by breaking large universities into smaller, semiautonomous units (Gaff and Associates, 1970). Many traditional institutions established innovative programs and subcolleges, such as the Residential College at

Michigan, the Centennial program at the University of Nebraska, Unit One at the University of Illinois, Collins College at Indiana University, Wautauga College at Appalachia State University, the Goodrich program at the University of Nebraska-Omaha, and Fairhaven College at Western Washington University, to mention just a few. (See Jones and Smith, 1984, for an account of many of these educational experiments.)

Some of these cluster colleges were also living-learning experiments. They tried to create a seamless educational experience that brought curricular and co-curricular experiences together. In many instances, they provided a small college environment, an interdisciplinary curriculum, and opportunities for students to design their own course of study. Other harbingers of the future were early efforts to move beyond credit hours and courses to assess student learning through competency-based self-paced learning, the examination system at Hampshire College, and the practice of assessing student abilities at Alverno College.

In 1970 Colorado College moved boldly into curriculum restructuring by creating the "block plan," whereby the curriculum was reorganized into eleven three-week intensive blocks in which students would take disciplinary courses. Though motivated by many of the same factors as the contemporary learning community movement (class size, fragmentation of effort, lack of sustained interaction, and the desire for time flexibility for fieldwork), the Colorado plan developed independently and was replicated in a number of independent colleges, including Cornell College of Iowa, where it remains operative.[8]

Innovative new public and private colleges were also founded in this era, including The Evergreen State College, the University of California-Santa Cruz, Pitzer College, Hampshire College, New College in Florida, Ramapo College in New Jersey, University of Wisconsin-Green Bay, and Empire State College. As Gerald Grant and David Riesman point out in their classic early study of major educational experiments of this period, *The Perpetual Dream* (1978), these colleges varied considerably but most had distinctive missions, an interdisciplinary focus, and a stress on active learning. Most were what they termed "popular reform efforts," which sought to liberalize the existing educational approaches. Many of these efforts would probably trace their lineage back to the work of John Dewey, with his emphasis on experiential learning and his insistence that teaching consider first the interests and passions of the individual. Many of the innovations in these programs—such as writing across the curriculum, active learning, cooperative education, independent study, and interdisciplinary education—were later broadly appropriated by more traditional institutions.

A few of these reform efforts aimed at fundamentally rethinking educational goals and structures. Grant and Riesman called these more fundamental reform efforts *telic reforms:* St. John's College and its Great Books program, Kresge College at Santa Cruz, and the College for Human Resources (now called Metropolitan College of New York) represented telic reform efforts (Grant and Riesman, 1978). Whether any of these efforts could sustain themselves, whether they could scale up and become cost-effective, and whether they would influence higher education broadly, were open questions for decades to come.

Most of these innovative programs were insular and understandably preoccupied with survival in their founding years, seldom interacting with one another. It would be quite a few years before their leaders would begin to meet and actively discuss their role in the larger education reform efforts and the century-long debates about the purposes and practices of higher education. Two conferences held at Rollins College in 1983 and 1995 were landmarks (Lane, 1984). Dewey had given an important lecture at Rollins in 1931, and the college had continued to celebrate the Dewey connection with occasional conferences. These gatherings became important in resurfacing the work of Dewey, bringing the several traditions of the progressive education movement together and challenging them to address contemporary issues about education reform and liberal education (Hill, 1984a; Cadwallader, 1984b).

The 1983 conference attendees were notable, including representatives from older progressive colleges such as Antioch and Bennington, the leading innovative institutions of the 1960s and 1970s such as Hampshire, Evergreen, Alverno, Pitzer, State University of New York-Old Westbury, and newly emerging centers for innovation at LaGuardia Community College and Miami Dade Community College. Eventually the learning community effort would draw together a broad spectrum of colleges and universities and many elements of the work of John Dewey and Alexander Meiklejohn.

Tussman's Experiment at Berkeley

Two of the programs directly related to Meiklejohn's Experimental College that emerged in the 1960s were in California, one at Berkeley and the other at San Jose State College. The University of California successor to the Meiklejohn Experimental College was created by Joseph Tussman, a Berkeley professor. Tussman had studied philosophy with Meiklejohn at Wisconsin after the Experimental College closed. He was taken with his mentor's vision, and the two men became lifelong friends. When

Meiklejohn eventually moved to California, Tussman followed him and enrolled in a graduate program at Berkeley. Tussman later joined the Berkeley faculty.

In 1965 Tussman convinced the administration to establish a program modeled on Meiklejohn's Wisconsin experiment. Like its predecessor, the Berkeley learning community effort was short-lived (1965 to 1969), but it too established a model for other reform efforts, including many programs in the United States and Canada.[9] Tussman's lively and detailed account of the *Experiment at Berkeley* (1969) had a significant influence on many later learning community initiatives. His book offers a detailed and provocative structural argument for an integrated curriculum, resituating the rationale for learning communities in a more contemporary context.

Tussman contended that the most significant conflicts in our universities are not necessarily the most obvious ones. Most important, he thought, was the internal tension that resulted from being both universities and colleges at the same time. Tussman wrote eloquently about these two sides of the modern American university (1997, p. 53):

> The university is the academic community organized for the pursuit of knowledge. It is arrayed under the familiar departmental banners and moves against the unknown on all fronts. Its victories have transformed the world. The university is a collection of highly trained specialists who work with skill, persistence, and devotion . . . but it pays the price of its success. The price is specialization, and it supports two unsympathetic jibes: the individual specialized scholar may find that, as with Oedipus, the pursuit of knowledge leads to impairment of vision; and the community of scholars, speaking its special tongues, has suffered the fate of Babel.
>
> The men who are the university are also, however, the men who are the college. But the liberal arts college is a different enterprise. It does not assault or extend the frontiers of knowledge. It has a different mission. It cultivates human understanding. The mind of the person . . . is its central concern. . . . The university [strives] for multiplicity and knowledge; the college for unity and understanding. The college is everywhere in retreat, fighting a dispirited rear guard action against the triumphant university. The upper division dominated by departmental cognitive interests, has become, in spirit, a preparatory run at the graduate school, increasingly professional. Only the lower division remains outside the departmental fold—invaded, neglected, exploited, misused. It is there that the college must make its stand.

Although Tussman's argument focused on the research university, it has now become relevant to many other types of institutions because many of the nation's colleges—public and private, large and small—have adopted the structure, culture, and aspirations of the "flagships." In many ways, the issues about the role of general education during Tussman's time had deepened and shifted to other institutions, especially community colleges, which were becoming more and more important in providing students with their general education experience. Although community colleges might have become beacons of new visions of general education, that was not their primary mission, though learning communities are increasingly tied to general education today (see Fogarty, Dunlap, and others, 2003, for a history of this effort). Instead, the research university's transfer requirements have increasingly set the tone and called the tune, prescribing the curriculum in conventional modular terms largely organized through the elective system of course offering and course taking.

Tussman believed a new way of thinking about general education was required to resolve the dualisms in the modern university. Drawing upon the Experimental College model, his solution was to abolish courses as the basic curricular planning units and to see the lower-division curriculum as a "program" rather than a collection of courses. His trenchant analysis of the negative impact of the course remains compelling and central to the learning community rationale (1997, pp. 56–57):

> The course forces teaching into small, relatively self-contained units. Horizontally, courses are generally unrelated and competitive. . . . No teacher is in a position to be responsible for . . . the student's total educational situation. The student presents himself to the teacher in fragments, and not even the advising system can put him together again. . . . Horizontal competitiveness and fragmentation of student attention are limiting conditions of which every sensitive teacher is bitterly aware. But there is nothing he can do about it. He can develop a coherent course, but a collection of coherent courses may be simply an incoherent collection. For the student, to pursue one thread is to drop another. He seldom experiences the delight of sustained conversations. He lives the life of a distracted intellectual juggler.

Structuring the curriculum around *programs* proved to be revolutionary, as Tussman predicted. Programs required the re-creation of community among faculty, because programs, unlike courses, could not be usefully taught by a single teacher or from the perspective of a single discipline. Programs asked faculty teams to examine publicly the content and purpose of each offering. They liberated the planning process, making it dynamic and creative. This led to new ways of thinking about how teachers would interact with one another and with their students.

In writing about his program, Tussman stressed the importance of an emergent, creative process of constructing the curriculum, an insight that flies in the face of many contemporary approaches to education reform. He said, "A dominating idea must come first. Without it nothing happens. This has some implications for first program curricular planning and educational reform. It means, I think, that we should expect nothing, or very little, from academic committees, commissions, or task forces in the way of real innovation or reform. They are, at best, midwives; they may encourage fertility and even help with the delivery, but they neither conceive nor bear. . . . The curriculum must grow out of a simple idea and be developed by a group committed to the idea" (1997, p. 89).

In content and structure, the program at Berkeley was similar to Meiklejohn's, but as Tussman put it, "We were captivated, not enslaved" by the Meiklejohn curriculum. Again, the curriculum was organized as a team-taught interdisciplinary program rather than a set of courses. It was based on the central theme of democracy and the Athens-America concept. It began with study of the Greeks through the Hebraic tradition to seventeenth-century England and America. In the process students read Shakespeare, Hobbes, Homer, Plato, Thucydides, and others. The second year focused on Tussman's passion—the U.S. Constitution.

Primary texts, seminars, and a pass-fail grading system were critical elements of the structure. Writing was heavily stressed, with tutorials on the papers with the program faculty. Students were also invited to share and comment on each other's journals. Once a week there was an "unattended seminar" that was run entirely by the students, without faculty present. In her lengthy retrospective study of alumni of the Tussman program, Catherine Trow (1998) reported that the unattended seminar was identified as a key program element in building skills in working in groups and participating in discussions.

The Berkeley program also had a place—an old house next to campus— that helped create a sense of community. As one alumni recounted, "The greatest impact of the program for me was the idea of a community of scholars, of having been associated with the same faculty members, the same students over two years, with a physical location identified with this house" (Trow, 1987, pp. 19–20).

Looking back twenty years later, many alumni mentioned *community* as a strong element of the program. They described community in multiple ways: an abstract idea explored through the curriculum, a descriptor of the social environment where they found friendships, and the "academic learning community" in which they experienced sharing of ideas and intellectual growth through common readings and discussion (Trow, 1998). The overall ethos of the program made it a powerful experience for many of them, often the high point of their undergraduate career.

The Berkeley curriculum was based on what Tussman saw as the most fundamental goal of general education: education for democracy. In a somewhat ironical twist on how the term is now generally used, Tussman speaks of general education as "vocational education," arguing passionately for its importance. "Democracy imposes on everyone a political vocation; this vocation demands a special education. . . . The purpose of the first program [the Experimental College] is to lead the student into a broad and sustained examination of the 'moral' dimensions of the situation in which he and we find ourselves . . . and [this] must be related to the deep controversial issues of our time" (Trow, 1998, p. 379).

As Trow points out in her study of the alumni, Tussman was asking students to make a commitment to the political vocation: doing so required advances in their moral and cognitive development. "'Reconciling yourself with authority,' as one participant put it, was certainly one developmental component, [making a] commitment to community and understanding the citizen's obligations to society were others" (Trow, 1998, p. 379).

Although the commitment to education for democracy was partially about the content of the curriculum, it also guided the program's admissions policy and pedagogical strategies. The faculty were committed to working with average students along with the gifted. Many later learning communities have also shared this commitment to providing all students with this powerful form of education. As Trow points out, "Faculty considered each and every student in the program capable of 'getting' the program curriculum. Tussman was very Deweyian. . . . His intensive individualized teaching methods were based on the progressive nature of cognitive development—when students weren't thinking clearly it wasn't because they were dumb and couldn't get it, it was because there was a snag somewhere in the course of their intellectual development that needed to be and could be overcome" (Trow, 1998, pp. 290–291).

Thirty years later, Tussman remained convinced that the lower-division curriculum should be an education for citizenship. While acknowledging that his position is widely rejected by many scholars and humanists, he continued to raise pointed questions of educational purpose (Tussman, 1997). In 1994, he attended a learning community conference in Washington State and was amazed at the large number of programs describing themselves as learning communities. Although he was impressed with the proliferation of the concept, he asked, "Where is the U.S. Constitution? Where is the Bible? Where are the great moral questions?" This was his way of asking the fundamental question: To what end and purpose are these programs designed, and how do they serve the betterment of society? Altering structure and pedagogy is all well and good, he observed, but if we do not also address the deeper questions in society, contemporary learning communities are not seriously addressing societal needs.

Tussman's accounts of the experimental program at Berkeley are filled with paradox and self-revelation (Tussman, 1969, 1997). They offer poignant insights into the personal dilemmas of being a change agent in a large university and the difficulty of maintaining personal commitments that contradict the dominant value systems. His writing also vividly describes the realities of building a teaching team.

During the first two-year program cycle, the teaching team consisted of regular Berkeley faculty. Tussman describes the first year as tumultuous, and recounts in detail the trauma of becoming a teaching team and getting the students to do their work. Finding it difficult to recruit regular faculty for the second cycle, Tussman brought in non-Berkeley faculty. The second cycle, he said, restored his faith that "education could be thought of as initiation of the new generation into a great continuing and deeply rooted civilization" (Tussman, 1997, p. 42). Although using non-Berkeley faculty members may have proven "easier" in the short run, it exacerbated the problem of establishing the program more permanently in the university structure.

As the program neared the end of its second cycle, the question of its continuation was raised. It had proved difficult to attract faculty, and the students constantly tested the boundaries of the program and the faculty expectations, but Tussman thought it had been successful. The prospects for continuation were favorable, but he was undecided about what to do. In a retrospective published many years later, he described his dilemma:

> I had done nothing to get the program rooted in Berkeley's soil. The first run faculty had returned to their departments and had no continuing connection with the program. The visiting second run group had gone home. I was left, panting, in my home department. Where was the program? Who cared? . . .
>
> Everything was in limbo when I got a call from a newly appointed vice chancellor. He wanted the program continued. . . . Would I draw up a proposal? So I drew up a modest proposal. . . . A program to start each year with about 150 students and six professors. I suggested that

three faculty be permanent tenured, faculty who understood and were committed to the program and who could guide the three transient faculty members and provide stability and experience. . . . By inviting the right visiting faculty, I wanted to foster imitation by other state and community colleges. And I proposed that we become a center for the study of higher education teaching, the absence of which had seemed to me to be a scandal not mitigated by Schools of Education. . . .

But tenure slots were a different proposition. They were precious, and departments fought over them. . . . And I was unnerved by other doubts . . . about myself. Life in the program . . . was enormously exciting. . . . But why was I so exhausted? . . . I felt the seductive charm of "normal" academic life—the intellectual tension, the pervasive wit, the intellectual privacy, the leisurely autonomy, the cool arm's length, controlled, well-mannered involvement, on one's own terms, with others. I missed it, and I shrank from the thought of giving it up for the unremitting intensity of life in the program. . . . Was I really prepared to wrestle endlessly with the recalcitrant to live the life of a missionary in a corner of a gaudy Rialto? The very question was enervating, demoralizing. So, when the vice chancellor told me there would be no tenure slots, I did not argue. [Tussman, 1997, pp. 40–44]

Tussman made these further observations: "For the student of institutional reform the situation was not without interest. I see it now as an encounter between the enduring and the ephemeral. The enduring university is rooted in departments, themselves based upon the great cognitive disciplines that, over time, may merge and split, slowly altering the geography of the mind. . . . The key to the relation between the enduring and the ephemeral is the institution of tenure. And tenure is something you have (with a few notable exceptions) in departments" (1997, p. 39).

Finally, Tussman noted: "The fundamental delusion may have been to suppose that it was possible for a great organism like the university to sustain for long an enterprise so at odds with its essential nature. The mode of life required by the program was not congenial to the normal Berkeley professor. In the end, the program must be judged to have made no enduring difference to the quality of education at Berkeley" (1997, pp. 44–46).

And so Joseph Tussman returned from the program house to the usual halls and habits of academe. The University of California, like the University of Wisconsin, had not proven hospitable to such innovations. Despite the administration's support, it was clear that the program was not compatible with the existing values, decision-making processes, and resources of a large research university. It ran against the mainstream in terms of faculty roles and rewards. Without administrative status the program had no reliable means of recruiting faculty. Although the university might have continued the program under its "experimental status," that wasn't enough for Tussman (1997). Other, later learning communities would struggle with this issue of institutionalization and the reshaping of institutional environments to structures, processes, and value systems that could sustain them over the long run.

San Jose State College

Although Berkeley never embraced Tussman's notion of aligning with the more teaching-oriented state universities and community colleges, San Jose State College simultaneously offered a program (1965 to 1969) very similar to Berkeley's. A number of the San Jose faculty involved with this program eventually joined the founding faculty at The Evergreen State College. Mervyn Cadwallader, then on the faculty at San Jose, played an important role in bringing learning communities to San Jose, then to SUNY-Old Westbury, and finally, to Evergreen. Cadwallader was one of the first in a growing tradition of charismatic leaders committed to learning communities as an idea that could be broadly disseminated (Cadwallader, 1982a, 1982b, 1983, 1984a).

Innovations often spring from serendipitous events and chance encounters, and this is certainly true of the Meiklejohn-Cadwallader connection. Cadwallader's cousin was married to Joseph Tussman. One evening in 1963, Cadwallader met Meiklejohn at a dinner party at Tussman's home. Cadwallader recalled being "bowled over" at Meiklejohn's vitality at age ninety as he avidly recounted a story about a speech given by Brown University's president during his freshman year. The president had asked the eager freshmen what difference it might have made if Alexander the Great had not died so young. Cadwallader was immediately taken with Meiklejohn's energy and ideas and particularly with his account of the Experimental College.

After that initial meeting, Tussman, Meiklejohn, and Cadwallader continued to see one another periodically. At one of these meetings in 1964, Tussman mentioned that he was going to propose a Meiklejohn-type program at Berkeley, and Cadwallader decided to try to establish a similar program at San Jose as well. On both campuses, the initial response from the administration was favorable.

At San Jose the new program, called the Tutorial Program, was up and running by 1965. The San Jose and Berkeley curricula were similar but not identical. Both were team-taught, yearlong programs of full-time study based on primary texts and seminars. Both studied the roots of modern democracy through the Greeks, then moved through the romantic and industrial revolutions, and concluded with the American experience and contemporary issues and problems. In the succeeding years, the San Jose program developed some quite different curricular content, including a program called "Political Ecology" that brought in the sciences and environmental themes that were emergent in the late 1960s. This program theme would eventually be taken up at other institutions.

Cadwallader was quite taken with the idea of exporting the integrated curricular approach to other institutions. He thought the benefits were so obvious that if he just described the approach, people would want to launch interdisciplinary programs of their own. To this end, he visited other campuses, including Sonoma State College. Sonoma subsequently established the Hutchins School of Liberal Studies in 1969, an integrated general education program of four twelve-credit programs based on team teaching, narrative evaluations, and a book seminar–based pedagogy. This strongly rooted program is thriving today and has become a leadership center for learning community work in California.[10] The approach proved interesting to faculty members at other colleges as well. By Cadwallader's account, colleagues were invariably drawn most to the notion of a coherent curriculum and the possibility of deep learning in an interdisciplinary, full-time structure. Perhaps predictably, the specific content of these learning communities was generally of less interest.

Cadwallader was also greatly sobered by his experiment at San Jose, especially the need to build congruent expectations among the students and the faculty. After a turbulent first year, the program became much more structured and intentional in building a sense of community and responsibility.

> The mistakes made in the first program were clear. There was too much committee and not enough commitment. Accustomed to academic sovereignty in the classroom, the first faculty team continued to cherish and exercise sovereignty despite the program. Someone was always spending an extra month on his favorite book while some books on the list were ignored and others added. We really did not want close collaboration.
>
> The second time around we had a coherent program and a collegial faculty. The program had a clearly elucidated political theme and the theme was stated over and over again. The teachers collaborated as a team in the teaching of the theme all the way through the program. Each member of the faculty understood that he was a voluntary member of something that would become a fellowship, and that if he could not continue to accept the obligations of that fellowship, he must resign from it, rather than divide and destroy it. . . .

We discovered (also) that there was a lot to learn about winning over students, signing them up as members, getting them to make the necessary commitment. Our students were constantly distracted by identity crises, family crises, sexual dilemmas and debacles, dates and drugs, beads and boots, cars and rock concerts, and even jobs. . . . We learned the hard way that for them the essence of good communication was trusting and being trusted. Neither trust nor the lack of it have relevance for the traditional college course in which a distant professor lectures and dutiful student-stenographers take it all down. But trust is at the heart of a program built on a sense of community, and we realized that reconciliation had to come first, and good conversation about Plato or de Tocqueville could only come later. [Cadwallader, 1984a, p. 356]

In many ways, the San Jose program was a successful venture but it too disappeared in a few years, failing to root itself in the larger institution when Cadwallader and two of the original faculty left to start a similar program at SUNY-Old Westbury. The faculty who had taught in the San Jose program were older and wiser. As it turned out, they would be given other opportunities to use what they had learned in different institutional settings.

State University of New York-Old Westbury

In 1969 Cadwallader was recruited to SUNY-Old Westbury, one of the new innovative universities on the East Coast. He negotiated a place for his program in the humanities honors program, bringing two of the San Jose faculty with him. They joined four others to form a teaching team of six full-time faculty. The new integrated program was one of several alternative programs available at Old Westbury. The program barely limped through one year with disappointing enrollment. Old Westbury, it turned out, was an institution in a state of turmoil. The following year, the entire campus was shut down and reorganized into more conventional structures.

But Cadwallader was not ready to give up on the idea. Midyear he was hired away to be one of the founding deans at the newly established Evergreen State College. He spent much of the next six months commuting back and forth to Olympia, Washington. Eventually four Old Westbury faculty and administrators, including the acting president, Byron Youtz, came to Evergreen, all more careful about setting boundaries on curricular innovation and faculty governance. Reflecting on his experience, Cadwallader said: "What I learned at Old Westbury is how risky it is to start an alternative program with people who'd never done it before.

When I went to Evergreen, I advised the president to hire a number of people with this kind of experience" (personal communication with the authors, October 2000). This advice was followed. One-third of Evergreen's seventeen planning faculty were protégés of Cadwallader. Many of the others came with experience at strong liberal arts colleges or other nontraditional institutions, such as New College or Santa Cruz.

The Evergreen State College

The Meiklejohn-Tussman ideas about a reformed curriculum structure and integrated study were to take root next in the state of Washington. In 1970, The Evergreen State College, a new public alternative college, was being established. The seventeen planning faculty were given the luxury of spending an entire year planning the curriculum and the institutional structures and practices. (For an account of this early history, see Jones, 1981.) At Cadwallader's suggestion, the founding faculty read Tussman's book *Experiment at Berkeley.* Tussman's trenchant analysis of the dualistic structure of the American university and his integrated program approach captured their imaginations. Many of the founding faculty came with aspirations to create an innovative *public* institution that could address the serious social issues of the times. Agreeing that academic departments and discipline-based discrete courses were a major obstacle to meaningful interdisciplinary undergraduate education, the Evergreen founders decided to design much of the new college around yearlong coordinated studies programs that would be full-time, team-taught, and organized around interdisciplinary themes. "Democracy and Tyranny," "The Individual and Society," and "Political Ecology" were titles of early programs.

By making a commitment to team-taught, yearlong integrated programs at the outset, much controversy was avoided about the mission and approach of this new institution, and new faculty were hired with clear expectations. The pedagogy was based on team teaching, seminars, narrative evaluations instead of grades, writing across the curriculum, cooperative education, and experiential learning. Most important, the entire organizational structure and the faculty role and reward system were designed to support this curriculum and pedagogy. Other important structural components included no faculty rank, no faculty titles, no departments, a uniform pay scale, rotating academic deans from the faculty, and reappointment procedures that required team teaching. These structures and values were later articulated as the five foci of an Evergreen education: interdisciplinary education, collaboration, active learning, connecting theory and practice, and teaching and learning across significant differences.

Evergreen represented an ambitious attempt to design a coherent institution around the notion of a team-taught integrated curriculum without the conflicts inherent in existing institutions. (For a history of the college, see Smith, 2001b.) Furthermore, the college would test whether this could be cost-effective, since Evergreen would operate under the same funding model as the other regional state universities but reconfigure the manner in which the resources and faculty load were distributed. Comparability was seen as necessary if the college was to survive in the competitive and often uniform policy environment of public education. In the early 1970s alternative institutions had been widely criticized for being unaffordable, but Evergreen was determined to demonstrate that this was not necessarily true.

Mervyn Cadwallader, then at the forefront of his third educational experiment, was Evergreen's most influential early dean. He argued forcefully for both the structure and content of the Meiklejohn-Tussman curriculum, advocating for a "moral curriculum" grounded in the humanities and the social sciences that would help prepare students for civic engagement. When the college opened, a number of programs were offered (and continue to be offered) that fit this conception, but the Evergreen faculty as a whole chose to emulate the pedagogy and the structure of the Meiklejohn curriculum but not the specific content. The Evergreen structure and culture remained basically permissive about curricular content, allowing the college to expand the audience for its programs greatly. The learning community model of yearlong, team-taught programs proved remarkably adaptable to any subject matter and level of student preparation.

Innovations face challenges, especially in their early years when enrollments are often equated with success. How an institution addresses these early enrollment issues can shape its future. During its third year, the Washington economy slipped into recession and all of the state's colleges experienced a large enrollment slump. Thinking that yearlong integrated programs could only work in certain subject areas and that the college needed to attract more students, Cadwallader recommended establishing two colleges at Evergreen—one traditionally structured around departments and courses and the other based on coordinated studies programs. This was, in fact, the model at Wisconsin and Berkeley where the Meiklejohn-Tussman colleges provided the lower-division, general education program and students then went on to take conventional departmental majors.

This enrollment crisis and the proposed response to it presented a critical turning point. Thinking that it would allow the traditional college eventually to kill the innovation, the Evergreen faculty emphatically rejected the two-college idea. Instead, the college decided to stay the course and committed fully to its coordinated studies curriculum.

For many years it was not clear whether Evergreen could "scale up" to accommodate a larger enrollment, whether it could be cost-effective, and whether its educational ideas could be adapted to traditional institutions to improve undergraduate education. All of these questions remained open well into the late 1980s, but the answers became clear in subsequent years. By 2004 the college enrolled more than four thousand students, and numerous significant studies had demonstrated that it was a highly effective learning environment (Astin, 1991; Kuh, Schuh, Whitt, and others, 1991). At the same time, Evergreen had become a leader in the learning community movement, finally realizing early hopes that it would play a broader role in education reform. Continuing to operate within the budgetary expectations of the other regional public universities, the college demonstrated that this type of restructured learning environment was financially viable.

East Coast Learning Community Development

In the mid-1970s, a number of learning community experiments were emerging on the East Coast as a result of two highly visible programs, the federated learning communities at SUNY-Stony Brook, under the leadership of Patrick Hill, a philosophy professor, and learning clusters at LaGuardia Community College in New York, under the leadership of Roberta Matthews, an associate dean. These two individuals were important in further articulating the idea of learning communities and developing new models for very different institutional environments. Matthews later teamed up with Hill to disseminate the idea to a large number of institutions, but they came to their structural innovations separately. When Hill and Matthews co-presented, as they often did, the juxtaposition of the research university and the community college made the idea of linking courses appeal to a much broader audience.

With the dramatic expansion of the community college system in the late 1960s and 1970s, more and more students began their college careers in a two-year institution. This made the introduction of learning communities in a leading-edge community college like LaGuardia an important bellwether of the future (Matthews, 1986, 1994). LaGuardia Community College developed the idea of paired and clustered courses in 1974 as a result of Matthews' interest in making collaborative interdisciplinary teaching and learning possible in the community college. These programs were seen as a means of overcoming faculty isolation and promoting curricular coherence (Matthews and Lynch, 1997). Building the program around existing general education courses also facilitated transfer to four-year institutions.

Team teaching was not seen as financially feasible, so the LaGuardia course cluster model involved careful team planning, but not team teaching, around themes relevant to the mission of this diverse, urban institution. The cluster course themes were organized to reinforce the college mission and audience. Liberal arts majors and students could choose between learning communities grouped around two themes: one was "Work, Labor, and Business in American Life," the other, "Freedom and Seeing." The freedom theme was especially appropriate to the college's large immigrant population. The work theme was reinforced through an institutionwide cooperative education program. Each cluster contained a composition course, a course in writing the research paper, an integrating seminar, and a combination of philosophy, social science, or humanities courses. Although the cluster was often a full academic load for the students, the faculty taught a combination of cluster and non-cluster courses each term. It quickly became apparent that the cluster courses were highly effective and that the modest additional cost was easily offset by increases in student retention. Since 1978, all full-time liberal arts students at LaGuardia have been required to take one of the clusters to earn their associate degree, and LaGuardia now offers learning communities in a variety of other areas as well (see Matthews and Lynch, 1997).

Hill is primarily associated with the idea of federated learning communities, a model particularly well adapted to large research institutions.[11] Looking for ways to improve undergraduate education in large research institutions in the mid-1970s, Hill visited Evergreen and a number of other innovative programs at research universities in California. He came up with the idea of curricular restructuring through federated learning communities after thinking about how to adapt some of the ideas he saw to a research university environment.

Hill became an active advocate for learning communities in the late 1970s. He brought a new language to the Meiklejohn-Tussman rationale for learning communities that was squarely rooted in the realities of life in research universities in the 1970s (see Hill, 1975, 1982; Gamson and Associates, 1984). Though Meiklejohn had first introduced the terms *communities of learners* and *learning community,* Hill resurfaced the latter term, choosing it quite intentionally to respond to what he saw as deep social and intellectual atomism in universities, held in place by their prevailing structures.

Well-versed in the work of John Dewey, Hill agreed with many of his views about community, active learning, and the value of letting student interest guide the classroom. He became a well-known advocate for diversity in the 1990s (Hill, 1991, 1984a), strongly echoing the Dewey point of view that diversity is a huge resource for higher education (Hill, 1991).

Hill was aware of and influenced by Tussman, but the program at Stony Brook was in many ways differently rooted. Hill is quick to point out that he never uttered a word against specialization or departments. Indeed, he hardly ever used the word "interdisciplinary." Nor was the focus on the lower-division curriculum (although they were later forced by the administration to become involved with it). Hill's primary concern was with the kind of community that existed and the lack of interaction among departments. A central issue for him was the kind of compartmentalized education students were receiving as a result.

Hill recognized that research universities were already communities in many ways. They were richly funded residence-based academic communities, and they were also departmental communities. But they were not the kind of community Hill envisioned. He thought these were elitist communities, resting on social relations that fostered dominance and dependency, not the communities of inquiry needed in contemporary society. He also saw deep problems in these communities as a result of mismatched expectations between a research-oriented faculty and a career-oriented student body, among the faculty themselves (and also their administrators), and between the university and the larger society.[12]

When faculty at Stony Brook complained about students being passive, Hill responded that this was a consequence of the educational structure and the organization of the curriculum. "There was neither time nor space nor opportunity nor guidance for students to engage in active or integrative learning" (Patrick Hill, personal communication with the authors, May 2001).

In thinking about institutional change, Hill was very much a pragmatist. Creating the conditions for a liberating education was a sociological as well as a philosophical issue, he contended, and it required carefully working within the parameters of the existing institutional environment. Would-be reformers must "design structures that overcome the isolation of faculty from one another and from their students. They must build communities that encourage faculty members to relate to one another not only as specialists but also as educators. And they must provide continuity and integration of the curriculum" (Gamson and Associates, 1984, p. 85).

The federated learning communities (FLC) program was Hill's solution to the dilemma of building new types of learning communities in a research university environment. This program took unchanged existing courses in the curriculum and essentially "federated" them around an integrating seminar and theme. The learning community itself was a subset of these larger classes, a cohort of twenty to forty students taking the federated classes together, and also enrolling in an additional integrating seminar. A "master learner"—a faculty member from a different discipline, freed of usual teaching responsibilities—was a key member of the community. He or she took all the federated courses as a student and facilitated the integrating program seminar. The model provided a novel and stimulating approach to faculty development because it put a faculty member—the master learner—into the unique role of observing other faculty members and integrating their disparate material along with the students. Many of the FLC programs addressed major social and civic issues of the day, a special concern to Hill and his colleagues. Examples of early program titles included "World Hunger," "Technology, Values, and Society," and "Social and Ethical Issues in the Life Sciences."

Hill regarded his credit-bearing, no-books, no-predetermined-content, no-expert-led program seminar as the hardest thing to sell to faculty members and also the most radical and important innovation. This was the "mediated space" for students to explore, exercise their own creativity, and (perhaps) find coherence. "Coherence was most importantly a property of the interaction of the students' interests with disparate materials to be worked over. Only in the context of the unstructured program seminar could you observe how prepackaged, initiative destroying, and creativity limiting were the questions and projects of the overly planned courses" (Patrick Hill, personal communication with the authors, May 2001).

Hill's federated learning communities program opened at Stony Brook in 1976 with support from the Fund for the Improvement of Postsecondary Education (FIPSE). Although it never became a large-scale innovation there, it was quite influential in attracting prominent faculty members to Stony Brook, and within a few years, garnered significant national publicity.

Faith Gabelnick, an honors program leader at the University of Maryland and later Western Michigan University, was especially influential in disseminating the idea of learning communities into the honors program networks. She also expanded the conceptual underpinnings of learning community practice by bringing her work on cognitive development, interpersonal relations, and active learning into the learning community discussion. Gabelnick was interested in seeing the seminar portion of the learning community model explicitly developed as a site for work on critical thinking and cognitive development. She had a special interest in William Perry's work on intellectual and ethical development (Perry, 1970). Gabelnick was also vitally interested in connecting higher education to the K–12 schools. With John Howarth, she created federated learning communities program at Maryland whose master learner was an experienced high school teacher on sabbatical. This approach helped support the program financially, because the public school's sabbatical program essentially paid for the master learner.

By the early 1980s different types of curricular restructuring efforts began to spread on the East Coast to different types of institutions. A number of institutions started programs as a result of meeting Hill and hearing about the FLC program, including the University of Maryland, the University of Tennessee, Gallaudet College, SUNY-Plattsburgh, the University of Nebraska, Denison, Lesley, and Rollins College. Adopting ideas from Stony Brook, LaGuardia, and Evergreen, Daytona Beach Community College developed a yearlong, interdisciplinary team-taught learning community program in 1983 that continues today. With the exception of the long-standing Quanta program, however, most of these institutions did not continue their learning community programs past the first few years because they made the fatal mistake of resting the innovation on the shoulders of a single person or a small group of supporters.

In the years since, many new adaptations of this model have developed and are thriving throughout the United States. Few institutions, unfortunately, continued the master learner role and the program seminar that Hill considered central to his model, providing a crucial element of self-reflection to both a faculty member and a student community trying to make sense of the curriculum and the pressing issues of the day. The mediated space and freedom of the program seminar, in particular, gave the students the opportunity to develop their own voices and sense of the curriculum. With only a few exceptions, this subtle perspective and structure has been lost as the model has been adapted to other institutional circumstances.

As with many small and struggling innovations, learning community programs came and went in the late 1970s and early 1980s. A number started one model and then moved to another. It was not unusual for campuses to start and then end programs, and then start them all over again, often under new leaders. Some institutions had great continuity in learning community leadership, whereas others experienced rapid turnover. In 1983 the East and West Coast learning community efforts converged with the appointment of Patrick Hill as provost of The Evergreen State College.

Learning Community Expansion and the Washington Center for Improving the Quality of Undergraduate Education

When Evergreen was founded in 1969, many had hoped the college would play a leadership role in higher education reform. Although many aspects of the college were innovative and potentially transferable, this alternative college's first decade focused on establishing itself and surviving the assaults of skeptics in the Washington legislature. By the early 1980s, though, the institution stabilized and began to turn outward, realizing early hopes that it would play a larger external role in education reform, reaching out and sharing its innovations with others.

In 1981 Evergreen sponsored the first of several national conferences on alternative education. The conference drew many representatives from the nontraditional institutions established in the 1960s, the early 1970s, and more recent endeavors. Many of these institutions were grappling with issues of sustaining innovations in increasingly restrictive traditional institutional environments. Lively debates simmered on reforming faculty roles and rewards, creating student-centered classrooms, and working with more diverse learners. Patrick Hill attended the conference and gave a workshop on the federated learning communities program he was leading at Stony Brook. A dozen or so alumni of the original Experimental College at the University of Wisconsin also participated, wrote a paper, and enthusiastically shared their experiences. This conference represented the first broad-scale coming together of the East and West Coasts and the past and the future, and it resulted in the book *Against the Current: Reform and Experimentation in Higher Education* (Jones and Smith, 1984).

In 1983 Evergreen hired Patrick Hill as its provost. With Hill's appointment, important connections began to be forged between the different curricular restructuring efforts. Having seen the adoption of learning community strategies at a variety of campuses on the eastern seaboard, Hill had a strong interest in finding ways for Evergreen to connect with these related efforts and share its approaches with other institutions. A variety of learning community models had already been developed to implement the idea of curricular restructuring in different institutional settings and a number of these had sustained themselves for several years. What was needed was a vehicle and a language for further developing and disseminating the idea and the lessons learned in sustaining these innovations.

In 1984 a chance encounter between Evergreen's academic dean, Barbara Leigh Smith, and Ron Hamberg, a dean at Seattle Central

Community College, provided the triggering opportunity. Hamberg had heard about Evergreen's coordinated studies approach at a general education conference. Intrigued, he decided to bring a group of his faculty and student affairs leaders to visit. The visit captured the imaginations of the Seattle Central group, and they immediately decided they wanted to try teaching in an interdisciplinary coordinated studies format. A faculty exchange seemed to be a good way to learn how, so on short notice two Seattle Central faculty members were reassigned to Evergreen to spend spring quarter 1984 team teaching with an Evergreen veteran. The following fall, two Evergreen faculty went to Seattle Central to help start the new coordinated studies program. The exchange was so successful that the two colleges have continued it for more than fifteen years, creating an ongoing, deep relationship between the two schools and a seamless learning community experience for Seattle Central students interested in eventually transferring to Evergreen.

The Seattle Central initiative and the faculty exchange opened everyone's eyes to what institutions could do together. Other Seattle-area community colleges became interested in interinstitutional faculty exchanges, especially as a way of launching similar coordinated studies programs. Recognizing the power of the serendipitous opportunity, leaders at Evergreen decided to seek funding for a center to work statewide on education reform through learning communities. The Exxon Education Foundation and then the Ford Foundation provided seed money to start the Washington Center for Improving the Quality of Undergraduate Education, under the leadership of Barbara Leigh Smith and Jean MacGregor. Smith had previous experience at the University of Nebraska running a small cluster college. Her position as a senior academic dean at Evergreen gave the new consortium access to highly placed administrators, which was unusual and important in giving the Washington Center immediate connections and credibility. MacGregor brought to the project extensive experience in collaborative learning, community development, and community organizing. These skills proved crucial as the Washington Center developed its distinctive grassroots approach to education reform in Washington State. Because of their connection to Patrick Hill, Roberta Matthews and Faith Gabelnick became involved with the center in its early years, frequently serving as speakers, consultants, and workshop leaders for its conferences and outreach activities. The collaboration with these East Coast leaders gave the emergent effort on the West Coast both depth and broad connections to other networks and ideas.

In 1987, recognizing the potential of a statewide higher education network, the Washington legislature provided ongoing funding to the

Washington Center as a public service initiative of The Evergreen State College (Smith, 1988, 2001b). The center's focus was to be on curricular restructuring through learning communities. *Learning communities* became the term that the center used to describe a variety of curricular restructuring approaches, many of which were springing up independently of one another. Smith and MacGregor stressed the value of shaping learning community designs to local circumstances, student needs, and faculty intentions.

With a continuous stream of support from the Washington Center in the form of conferences, consultants, publications, faculty exchanges, and statewide working committees, learning communities of various types spread rapidly in Washington State, reaching thirty-four campuses by 1994. The center pursued a strategy of encouraging experimentation and carefully disseminating promising practices that consciously linked the Washington effort to important national efforts in assessment, active and collaborative learning, writing across the curriculum, inquiry-based approaches to science education, and multicultural education. Status differences between institutions and roles were purposely downplayed to encourage an environment of sharing and collaboration. The necessary partnerships between faculty members and academic administrators were built through explicit strategies, such as having pairs of participants—a dean and a faculty member—from the various schools serve on the center's planning committee.

During the first four years, twelve institutions in Washington State established strong learning community programs. The community colleges were initially at the forefront, but by the late 1980s the four-year institutions were also involved. The University of Washington established a robust Freshman Interest Group program that would eventually enroll nearly 75 percent of its freshmen.

In the early years, faculty exchanges were an important dissemination strategy for the Washington Center. More than four hundred faculty were involved in faculty exchanges, either by going to another institution or by team teaching with an exchange faculty member. This proved to be a powerful and low-cost vehicle for disseminating curriculum ideas and practices. It also stimulated students to transfer, because they now had familiarity with the learning community idea and a personal relationship with a faculty member at the transfer institution.

By the mid-1990s more than two dozen Washington colleges were regularly offering learning communities, and a number of institutions had successfully institutionalized them. Seattle Central Community College, North Seattle Community College, the University of Washington, Skagit Valley College, and Evergreen became the sites for dozens of visits from other colleges interested in exploring the learning community approach. In Washington State, visitors could see how a diverse array of learning communities had been implemented in two- and four-year schools, private and public institutions, and in research universities as well as liberal arts colleges.

The learning community reform effort in Washington State is notable for its scale, its diversity, and its longevity. The higher education climate there provided fertile ground for the change effort. It already had a long-standing tradition of two- and four-year colleges working together in a relatively egalitarian fashion on such issues as transfer and articulation. The Washington Center built on these good relationships, and created a unique support system for the learning community effort, fostering frequent interinstitutional sharing and dissemination of both pedagogical practices and assessment and implementation strategies. The center also played an active role in the commitment of the Washington higher education system to assessment and diversity, often organizing collaborative statewide initiatives, frequently working on them with the State Board for Community and Technical Colleges. All these threads reinforced and deepened the learning community effort and broadened its appeal (Smith, 2001b). In all of its activities, the center's continued emphasis on collaborative efforts on behalf of organizational change helped to stimulate leaders in all these movements to see themselves in new ways. Many of these leaders now describe themselves as change agents and builders of a statewide reform community.

A Learning Community Movement

By the year 2000, learning communities had become a national movement. More than five hundred institutions, public and independent, urban and rural, residential and commuter, two-year and four-year, had adopted the learning community approach and they are continuing to adapt it to their own purposes and needs. Learning communities are being used in a variety of curricular settings—in general education, in freshman-year initiatives, in honors, in developmental education, in study in the major, and in vocational and professional programs. On some campuses, the learning community effort is just one small offering involving a few faculty members and students; at others programs enroll substantial portions of an entering class. Some institutions have established learning community requirements as part of their general education program. On some four-year college campuses, such as Wagner College, St. Lawrence University, Babson College, and Portland State University, and leading community colleges such as Skagit Valley and the Seattle community colleges, learning communities are a signature program in an overall effort at institutional transformation. On many others, they are simply one of many avenues for improving undergraduate education.

As Chapter One pointed out, these programs have evolved in response to a whole range of issues in higher education: the fragmentation of the curriculum, the growing diversity of students, problems in student retention, new research about student learning, calls for higher expectations from the public, and interest in faculty revitalization. Although two significant studies of higher education, *Involvement in Learning* (National Institute of Education, 1984) and *Integrity in the Curriculum* (Association of American Colleges, 1985), provided an early rationale for learning communities in the 1980s, the effort really took root in the 1990s.

Both individual leaders and various organizations played important roles in learning community dissemination. Books and articles by Vincent Tinto, K. Patricia Cross, Barbara Leigh Smith, Jean MacGregor, Roberta Matthews, John Gardner, Faith Gabelnick, Patrick Hill, W. Norton Grubb, Jodi Levine, Nancy Shapiro, Grant Cornwell, and Richard Guarasci were important. These leaders spoke regularly at national forums such as the American Association for Higher Education, the Association of American Colleges and Universities, and the Freshman Year Experience conferences, which featured learning communities as continuing threads in their conferences and publications over the last fifteen years.

The leadership and work of Vincent Tinto of Syracuse University has been central to the increasing interest in and credibility of learning communities. Known for his cutting-edge work on student retention and his landmark book *Leaving College: Rethinking the Causes and Cures of Student Attrition* (1987), Tinto turned his attention to learning communities and collaborative learning in 1990 when he became one of the principal researchers at the federally funded National Center for Postsecondary Teaching, Learning, and Assessment (NCTLA) at Pennsylvania State University. With two of his graduate students, Anne Goodsell Love and Patricia Russo, he did an in-depth study of the University of Washington's freshman interest group program, LaGuardia Community College's learning clusters, and Seattle Central Community College's coordinated studies program. These three institutions were quite different, providing rich opportunities for studying different models and different contexts. Tinto's NCTLA effort culminated in a series of reports and a large national conference on learning communities and collaborative learning at Pennsylvania State University in 1994 (see Tinto and Goodsell, 1993a, 1993b; Tinto, Goodsell-Love, and Russo, 1993; Tinto, 2000, 2002; Ratcliff and Associates, 1996). Both the publications and the conference widely disseminated the message that learning communities address a variety of significant issues in higher education.

Tinto's research demonstrated learning community effectiveness with extensive quantitative and qualitative detail, confirming that students in learning communities persist in school and learn more. His studies highlighted the positive contribution of the peer group, demonstrating that learning community students "learn from each other and develop a sense of responsibility for the learning of others" (Ratcliff and Associates, 1996, p. 10). Although his previous work suggested that student involvement was key, his landmark learning community study carefully described how student involvement could be fostered through collaborative learning. The research produced the dramatic insight that involving and academically challenging campus environments could be purposefully built, even on commuter campuses, and within the constraints of current budgets.

Active nationally as a speaker, Tinto's presentations increasingly turned toward issues of wider purpose as he drew significant connections between learning communities and democratic practice. Tinto's alliance with the learning community effort was an unusual and productive partnership between a leader in the educational research community and the practitioners working with learning communities in the field. It also brought academic and student affairs practitioners together, again broadening the movement's scope and audience.

In 1999 W. Norton Grubb and Associates produced a major study of teaching in community college that added further to the literature about learning communities. The book, *Honored But Invisible: An Inside Look at Teaching in Community Colleges,* studied 275 classrooms in thirty-two community colleges. Many of the institutions the research team visited offered learning communities. In this provocative and critical look at teaching in two-year institutions, the authors concluded that appropriately designed learning communities are a powerful approach to teaching and learning and an ideal vehicle for these institutions to address their multiple missions. At the same time, they saw disturbing variations in implementation and the quality of teaching and little institutional support for faculty development. The authors concluded their book with a clarion call for community colleges to invest deeply in becoming more effective teaching colleges and aggressively develop a culture of teaching.

Several other influential books appeared in the 1990s that supported learning communities and collaborative learning: Alexander Astin's *What Matters in College?* (1993b; see also Astin, 1993a), Ernest Pascarella and Patrick Terenzini's *How College Affects Students* (1991), and Lion Gardiner's *Redesigning Higher Education: Producing Dramatic Gains in*

Student Learning (1994). These works clearly described some of the problems of undergraduate education and offered some solutions. They affirmed the finding that challenging, involving learning environments fuel student performance while raising the paradox that student learning is also strongly affected by many of the uncontrollable features of our institutions—their size and student profile, for example. In a more recent summary of the literature, Ernest Pascarella (2001) concludes that admissions selectivity makes little difference in student growth; programmatic differences matter far more.

John Gardner also played an important role in the development and expansion of learning communities. A tireless promoter of ways to improve the critical transition points in higher education, Gardner established the infrastructure to support this work. In 1972 he launched the first University 101 course, which was designed to help students make a successful transition into college. Many institutions have established what have come to be referred to as "University 101 Freshman Seminars." Some of these seminars have become the anchor in a constellation of learning community courses. (Learning communities in freshman seminars are discussed in more detail in Chapter Five.) In 1986 Gardner established the National Resource Center for the First-Year Experience and Students in Transition to support the burgeoning interest in improving the freshman year. (The Web site is www.sc.edu/fye.) The center collects and disseminates information about the first year of college and other significant student transition points. For many years, this center has held conferences and provided technical assistance to institutions trying to improve student success in the freshman year. Freshman Year Experience conferences have regularly brought academic and student affairs practitioners and leaders together. In 1999 Gardner founded the Policy Center on the First Year of College hosted by Brevard College in North Carolina (www.brevard.edu/fyc). Current projects include research on best practices, forums and institutes for institutional leaders, and new assessment tools. Gardner's alliance with the emerging learning community effort deepened both endeavors.

Learning communities also evolved into a movement as a result of concerted regional and national efforts to learn about evolving practice, disseminate information, and help create a more general climate focused on teaching and learning (Lazerson, Wagener, and Shumanis, 2000). Organizations such as the Washington Center for Improving the Quality of Undergraduate Education have been key in building "the movement." The Washington Center's leadership has focused on Washington State because it is a state-funded public service center, but its influence became national.

In 1996 it launched the National Learning Community Project, first with FIPSE funding (1996 to 1999) and then with support (2000 to 2003) from The Pew Charitable Trusts. The effort has included conferences, resource dissemination, and strengthening both regional and national leadership for learning communities.

Recently, additional centers of leadership have started to emerge. Since 1995, Delta College in Michigan and William Rainey Harper College in Illinois have jointly sponsored an annual regional learning community conference. The Metropolitan Community Colleges of Kansas City and Indiana University-Purdue University Indianapolis (IUPUI) recently joined the leadership group for this midwestern conference, further extending the regional collaboration. In the Southwest, the Maricopa community college system has assumed an increasing leadership role with learning communities. Similar convening campuses are emerging in California at Sonoma State University, De Anza Community College, Cerritos, and Moorpark Community College. Wagner College in New York, George Mason University, Portland State University, and Temple University have also become centers of dissemination, along with the early leaders in learning communities such as LaGuardia. In 2003 the Atlantic Center was formed as an East Coast analogue to the Washington Center to support learning communities. The new center is hosted by Brooklyn College and Wagner College and brings many campuses together for periodic open houses and curriculum planning events.

At the same time, funding organizations such as the U.S. Department of Education's Title III, IV, V, VI, TRIO, the Fund for the Improvement of Postsecondary Education, the National Science Foundation, the National Endowment for the Humanities, and various private foundations, such as Hewlett, Pew, Exxon, Packard, and Ford, have been highly supportive of learning communities reform efforts, often funding projects that have a movement-building, networking quality about them. Many of the federally funded learning community programs focused on increasing access and student success for underserved populations. Some of these funding agencies were interested in building learning communities in like-sector institutions through collaborative work. The Pew RUSS (Restructuring Urban Student Success) project funded by The Pew Charitable Trusts, which involved IUPUI, Portland State, and Temple University, for example, focused on urban, public universities that are primarily commuter institutions. A consortium of institutions in California headed by De Anza College and funded by the Packard Foundation is another example of a group of institutions joining forces, in this case around a common interest in developing learning communities to serve underprepared students more effectively. In addition, several of the National Science Foundation–funded coalitions of engineering schools have focused on integrated math-science learning communities as a way to strengthen student success and retention in the first year.

A Movement at a Crossroads

The history of learning communities remains an evolving story of reformers and innovators embracing daring ideas and working to put them in place. It is a story about the power of personal commitments and relationships in building reform efforts. It also reveals the power of institutional structures, processes, and value systems in shaping our institutions. Most of the early learning community innovations survived for only a few years, but in a sense these programs were not failures. Their transformative structures and powerful potential inspired other leaders, who established them anew in different places.

There are a number of persistent themes in learning community history. The themes of democracy, access, and classrooms as communities particularly stand out. Early learning communities dating back to the early twentieth century were concerned with the role schools play in preparing students for responsible citizenship. Education for what was the question at the forefront in early learning community history. This concern influenced not only the content of the curriculum but also the educational methods and practices. It expressed a clear point of view about the relationship between the larger society and the academy. Early learning communities were also concerned with access. These were not elitist enclaves. Continuing to expand access to higher education was seen as critical to the evolving American experiment with democracy. This thread is continuous from Meiklejohn and Dewey to Tussman and Cadwallader to more recent efforts focusing on access and student success at LaGuardia Community College, Stony Brook, The Evergreen State College, and other leading early innovators such as North Seattle and Seattle Central Community College. The themes of expanding access, student success, and preparation for democracy also figure prominently in the work of significant learning community philosophers and educational researchers, including Patrick Hill, Vincent Tinto, and Alexander Astin. All believed that access was not simply an admissions task but an urgent need for student success. All acknowledged the words of Meiklejohn—that "we do not yet have the educational system required for this task." With a resurgence of interest in civic engagement and expanding access, colleges and universities are revisiting issues about their role and responsibilities to the larger society and looking toward learning communities as a promising strategy.

If we review these generations of leaders, we also see dramatically different leadership styles, organizational strategies, and settings. Learning communities in the latter part of the twentieth century are characterized more by collaborative leadership models, which came in with the feminist and civil rights movements and a variety of wider social and educational reform efforts in the 1960s and 1970s. There has been a shift toward community organizing strategies in the contemporary learning community movement. The effort is more purposefully interinstitutional with the rapid dissemination of ideas and strategies across institutions. There is also a systematic effort to build bridges to related enterprises, such as writing across the curriculum and assessment and service learning, and to broaden leadership across the movement. This bridge building and collaboration is a promising new direction that needs to go even further.

The learning community effort now stands at a crossroads, both at the institutional level and as a national movement. Because it is now a large-scale effort, pointed questions need to be raised about how quality can be maintained and strengthened as this endeavor expands. As one longtime learning community participant put it, "I worry about the tendency on the part of educators to adopt innovative practices without a clear and coherent vision of learning. I think this often leads to shallow and scattered adaptation of the work, and ultimately can undermine the effectiveness of the whole movement. This is at the heart of the continual rise and fall of educational fads over the years and the resulting faculty cynicism it produces. Although structural changes and organizational practices are important, we also need close attention to the microprocesses of teaching and learning that embody the best elements of what makes learning communities successful."

For a broad-scale reform effort that has reached what Malcolm Gladwell (2000) calls "the tipping point," the history of education reform is sobering. Few reform efforts expand and last long enough to have broad impact. In fact, the usual pattern is for institutions to change the reforms more than the reforms change them, usually through a process of dumbing down and turning big ideas into small ones (Cuban, 1999, 2000). In a provocative essay examining past failed attempts to scale up significant reforms, Richard Elmore suggests ways to build firmer connections between big reform ideas and the practices in institutions that might lead to greater success:

○ Develop strong external normative structures to compensate for the typical failures that result from attempting to sustain reforms through the commitment of early adopters.

○ Develop organizational structures that intensify and focus intrinsic motivation to innovate and engage in challenging existing practice. Small structures that encourage face-to-face relationships may be important in accomplishing this.

○ Create processes for the reproduction of success with a practical theory of change about how to work with institutional complexities.

○ Create structures that promote learning new practices and incentive systems that support them. (Elmore, 1996)

Both the learning community movement and the efforts on individual campuses have developed and grown by using change strategies that are quite different from many other attempts at broad-scale change. Starting small with the right people and expanding gradually on individual campuses has been key in giving quality and credibility to the effort. Working to sustain the reform by developing normative structures, changes in the role and reward systems, and in the incentives has been important too. At the same time, many institutions recognize that if this change effort is to be highly effective, it needs to reach larger numbers of students. Indeed, sustaining and expanding the effort may well pose greater challenges than getting it started, especially because many of the early learning community leaders are retiring.

There are other challenges beyond succession that the learning community movement now faces. As the effort continues to grow, we need to continue to ask whether there are ways in which it can even more powerfully affect student learning and institutional reform. While being realistic about organizational change, we also need to hold onto the kind of idealism that pushes us up toward higher goals. As we move to the next stages of learning community development, we must continue to engage the fundamental questions raised at the beginning of this chapter. For what purposes are we building learning communities and for whom? What are some of the most critical arenas for learning communities? Which students are not being well served by our current efforts, and how might their needs be better addressed?

In the following chapters, we explore many of the issues involved in both launching learning communities and taking them to the next step. We will look at learning community frameworks and core practices, critical arenas where learning communities may be situated, and the challenges of initiating and sustaining learning communities.

PART TWO

LEARNING COMMUNITY STRUCTURES AND PRACTICES

3

LEARNING COMMUNITY CURRICULAR STRUCTURES

---

*This is a fundamental view of the world. It says that when
you build a thing you cannot merely build that thing in
isolation, but must also repair the world around it, and within
it, so that the larger world at that one place becomes
more coherent, and more whole.*

—Christopher Alexander

LEARNING COMMUNITIES are a variety of curricular approaches that intentionally link or cluster two or more courses, often around an interdisciplinary theme or problem, and enroll a common cohort of students. This represents an intentional restructuring of students' time, credit, and learning experiences to build community, enhance learning, and foster connections among students, faculty, and disciplines. At their best, learning communities practice pedagogies of active engagement and reflection. On residential campuses, many learning communities are also living-learning communities, restructuring the residential environment to build community and integrate academic work with out-of-class experiences.

In the past twenty years, learning communities have proliferated; they are now found at all levels of the curriculum, from developmental-level offerings through graduate school. The most precise estimate we have of the reach of these programs comes from a recent study of first-year curricular practices (Policy Center on the First Year of College, 2002), which indicates that learning communities have been established for entering freshmen at more than five hundred institutions—large and small, two-year and four-year, liberal arts colleges and research universities. Although there are no national data on the number of learning community programs that serve students after their first year in college or in the major, we are aware of dozens of programs tailored to more advanced students.

There is wide variability in learning community structure and curricular emphasis, but similar broad intentions recur in all these programs. Learning communities aim to foster a sense of community and shared purpose among learners and their teachers. They attempt to create curricular coherence and connections among courses and ideas, and to teach skills in meaningful contexts. They aspire to develop students' capacity to make both academic and social connections as maturing college learners. Learning communities offer a more intensified learning environment by providing more time for students to develop these connections, both through the classroom learning afforded by taking multiple courses together and out-of-class activities such as study groups, project work, and co-curricular experiences. These academically and socially reinforcing experiences enable them to be both autonomous and interdependent learners. These programs also aspire to become learning communities for the teachers who are involved, and here we use the word *teacher* in its broadest sense because many different individuals on campus—full-time and part-time faculty members, student life professionals, academic advisers, librarians, and even students themselves—may assume teaching roles in learning communities.

As both Alexander Meiklejohn and Joseph Tussman eloquently argued, the goal of improving undergraduate education cannot be realized by simply adding a reformed course or a promising pedagogy here and there in the curriculum. These early learning community pioneers maintained that although well-taught individual classes might be helpful to students' learning, they seldom have a transformative impact on students, teachers, or the curriculum. The power of the learning community approach springs from its structure, the explicit linking together of courses into larger programs of study, and the commitment to creating a community through the enrollment of a cohort of students. This reformed curricular architecture can create reinforcing patterns in numbers of classes all at once. It can provide larger, more holistic spaces for developing and deepening social relationships, making intellectual connections, and involving students in any number of active and collaborative pedagogies. Architect Christopher Alexander made an analogous argument in his classic book on design,

A Pattern Language. The central thesis of Alexander's approach was that good design cannot be piecemeal; multiple patterns of the design of a room must connect to the house, the garden, the neighborhood, the town. Alexander wrote, "This is a fundamental view of the world. It says that when you build a thing you cannot merely build that thing in isolation, but must also repair the world around it, and within it, so that the larger world at that one place becomes more coherent, and more whole" (Alexander and Associates, 1977, p. iii). Similarly, a learning community creates for students a more coherent whole for learning.

In this chapter we will describe the main curricular frameworks that learning communities take, and comment on some variations. Then, in Chapter Four, we will discuss the core practices that we believe make learning within these structures most engaging and educationally effective.

Principal Curricular Structures

For the past thirty years, colleges and universities have been "inventing" learning communities and modifying them as student needs, curricular imperatives, and institutional opportunities and constraints have evolved, and as newly involved individuals have brought different perspectives. Nonetheless, some patterns of learning community structures have emerged and endured as campuses found them to be effective and engaging for teachers and students. Individual learning communities rarely share the exact same structure or practices, yet they *resemble* one another in their attempts to make curricular connections and align practices across multiple courses.

Figure 3.1, depicting the "Ascending Steps of Learning Community Goals," summarizes the many and varied goals set out for these programs. Creators of learning communities often describe goals for students and teachers and even goals that their institution might realize from the learning community initiative. Although we describe them as steps on a staircase, we do not mean to suggest that one goal precedes or leads to another; rather, the most frequently stated and concrete goals are shown on the lowest steps, while more ambitious and ineffable goals are shown on the higher steps. The idea is to suggest the multiple layers of learning community outcomes that might be considered, articulated, and assessed by program creators. Learning community planning and implementation afford the opportunity to set clear goals for the initiative, and then align them, reach toward them, and assess them.

Figure 3.1. Ascending Steps of Learning Community Goals

STUDENT LEVEL

New or reaffirmed values, aspirations, commitment

Enhanced leadership skills

Increased intellectual development, cognitive complexity

Academic maturity, self-confidence, and motivation

Deepened diversity and citizenship understandings and skills

Demonstration of learning outcomes (related to courses, LC program, gen ed, study in major/minor)

Achievement (grades, overall GPA, entry into majors, pass rates for proficiency tests, licensing exams)

Retention, progress to degree, grad rates (course completion, persistence, completion of requirements)

Increased interaction with other students, faculty, student affairs professionals

General response: level of satisfaction, perceived benefits, or challenges

Participation and enrollment

FACULTY, STUDENT AFFAIRS, AND STUDENT FACILITATOR LEVEL

New or reaffirmed values, aspirations, commitment

Enhanced leadership skills

Increased self-confidence and motivation

Widened scholarly interests and efforts

New understandings of other disciplines and the nature of interdisciplinarity

New understandings of discipline or professional specialty

Deepened understandings about diversity and citizenship, multicultural teaching skills

Enlarged pedagogical repertoire

Deepened understanding of students, student development, and student needs

Increased interaction with students

General response: level of satisfaction, perceived benefits, or challenges

Participation

INSTITUTIONAL LEVEL

Enhanced institutional reputation

Strengthened institutional culture (focus on learning and community)

Hiring, tenure, promotion, and other reward systems supportive of LC goals

Increased cost efficiencies

Achievement of diversity- and citizenship-related goals

Strengthened curricular offerings

Improved campus climate

Fit with and movement toward institutional mission and goals

Positive interdepartmental or inter-unit collaboration (academic affairs/student affairs)

General response: level of satisfaction, perceived benefits, or challenges

Understanding (degree to which institution is aware of, understands program)

In the following paragraphs we describe three general structural frameworks for creating learning communities and specific examples of how these frameworks have been adapted on a variety of campuses.[1] These different structures represent a range of approaches and adaptations in particular institutional or curricular settings and are meant to stimulate invention. The main differences between the three have to do with the degree to which the teaching teams work together to foster connections among their courses.

Learning Communities Within Courses That Are Unmodified

The simplest learning community structure involves students in two or three (often large) standing courses that are taught autonomously without any modification (Figure 3.2). A small group of students—generally ten to thirty—enroll as a cohort in these two or three classes, which are taught by faculty members who do not modify their syllabi or teaching methods. However, this small cohort of students also enroll in an *additional* course where they are a self-contained group. It is in this important, additional course that the community building and connection making can occur. This type of learning community structure has two main adaptations: the freshman seminar or interest group learning community, and the integrative seminar or colloquy learning community.

FRESHMAN SEMINAR OR INTEREST GROUP LEARNING COMMUNITIES. Most frequently, the additional seminar in this framework is a Freshman Year Experience course. Most of these types of learning community initiatives focus on a specific interest that students might have—an

---

Figure 3.2. Communities Within Courses That Are Unmodified

+

Integrative Seminar

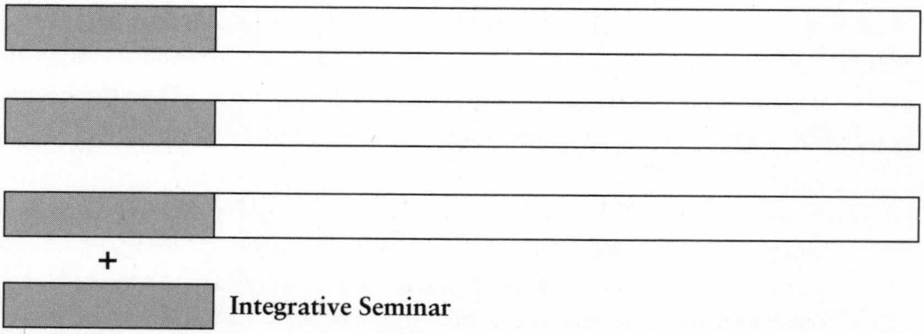

The shaded area represents the learning community students;
the unshaded area represents other students taking each individual class.

appropriate set of freshman classes for a specific major, or a set of classes that speak to an interdisciplinary theme while fulfilling general education requirements. These programs are often called "Freshman Interest Groups" to reinforce the thematic connection and foster a group identity around a field of study or a topic of interest. The additional seminar itself ranges from zero to three credit hours and usually focuses on an orientation to the college or university, building community around shared academic interests, career exploration activities, creating student study groups, and an introduction to university services. It offers assistance with academic planning, and in some instances, local field trips and service learning projects. These seminars might be convened by an undergraduate student peer mentor or graduate teaching assistant, an adviser or other student affairs professional, a faculty member, or a teaching team made up of any combination of these. Variations on this approach are more fully described in Chapter Five. Exhibit 3.1 presents examples of Freshman Interest Group (FIG) communities offered in recent years at the University of Washington. All of these were offered on the quarter system. Each of the individual classes carried five credits; the FIG seminar itself carried one credit.

This interest group structure has developed primarily in larger research institutions where lower-division classes tend to carry high enrollments. Beginning students can easily feel overwhelmed by the sheer size and anonymity of these classes, and reward systems and expectations for faculty members do not support the time required to coordinate linked classes or make close connections with beginning undergraduates. Over the past decade, significant numbers of large research institutions developed freshman interest group programs, and several now offer over one hundred of them, enrolling 50 percent or more of their freshman classes. On residential campuses, community can be more intensively fostered with a residence life component, where members of each FIG live in a common residence hall or even on a common floor, with a student peer mentor in residence there as well. Because enrollment patterns and syllabi do not need to be modified for this type of learning community, these interest group communities are inexpensive and can be easily placed in and alongside standing curricular offerings. Furthermore, these programs can begin with one or a few offerings and then expand over time.

INTEGRATIVE SEMINAR OR COLLOQUY LEARNING COMMUNITIES. Using the same curricular architecture (as depicted in Figure 3.2), another adaptation brings together students from two or more regularly scheduled classes and makes the additional course an integrative seminar or colloquy. In this structural framework, a *faculty team,* usually the

Exhibit 3.1. Freshman Interest Groups at the University of Washington

Pre-med
- College Chemistry
- Calculus
- Ethnic Studies
- FIG Seminar

Business
- Microeconomics
- College Algebra
- English Composition
- FIG Seminar

"Global Preservation"
- English Composition
- Environmental Sciences
- Geography
- FIG Seminar

Physical science and engineering
- English Composition
- Chemistry
- Calculus
- FIG Seminar

"Law and Order"
- Political Theory
- English Composition
- Philosophical Issues and the Law
- FIG Seminar

"Women in History"
- English Composition: Social Issues
- World History
- Women's Studies
- Service Learning Fieldwork
- FIG Seminar

Source: Brochures of the University of Washington's Freshman Interest Group
Program, 1998–2001. Used by permission.

teachers of the larger classes associated with the learning community,
convene the additional seminar. The purpose is to explore interdisciplinary themes and draw connections—or contrasts—between the larger
courses. Examples are provided in Exhibit 3.2. All of these program clusters carried a total of ten quarter hours of credit.

Exhibit 3.2. Examples of Integrated Seminar Learning Communities

University of Wisconsin-Marinette

"U.S. Minority Experience"
- Multicultural Literature in America
- History of Minorities in America
- Sociology of Race and Ethnicity
- Integrative Seminar

"Environmental Topics"
- Environmental Ethics
- Composition II
- Human Environmental Biology
- Integrative Seminar

"Issues in Education" (for education majors)
- Physical Education
- Math for Elementary Teachers
- The Exceptional Individual
- Integrative Seminar

University of Wisconsin-Marathon

"Playing War: A Learning Community About Gender, Vietnam, and Theatre"
- Images of Gender in Drama and Performance (co-listed in Communication and Theatre Arts and Women's Studies)
- Themes in Literature: Literature about the Vietnam War
- Theatre Lab

"A Midsummer Night's Dream"
- Literature in Performance
- Introduction to Shakespeare
- Theatre Lab

Diablo Valley College

"Water, Water, Everywhere"
- Economics in Action
- Fundamentals of Oceanography
- Critical Thinking
- Colloquy

"Borders as Barriers and Frontiers"
- English Composition
- Multicultural Perspectives in American Theater
- The Political Economy of Democracy
- Colloquy

Sources: University of Wisconsin-Marinette, University of Wisconsin-Marathon, Diablo Valley College, 2002. Used by permission.

This learning community structure has developed on campuses of all types and sizes. Several colleges in the University of Wisconsin system, most notably Marinette and Marathon, have used this framework to enhance general education coursework, as has Diablo Valley College, a large community college in the San Francisco Bay Area. The integrative seminar usually carries one to three credit hours and is built around reading, discussions, and research projects on a theme related to the associated courses. At University of Wisconsin-Marathon, the integrative course has occasionally been a theater lab (see again Exhibit 3.2). At other institutions, it has been a field study course or a service learning experience, complementing and extending the on-campus associated courses. Faculty members who teach in these communities report that this structure offers a rich opportunity for building academic community among students and faculty and requires minimal effort to rearrange regular enrollment patterns or course syllabi.

A much more ambitious use of the integrated seminar model is Fairhaven College at Western Washington University's Law and Diversity Program, an upper-division, pre-law concentration. This multidisciplinary program brings together students with interests in diversity, legal representation, and justice for underrepresented groups. It provides an intensive two years of study in a number of disciplines, designed to build and hone the abilities necessary to succeed in law school and in careers in law and related fields. Exhibit 3.3 lists the full six quarters of academic work in this program. Each quarter, the students in the program take classes together—some classes are for them alone, others are open as well to students who are not in the program—and also meet in an integrative seminar led by the faculty member who directs the program. The seminar brings together each quarter's coursework with focused skill-building work related to the program's goals. The students also meet weekly with the program director for a "homeroom hour," in which they and the director build relationships with one another, discuss program logistics, and reflect on and provide feedback on the overall program. This model offers a promising strategy for creating community and intensive integration in any major course of study.

Learning Communities of Linked or Clustered Classes

Another widely used curricular structure for learning communities involves *explicitly* linking two or more separate courses. Social and curricular connections happen *within* the linked but discrete learning community courses, and teachers of these courses collaborate to bring this

Exhibit 3.3. Law and Diversity Curriculum at Fairhaven College, Western Washington University

Quarter 1		Credits
Political Science 250:	American Political System	5
Fairhaven 224:	Writing Logical Arguments	3
Fairhaven 211:	*LDP American Legal System*	5
Fairhaven 307:	*LDP Seminar: Conflict Resolution*	3
Homeroom:	*Weekly LDP meeting*	

Quarter 2		
Fairhaven 396:	Power, Privilege, and the Law	3
Philosophy 107:	Logical Thinking	3
Fairhaven 308:	*LDP Seminar: Legal Research and Writing*	4
Homeroom:	*Weekly LDP meeting*	
Optional elective		

Quarter 3		
Fairhaven 3xx:	*Any of several substantive law classes*	4
Fairhaven 395:	*Commercial Relationships*	4
Fairhaven Independent		
Study Project:	*Critical Reading and Thinking (LSAT)*	4
Homeroom:	*Weekly LDP meeting*	
Optional elective		
Fairhaven 262:	Swimming with the Sharks: The Life of a Lawyer	2

Quarter 4		
Fairhaven 415:	Constitutional Law I:—Government Powers	5
Economy 206:	Microeconomics	4
Fairhaven 407:	*LDP Seminar: Advanced Legal Writing*	3
Homeroom:	*Weekly LDP meeting*	
Optional elective		

Quarter 5		
Fairhaven 416:	Constitutional Law II:—Individual Rights	5
Fairhaven 398:	Political Economy and the Law	4
Fairhaven 408:	*LDP Seminar: Oral Advocacy*	4
Homeroom:	*Weekly LDP meeting*	
Optional elective		

Quarter 6		
Fairhaven 480:	*LDP Internship*	10+
Fairhaven 409:	*LDP Seminar: Legal Profession*	3
Optional elective		

Note: Courses in italics are open only to the program (LDP) students; in all other courses, they are enrolled with other students.

Source: Helling, 2003.

about. This interrelated coursework most often includes an introductory skill-building class linked to a content-heavy class. Linked courses or clusters also might become foundation courses for a major, a platform of courses for study in a minor, or a set of general education courses linked around an interdisciplinary theme. Skill-building classes (such as composition, speech, information literacy, or computer applications) are often seen as a target of opportunity in these curricular arrangements because many of these classes are required and because enrollments in them tend to be smaller, thus offering a natural locus for community building. Faculty members in composition and speech often relish the opportunity to link their classes to other disciplines; they often make the point that when writing assignments, research papers, or speeches relate to topics and questions in the linked class, it gives their class coherence. As one of our colleagues put it, "When I link my research writing class to cultural anthropology, my students can get on the 'same page'; and in their peer writing groups, they have enough baseline knowledge to be more interested in and responsive to each other's work."

In this type of learning community structure, two classes are usually referred to as *linked classes* or *paired classes*. When three or even four classes are offered as a learning community package, they are usually called a *cluster*. Enrollment arrangements for these linked courses or clusters are varied. Most learning communities of this type are established to create a "pure cohort" of students who form the entire enrollment of the two or three classes (Figure 3.3). For example, at Lane Community College, the "Psychologically Speaking: Science Versus Psychobabble"

Figure 3.3. Linked and Clustered Classes with Pure Enrollments

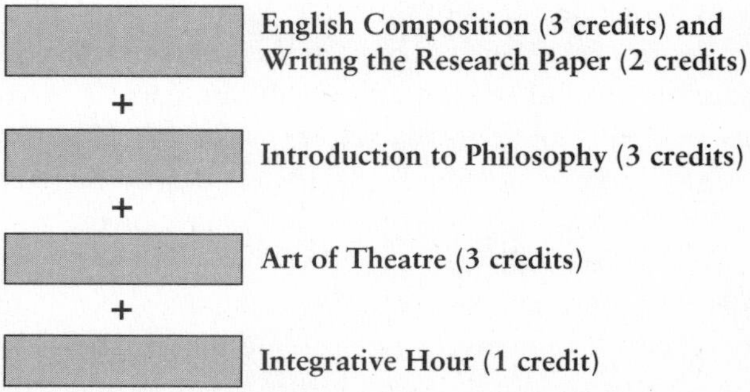

English Composition (3 credits) and
Writing the Research Paper (2 credits)

+

Introduction to Philosophy (3 credits)

+

Art of Theatre (3 credits)

+

Integrative Hour (1 credit)

The shaded area represents the learning community students; as a "pure cohort," they are taking all these classes together.

paired classes are English Composition and General Psychology, and the two classes include only the same cohort of students. In LaGuardia Community College's learning cluster titled "Identity, Performance, and Poetic Justice," the same group of students take English Composition (three credits) and Writing the Research Report (two credits), Introduction to Philosophy (three credits), Art of Theater (three credits), and the Integrated Hour (one credit). When paired and cluster learning communities are run as pure cohorts, as these are, the class size is usually twenty to thirty-five students. Having a pure cohort of students is important for two reasons: first, the students and their faculty become a community of learners having a common experience, and second, because everyone is taking both classes (or all three or four classes), thematic connections can be made and integrative assignments created.

Although pure cohorts of students in links or clusters are the ideal, some learning communities accept other students into a link or cluster as well. Often at the last moment of the registration period, in order to fill a few more seats in these classes, other students are permitted into some of them. At some small institutions there may be only one section of a certain course, so a small number of students from outside the learning community who need that course are permitted to take it. However, these administrative dilutions of the learning community cohort run the risk of encouraging faculty members to take the community building and curriculum integration focus less seriously. If these "broken cohorts" become a regular practice in learning communities, it will inevitably lead to reductions of quality. At some institutions this practice has devolved into situations in which only a handful of students are co-registered in both classes of the learning community, thereby creating no incentive for the faculty members to make any linkages at all.

We recommend that learning community planners and teaching teams be sensitive to the implications of broken cohorts, avoid them if possible, and agree to let in other students only in the kinds of special situations we have mentioned—and only in very small numbers. If broken-cohort registrations have to be undertaken, faculty teams should understand this in advance and plan accordingly to foster community and course integration in ways that include or provide choices for the non-learning-community students as well.

LaGuardia Community College requires that all its liberal arts students who are enrolled full-time take a twelve-credit liberal arts cluster, such as "Identity, Performance, and Poetic Justice," described earlier. Each of its liberal arts clusters runs with an enrollment of twenty-six students. The courses are taught separately, but the students and at least two members of the faculty team come together each week for the integrated hour. Learning community planners strive to schedule linked or cluster courses back-to-back, not only to provide students with a compact schedule but also to reinforce the connections and community in the overall offering (Exhibit 3.4). It is frequently but not always the case that the faculty teaching team requires completion of the entire package of paired or clustered courses, and announces that a course in the learning community may be dropped only in extreme circumstances. In consequence, the stakes are raised for the students and the tone set is quite different from the more permissive course-dropping culture of most campuses. As a result, these communities have consistently high rates of course completion.

Links and clusters are also designed to connect smaller classes with larger ones. In these cases, the responsibility for community building and connection making falls to the teachers of the smaller classes, where the learning community students are kept together as a group. Frequently, the smaller class is a writing or speech class that is linked to a larger general education class (Figure 3.4). Writing classes appear most often in these linkages: one or more subsets of students in a general education class simultaneously enroll in a writing class, where the reading and writing

---

Exhibit 3.4. Schedule for the "Identity, Performance, and Poetic Justice" Learning Cluster

Monday	Tuesday	Wednesday	Thursday	Friday
10:30–11:30 Philosophy	10:30–11:30 Philosophy	10:30–2:00 Art of Theatre	10:30–11:30 Philosophy	
1:00–3:00 Research Paper	1:00–3:00 English Composition	2:15–3:15 Integrated Hour	1:00–3:00 English Composition	

Source: LaGuardia Community College. Used by permission.

Figure 3.4. Small Class Linked to a Larger One

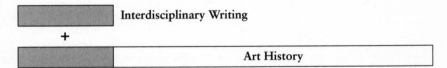

The shaded area represents the learning community students;
the unshaded area represents other students taking the Art History class.

work relates directly to the content of the larger class. The writing instructor and the faculty member of the linked class collaborate to develop the writing assignments, and sometimes they jointly grade them. These writing links can be found at any number of two-year and four-year colleges, but two universities, University of Washington and George Mason University, have mounted substantial writing link programs specifically to advance writing in the disciplines, to give depth and context to required composition classes, and to strengthen the learning in large general education lecture courses. The University of Washington's Interdisciplinary Writing Program (IWP), founded in 1977, is probably the oldest and largest program of linked writing classes; it involves sixty linked classes annually, reaching about 1,500 students. George Mason University has been offering linked writing courses since 1986. In its current design, its Mason Topics program now attracts more than 175 students each year to one of several two-semester sequences of linked classes organized around a theme; students have options of living on special living-learning floors in the residence halls and of continuing with more advanced linked writing courses in their sophomore year as well.

Many clusters involve two small classes, such as a freshman composition class and a freshman seminar (taken together by the student cohort), and two larger classes. Figure 3.5 depicts the liberal arts cluster at the University of Northern Colorado which enrolls students in this way. Freshman Composition and Freshman Seminar are the two pure cohort classes; these students also attend two general education classes that are open to other, non-learning-community students as well. The main centers of

Figure 3.5.   Clusters at the University of Northern Colorado

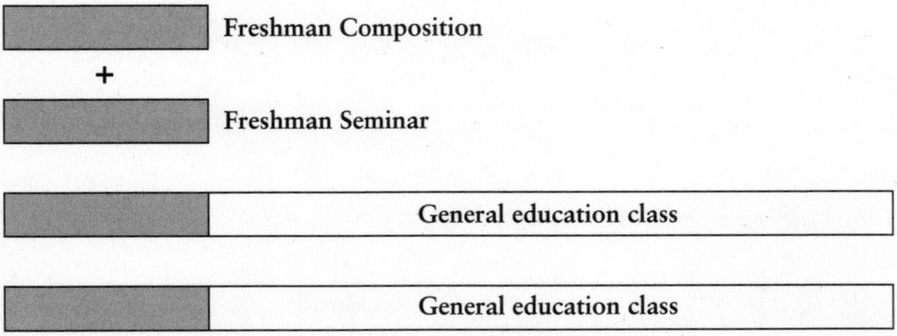

The shaded area represents the learning community students;
the unshaded area represents other students taking each individual class.

community building and connection making are naturally in the composition and seminar classes.

As we have seen, most of these linked or cluster class structures involve
two or three classes, and therefore, two or three faculty members.
Although many campuses put together communities of four or even five
classes in a semester-long, full-time package of academic credit, planners
for these more ambitious constellations often face daunting enrollment
and scheduling problems. Finding enough students with flexible schedules
to take a constellation of five classes is challenging, and chairs and deans
are generally reluctant to let five-course communities run with low enrollments. Furthermore, when four or five faculty members and their courses
are part of a learning community mix, the necessary, frequent communication among the team and effective curricular coordination become that
much more difficult. In addition, students in learning community programs
often report that although they enjoy being in the community for a few of
their classes, they also appreciate the opportunity to meet and work with
other students in the rest of their coursework.

Links and clusters provide a better opportunity to delve deeper
into content and build community than when groups of students
"block-register" in several unconnected classes. Block-registering,
or block-scheduling, the freshman class or a large segment of it has
become a popular strategy for efficiently filling large general education
classes and giving students a convenient first-term schedule of general
education coursework. Of course, block registering can create a structure in which students see each other in several classes and perhaps
make friends. But if no *intentional* effort is made to foster community
(through a residential, living-learning component to the program, for
example) or to take advantage of the curricular connections that the
related courses invite, the learning *and* the community are less powerful than they could be. Furthermore, students who share experiences in
different classes can form a community that excludes the isolated, individual faculty members and sometimes works against their intentions.
We believe, therefore, that campuses offering these types of block-
scheduled programs would do well to create both time and faculty
development support for teachers to engage in collaborative course planning in order to take greater advantage of the obvious opportunities
already in place with block-registered students.

Naturally, the degree to which faculty members plan collaboratively
and to which courses are integrated varies from program to program.
Exhibit 3.5 describes a range of both curricular integration and faculty
collaboration, with the levels of coordination shown rising from bottom

Exhibit 3.5. Levels of Integration in Linked or Clustered Classes

Degrees of Curricular Integration	Degrees of Teaching Team Collaboration
A common syllabus for all courses and activities (requires a pure cohort of students)	All aspects of the program are jointly planned and developed.
Integrative assignments and projects	⇧ Assignments and projects are jointly developed, jointly graded.
Assignments, research paper or project	
Discussion, integrative seminar	
On-line discussions	
Co-curricular activity	⇧ Co-curricular events are planned collaboratively.
Potlucks, socials	
Field trips, conferences away from campus	
On-campus play or exhibit	
Service learning or community-based projects	Regular meetings and communication occur throughout term.
Common goals, pedagogical approaches	⇧ There is collaborative planning around themes, topics, concepts, and student learning outcomes.
Active learning, cooperative-collaborative learning, student self-assessment, classroom assessment techniques	
Some common learning outcomes	There is a collaborative effort to reach out to students in difficulty.
Some common themes and topics	⇧ Calendar, tests, due dates are coordinated.
	There is an exchange of syllabi and cursory communication.

Created by: Jean MacGregor, Will Koolsbergen, and Phyllis van Slyck.
Source: National Learning Communities Project "Learning Commons" [http://learningcommons.evergreen.edu].

to top of the columns. It is often the case that faculty members who team up to teach course links or clusters repeat their offerings in successive years. As they do, the linkages and degrees of integration among courses deepen over time.

When students are enrolled in separate but linked courses in a learning community, there is both opportunity and challenge to make the connections explicit. After offering their liberal arts clusters for many years, the faculty at LaGuardia Community College added the "Integrated Hour" to them as a designated time for bringing concepts and disciplines more fully into play. This extra hour of class time may be a weekly gathering each Wednesday afternoon as shown in Exhibit 3.4, but often the hours are banked for special projects or field trips. Alternatively, at the University of Hartford, faculty members of linked and clustered courses do not come together for an integrative hour but the faculty teams are more consistently intentional about course integration. They have called the intersections among their courses *integrated learning blocks* (ILBs). University of Hartford has used the intersecting elements in the Venn-diagram visual (Figure 3.6) as its learning community logo to represent to both students and faculty the interrelatedness of the courses and to invite creative thought about their intersections. With the support of faculty development workshops, each learning community teaching team identifies hoped-for common concepts, skills, and understanding for their two (or three) learning community classes and then creates these ILB activities and assignments in which students can develop and demonstrate intersecting learning outcomes.

In recent years, both community colleges and baccalaureate campuses have put together robust offerings of linked or clustered courses, especially to serve beginning students. At community colleges such as Lane in Oregon; Cerritos, De Anza, and Moorpark in California; Collin County in Texas; LaGuardia in New York; Delta in Michigan; Harper in Illinois; and the Metropolitan Community Colleges of Kansas City, Missouri, linked and clustered courses are regularly offered in many areas of the curriculum: liberal arts, professional and technical, developmental,

---

Figure 3.6 University of Hartford's Learning Community Logo

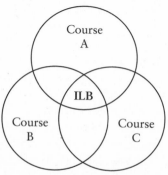

Source: University of Hartford [http://uhaweb.Hartford.edu/figs].

and English as a Second Language. Appalachian State, Georgia State, Iowa State, Northern Colorado, Temple, and a host of other universities now have a large percentage of their freshmen enrolled in course clusters. Some institutions, such as Ball State University, California State University-Hayward, and Texas A&M-Corpus Christi, have moved ambitiously to enroll their entire freshman classes in these types of programs. Texas A&M University, University of Alabama, and University of Massachusetts-Dartmouth enroll their freshman engineering majors in clusters, and University of Texas-El Paso provides entry clusters to both engineering and science-bound freshmen. Many of these universities have invested a lot of energy and resources to involve graduate teaching assistants in learning community teaching teams and to provide the necessary professional development and support for them.

Team-Taught Learning Communities

Fully team-taught programs are the third main type of learning community structure. These programs bring together the equivalent of two, three, or even four classes, which faculty members adapt to create a common syllabus around integrating themes or projects. Exhibit 3.6 presents some titles of team-taught programs and their respective constituent courses. Interdisciplinary questions and problems—some timeless and others contemporary—animate these learning communities. Thus, for the students, what is at the forefront is often not the English composition and the European history course they are taking but rather the program's integrating theme—The Fall of Empires, for example. The intentions for these communities are to examine broad questions or themes in an extended way, to explore interdisciplinary topics from multiple perspectives, and to practice academic skills in rich, meaningful contexts. Although programs are known to the students and faculty members by their titles—Disease as Metaphor and Reality, Rhapsody in Blue: Modern Art and Music History, or Molecule to Organism—at most institutions students receive credit for the embedded classes and only traditional course names and numbers appear on their transcripts. This makes it clear that the learning community coursework meets college or university degree requirements and like stand-alone classes can transfer to another institution.

The Meiklejohn-Tussman-Cadwallader legacy lives on in many of these team-taught programs in terms of both content and pedagogy. Coordinated studies programs continue to revolve around liberal arts themes at The Evergreen State College, the Hutchins School of Liberal Studies at Sonoma State University, the Arts One Program at University of British Columbia,

Exhibit 3.6. Titles and Coursework in Team-Taught Learning Communities

Program name, College	Courses Included	Credits
"The Wisdom of the East," Bellevue Community College	Anthropology, Philosophy	10 (quarter)
"Disease as Metaphor and Reality," Yakima Valley Community College	English Composition–Research Writing, Introduction to Literature, Human Biology	15 (quarter)
"The Paradox of Democracy: The Outsider in America," Delta College	Political Science, English Composition, American Literature Since 1865	10 (semester)
"The Televised Mind," Seattle Central Community College	Sociology, Freshman Composition, Introduction to Mass Media/Television, Video Production Lab	16 (quarter)
"Computability and Cognition: The Scope and Limits of Formal Systems," (yearlong program) The Evergreen State College	Mathematical and Symbolic Logic, Philosophy of Mind, Philosophy of Mathematics, Computer Programming, Discrete Mathematics, Formal Language Theory, Theory of Computability, Cognitive Science	45 (quarter)
"Land, Water, and People," University of North Dakota	Humanities, Composition, Geology	9 (semester)
"Self as Citizen," George Mason University, New Century College	Government, Art, Literature	8 (quarter)

Sources: Bellevue Community College, Seattle Central Community College, Yakima Valley Community College: The Washington Center *News,* The Evergreen State College catalogue, University of North Dakota: Integrated Studies Program Web site, University of North Dakota, New Century College catalogue.

the Integrated Studies Program at University of North Dakota, and New Century College at George Mason University. Following the example of The Evergreen State College and as a result of the leadership of the Washington Center for Undergraduate Education, many community colleges in Washington State have adopted this team-taught, interdisciplinary structure as well, mounting programs that link general education courses around themes; they include Bellevue, Edmonds, Lower Columbia, North

Seattle, Seattle Central, Skagit Valley, Spokane and Spokane Falls, Tacoma, and Yakima Valley. Like their predecessors, these programs are committed to active and collaborative learning and to processes whereby students and their faculty construct understandings together.

Most of these learning communities continue to use book seminars as a primary pedagogy. In book seminars, students explore the program themes with their teachers through reading, writing about, and discussing primary texts in small discussion settings. Exhibits 3.7 and 3.8 provide examples of the assigned reading lists. Exhibit 3.7 lists the readings for the quarter-long program "Beginnings: The Shaping of Cultures, Myths, and Identities," a learning community designed for entering students at North Seattle Community College. Exhibit 3.8 presents the list for "Liberty and Order," a yearlong program at Arts One at University of British Columbia. Through seminar discussions, themes in these texts and in the students' and their teachers' meaning-making about them develop cumulatively over a term or year.

Although seminars continue to thrive as an important component of many team-taught learning communities, an impressive array of other pedagogical formats is also used. Experiential learning, field and laboratory investigations, service and civic learning projects, writing groups, simulations and debates, extended research projects, and problem-based learning might be found in these programs, and usually they are carefully designed to weave together the disciplines and the program themes.

Although the team-taught learning community structure is most often associated with liberal arts study as an alternative general education

---

Exhibit 3.7. Readings for "Beginnings: The Shaping of Cultures, Myths, and Identities"

A coordinated studies program for entering students at North Seattle Community College, providing academic credit in English composition, world history, and women's studies.

Rose, *Lives on the Boundary*
Nutting, *The Free City*
Johnson, *Privilege, Power, and Difference*
Kingston, *The Woman Warrior*
Lerner, *The Creation of Patriarchy*
Allen, *Spider Woman's Granddaughters*
Naylor, *Mama Day*
Additional articles and short stories

Source: North Seattle Community College; used with permission.

Exhibit 3.8. Readings for "Liberty and Order"

A coordinated studies program of the Arts One program at the University of British Columbia.

Fall Semester

Socrates, *Clouds,* Plato, *Apology*
Thucydides, *The History of the Peloponnesian War*
Plato, *Republic*
St. Paul, *Epistle to the Romans*
Luther, *The Freedom/Dignity of the Christian*
Shakespeare, *Measure for Measure, King Lear*
Milton, *Aeropagitica*
Reid and Bringhurst, *The Raven Steals the Light*

Spring Semester

Burke, *Reflections on the Revolution in France*
Pope, selected poems
Blake, selected poems and engravings
Shelley, selected poems
Bronte, *Wuthering Heights*
Mill, *On Liberty*
Dostoyevsky, *The Possessed*
Camus, *The Rebel*
Morrison, *Beloved*

Source: University of British Columbia, Arts One, http://artsl.arts.ubc.ca/.

pathway, it has been adapted to a number of other curricular settings. At The Evergreen State College, team-taught programs are prevalent throughout the entire curriculum, both in lower-division and upper-division work and in three graduate programs (public administration, teacher education, and environmental studies). Many colleges' developmental programs interweave reading, writing, and an introductory course in a discipline to accelerate skill development in underprepared students. Several engineering schools have developed team-taught learning communities to integrate introductory-level science and engineering courses. Babson College and the College of Business at Ohio University have created ambitious team-taught programs built around intensive problem-based learning.

Each week of the term, most team-taught programs meet like a conference, with plenary sessions that all the students attend, and concurrent sessions with the community dividing into smaller working groups for discussions, workshops, studio work, or laboratory sessions. In many of these learning communities, each faculty member on the teaching team has a seminar group with which he or she meets each week. This seminar group functions as a kind of homeroom and becomes an important social and intellectual focal point within the larger learning community program. Many team-taught programs fulfill only part of a student's credit load, whereas others constitute the full load for all the participants, both the students and their teachers. Exhibit 3.9 portrays a typical weekly class schedule for a full-time coordinated studies program, for which students receive fifteen credits of coursework. This class schedule plans for plenary class meetings two mornings a week and concurrent seminar and workshop meetings at other times. (Also included in this schedule is a faculty seminar, a tradition in some communities in which faculty members set aside time for their own conversations and program work; this will be more fully described in Chapter Eight.)

A single syllabus, interdisciplinary or overarching themes, extended class meeting times, and teachers who also play learning roles in class— all these combine to blur many of the traditional boundaries of undergraduate classrooms. In these programs, students are regularly challenged to see issues from multiple perspectives, not just from different disciplinary points of view but also from the different perspectives of fellow students. This kind of learning environment is complex and challenging for students and teachers alike, but it is also highly stimulating. When students see their teachers in a learner's role, asking questions, expressing confusion, or even disagreeing with another teacher in the classroom, it can be a transformative experience. As a colleague put it, "It is at those points that students experience breakthroughs in their thinking. They realize there is no one 'right answer' and now, based in the evidence before them, they have to make up their own minds."

Obviously, fully team-taught programs require extensive planning both in advance of and during the program itself. Not every faculty member is prepared to commit the amount of time necessary, nor is every teacher comfortable with the intense, public nature of team teaching, the give-and-take of collaborative planning, and the demands of designing and giving

---

Exhibit 3.9. Example of a Class Schedule in a Full-Time Coordinated Studies Program

Monday	Tuesday	Wednesday	Thursday	Friday
No class, preparation day	Plenary program meeting (9–11)	Seminar (9–11)	Plenary program meeting (9–11)	Seminar (9–11)
	Writing workshop (12–2:30)	Faculty seminar (12–2)	Group workshops (12–2:30)	Faculty office hours (12–3)

students feedback on integrative assignments. Team teaching does indeed require an investment of time, but it is a different kind of time investment than many teachers have previously experienced on their own. Many of these programs put substantial responsibility on students to prepare for, participate in, and even lead student seminars and other forms of collaborative learning. In these programs, students may also be asked to work in teams on extended projects or problems. For faculty members, then, time spent teaching in the program often is less about preparing lectures or holding forth as an expert, and more about designing engaging learning opportunities for students, facilitating discussions, and coaching student project teams. Moreover, the faculty members who make the commitment to teach in these programs often remark that this is the most stimulating and satisfying teaching experience that they have ever had. As a result of team teaching in these learning communities, faculty members come to see their own disciplines in a new light and build strong interests in interdisciplinary topics, they discover new research interests, they learn and strengthen new teaching strategies, and they build important relationships across their institutions (Eby, 2001; Cornwell and Stoddard, 2001; Finley, 1990; Bystrom, 1997; Tommerup, 1993; Rye, 1997; Brown, 2003; Tollefson, 1990).

Variations and Elaborations on Learning Community Structures

There is considerable variability in learning community designs besides the three general structures just presented, and we encourage invention and adaptation to local curricular needs and circumstances. Some important variations are presented next.[2]

Living-Learning Communities

The classification of learning community curriculum structures that we have presented focuses on different *course*-linking structures and the degree to which teaching teams collaborate to develop an integrated, holistic curricular experience for students. These course-linking structures do not do justice to the variety of co-curricular arrangements embodied in residential learning community programs. *Living-learning programs* or *residential learning communities* can both underpin and extend curricular learning communities in important ways. As David Schoem recounts in his chapter on living-learning programs in a new book about sustaining learning communities (Levine Laufgraben and Shapiro, 2004), residential learning communities have a long and distinctive history of their own. There is considerable variability in these types of programs when it comes to focus, duration, type of faculty involvement, type of coursework, and administrative sponsorship and oversight. Meiklejohn's Experimental College is one of the roots of the living-learning program tradition. Students both live and take courses together, often with classes held in the residence hall and with the associated faculty members maintaining offices there. Schoem asserts that learning *and living* together creates the opportunity for carrying academic discussions beyond classrooms and into the night, for building relationships with teachers and scholars on a daily basis, and for practicing the ideals of community and democracy in a residential setting. Furthermore, in a careful assessment of living-learning programs at University of Massachusetts-Amherst, Martha Stassen (2003) shows that even if the classes that students share are not intentionally integrated, when they live and learn together it can be very effective in improving student adjustment and engagement, retention, and academic success.

Additional Co-Curricular Elements

Regardless of whether learning communities have a residential component, many of them incorporate additional co-curricular features and other elements that take students out of the classroom. Special new-student orientation activities, visiting speakers or artists-in-residence, field trips, theater and arts events, and service projects are typical features of learning communities. These activities are planned to extend students' learning community coursework, strengthen social ties among students, provide experiential learning opportunities, and broaden the curricular themes of the academic program. For example, a several-day field trip to visit architecture and design firms in Minneapolis is an annual event for "Design Exchange," a learning community program for freshmen considering majoring in architecture or design at Iowa State University. All undergraduate students at Portland State University and Wagner College undertake service learning projects as part of their general education, and this community-based work is usually done in the context of learning community coursework (Eaton and Patton, 2003; Guarasci, 2001, 2003a; Guarasci, Cornwell, and Associates, 1997). Projects that students undertake in their learning community programs often become extracurricular events themselves, presented to the campus or the wider community. For example, the "Ancient World" cluster at California State-Hayward holds an annual symposium at which faculty members, students, and an invited speaker make presentations. At Seattle Central Community College and University of Wisconsin-Marathon, learning communities involving drama classes have produced theatrical productions for the campus and community.

Curricular Cohort Programs

For decades, colleges and universities have had programs in which student cohorts enter in cycles and take a sequence of required classes, often with no elective space. This is common in professional and technical programs in community colleges, specialized majors in the upper division, and certain graduate programs. As Oscar Lenning and Larry Ebbers (1999) point out, these programs often achieve extraordinary levels of student engagement and rates of completion. There is wide variation in these programs, from block registration of students and no curricular coordination on the part of teaching faculty all the way to high degrees of integration, collaborative learning, and at the program's close, synthesis assignments. Curricular cohorts, with their common group of students, present a natural learning community opportunity. The challenge is in taking advantage of the structure to strengthen students' learning through reinforcing skills and concepts, to gain efficiencies through eliminating overlaps or possible confusions in how material is presented, and to plan in a coordinated fashion for the integrative projects or applied work that often conclude these kinds of programs.

Sequential Course Learning Communities

Some colleges and universities have developed "horizontal" or sequential course types of learning communities—that is, a cohort of students enroll in a sequence of two or three *individual* courses that follow one another over consecutive terms and are usually organized around a theme. These programs are often situated in the freshman year and offer students an opportunity for several general education classes to become more meaningful. Sequential course learning communities offer promising opportunities for deepening curricular connections from one term to the next, but they often lack the depth, intensity, and synergy that comes with intensive immersion in multiple courses during a single term. Still, a number of institutions have designed effective sequential course models. Those that have realized the strongest outcomes for students have made significant investments in curriculum planning and faculty development so that both community and curricular emphases are sustained from one term to the next. Portland State University's Freshman Inquiry Program reflects this kind of investment. This program enrolls its entire entering class in a three-quarter sequence of interdisciplinary classes organized by themes and team-taught by faculty members and student peer mentors. Here, program leaders have made an ambitious commitment to engaging students and their teachers in collaborative learning, community building, self-assessment, and synthesis of ideas across the span of a year's work.

Multiple Learning Community Structures on a Single Campus

Many campuses have settled on just one of these learning community structures, whereas others quite successfully offer multiple configurations to reach multiple curricular goals and serve students at different points in their undergraduate careers. Many universities, including Iowa State and the Universities of Hawaii-Manoa, Michigan, Washington, and Wisconsin, to name a few, have in place several kinds of learning community configurations, both curricular and residential, focusing on different themes and serving different student populations. Some are more administratively driven from offices of undergraduate affairs or university colleges, others are led by residence-life staff in collaboration with faculty, and still others are mostly faculty-driven. Similarly, many community colleges offer both linked classes and fully team-taught learning communities.

Fixed-Content and Variable-Content Learning Communities

Some learning communities have the same courses and teachers year after year, and these become predictable fixtures in the curriculum. Ideally, teaching teams build close teaching relationships and refine their curriculum and assignments each time they teach their program. Although this can happen because a pair or trio of teachers enjoy teaching together, it can also occur because a department or unit believes enough in the curricular value of an offering to support it year after year. Edmonds Community College regularly offers CheMath (a 100-level chemistry class linked to intermediate algebra) to science-bound students who are underprepared in mathematics. Bellevue Community College regularly offers "Of Mice and Matter" (biology, chemistry, and study skills or speech) to both science and nonscience majors. Grossmont College offers integrated combinations of reading and writing to hundreds of developmental students each year. The University of Ohio College of Business requires one quarter in its integrated problem-based learning program for the undergraduate degree.

However, at Evergreen and many other colleges, there are both fixed offerings, the learning communities that recur year after year, and variable offerings that change each year. They change because different faculty members want to form new teaching teams and bring their disciplinary expertise and interests together in new ways. Creating new learning communities not only appeals to many faculty members' interests in freshness and invention but also enables curricular emphases to respond to contemporary issues in the world, such as crises in the Middle East, globalization, ethics and medicine, or environmentally sustainable communities. Some learning community titles such as "Problems Without Solutions," "The Search for Meaning," and "Political Ecology" have been used for years, but the specific content has varied depending on both faculty interests and contemporary issues. At institutions where variable learning community offerings occur, there is an annual planning calendar and a predictable cycle for making proposals for learning communities. At increasing numbers of these schools, guidelines are developed to set forth standards for learning community offerings, including learning outcomes, integration across courses, requirements for writing, and expectations about active and collaborative learning.

The Importance of Fit and Getting to Scale

Whatever curricular structure is chosen, what is most important is the fit between the learning community idea, the individuals who are likely to undertake the program, and the campus's existing mission, culture, and structures. Most institutions start small and take the time to plan and assess their pilot offerings with careful attention to institutional fit.

Adaptations of the different curricular structures described in this chapter can be found in all sectors of colleges and universities. Figure 3.7, drawn from a recent study by the Policy Center on the First Year of College, shows the relative percentages of different types of institutions that report offering learning communities to 10 percent or more of their first-year students. At this point, learning community programs for freshman students have been created in all types of institutions, but they are most common in research-extensive universities. There is a growing commitment among these large institutions to creating small, companionable groups of freshman students within what are often overwhelmingly large and impersonal environments. The learning community structure most often put in place is the freshman interest group model. This is the most modest strategy in terms of faculty involvement and coordination, curricular

Figure 3.7. Percentage of Institutions Offering First-Year Learning
Communities to at Least 10 Percent of Entering Students,
by Carnegie Classification

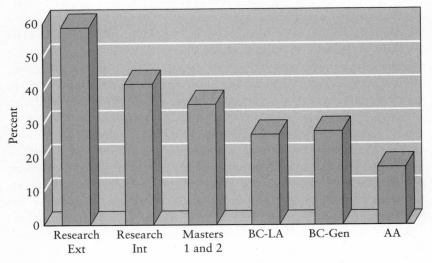

Source: B. O. Barefoot, 2002. Used with permission.

connections, and pedagogical interventions. Although these institutions
offer large numbers of learning communities that reach hundreds or even
several thousand freshmen, both the intentions and the outcomes of these
programs may be situated on the lowest steps of the "Ascending Steps of
Learning Community Goals" (Figure 3.1).

In contrast, there are dozens of learning community initiatives with
much more ambitious curricular and pedagogical intentions in community colleges and liberal arts colleges, although they occur occasionally as special alternative programs in research universities. The goals
and outcomes of these more far-reaching programs may be situated not
only on the lower steps of the staircase but on certain higher ones as
well, with stronger attention to having the courses and co-curricular
activities reinforce both program themes and social connections.
Yet these programs can remain small, engaging relatively few students
and faculty members and sometimes remaining on the margins of the
institution.

This raises an interesting point about getting to scale. The getting-to-
scale issue increasingly concerns leaders in both K–12 and higher education (Elmore, 1996; *Greater Expectations,* 2002; Seymour, 2001;

Lazerson, Wagener, and Shumanis, 2000). We have increasingly high expectations for student success and student learning. And with the development of many proven teaching and curriculum reform endeavors such as collaborative learning, inquiry-based science, problem-based learning, service learning, and so forth, we have a repertoire of strategies to help us achieve these goals. Yet at many institutions, reform efforts remain modest, in the hands of a few faculty members working in isolation. In contrast, traditional patterns of teaching and learning at our colleges and universities have remained the same overall (Schneider and Schoenberg, 1999). If getting to scale is simply about the reach of the innovation—the number of students it serves—one could argue that interest group types are the learning communities to have attained the largest scale at large research universities. But if getting to scale is about the spread of promising teaching practices that promote community and foster deep learning, then these learning communities are just small pockets of promising work and are not nearly getting to scale.

It may be too early in the learning community movement to resolve this issue fully, but the patterns of learning community development on some campuses over time are promising. Some programs seem to be evolving toward greater aspirations for curricular connections and pedagogies that foster deeper student engagement. Programs that involve freshman seminars often move to make that component more academically integrated with the other courses in the learning community. This is particularly significant when it happens at large institutions and involves substantial numbers of students. And in course pairs and clusters, as the faculty members teach the same or new offerings over successive years, they often deepen curricular connections, share pedagogical approaches, and invent assessments that bring the courses together in more substantial ways. As they initiate learning community programs, many institutions put their energy first into remaking the course structures so that students can enroll in coherent sets of classes. Subsequently, they begin to invest more in faculty recruitment for learning community teaching, and in faculty and staff development to explore different teaching strategies and deeper curriculum integration. So the evolutionary pattern appears to be moving toward increasing the degrees of integration and faculty collaboration, as depicted in Exhibit 3.5. The learning community movement may yet get to scale in both reach and quality.

Learning community initiatives, then, are not designed in a vacuum. They are intentional structures designed to address specific issues and raise collective aspirations in the context of a campus's mission and culture, and they often develop out of the passion and energy of certain faculty and staff leaders. Reflecting on the campus's mission and its needs and opportunities, selecting a curriculum structure, and planning for the incorporation of proven teaching practices all can combine to ensure a strong start for a learning community program. In the next chapter, we will discuss five core practices that we believe are essential to making learning community initiatives effective.

4

CORE PRACTICES IN
LEARNING COMMUNITIES

*It's time we applied what we know about learning generated in
our own cognitive laboratories and applied research settings to
systematically enhance teaching and learning practice in college.*

—Diane F. Halpern and Milton D. Hakel

WHEN LEARNING COMMUNITIES ARE CREATED, the initial focus is
on the type of curricular structure they will have. However, an equally
important consideration is the learning environment that will be generated
through that structure. Just putting students together in classes does not,
in and of itself, stimulate learning or guarantee a positive experience of
either learning or community. The challenge, therefore, is to take creative
advantage of the learning community structure to capture and intensify
the synergistic possibilities for meaningful community building and learning. When appropriately designed, learning communities become spaces
to bring together the theory and practice of student development and diversity, of active inclusive pedagogies, and of reflective assessment. All of these
areas have been the subject of much research, foundation support, and
classroom experimentation. When we focus on these areas, we have powerful opportunities to do our best work in undergraduate education. Therefore, we recommend that all learning communities be implemented with
five *core practices* in mind: community, diversity, integration, active learning, and reflection/assessment. Because they are so complementary and
interrelated, they are represented as interlocking circles in Figure 4.1. In
this chapter, we will discuss each one of these in turn.

97

Figure 4.1. Core Practices in Learning Communities

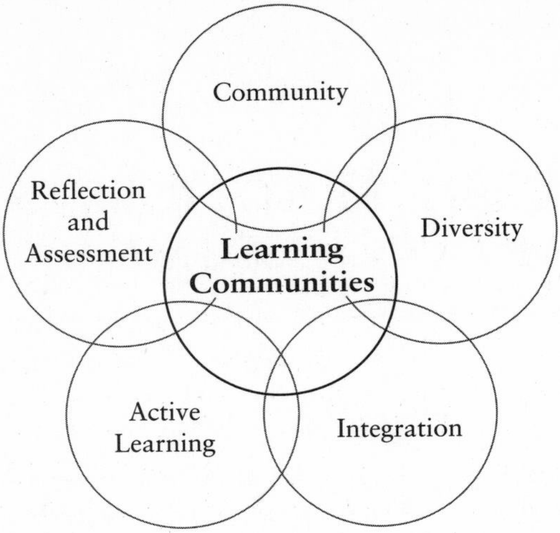

Community

Both learning and the development of community are *processes* that are dynamic and continuous. They also can be viewed as *outcomes* that may be described and even assessed to determine the degree to which they were attained. In learning communities identified as successful by both students and teachers, *learning* and *community* have been highly interrelated. The sense of community has stimulated student involvement and learning, and at the same time, students and teachers have come to a more expanded understanding of community—not only what it offers but also what it requires. The meaning of *community* can be, of course, quite varied, as are the strategies that teachers use to create an ideal community for learning. In this section, we will discuss four dimensions of learning in community: communities of inclusion, communities of collaboration and interdependence, community as focus for study and learning, and communities of practice for teachers.

Communities of Inclusion

When students are asked to define community, they describe it as a sense of belonging and connectedness in both the academic and the social contexts of the college or university. These reflections have been repeatedly reinforced in the extensive literature on college student socialization, which underscores the power of the peer group and the value of positive relationships with peers and faculty members (Astin, 1993b; Newcomb, 1966; Tinto, 1997; Pascarella and Terenzini, 1991; Chickering and Reisser, 1993; Light, 1992). Yet the anonymity of large campuses, large introductory classes, and large residence halls can all militate against the natural development of positive peer groups and meaningful relationships with faculty. Although the factors influencing whether students stay or leave college are complex, most researchers agree that positive social relationships and feelings of belonging figure into the equation, regardless of whether students live on campus or commute. Student retention researcher and theorist Vincent Tinto (1987) argues that developing these relationships is key during the first six weeks of college, when students must not only get acclimated to a new and different social setting but also feel accepted for membership into the college community. Tinto further contends that, especially for commuting students, the classroom is *the crucial place* for fostering social relationships and building the kind of academic and social communities that encourage student success and persistence in college.

Laura Rendón (1994) and William Tierney (1993) offer important amendments to Tinto's theories, particularly with reference to first-generation learners and students of color. Rendón's research on first-generation learners indicates that the "accepted for membership" issue is especially critical: she found that newcomers to academia have a deep need for validation that their ideas are worthwhile and that, in fact, they belong in college at all. Similarly, reflecting on his research on Native American participation in higher education, Tierney notes that minority students in particular come to college from communities with cultural identities that are often markedly different from the mainstream academic communities. Integrating into the community of college learners, although ideal, is not necessarily a positive experience if it requires assimilation and the setting aside of one's ethnic heritage and culture. Tierney argues that in higher education we have much work to do, "shifting our emphases so that alternative discourses can be heard," honoring the histories and cultures of all students, and searching for other strategies by which minority students can "maintain their identities while grasping the tools that a college education offers" (Tierney, 1993, pp. 322–323).

To accomplish the core practice of building an inclusive community, learning communities must create safe spaces for all students to interact more closely with teachers and with fellow students. Teaching teams can strengthen community by offering activities that foster hospitality, inclusion, and validation for all members. In-class and out-of-class activities might include extended introductions of both students and teachers, explicit recognition of all the disciplines and co-curricular elements of the learning community, opportunities for dialogue and collaborative work, informal social occasions and excursions, the creation of study groups, and service learning projects. Physical spaces to meet outside class are valuable, whether they are shared living spaces in a residence hall or a corner of the library, dining hall, or study lounge. Occasions for sharing food are particularly appreciated: potlucks are mainstays of many programs. Teachers and students often invent their own rituals to signify the beginning of the community's time together. Special retreats might be arranged to plan the term's work, celebrate special events, recognize culminating projects or productions, or reflect back on the experience. Through these experiences, learning community students can develop a positive sense of shared identity. And perhaps they can also become skilled practitioners in creating community in other contexts.

Communities of Collaboration and Interdependence

In communities of collaboration, students literally *learn in community*—that is, they engage in collaborative work. When they work together to make meaning, debate issues, solve problems, create products, or undertake a host of other learning tasks, students have to practice the skills of articulating their own perspectives and listening to those of others, contributing their ideas, negotiating decisions, and working constructively through disagreements—in short, they have to learn to work together. These are vital skills for working and living in the world today, as alumni and employer surveys repeatedly attest. But collaborative learning has a more immediate role as well in the creation of community and in stimulating students to rely on one another.

Kenneth Bruffee, an eloquent proponent and theorist in the field of collaborative learning, offers a compelling rationale for these types of practices, which are key to developing community. He begins his book *Collaborative Learning* (1993) with the story of his agreeing to become the new freshman composition director at Brooklyn College in 1970, the year that City University of New York (CUNY) began its open admissions policy. Inundated by underprepared students and daunted by their multiple needs, Bruffee and his counterparts at sister CUNY schools began to meet to explore ways to understand these new students and develop strategies for helping them be successful. Bruffee (1993, p. 17) recounts a key discovery that they made:

> Our students, however poorly prepared academically, did not come to us as blank slates. They arrived in our classes already deeply acculturated, already full-fledged, competent members (as we were, too) of some community or other. In fact, they were already members of several interrelated communities (as we were, too). . . . The community that the students were not yet members of and were asking to join by virtue of committing themselves to attend college was of course the (to them) alien community of the "literate" and the "college educated." In a word, us.

As Bruffee and his colleagues continued to work with these students, they came to realize that their work was not so much to correct the students' errors but rather to "reacculturate" them to the world of college learning and devise ways for them "to become members, to one degree or another, of the knowledge communities to which their teachers belong" (1993, p. 3).

Bruffee believes that this reacculturation process, this learning to join academic communities, takes time and a great deal of active practice in the company of supportive others. These bridges into college must revolve around collaborative work with peers in what he calls "transition communities," where, with the guidance and support of teachers, students can struggle to learn the new moves and the new languages of the academy and also cope with the stress of change. Much of this is centered in talk, Bruffee contends, because it is only by talking, sometimes accurately, sometimes not, that fluency can develop. He comments, "In collaborative learning the route to fluency in the language of a new community is paved with ad hoc intermediary languages that students devise themselves to serve their own purposes as they work through the assigned task" (1993, p. 77).

It seems ironic that, in some sectors of our campuses, learning the crafts of collaboration and interdependence is seen as utterly fundamental to practice and accomplishment. Athletic teams, debate teams, dance groups, marching bands, and orchestras come to mind. Yet, in contrast, the general expectation for classroom learning is that it should be individual and competitive. Bruffee thinks the reason for this is deep and epistemological. It is not just that faculty members have not yet added the collaborative learning arrow to their "quiver of pedagogical tricks" (1993, p. 9). Instead, most faculty members believe that knowledge is "foundational"—that is, that knowledge is an entity, "out there," that students have to receive from texts and teachers, rather than a complex scheme of understanding that is socially constructed and reconstructed by "negotiating with one another in communities of knowledgeable peers" (p. 9). It also has to do with how college teachers were taught themselves (largely through the practices shown on the left side of Exhibit 1.2 in Chapter One) and the strong pull of historic classroom norms that too often keep the teacher as the sole source of expertise and the manager of the classroom agenda.[1] Still, the idea of engaging students in cooperative and collaborative learning is gradually gaining acceptance, and there are many excellent resources on classroom strategy (Johnson, Johnson, and Smith, 1998; Finkel, 2000; Johnson and Johnson, 1995; Mazur, 1997; Brookfield and Preskill, 1999; Millis and Cottell, 1998; Matthews, Cooper, Davidson, and Hawkes, 1995).

A productively functioning community of students and teachers is a worthy goal to aspire to, but of course, it is not a given. Life in any community can be engrossing and wonderful, and yet challenging, unpredictable, and outright baffling at the same time. Beginning college students often come to us with little experience working in teams on academic tasks and have often never been asked to sustain an idea in a discussion setting. And there is no getting around it: putting students in several classes, and perhaps in a residence hall as well, sets up conditions for intense interpersonal dynamics, for better or worse. In fact, some learning community practitioners have come up with the term *hyperbonding* to refer to the behavior of certain groups of first-year students who become empowered around their own norms of immature behavior, sloppy work, and incivility. So those who teach in learning communities, particularly communities that enroll just freshmen, need to consider these dynamics and find ways to establish both learning activities and classroom norms that foster student responsibility and mature behavior from the start. It can be helpful to have more advanced students serve as peer mentors. Also valuable is the construction of social contracts or "program covenants" that contain ground rules for etiquette and mutual support as well as processes for resolving conflicts. Involving the students in the creation of these covenants is a good first step in taking community seriously and engaging students as shapers of their own experience, because it demonstrates that the creation of community and the development of trust are as important as mastering skills and content.

Community as Focus for Study and Learning

Some learning community initiatives include a third dimension: the study of or work in the surrounding community. This may even be the organizing feature of these programs. The leaders of these programs are interested in cultivating an experience of civic engagement among both students and the local communities. In describing the rationales for their programs, they cite voter apathy, the nation's drift toward disengagement and individualism, and the loss of "social capital" associated with the continuous decline in participation in community-based civic organizations over the past thirty years (Putnam, 2000; Bellah and others, 1996). Learning outcomes here include deeper multicultural understanding, knowledge of public issues and democratic processes, engagement in the civic life of the communities surrounding the campus, the linking of theory and practice with real-world problems, and the development of motivation, skills, and commitment to work individually and collectively to make the world a better place.

These goals, and a commitment on the part of the academy to greater civic engagement, have been put forward as a national imperative for some years (Barber, 1992; Zlotkowski, 1996). National higher education organizations have recently organized major initiatives to provide visibility and share practices with institutions: the Association of American Colleges and Universities' (AAC&U) Shared Futures Project; the American Association of State Colleges and Universities' (AASCU) Democracy Project, and the American Association for Higher Education's (AAHE) Engaged Campus for a Diverse Democracy. Over the past decade, leaders in service learning have consistently argued for depth in students' learning experiences, insisting that their learning in service and civic issues must have enough academic integration to affect their intellectual conceptions, not to mention their attitudes and their values when it comes to the origins of community needs, the nature of inequalities, and the complexity of public issues (Eyler and Giles, 1999; Zlotkowski and Williams, 2003; Jacoby and Associates, 1996; Kupiec, 1993). Yet as Caryn McTige Musil (2003) has recently observed, although campus leaders indicate renewed commitment to the ideal of civic engagement and although more undergraduates than ever (78 percent) are participating in some sort of service experience, few colleges and universities are demonstrating a commitment to civic learning. Too often, the actual structures for linking campus and community reside on the margins of campuses in small service learning offices or research centers without substantially changing courses, research, or faculty work.

With these realities and needs in mind, many campuses have integrated service learning into their learning community programs. Marie Eaton, Jean MacGregor, and David Schoem (2003) point out in a recent monograph on integrating learning communities with service learning that linking these two efforts has the potential to strengthen them both. Because learning community structures involve more than one course during a given academic term, learning communities can enhance service learning experiences simply by providing more time and space—and often more academic credit—for community-based work. Service learning, which is too often uneasily tacked onto a single course, can become a larger and more significant element of a student's experience in a learning community program, thereby affording more time for needed reflection and academic integration of the service experience itself. In addition, because learning communities generally link classes across disciplinary lines, they can provide multiple disciplinary lenses through which to examine community issues and a more substantial platform for embracing their complexity. At the same time, service learning can enrich and deepen classroom-based learning communities by adding a component of experiential learning and immersing students in real issues and problems that exist in the wider community. Several institutions have made service learning a centerpiece of their learning community initiatives, including Collin County Community Colleges in northern Dallas, Texas, Wagner College in Staten Island, New York, and Portland State University.

In addition, some learning community programs are making *community* itself the center of focus and study. For example, with its partner campus Arizona State University-East, Chandler Gilbert Community College in Phoenix has for several years offered a yearlong learning community whose theme is the concept of community. Entitled "Finding Community in a Changing World," this program allows freshman students to explore this theme through film and literature, and they also participate in a service learning program at a transitional housing facility for homeless families that is located nearby (Hesse and Mason, 2003). At Bellevue Community College in the Seattle suburbs, "The Power of Place," an American studies learning community, examines both historical and contemporary relationships between people and their landscapes in North America, with a particular emphasis on Seattle's urban sprawl. "Local Knowledge" and similar programs at The Evergreen State College focus on community-based research in which students explore relationships between knowledge, authority, and democracy both in and with the communities that surround South Puget Sound (Nelson, 2003).

Other learning communities have focused their community-study lenses on regions. Among the oldest forms of learning communities are semester-abroad or year-abroad programs, many of which provide a fully integrated program of study in another country. The Audubon Expedition Institute, based in Maine and associated with Lesley College, takes students on the road in buses to travel and study both environmental and cultural issues in different regions of the United States. Other programs focus on a region that is near the campus; sometimes these have a cultural emphasis, sometimes an ecological one. Some examples of such programs are "The Adirondacks" (offered by both St. Lawrence University and SUNY-Potsdam), "The Appalachian Semester" (Union College), "Harlem on My Mind" (LaGuardia Community College), and "Asian Pacific American: Whose Values/Who's Valued?" (Seattle Central Community College).

Communities of Practice for Teachers

Learning communities involve teams of faculty and staff members who teach in these programs; therefore the communities of practice that their relationships create must also be considered. The phrase *community of practice* is an intriguing one that has important implications for higher education. It appeared in the early 1990s with Jean Lave and Etienne Wenger's *Situated Learning: Legitimate Peripheral Participation* (1991), a book that explores how people learn their crafts in apprenticeship communities, specifically midwives, tailors, butchers, and even alcoholics, who learn to live a sober life in Alcoholics Anonymous meetings. These scholars particularly examined the dynamic relationships between novices and experts and built an epistemology of learning a craft that involved increasing degrees of social participation and practice. Subsequently, Wenger (1998) continued to study and develop this idea by examining informal communities of practice that frequently arise in workplaces, groups of people who come together informally to share work-related problems and deepen their expertise by interacting on a frequent basis. You would not see this "community of practice" on an organizational chart, but it could be a significant arena for crucial learning and community building to take place.

What began as theory has swiftly moved into practice, with ideas and guidance for strengthening workplaces by taking advantage of the apprenticeship, community knowledge sharing, and growth that occur naturally when people work together. In short, the idea is to *cultivate* nourishing communities of professionals (Wenger, McDermott, and Snyder, 2002). In higher education, both formal and informal communities of practice are common. Yet for the most part, they are centered in separate areas, such as faculty members' disciplinary and professional networks, or student affairs professionals' work in advising, career planning, student activities, and residence life. Ongoing communities of professional practice focused on issues of curriculum development and teaching and learning (which, presumably, is the core work of colleges and universities) are much less common (Shulman, 1993; Grubb, 1999). When learning community teaching teams (often made up of faculty members and student affairs professionals) work collaboratively with one group of students for an entire academic term, new communities of teaching practice can emerge. These groups have much to share with each other about enhancing the student experience. These communities not only are important for developing a culture of teaching on a campus but also can be vital to the rebuilding and regeneration of relationships in our institutions as large numbers of faculty retire and new faculty arrive. Often, learning community leaders encourage newer faculty members to join their programs as a strategy for introducing them to new colleagues and institutional values; they also encourage older, respected teachers and student affairs professionals to join learning community teams and pass along their perspectives and expertise.

Diversity

That learners are diverse in numerous ways is not a new insight, of course, but it is too often overlooked in teaching and learning environments. As Chapter Two notes, John Dewey's work rested on the central observations that students are highly variable individuals and that creators of successful learning environments respect and build on this individuality. Early in the twentieth century, both Dewey and Alexander Meiklejohn were strong advocates of community, but they also wrote about diversity as a core value in an evolving democracy and about schools as critical transmitters of democratic habits of mind. For them, diversity was an ongoing source of renewal in America, and that is precisely what it has proven to be.

As students in our colleges have become more diverse in socioeconomic status, cultural background, ethnicity, gender, and learning style, attending to diversity should be a fundamental core practice throughout our institutions. First and foremost, attending to diversity is a value commitment in education, a statement of our aspirations for social justice and equality in a democratic society. Higher education has enjoyed public support in part because it is seen as a key way to build public competence for self-governance and as a ladder to economic success. Diversity themes having to do with opportunity, equity, and a fully participatory democracy run deep in both of these goals. In our colleges and universities, diversity is a multifaceted issue that relates to how different people learn, who participates (students and faculty), what the curriculum is, and how the formal and informal teaching and learning environments are structured.

Daryl Smith (Smith and Associates, 1997, 2000), a leading scholar on diversity, suggests that the national conversation about this subject has become more sophisticated in the last fifteen years, having moved from an initial focus on access and success (measured by participation rates in college of different demographic groups) to an exploration of the multiple factors that foster academically successful learning environments. Smith and her associates describe four ways in which to think about diversity:

- *Diversity as access and success* refers to the inclusion and achievement of underrepresented groups. Perhaps the oldest notion of diversity, the focus here is on numerical representation of people of color on campuses and in different programs and on their success.

- *Climate and intergroup relations* refer to the campus environment, especially for groups that have been traditionally underrepresented and the ways in which campuses create supportive and inclusive environments.

- *Diversity efforts in education and scholarship* refer to the curriculum and research as well as teaching practices and faculty development. The last twenty-five years has seen a blossoming literature on cultural pluralism, women's studies, and American ethnic studies, supporting and offering important opportunities for enriching the curriculum. Recognition has grown about the need to understand better the impact of diversity on the learning environment and the relationship between campus diversity and pedagogy. Questions include the following: How do active and collaborative learning and service learning work for diverse student populations? How effective are learning communities among different student populations? What relationship does faculty diversity have with student success?

- *Institutional vitality and viability* refer to the role of diversity in fostering vital institutions and the characteristics of institutions that are effective in this regard. How does diversity affect leadership and decision making? Why do some institutions make broad commitments to diversity initiatives while others do not? What is the impact of these commitments? How are such institutional commitments maintained?

Daryl Smith and Associates (1997, 2000) suggest that all these conceptions of diversity are important for institutions making diversity an essential component of their mission and practices. Smith and her colleagues looked at the recent research on diversity in their publication *Diversity Works: The Emerging Picture of How Students Benefit* (Smith and Associates, 1997). This valuable synthesis articulated the benefits of diversity for all students and suggested how to promote both access and success for students from underrepresented groups:

1. Diversity initiatives benefit both majority and minority students on campus, affecting student attitudes and feelings toward intergroup relations as well as institutional satisfaction, involvement, and academic growth.

2. Programs that focus on the transition to college are important for the recruitment, retention, and academic success of underrepresented students.

3. Mentoring programs result in improved adjustment, retention, and academic success rates.

4. Specialized student support programs and larger campus community-building programs benefit students.

5. Opportunities for interaction between groups are desired by virtually all students and produce increases in understanding and academic success.

6. The conditions for effective intergroup dialogue cannot be assumed and must be carefully structured. (Intergroup dialogues are "a form of democratic practice . . . involving face-to-face, focused, facilitated, and confidential discussions occurring over time between two or more groups of people defined by their different social identities" [Schoem and Hurtado, 2001, p. 6]).

7. Serious engagement of issues of diversity in the curriculum has a positive impact on cognitive development, attitudes toward racial issues, and overall satisfaction with the institution.

Resonating with these research findings, many learning community designs focus on the first year of college, make use of peer mentors, and feature community building. Program leaders often make special efforts to recruit broadly so that the demographic makeup of the learning community offerings reflects that of the institution as a whole. Some programs engage cultural pluralism in the curriculum content or the co-curriculum and provide opportunities for intergroup dialogue among students. It is, therefore, not surprising that the *National Survey of Student Engagement* (2001) found a positive correlation between learning communities and diversity experiences.

As Emily Lardner (2002) points out, learning communities can be ideal places to approach diversity on multiple fronts: to reach particular groups of students, to design a more inclusive curriculum and to develop pedagogical practices that support diverse learners. We will briefly discuss each of these three intentions.

Learning Communities That Serve Special Student Groups

Numerous learning community initiatives have been developed specifically for particular groups of students to enable them to achieve greater academic success. Federally funded Title III programs (serving first-generation and low-income students) and more recently Title V programs (serving Hispanic students) are frequently sites for learning communities. Many of the educational opportunities programs (EOP) in the California State University system have built successful learning community initiatives for students admitted under their EOP guidelines. The Law and Diversity Program at Western Washington University, whose curricular structure was described in Chapter Three, was established to enable both students of color and white students interested in issues of diversity and justice to prepare for law school or related careers. At The Evergreen State College, the reservation-based and community-determined Native American studies program has been instrumental in enabling large numbers of Native American students to earn a bachelor's degree. Chapter Six discusses learning communities in developmental education, often a perilous area in the curriculum for students of color and first-generation learners.

In the sciences and engineering, learning communities have been established to foster greater success among women and underrepresented minorities. Several research universities have established Women in Science and Engineering (WISE) programs, living-learning communities that intentionally create a support system for women entering these fields. Building on Uri Treisman's landmark project to increase African-American and Hispanic students' achievement rates in the calculus sequence (Treisman, 1992; Fullilove and Treisman, 1990), over one hundred campuses have "Emerging Scholars" programs that link an introductory math or science class to a credit-bearing, problem-oriented workshop course, often facilitated by a more advanced undergraduate or graduate student. One of the largest learning community initiatives in science and engineering is at the University of Texas-El Paso, where a course-cluster program for entering students, the CircLES (Circles of Learning for Entering Students) learning community, has successfully strengthened retention, academic achievement, and entry into science and engineering majors among Hispanic students (Della-Piana and others, 2003).

Learning Communities as Sites for Inclusive Curricula

Many learning community teachers are working to offer a more inclusive curriculum, drawing on rich bodies of work in American ethnic studies and in non-Western literatures. At Seattle Central Community College, for example, program themes such as "Eyes on the Prize" and "Our Ways of Knowing: The Black Experience and Social Change" attracted significantly more students of color to the learning community offerings at this college and also created important places in the general education program for study and reflection about pluralism and justice in the American experience. At the University of Michigan, the Michigan Community Scholars Program is a residential learning community that has placed diversity, democratic practice, and student leadership at its center; it exemplifies an inclusive and transformed curriculum. The program leaders try to recruit a diverse student body; in addition, program courses, service learning projects, and intergroup dialogues, combined with living together in a common residence hall, ask students to study and work together as a diverse and interdependent community (Schoem and Pasque, 2003).

Learning Communities That Use Inclusive Pedagogies

Pedagogy can play an important role not only in engaging diverse learners but also in enabling all students to learn in a context of diversity. A number of studies note a mismatch between faculty teaching styles and student learning preferences. Teachers who are generally analytical learners may focus more on intellectual concepts while their students may favor more experiential and relational forms of learning (Rendón and Hope, 1996; Anderson, 2001). Some of the earliest research in this area focused on gender differences, finding that many women students felt alienated and voiceless in the traditional lecture-centered classroom's "chilly climate" that does not invite women to relate their new learning to their life experiences or situate new ideas in assumptions they bring to the learning experience (Association of American Colleges, 1982). The influential book

Women's Ways of Knowing suggested that more connected ways of learning, especially through conversational dialogue, could help some women students connect their life experience to their classroom education, find their voices, and feel validated through the connections they make with new knowledge and understanding (Belenky, Clinchy, Goldberger, and Tarule, 1986).

Our understanding of how cultural and gender differences relate to pedagogical strategies is gradually increasing and what we have learned is being incorporated into classroom and institutional practices. A number of recent studies summarized by Tierney, Colyar, and Corwin (2003) explore what it will take to prepare students successfully for college, especially Latino and African-American students. These studies point to the importance of core programmatic improvements in high school to ensure college readiness and create social support networks that foster student interest and awareness of college opportunities. Both high school and college programs need to consider issues of culture, cost, and appropriate timing interventions as they prepare underrepresented groups for college. Other studies examine enhancing the success rates of African-American and Hispanic students by making changes in the classroom and public policy (Kazis, Vargas, and Hoffman, 2004). Pedagogical approaches mentioned earlier, such as practices built around hospitality and inclusion, collaborative learning, and intergroup dialogue, are concrete ways to put a more relational and validating learning style into practice. They also create the kinds of bridging experiences that Kenneth Bruffee sees as crucial for both welcoming and acculturating students to college learning. All these approaches can easily be adapted to learning community settings.[2]

Teaching highly diverse students is challenging, especially when building community is an explicit goal. When difficult issues are confronted, differing values, identities, and biases of students and teachers are brought into the open. Learning communities can create an environment in which teams of teachers can work together to explore new practices with common cohorts of students and learn from and support each other in the process. Phyllis van Slyck (1997) and Will Koolsbergen (2001), faculty colleagues at LaGuardia Community College who often teach together in learning communities, made this point as they reflected on the complexity of embracing diversity issues in the curriculum and designing ways to engage students with those issues in productive ways. Describing LaGuardia, whose student body is heavily international, an English professor comments: "I'm not sure there's any place in the world where the conversation about 'difference' has the urgency that it has in New York City. It's an extraordinary thing that we are all in classrooms together;

no matter how much one talks about the mix of life in New York City, we often live in segregated communities; frequently, students have said to me how incredible it is to find themselves together in a learning community talking about very volatile subjects. . . . [The] opportunity to talk about difference through the materials is a powerful situation" (Matthews and Lynch, 1997, p. 108). Van Slyck believes that learning communities can (and should) provide an important dialogue space, a rare "contact zone" for her students, where they can "understand difference better and begin to define what they as individuals and as members of communities need to do to cross borders, to connect" (1997, p. 167). Sharing that perspective, Koolsbergen (2001) believes that productive dialogue rests on a set of "conversational ground rules" (similar to program covenants, mentioned earlier) that he develops with his students at the beginning of each class; he particularly stresses creating a safe atmosphere for dialogue about matters of racism, sexism, and heterosexism. These faculty members and many of their colleagues at LaGuardia have made a significant commitment to learning from each other through ongoing professional development activities that explore ways to work with diversity and the kind of pedagogical complexity it requires (Mellow, van Slyck, and Eynon, 2003).

Integration

Integration is increasingly mentioned as a goal in higher education, but the meaning of this term, like that of our other core practices, is often assumed but not precisely described. *To integrate* usually means to bring two or more things together. The *Oxford Dictionary* defines it as "to combine into a whole, to complete an imperfect thing by the addition of parts, and to fuse or unify."

Many years ago, educator Paul Dressel (1958), attempting to define integration more precisely, stated that there are two intertwined processes or purposes underlying the idea of integration in the curriculum and that a complete education should include both: an *integrated* curriculum, which provides learners with a unified view of knowledge, and an *integrative* curriculum, which motivates and develops learners' powers to perceive and create new relationships for themselves. This view stresses the teaching and learning process and the importance for learners to construct their own meanings in order to make sense of the world of knowledge.

As Chapter Two described, a principal feature of Alexander Meiklejohn's Experimental College at the University of Wisconsin and Joseph Tussman's learning community program at Berkeley was their *integrated* curricula organized around the theme of democracy. In fact, both of these programs incorporated *integrated* and *integrative* principles at the same time. The curricular content was organized around a powerful theme, but in addition, many other aspects of the experience and the setting reinforced the theme—from the living and learning residential environment, to the restructuring of the curriculum into a *program* (rather than discrete courses), to pedagogies of collaboration that included active learning in seminar discussions, inquiry-based assignments, and applications projects.

The literature on learning theory and cognitive development, interdisciplinary education, and integrative learning strategies and pedagogies further illuminates these dimensions and points to their importance in learning communities. We discuss this research in the following paragraphs.

Integration, Learning Theory, and Cognitive Development

The importance of deep learning through an integrated and integrative education resonates with a robust multidisciplinary literature on how people learn (Bransford, Brown, and Cocking, 1999; Zull, 2002). As James Zull put it in *The Art of Changing the Brain: Enriching the Practice of Teaching by Exploring the Biology of Learning*, we "continually blend the old and the new. . . . We construct our understanding using part of what we already know and part of what is new" (2002, p. 119). And it is becoming clear that this natural tendency to organize and generalize can be much more intentional and better developed if we create structures and opportunities that stimulate connection making and nurture deep learning.

Thanks to a growing body of international research, the terms *deep learning* and *surface learning* are gaining currency to describe the nature of memory, learning, and understanding as well as students' conceptions of learning and their approaches to tackling new material in classes. Surface learning refers to that information that resides only in the short-term memory and is usually not internalized into knowledge structures. Deep learning, in contrast, is more permanently embedded in the learner's evolving understanding of a subject and transforms the learner in some way (Ramsden, 1992). These terms, *surface* and *deep*, are used also to refer to students' *orientations* to learning. Noel Entwistle points out, "Some students see learning as mainly a matter of memorizing and reproducing knowledge in ways acceptable to the teacher. Others see learning as a way to establish personal meaning, by transforming the information and ideas in relation to their existing knowledge and experience" (2000, p. 10).

Ramsden, Entwistle, and other researchers of college students' learning strategies in the 1990s and 2000s, most of them working in Australia and Europe, echo and reinforce earlier research on student learning and development conducted by William Perry and his graduate students at Harvard in the 1960s and 1970s and extended in the 1980s and 1990s by Lee Knefelkamp, Marcia Baxter Magolda, William Moore, and others. As director of Harvard's counseling and advising center, Perry (1970) became intrigued with how students described their learning as they came to grips with intellectual complexity over the span of their undergraduate years and as they began to make judgments and personal commitments in a world they came to see as complex and ambiguous. Perry noticed patterns that began with a type of surface learning (dualism) and moved to a type of deep learning (contextual relativism). Perry's conversations with these students led to a scheme of student intellectual development reflecting the full range of meaning making involved in that journey.

Although many of the international researchers at first rejected a developmental explanation of the deep-surface learning differences they saw students making, close parallels to Perry's description of intellectual development in terms of students' emerging conceptions of learning remain. That is, many students arrive at college with expectations that they will be successful by simply learning information provided by respected authorities such as teachers (and texts). They find it disconcerting and challenging to be confronted with complex problems having multiple solutions or to be asked to articulate their own point of view or understanding in the face of diverse perspectives. Yet, with a reasonable balance of challenge and support over time, students can move toward a more complex understanding of the world; and that complex understanding parallels—or perhaps engenders—deep approaches to learning.

Student conceptions of what learning entails affect how they tackle academic tasks, but their conceptions in turn can be influenced, for better or worse, by the learning environments that teachers establish (Tagg, 2003; Entwistle, 2000). For decades, educators have worried that too many classrooms are set up to do little more than elicit recall; they have advocated for academic environments that encourage the higher-order reasoning skills described in Bloom's taxonomy: analysis, synthesis, and evaluation (Bloom and Collaborators, 1956; Mehan, 1979; McKeachie, Pintrich, Yi-Guang, and Smith, 1986; Anderson and Krathwohl, 2001; Shulman, 2002). In integrative learning environments, teachers provide ways for students to learn these higher-order reasoning skills, to practice becoming deeper learners, to become more comfortable with intellectual complexity. Moreover, these environments often encourage collaborative student learning as well.

Integration as a Coherent and Connected Curriculum

As described in Chapter One, national reports have repeatedly called for undergraduate education to be more coherent and connected to co-curricular life. Although this search for more coherence and balance has most often focused on inadequacies in general education, it has also prompted debates over study in the major. In his classic study *College: The Undergraduate Experience in America* (1987), Ernest Boyer made the case for an "enriched major" that would foster broader perspectives in students. The Association of American Colleges and Universities has also been an advocate for greater curricular coherence and integration, both in general education (Association of American Colleges [AAC], 1985) and in the major (AAC, 1990). Most recently the Association of American College and Universities' *Greater Expectations* report (2002) expanded on Boyer's work, arguing for curricular integration that links the "practical liberal arts" with pedagogical practices that encourage students to become intentional, responsible, empowered learners. Boyer's work and the AAC&U reports ask educational leaders not only to address the curricular fragmentation of unrelated classes but also to encourage students to make their own connections between coursework and the world outside the classroom.

Curricular integration in learning communities does not abandon or ignore subject matter or skill development, but it sets the two into the context of significant themes and asks students and faculty to understand those themes and communicate about them. Thus, students are asked to make connections, use higher-order reasoning skills, and develop capacities for deeper learning. Learning communities, then, provide an ideal site and a stimulating context to foster the development of integrative skills that help students make sense of their learning across multiple courses.

An Integrated Curriculum Through Interdisciplinarity

Although learning communities and integrated curricula are not synonymous with interdisciplinary approaches—because there are learning communities that link two skill courses (such as developmental reading and writing) or two courses in the same discipline (such as the botany of woody plants and forest ecology, or Russian language and Russian literature)—many learning communities do employ interdisciplinary approaches to foster curricular integration. There are several arguments in support of interdisciplinary approaches. The primary intellectual argument is that interdisciplinary approaches can address the inherent limitations of disciplines (Gaff, 1993; Davis, 1995). Disciplines, by definition, establish boundaries and narrow the scope of knowledge, necessarily leaving out important ways of knowing, concepts, theories, and methods of other disciplines. As Grant Cornwell and Eve Stoddard point out, disciplines look at a small patch of ground and impose a kind of invisible "electric fence" around it through norms, practices, and various stratification systems. Interdisciplinary approaches turn off that electric fence and open up new horizons, new worlds of questions and practices (Cornwell and Stoddard, 2001). They can overcome the inherent limitations of single disciplines by drawing on other theories, knowledge, and methodologies.

Another rationale for curricular integration through interdisciplinary approaches has to do with social relevance. This argument rests on the recognition that the issues facing the world and the planet today are not neatly organized according to disciplines. Any significant issue is so complex that understanding and addressing it require an interdisciplinary approach (Hill, 1985; Gaff, 1993; Davis, 1995). The problems of polluted rivers or urban homelessness or HIV/AIDS—or terrorism—for example, can only be understood and addressed through a broad interdisciplinary approach that draws on diverse disciplines and practices.

Integration as Integrative Learning Strategies and Pedagogies

When we think of integration in terms of an integrative curriculum, it pushes us more into the realm of learning strategies and pedagogy. In his essay "Powerful Pedagogies," William Newell (2001) suggested that integration can be thought of as a variety of pedagogical strategies that invite integrative activity on the part of students, including collaborative learning, living-learning communities, study abroad, service learning, and multicultural education. All these are important complements to disciplinary and interdisciplinary notions of integration. As he pointed out (p. 197):

> These educational strategies share a concern for learning from diverse perspectives. The perspectives can emanate from academic disciplines, cultures, subcultures, or individual life experiences, and the learning can take place in the classroom, breakout groups, the residence hall,

field sites, other communities, or even foreign countries. Insights from these different perspectives must somehow be integrated. . . . They provide synthesis that complements disciplinary analysis, breadth to accompany its depth, and real-world personal application to go with abstract theory. In short, they offer educational balance. Students who experience integrative as well as disciplinary education should be more fully educated and should be better able to make use of what they have learned.

Newell suggests that these strategies, often used in combination with one another, are mutually reinforcing and have a multiplicative power as engines for deep learning.

Active Learning

In a way, active learning incorporates all of the core practices we have been discussing, because active learning environments include community building, encounters with diversity and pluralism, and the integration of interdisciplinary and diverse pedagogies. The concept of learning as an active, constructive process certainly is not new: throughout the twentieth century, educational theorists such as John Dewey, L. S. Vygotsky, Jean Piaget, Jerome Bruner, and David Kolb repeatedly described learning as a process of taking in experiences, attaching new knowledge to what one already knows, and making and remaking one's understanding of the world. In 1929, Alfred North Whitehead put forward his famous and prescient rationale for active learning: "Beware of inert ideas that are merely received into the mind without being utilized, or tested, or thrown into fresh combinations. By utilizing an idea, I mean relating to that stream compounded of sense perceptions, feelings, hopes, desires and of mental activities adjusting thought to thought, which forms our life" (Whitehead, [1929] 1949, p. 13). For Whitehead, education was the art of the utilization of knowledge—not only an active and continuous process, but, tellingly, one that was influenced by human emotions.

More recently, in advocating for active learning as one of their seven good practices in undergraduate education, Arthur Chickering and Zelda Gamson (1987, p. 3) asserted, "Learning is not a spectator sport. Students do not learn much just by sitting in class listening to teachers, memorizing prepackaged assignments, and spitting out answers. They must talk about what they are learning, write about it, relate it to past experiences, apply it to their daily lives. They must make what they learn part of themselves."

Decades of research on the learning process continue to reinforce these active knowledge construction rationales, and they corroborate Whitehead's belief that human emotions and motivation are key elements in the learning process (Bransford, Brown, and Cocking, 1999; Zull, 2002). Moreover, the past twenty years have seen a proliferation of practices in the active learning realm. Active learning can be viewed as an umbrella term encompassing a range of activities that may occur both in and out of class. Figure 4.2 mentions some of the most widely recognized of these activities. Many, such as service learning, problem-based learning, writing across the curriculum, and undergraduate research, have their own rich literatures, professional networks, and recommended best practices for different types of educational settings. Importantly, all of these practices are used to one degree or another in learning community programs, and certainly one argument for learning communities is that the introduction and reinforcement of certain active learning strategies *across multiple classes*

Figure 4.2. Active Learning Strategies

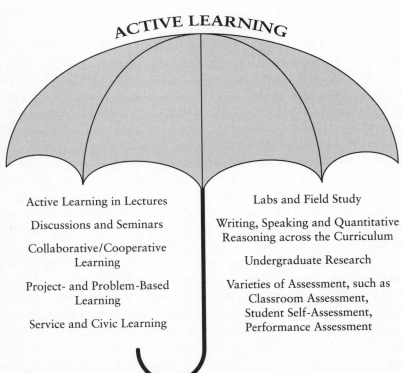

ACTIVE LEARNING

Active Learning in Lectures

Discussions and Seminars

Collaborative/Cooperative Learning

Project- and Problem-Based Learning

Service and Civic Learning

Labs and Field Study

Writing, Speaking and Quantitative Reasoning across the Curriculum

Undergraduate Research

Varieties of Assessment, such as Classroom Assessment, Student Self-Assessment, Performance Assessment enables students to master the strategies more intensely and quickly than when they pick them up here and there in discrete classes.

Although the different active learning strategies vary, they do share four important attributes: they involve meaningful contexts or questions, they engage studies in interactive learning, they require teachers to play multiple roles, and they require students to play new, demanding roles.

Meaningful Contexts or Questions

Most teachers who use active learning strategies intuitively design these educational experiences around interesting topics. Intriguing questions, issues that matter in the world, puzzling open-ended problems that engage student curiosity and stimulate thinking: any of these can create both reasons and platforms for learning. Rather than beginning with abstract content or practicing skills in preparation for application at some later date, these teachers often begin with immersion experiences—real contexts and problems that invite students to access their own knowledge and assumptions. In fact, a problem or question often determines what elements of a course can be most important and helpful. This approach has always been at the heart of experiential learning, but more recently, the importance of *contexts* as bases for learning have gained added support from theories about "situated cognition" and the value of learning to problem-solve in real-world situations (Brown, Collins, and Duguid, 1989). Learning community programs are often designed around contexts and issues that matter to students, for example, "The Search for Meaning," "Political Arabesques: Sources of Conflict in the Middle East," "The Race for the White House: Politics and the Media," "Rights and Wrongs in America," "China: The Waking Lion," or "Climate and Climate Change."

Interactive Learning

Active learning strategies usually involve interactive, interdependent activity. Much of the "activity" in active learning involves students' engagement with others—talking and listening, giving and receiving feedback, and undertaking collective or collaborative projects. Our overarching intention in education is to develop students' individual understanding of subjects, competence with thinking and communication skills, and ability to integrate knowing and doing. However, the path to these goals is often collaborative, when students explore, test, and refine ideas "by negotiating with one another in communities of knowledgeable peers," as Kenneth Bruffee puts it (1993, p. 9). In fact, collaborative activity is essential to students' emerging understanding of their own and others' capacity to be constructors of knowledge. Through carefully designed collaborative activities, students can begin to see themselves not just as receivers of truths from textbooks and teachers, or "procedural knowers" (going through the motions called for by the teacher), but as responsible creators of their own meanings and understandings in the company of others who are attempting to do the same thing—which is essential to intellectual maturity and lifelong learning (Smith and MacGregor, 1992).

In discussions promoting active learning approaches, the lecture usually takes a beating. The syntheses of the research do not have good news about student learning habits in lectures (attention spans fall off after fifteen or twenty minutes, and thoroughness of note taking generally declines throughout the lecture period), or about the levels of thinking most lectures ask of students (higher-order thinking and in-depth understanding are rarely expected), or about student retention of lecture information (it is disappointingly small) (Gardiner, 1994). In short, lecturing seems to reinforce surface learning habits and little more (Halpern and Hakel, 2003). A recent assessment of first-year college students reveals that the lecture is ranked as the most frequently used teaching technique in the classes they take but is also ranked as the teaching method they least prefer (Sax and others, 2000).

Many faculty members admit that lecture-centered classes are not engaging or useful to students. As one of our colleagues who has adopted active-learning methods in her very large (six hundred students) chemistry classes lamented, "What propelled me into this was watching colleagues in lecture working a problem for the students on the board: I saw it going into the students' eyes, down their arms, and into their notebooks, but their understanding of the problem was bypassing their brains! Over and over, I saw the students not able to do similar problems in the tutorial sections the very next day" (Cooper and Robinson, 2000, p. 17). This inventive instructor activated her lectures by designing them around short problems that students work out in pairs in class, but she is still something of a rarity among her peers: the research continues to be fairly consistent that most college faculty (in the 60 to 90 percent range) primarily teach their classes in the lecture method (Bonwell and Eison, 1991; Finkelstein, Seal, and Schuster, 1998; Outcalt, 2002).

In spite of this discouraging news, a lecture setting can stimulate active learning and mental processing. However, learners must have sufficient readiness and motivation to take in new ideas and reflect on them. And teachers must build interventionist strategies into their lectures that stimulate students to work actively with lecture material and integrate it into their own schemes of understanding. Strategies for "active learning in lectures" are becoming more widespread, and important and proven efforts are under way to transform lectures in ways that encourage deeper forms of learning, even in very large-class settings (deWinstanley and Bjork, 2002; Schwartz and Bransford, 1998; Ruhl, Hughes, and Schloss, 1987). The Course Redesign Project (described in Chapter One) represents the largest national effort to take on strengthening learning in large classes, with many of them previously lecture-heavy. Many course redesign efforts have reduced the number of lectures in a given week in favor of increasing active learning with discussion sessions, labs, or online learning elements, and have reconfigured the lectures themselves with some of the strategies mentioned here (Twigg, 2003).

Multiple Roles for Teachers

Environments designed for active student learning naturally require that teachers assume new roles in the classroom. Although the late Don Finkel of The Evergreen State College gave his book on active learning the intriguing title *Teaching with Your Mouth Shut* (2000), he carefully described the multiple, important roles that teachers must play in creating active learning environments. Teachers become *designers* of environments that engage students' curiosity and motivation. As students move into the actual work of active learning, teachers become *expert observers* of their work and act as *coaches* in the sense of providing both encouragement and feedback. Or, as the authors of *Women's Ways of Knowing* suggest, they may act as *midwives,* assisting at the birth of inchoate ideas (Belenky, Clinchy, Goldberger, and Tarule, 1986). When collaborative activities such as discussion, debate, peer feedback, and group projects are used, teachers play the role of *facilitator* (keeping groups on task and encouraging or modeling constructive contributions) or *referee* (helping conversations be civil or adhering to agreed-upon ground rules). Another critical function is to act as a *spotlight,* helping the group slow down and focus on an important comment or point (Finkel, 2000). In many classes and particularly in learning communities that are team-planned or team-taught, teachers can also become *co-learners* with other teachers and students as they engage in mutual inquiry.

When faculty members assume these new roles, classrooms become new kinds of social systems that are quite different from those associated with a more traditional, lecture-centered setting. Active learning classrooms challenge teachers to rethink matters of authority and expertise, power and control. When students are asked to take more responsibility for their learning, these elements are not so much relinquished as they are reshaped. These new social systems are also rich in data about the quality of student learning. When students try out their ideas publicly "live, on the air, bloopers and all" (as one of our colleagues puts it), teachers are immediately confronted with evidence of their learning progress, their degree of understanding or misunderstanding. Thus, another important role for faculty members is *continuous observer* of student learning. Watching students engaged in learning activities can provide valuable information with which to continue shaping the learning environment and with which to provide students with feedback.

New, Demanding Roles for Students

Active learning situations also require that students assume a variety of new roles in class—roles with which they may not be familiar. Active learning carries with it a set of expectations about both workload and accountability to others that might be quite unfamiliar to students accustomed to classroom norms that do not ask as much of them. There are several important shifts (MacGregor, 1990):

- Students go from listener, observer, and note taker to active discussant, contributor, and problem solver.
- Expectations of students' preparedness for class rise from low or moderate to high.
- Students' previously private presence in the classroom, with few risks, is transformed to a public one, with many risks.
- Attendance, which is usually dictated by personal choice, is now often dictated by community expectation.
- Rather than competing with peers, students now do collaborative work with them.
- Responsibilities and self-definition having to do with learning independently are transformed into those associated with learning interdependently.
- Instead of assuming that teachers and texts are the sole sources of authority and knowledge, students find that they themselves, their peers, and their community (in or out of class) are additional and important sources of knowledge.

Although many students resist active learning activities or take some time getting used to them, others welcome them. Discussing these new expectations with students is essential, as is framing clear rationales for the different kinds of learning and assessment activities being undertaken.

Frequent check-ins and classroom assessment techniques are also important to evaluate how students are coping with these new and often demanding, interactive learning responsibilities.

Learning communities present singular opportunities to engage students in types of active learning that can be reinforced in multiple classes. If carried out haphazardly, though, active learning can seem incoherent and confusing for students. Just as they coordinate curricula in learning communities, teaching teams need to think through the kinds of active learning they want students to engage in. Planning these learning activities, and setting them up and reinforcing them across multiple classes, can greatly strengthen learning community programs.

Reflection and Assessment

The fifth core practice for learning communities—reflection and assessment—should bring together and underscore all the previously described practices in the context of both coursework and co-curricular activities. Reflection and assessment not only ask students to demonstrate what they have learned but also ask them to reflect on their work and consider what matters most in their learning community experience. These activities should not be undertaken just as terminal episodes; they are most effective when they are part of ongoing classroom practice. In learning communities, the ongoing work of reflection and assessment should create (for students and teachers alike) a kind of connective tissue among disciplines and ideas, the skills and content of the coursework, and the teachers' goals and actual student learning. We see reflection and assessment in three ways: assessment as learning, reflection as learning, and communities of reflection.

Assessment As Learning

Both the theory and practice of assessment of student learning have greatly expanded in the last twenty years, and much of what has been learned reinforces constructivist theories of learning. Much as we have begun to understand learning as a complex, multifaceted process, we have also begun to understand the assessment of learning as an equally complex and multifaceted activity in which learners and teachers alike attempt to become more aware of the learning process and improve their work over time. Alverno College, which has developed an impressive body of theory, practice, and research about assessment, calls its approach *assessment as learning*, "a process integral to learning that involves observation and judgment of each student's performance on the basis of explicit criteria, with resulting feedback to the student" (Alverno College Faculty, 1994, p. 3). Student learning and the developmental improvement of this learning is at the center of assessment practice. So is teacher learning, in that closely observing how students demonstrate their learning can provide teachers with immediate and critical information for shaping and reshaping their teaching.

The process of assessing learning outcomes asks teachers to clarify the outcomes (knowledge, abilities, understandings) they intend for a course and make these outcomes clearly understandable to students. It also requires that the learning activities and the assessment occasions in the class be aligned around these intended outcomes. Ideally, students are asked to demonstrate their competence relative to these outcomes through both small and large assessment occasions. These are often called *performance assessments* to emphasize that students are not simply displaying their knowledge or abilities in the abstract or in a narrow academic exercise but rather are situating what they know and can do in a context—for example, designing a research project, developing a grant proposal or a business plan, or making a Web site to serve a particular need. Observing students' performances in these settings, teachers use explicit criteria to provide them with feedback. They can also invite students to reflect on their own work and make judgments about it. A growing body of literature, geared to both K–12 and higher education audiences, offers valuable rationales and resources for assessment practice (Wiggins and McTighe, 1998; Huba and Freed, 2000; Walvoord and Anderson, 1998; Alverno College Faculty, 1994; Loacker, 2000). This kind of assessment, which begins in classrooms and focuses on strengthening student learning, is what accrediting bodies are asking colleges and universities to undertake.

Providing students with clear expectations for learning, criteria for what constitutes good work, opportunities to demonstrate what they understand, and ongoing feedback makes assessment an active learning process that focuses on accomplishments and progress rather than grading and ranking. Assessment, then, is another powerful pedagogy (to use William Newell's phrase) that invites integrative activity. Learning communities are natural sites for developing assessment as learning: their multiple course linkages invite integrative assignments and performance occasions in which students can demonstrate their understanding in the context of broad learning community themes. Furthermore, faculty members teaching on learning community teams have the benefit of working collaboratively to construct integrative learning activities and assessment occasions. We will present suggestions for integrative planning and examples of assessment occasions in Chapter Seven.

Reflection As Learning

A critically important dimension of assessment is how students are asked to contribute actively to their own learning and to the learning of the larger community. In recent decades, with the emergence of both research on student learning processes and the dissemination of various active learning strategies, we have discovered that student learning can be strengthened when student self-awareness and reflective activities are seen as distinct skills that should be developed through practice (Bransford, Brown, and Cocking, 1999; Mentkowski and Associates, 2000; Perkins, 1995). In other words, students should be asked to examine their own prior knowledge and assumptions explicitly. They should pay attention to how their new learning is causing those understandings to develop or change. They must work to make sense of what they are experiencing or examining, try out new ideas, revise previous conceptions, and make new connections.

MIT educator Donald Schön (1983) wrote that reflective habits of mind are not only useful but utterly essential to grappling with complex problems in the world. Schön observed that skilled professionals were "reflective practitioners" whose conscious attention to their practice would continually adjust it in subtle ways. As they worked through problematic and ambiguous situations, these professionals could both tap into and deepen their expertise in a kind of internal "conversation" with those situations. Schön called this kind of thinking "reflection in action." He argued that this capacity was not simply intuitive competence; it was a skill that needed to be developed over time. Schön later advocated (1987) for complex learning environments in which students could learn to integrate not only their developing knowledge and abilities but also their developing habits of reflection.

To translate active learning into something that is meaningful and lasting, students need to learn, in Schön's terms, to reflect in action about the learning process itself. They must build their habits of monitoring their prior knowledge and their learning, consciously connecting new learning to what they already know, noticing what is confusing, or inventing a new strategy if the one they are using does not seem to work. This involves critical, creative, applied thinking about the academic content at hand. Equally important, reflective thinking should be metacognitive. Metacognition—that is, "thinking about one's thinking"—is now considered essential for effective learning and problem solving (Pelligrino, Chudowksy, and Glaser, 2001). The idea of this kind of reflection becomes more concrete and familiar for students when they are asked to communicate both their learning strategies and their sense making by talking with others, writing in their journals, preparing response or synthesis papers, or doing self-assessments.

Students' capacities for self-awareness and self-reflection can be developed through ongoing informal and formal self-assessments, occasions when students are asked to make qualitative judgments about the quality of their work or describe what stands out as most significant and meaningful in it. This is not about students proposing grades for themselves but rather about their examining their learning, the assignments they have carried out, and the products they have created. One goal of self-assessment is for students to develop a more sophisticated understanding of the evaluation process: that demonstrations of competence are evaluated with criteria, that they (and their teachers) can begin to use those criteria to examine the quality of their work, and eventually, that they can develop their own criteria for what constitutes good work. Another important goal is for students to be able to discern what matters to them in a particular learning experience and what they will take away from it, and to describe this in their own words. As Marcia Mentkowski and Associates describe in *Learning That Lasts* (2000), the self-awareness required by this kind of nuanced judgment making often does not come easily to students, but it can develop over time. And it can lead to greater independence and personal self-directedness about learning.

Communities of Reflection

In a learning community, or in any setting where collaborative learning is practiced, reflection is often a communal experience. In these environments, students and teachers not only share a common identity and a series of learning experiences but may also be sharing responsibility for one another's learning through academic discussions, study groups, peer critique of work, or team projects. Through these activities, students naturally become familiar with other students' ideas and work, and as friendships and mutuality develop, reflection on the learning community occurs informally. Faculty members can formalize both individual and community reflective occasions as a strategy to strengthen the learning community and enable it to learn from its own experience. In short formative classroom assessments, students may be asked to report individually or collectively on their learning progress. Debriefing sessions can stimulate discussion groups, peer critique groups, or project teams to reflect on both their group process and the academic tasks in which they are engaged and to think together about how to strengthen group communication and teamwork. As the term comes to an end, many learning communities hold retreats or meetings to look back on the entire experience and to integrate more fully and bring closure to both the academic and the social learning that occurred. Activities such as these invite students to notice how they and others are experiencing learning in community, how individuals contribute to community, and how community can be strengthened through ongoing reflection and commitment to improvement.

Integrating Core Practices into Learning Communities

After countless encounters with highly effective learning communities, we believe that these core practices are essential for realizing the full potential of these programs. Furthermore, an abundance of findings from educational researchers and cognitive scientists point to the value of these practices for student engagement, learning, and intellectual development. As Diane Halpern and Milton Hakel argue in the epigraph that opens this chapter, we now have growing bodies of evidence about what strengthens student learning; the time has come to apply what we know in systematic ways (Halpern and Hakel, 2003).

In calls to improve higher education, these core practices often appear on lists of best practices or menus of promising pedagogies. In fact, these practices are highly interrelated and work synergistically. A sense of community is usually developed through active, collaborative learning experiences; integration is made tangible for students through reflection and assessment; collaborative learning activities must be designed with diverse students in mind. In colleges and universities, different individuals or academic departments might adopt one or more of these practices. Yet, deep competence in these strategies remains an unrealized ideal. Although it is not essential to embrace all of these practices simultaneously when a learning community initiative is launched, we do recommend adopting one or more, with a commitment to acquiring and learning from experience as each is developed.

Making a collective commitment to these core practices requires a substantial and long-term institutional commitment to faculty and staff development. As we have already said, generally faculty and staff members have not experienced these practices in their own education; therefore, they need time and institutional support to gain proficiency and confidence in them. They also need reflective spaces to share their experiences and approaches and come to deeper understandings of how learning communities lend themselves to these practices and vice versa.

Does publicly naming these practices as essential set too high a standard for learning community teaching practice? We do not think so. Several institutions that have made learning communities a primary feature of their mission and curriculum have already moved to codify one or more of these practices in formal and public ways and regularly organize both curriculum planning and faculty and staff development around them. For example, Wagner College's general education program is entitled "The Practical Liberal Arts," and experiential education, including service learning, is a foundation of its conception of undergraduate education. Furthermore, all beginning Wagner students link their first service experience there to a formal course called the Reflective Tutorial. St. Lawrence University's living-learning community program for first-year students describes its goal as to cross "the divide between classroom and social life, between books and bodily experiences . . . to educate the whole person . . . to create a dialectic between experience and critical reflection" (Cornwell and Stoddard, 2003, p. 29). The motto of New Century College at George Mason University is "Connecting the classroom to the world"; service learning, collaborative learning, and outcomes assessment are central features of its program. Portland State University's Freshman Inquiry Program, built around interdisciplinary inquiry and collaborative learning, asks each first-year student to create a portfolio of his or her entire year's work in this class around the stated university studies learning outcomes. The Evergreen State College's pedagogical approach is summed up in the five foci of an Evergreen education: interdisciplinarity, collaboration, personal engagement, connecting theory and practice, and learning across significant differences.

These institutions made deep commitments to effective practices that have now become hallmarks of their learning community programs. They demonstrate the synergy that can emerge from linking a reformed curriculum structure to pedagogies built on community, diversity, integration, active learning, reflection, and assessment. Yet that synergy is possible at any institution where learning community teaching teams embrace practices that foster community building and meaningful learning.

The subsequent chapters of this book provide further illustrations and information on initiating and sustaining learning communities. We begin by focusing on the two areas in which we see the greatest need and opportunity for learning communities: general education and developmental programs.

PART THREE

RICH ARENAS FOR REFORM

5

GENERAL EDUCATION, THE FIRST YEAR OF COLLEGE, AND LEARNING COMMUNITIES

The real question, I suppose, is whether we and our faculty colleagues are willing to consider the possibility that the student's "general education" consists of something more than the content of what is taught and the particular form in which this content is packaged.

—Alexander Astin

LEARNING COMMUNITIES have a growing presence in general education and first-year programs. They provide a promising approach to some of the most perplexing problems in these areas, long beset by seemingly intractable issues of purpose, student disinterest and attrition, and low institutional commitment. As we saw in Chapter Two, there has been a century-long debate over the purpose of general education, its form, and the functions it should serve. As the classical common curriculum gave way to the elective system, Alexander Meiklejohn and others predicted that general education would become increasingly beleaguered and that faculty ownership and interest would disappear in a university structured for a different purpose. Students would quickly follow suit, lacking interest and motivation in an area they saw as irrelevant to their major and peripheral to faculty interests. A silent agreement was struck:

a decentralized, negotiated general education curriculum prevailed, giving students, faculty, and academic departments maximum flexibility and autonomy. General education became a political compromise, a collection of courses, and ultimately an incoherent program with no overall purpose or educational rationale. At the same time, the first year of college was structured around large classes to subsidize smaller upper-division courses and faculty interests in research. And for too many students, the first year of college became their last.

General Education and Liberal Education

Although the terms *general education* and *liberal education* are often conflated and used interchangeably, they can be distinguished. As we saw in Chapter Two, Meiklejohn's notion of a lower-division education *program* encompassed both general and liberal education goals. As he put it, "The liberal college . . . intends to build up in the student the power of self-direction in the affairs of life. . . . Intelligence, it seems, is readiness for any human situation; it is the power, wherever ones goes, of being able to see, in any set of circumstances, the best response which a human being could make to those circumstances. And the two constituents of that power would seem to be, first, a sense of human values, and second, a capacity for judging situations as furnishing possibilities for the realizing of those values" (Meiklejohn, [1932] 2000, pp. 5–6, 8).

General education is now usually defined as exposure to various fields of inquiry and the skills and literacies that all students need, regardless of major. Over time, the list of general education goals and objectives for students has become longer, often including all of the following:

o Making a successful adjustment to college

o Learning and honing academic skills in writing, speaking, quantitative reasoning, critical thinking, and technological and information literacy

o Developing the academic maturity needed to undertake study in the major

o Establishing patterns of academic effort

o Attaining breadth of knowledge that is meaningful and lasting

o Gaining content knowledge

o Exploring possible majors

o Gaining civic sensibilities

o Understanding diversity

o Gaining integrative abilities

o Developing values, ethical thinking

In contrast, liberal education goals usually focus more on developing the higher-order and integrative skills necessary for social responsibility and civic engagement, as well as the student's capacity to deal with unscripted problems and the complex issues of the modern world. This definition is closer to Meiklejohn's notion of intelligence and the goals of the liberal college. Contemporary observers often describe liberal education more as a *way of learning* than a specific content. There is strong synergy between this notion of liberal education and the learning community core practices described in Chapter Four. Inquiry-based approaches are often used to promote liberal education goals because they provide a way of organizing the curriculum to involve students in the active process of investigation and problem solving. Collaborative learning, problem-based learning, service learning, and discovery methods in various fields are just a few of the pedagogies often associated with inquiry-based learning. Liberal education should occur throughout the student's educational career, in the major as well as in general education.

This notion of paying attention to both liberal and general education goals is now again at the forefront of national discussions about undergraduate education. The Association of American Colleges and Universities' report *Greater Expectations* (2002), which argues for liberal learning for *all* students, is the most recent statement of this position. The authors of this report envision a new form of liberal education that they call the "practical liberal arts," paralleling what others have called a "pragmatic liberal education."

The leading proponent of pragmatic liberal education, Bruce Kimball, argues that a consensus is emerging around this new, distinctly American educational concept (Orrill, 1995). He contends that this consensus includes seven major points about liberal education (Kimball, 1995a):

o Make a commitment to multiculturalism.

o Elevate general education and integration rather than specialization.

o Promote the commonweal and citizenship.

o Regard all levels of education as belonging to a common enterprise and working together.

o Reconceive the purpose of teaching as stimulating learning and inquiry.

o Promote the formation of values and the practice of service.

o Employ assessment.

Kimball believes that this emerging consensus has sparked a renewal of interest in John Dewey's writing (discussed in Chapter Two). Although not all would agree that there is this "emerging consensus" about liberal education, it is clear that we are in a fertile period of rethinking both general education and liberal education (Orrill, 1995, 1997). Learning communities are clearly part of this discussion, which reaches into all sectors of higher education.

The usual manner of addressing general education and liberal education goals by adding random courses is not viable now that the general education–liberal education agenda has become larger, more complex, and more fragmented. Without a larger framework and intention, a coherent and effective solution appears increasingly out of reach. The whole remains much less than the sum of the parts. As a result, the search for a more effective approach remains very much alive.

The Continuing Drumbeat for General Education Reform

As Peter Stearns (2002) points out, many of us remain uncomfortable with too much specialization, and few take pride in their general education program. Debates continue, with periodic cycles of tightening up and loosening general education programs. From The Carnegie Foundation for the Advancement of Teaching's 1977 study that declared general education a "disaster area" to the Association of American Colleges and Universities' 1985 report *Integrity in the Curriculum,* and 2002 report *Greater Expectations,* there is a continuing drumbeat for the faculty to take collective responsibility for strengthening general education.

In his prolific writing on general education, Jerry Gaff (1992) describes several waves of reform over the past twenty-five years and sketches a number of significant trends. These are summarized in Exhibit 5.1.

As Gaff notes, there has been some progress in defining general education in a more cross-disciplinary way and situating it more broadly in the curriculum. There has also been greater attention to pedagogy. The writing-across-the-curriculum movement, for example, has touched hundreds of institutions with similar cross-curricular efforts in quantitative reasoning, speech, diversity, technological and information literacy,

Exhibit 5.1. Trends in General Education

- Renewed emphasis on liberal arts and sciences subject matter, extending into professional and pre-professional programs
- Higher standards and strengthened programs required of all students
- Attention to fundamental intellectual skills such as writing, speaking, critical thinking, quantitative reasoning, and computing, often through across-the-curriculum initiatives
- Interest in active, experiential, technological, and collaborative forms of learning
- Interest in interdisciplinary study and integration of knowledge
- Commitment to the study of diversity in the United States and inclusion of new scholarship in these areas
- Incorporation of global studies into general education courses
- Interest in the moral and ethical aspects of each field of study
- Concern about student retention and recognition that the freshman year is a critical transition
- Creation of special courses and support systems; greater attention to "gateway" courses, which can be obstacles to student progress
- Extension of general education throughout four years of college
- Attention to the senior year as an opportunity for students to bring together what they have learned through senior projects and capstones
- New approaches to define and assess learning outcomes and greater use of results to improve programs; more administrative support for faculty to collaborate in curriculum planning, course development, and teaching of core courses

Source: Adapted from Gaff, 1992, pp. 52–53. Used by permission.

following in its footsteps reflecting similar assumptions about the necessity of embedding essential skills throughout content areas. But at the same time, Gaff indicates that the depth of the reform efforts is highly uneven.

Most institutions continue to rely on the loose distribution model of general education. The term *loose distribution model* covers a broad territory, of course, and many general education programs are, in fact, hybrids that combine some distribution areas with a few areas that are more prescriptive (Locke, 1989). In some institutions, there is a long list of courses that resembles a sizeable telephone book; in others, especially smaller institutions, the number of options students can choose among are more limited. How general education is situated also varies widely. In many large universities, there are few all-university standards for general education and the responsibility for defining general education resides with the schools and colleges. Solutions to the general education issue, however framed, must take into account the varied institutional contexts and cultures.

Thus, despite some progress in defining the overall purpose of general education and tying it to contemporary needs, the most recent national survey concluded that basic issues about the values and organization of the academy that affect general education remain largely unresolved, and reform efforts are difficult. As the authors asserted, "General education programs usually fail not because of a lack of good people or solid design, but because organizational barriers prove to be insuperable, strategies for change are flawed, and implementation processes are inadequate" (Ratcliff, Johnson, La Nassa, and Gaff, 2001, p. 18).

New Emphases in General Education Reform

In recent years the discussion has turned to the structural, policy, and implementation issues affecting general education (Kanter, Gamson, and London, 1997; Gaff, 1999). Gaff (1999) notes the following important new developments:

1. *A strong focus on the major.* In the interest of harmony, early reform efforts tended to ignore questions about the relationship between general education and the major, but it has become clear that this issue needs to be on the table. "One reason is that the majors have grown, gradually nibbling away at the size and moral authority of general education" (Gaff, 1999, p. 3). More importantly, there is increasing recognition that fundamental skills cannot be relegated to general education but must continue to be practiced throughout students' educational careers and in their major.

2. *Emphasis on pedagogy.* Campus discussions now focus not only on what general education is in terms of content but also on how it is delivered.

3. *Convergence of various reform initiatives.* With the recognition that the various reform efforts (such as service learning, learning communities, area studies, writing, diversity, and so on) have similar goals and make similar assumptions about learning, more attempts are being made to combine these efforts to create a stronger platform for reform.

4. *Technology.* Familiarity with various forms of technology and technological-information literacy is a focus of general education. Technology is being integrated into large introductory courses in many institutions as a means of improving learning and gaining efficiencies.

5. *Efficiency and effectiveness.* There is greater emphasis on finding general education approaches that are both efficient and effective. The loose distribution form of general education is inefficient and ineffective simply because the offerings are extensive and not well aligned around clear, common goals.

6. *Implementation.* Implementation is being recognized as a neglected issue in general education reform, often undermining thoughtful efforts. The implementation process is gaining more attention, including new ways of thinking about administrative organization and leadership.

7. *Convergent forces for change.* The external pressures (that is, state higher education coordinating boards and accrediting societies) and internal pressures for reform are increasingly convergent, resulting in a greater need to change accreditation, program review, and other accountability processes.

The Status of General Education in the Year 2000: Summary of a National Survey gives us specific information on the extent of recent general education reform efforts. This survey of campus academic officers indicated that 57 percent of the nation's colleges and universities were reviewing their general education programs. Both faculty and administrators have become more favorable to general education, saying it has become a more important institutional priority. Student attitudes, in contrast, remain unchanged from ten years ago (Ratcliff, Johnson, La Nassa, and Gaff, 2001).

Most respondents indicated that their current general education program originated in the 1990s, a robust period of innovation in which learning communities, freshman seminars, undergraduate research, and service learning became more common, especially in research universities. Nonetheless, only learning communities and freshman seminars (often overlapping efforts) reach a majority of students today. Other studies corroborate the findings that reform efforts are widespread but shallow in their reach (Boyer Commission on Educating Undergraduates in the Research University, 1998; *Reinventing Undergraduate Education,* 2001; National Resource Center for the First-Year Experience and

Students in Transition, n.d.). Ratcliff and his colleagues (Ratcliff, Johnson, La Nassa, and Gaff, 2001, p. 18) concluded that much more needs to be done:

> Despite the high level of interest in general education from campus and external sources, there is little evidence that academic leaders have made much advancement in the science or art of developing shared educational values and embedding them in the life of institutions. Leaders report a good deal of slippage in connecting learning goals to curricula and courses. Coherence remains an enticing but elusive goal at most campuses. Assessment of complex learning goals remains an aspiration rather than a reality in most institutions.

Most troublesome, the practice of assessing student learning in terms of general education goals was reported by only 32 percent of the respondents, and this encourages what the authors call "churning"—the continuous reinvention of general education without clear purpose and with no evidence of the impact on student learning. Where they exist at all, assessment efforts tend to be piecemeal, and as Ratcliff points out, "A piecemeal approach to general education assessment yields little evidence of holistic student development. Yet, such a holistic view of student development is often at the heart of general education aims" (Ratcliff, Johnson, La Nassa, and Gaff, 2001, p. 11).

This recent study, like many previous ones, points to endemic problems in general education—a piecemeal approach to change, student feelings that general education serves no real purpose for their majors or their careers, a divide between student and academic affairs, and resource allocation and staffing patterns that marginalize general education and any efforts aimed at freshmen (Ratcliff, Johnson, La Nassa, and Gaff, 2001). Of course, organizational challenges loom large because of the hegemony of academic departments and schools and the accompanying manner of rewarding faculty and accounting for student credit hours. This situation creates a competitive environment that often overshadows efforts at a more collective sense of what a general education program should be. Other substantial structural impediments include historical funding and staffing patterns, where large freshman classes subsidize the upper-division courses, and role and reward systems that encourage faculty to invest their time in research. The growth of academic majors as a total proportion of the academic degree, especially in the sciences and some professional fields, challenges the support of the rest of the curriculum. Although the trend for many majors to become longer has been somewhat curbed by efforts to contain the time it takes students to earn a degree, it has also encouraged doubling up of general education courses and introductory courses in the major in order to squeeze in more credit for the major. This clearly has an impact on the design of courses that count for both general education and the major and may compromise broader general education aspirations.

In a voice reminiscent of Meiklejohn and Tussman's concern about academic specialization, Robert Holyer (2002) asserts that faculty culture may well be the most central issue in the vitality and success of general education. He contends that we should think less about the right general education curriculum and more about how to rebuild a common faculty life and culture that are supportive of general education.

Meanwhile, a number of new factors are now in play that further exacerbate the problem of developing effective and coherent general education programs. As mentioned in Chapter One, student attendance patterns have changed dramatically. More students commute and attend college part-time. As the residential campus experience becomes less common, many of the built-in opportunities for creating a sense of involvement and community have disappeared. Student mobility is now a pervasive feature of higher education, with students transferring between institutions and often enrolling in several institutions at the same time. The transitions between both two-year and four-year colleges and high school and college are receiving increasing attention, with pressure to make these boundaries more permeable. Early college programs of various types are being developed that allow high school students to enroll in college classes. Meanwhile, transfer between two-year and four-year colleges is now commonplace, making community colleges the locus of many students' general education experience. If community colleges are to step up to a more significant leadership role in this arena, both they and the four-year institutions will have to rethink their historical roles and relationships.

In sum, it is no longer possible for a single institution to take responsibility for ensuring that students receive a coherent general education. The majority of students now attend two or more colleges before earning a degree (Adelman, 1999). Furthermore, it is clear that effective general education cannot be relegated to the freshman year. Sustained practice is important in developing many academic skills, so these skills need to be woven into the major. To reach high levels of student learning and performance, many believe we need a new approach that is less focused on credit and course accrual and more focused on assessable, portable learning outcomes. In addition, students must learn to take more initiative in charting and justifying their educational pathway. This requires very different skills than we traditionally associate with general education: planning one's own academic path, appraising alternatives, assessing oneself, and becoming a more intentional learner become especially important for students (Ewell, 2002c; *Greater Expectations,* 2002).

Discussions about general education now involve various external players, from regional and specialized accrediting associations to the state and federal governments. In an attempt to create a more efficient and seamless education system, many states are enacting public policy to facilitate transfer, often through interinstitutional agreements and various efforts at standardizing the curriculum. All of these internal and external forces make general education an increasingly complex negotiating zone with many stakeholders, interests, and constraints.

As access to higher education has become more universal and resources more limited, there is rising concern about serving an increasingly heterogeneous student body. Issues of both efficiency and effectiveness are being raised. On the one hand, there is concern about students' levels of preparation; on the other, there is concern about their performance, retention, and graduation rates. Nearly half of all first-year students test as underprepared and are advised to enroll in remedial courses, and only about half of the students succeed in even the best developmental education programs (Roueche and Roueche, 1999). College graduation rates in the United States are low, and attrition rates are especially precipitous in the freshman year. All of these circumstances create troublesome transition issues and new challenges for general education.

Finally, it is clear that we are in a period of redefining the purpose of general education and the kind of education needed for the twenty-first century. Fundamental questions are being raised about the skills that will be needed in a rapidly changing global society permeated by information overload, media, and technology. The practical and social relevance of our curriculum is in question. Advocates of reform contend that general education needs to be more consciously aimed at the big issues and questions, developing the *national intelligence of our citizens,* as Alexander Meiklejohn would have put it. How can we more effectively develop student capacities for civic engagement? How can we promote global understanding and an environmentally sustainable future? How do we reverse the growing divide in our society and in our universities between the haves and the have-nots, especially in mathematics, science, and technology? These questions require us to go considerably beyond the usual debates about tinkering with the distribution list of 101-level introductions to the disciplines.

What Works in General Education

Although much of the debate remains centered on the form and content of general education, Alexander Astin's study of more than two hundred institutions, *What Matters in College,* suggests that the only curricular structure that makes a real difference is a true core interdisciplinary approach to general education in which all students take the same set of courses. But this type of curriculum is found in less than 5 percent of all undergraduate general education programs (Astin, 1993a).

So what *does* make a difference in the majority of institutions? Astin's research uncovers a pattern of factors that deserve close attention. He suggests that "curricular planning efforts will reap much greater payoffs in terms of student outcomes if we focus less on formal structure and content and put much more emphasis on pedagogy and other features of the delivery system, as well as on the broader interpersonal and institutional context in which learning takes place" (Astin, 1993a, p. 427).

Astin's research also indicates what hinders student learning. At first glance, many of the environmental factors negatively associated with general education outcomes seem difficult to change—the size of an institution, having a large commuter population of students, heavy reliance on teaching by graduate students, an emphasis on research rather than teaching by the faculty, lack of community among students, and a large number of students who work full-time (Astin, 1992). But as we shall see, learning communities are a response to many of these environmental challenges, especially prevalent in large public colleges and universities.

Astin's research on what enhances general education outcomes, described in Exhibit 5.2, corroborates an extensive literature on what promotes student learning (see, for example, Pascarella and Terenzini, 1991, and Gardiner, 1994). By order of impact, the amount of interaction among students themselves and between students and faculty matter most.

Exhibit 5.2. Environmental Factors That Enhance General Education Outcomes

- Students interacting with other students
- Students interacting with faculty
- A very student-oriented faculty
- Students discussing racial and ethnic issues
- Hours devoted to studying
- Students tutoring other students
- Students socializing with students of different race or ethnicity
- A student body with a high socioeconomic status
- An institutional emphasis on diversity
- Faculty who are positive about the general education program

Source: Adapted from Astin, 1992, p. 30. Used by permission.

Student development is enhanced when there is extensive interaction among students who study together, tutor one another, and discuss issues that matter. The overall climate of an institution is also important in terms of diversity and the orientation of the faculty.

The amount of interaction with faculty and the quality of those interactions make a difference; interaction includes the advising process, overall faculty accessibility, their interest in the student's academic and personal development, and the overall attitude of the faculty toward teaching and learning and general education. Many of the practices that support student peer interaction and student-faculty interaction are most characteristic of small teaching-oriented institutions. Finding ways to embed these practices in institutional structures designed for different purposes has been the challenge, a structural and cultural challenge that learning communities appear able to meet. Astin's research also provides an important caution for us in terms of learning community design, clearly demonstrating that merely block-scheduling courses will not be enough to promote substantial gains in student learning. Student interaction with each other and faculty is necessary, and this often requires deeper forms of curriculum restructuring.

In the following sections of this chapter, we describe an array of learning community programs that respond to the general education and freshman-year challenges. We differentiate first-year initiatives from general education programs because they have different goals and purposes and they often develop separately from each other. Often called "student success initiatives," first-year programs usually originate in student affairs to address the transition issues new students face. Although they may link general education courses, there is usually little faculty involvement and no curricular integration.

Learning Communities as First-Year Initiatives

Learning community development has been most robust in the arena of first-year programs: there are now hundreds of such initiatives. Although the designs are diverse, program leaders see learning communities as a promising strategy for creating knowable communities that make a new place, and especially a large place, more welcoming and more navigable. As Vince Tinto puts it, these learning communities meet "two needs, social and academic, without having to sacrifice one in order to meet the other" (Tinto, Goodsell, and Russ, 1994, p. 9). Many of these initiatives involve collaboration between faculty and student affairs professionals, creating a human support system for new students and allowing them to become aware of the many resources of a large campus. In those learning communities with a purposeful linking of courses, there are additional opportunities to create more coherence in the curriculum and high expectations for college work.

Anyone who teaches or advises beginning students recognizes the huge transition they must make as they enter college—living away from home and parents for the first time, navigating a set of expectations quite different from high school. Older, working students and commuter students face other challenges as they learn to balance coursework with work on the job, family obligations, and the logistics of commuting. For the beginning student of any age, large campuses can be overwhelming and inhospitable; the sheer magnitude of these institutions with their predominant lecture-centered classes do little to communicate a sense of welcome. Few colleges purposefully initiate learners into the new academic community.

In his authoritative book on student retention, *Leaving College,* Vincent Tinto (1987) uses Van Gennep's (1960) theory of "rites of passage" to frame the transition to college as its own particular rite, in which students experience separation from a previous world and then acculturate into a new one. Students who do not successfully negotiate this transition are likely to withdraw from college. Tinto's analysis (1987) of attrition studies concludes that close to half the students who aspire to a college degree drop out, and that the first six months in college is the critical threshold, when students either engage with college or leave.

For first-generation students, those coming from backgrounds of poverty, and some students of color, this transition is particularly challenging. They are expected to adapt to a new setting with "attitudes, beliefs, and values quite removed from those of their cultures" (Rendón, 1994, p. 43). Laura Rendón's research reveals that many of these students come to college with doubts about their ability to succeed. Many feel intimidated by the college culture that is taken for granted by their more privileged peers. Some are so unsure of their direction in college that they do not even know what questions to ask (Rendón, 1995). Rendón agues that it is not enough to have mechanisms for involvement such as tutoring centers, student organizations, and extracurricular opportunities. There also must be *validating occasions* both in and out of the classroom where students can begin to "trust their capacity to learn and to acquire confidence in being a college student" (Rendón, 1994, p. 40).

The first year is a critical period for establishing patterns of academic effort. Throughout the 1990s, data from the national Cooperative Institutional Research Profile, a national survey for entering freshmen carried out by the University of California-Los Angeles, indicated that students reported spending only about an hour a day studying or doing homework while they were high school seniors. New freshmen expect they will have to study more in college, but a startling gap exists between the amount of time they think they will need to devote to course-work and the amount of time faculty expect them to spend.

A recent FIPSE-funded project (Fund for the Improvement of Postsec-ondary Education), "Setting High Expectations for Academic Perfor-mance," found that faculty members expected students to spend two to three hours studying out-of-class for every hour in class, whereas enter-ing students expected to spend only one hour and then reported engaging in even fewer hours than they had originally expected (Schilling and Schilling, 1999). Furthermore, the study found that the students' use of time established in the first year does not change appreciably later, suggesting that the pattern established in the first year is crucial.

Freshman Seminars

To address these challenges of adjusting to college, providing validating settings for students, and setting high expectations, many institutions have developed freshman seminars that are part of the learning community ini-tiatives. Freshman or first-year seminars have a long history. As John Dwyer and Virginia Gordon point out in their two histories of this effort, freshman seminars date back to the beginning of the twentieth century. As we saw in Chapter Two, Meiklejohn was aware of such seminars but thought the stand-alone freshman seminar was too small an intervention to make a difference in general education. Freshman seminars became large-scale after World War I (Dwyer, 1989; Gordon, 1989). By 1938, nine out of ten freshman were involved in such courses and the results indicated that they were effective (Gordon, 1989). The number of fresh-man seminars then began to decline, partly as a result of faculty objec-tions to offering credit for "life adjustment courses" (Gordon, 1989, p. 188). With the loosening of curriculum requirements in the 1960s, freshman seminars became nearly obsolete.

Since the mid-1970s there has been a resurgence of interest in freshman seminars in response to concerns about student retention and the complex choices today's students face. Numerous recent surveys indicate that large numbers of institutions now offer first-year seminars or extended orien-tation programs (National Resource Center for the First-Year Experience and Students in Transition, n.d.). The numbers continue to grow.

Also called "first-year seminars," or "University 101" classes, these programs differ in their staffing and emphasis. Some provide an orienta-tion to university resources, study skills, time management, and other fundamental strategies for academic success; others provide a stimulating introductory experience to learning in a discipline or an interdisciplinary theme. Debates continue about what the course content should be, who should teach these programs, whether they should be credit-bearing, whether student peer tutors should be involved, how training should be structured, and how to bridge the divide between student and academic affairs (Gordon, 1989). At most institutions, these seminars are elective, credit-bearing courses, usually carrying one credit. About half are taught in the pass-fail mode. Faculty members teach these courses on some campuses, but usually academic advisers, other student affairs professionals, or undergraduate or graduate students have responsibility for them.

These seminars are often stand-alone offerings that we would not consider to be learning communities, but they may still be an important means for promoting student success. Participation is associated with greater student satisfaction, more contact with faculty, stronger feelings of success in adjusting to college, and gains in self-rated skills and abilities (Sax, 2001). These seminars can be even more powerful if they are intentionally linked to other courses as part of a learning community that includes community building, student engagement and interaction, and curricular connections (Henscheid and others, 2004). More and more campuses are linking these first-year experiences to courses in the disciplines, often general education courses.

Two robust learning community designs are described here: the first-year seminar communities at Indiana University Purdue University-Indianapolis (IUPUI) and the freshman seminars at Washington State University. These programs are noteworthy for their reach, level of faculty and staff collaboration, interactive pedagogy, and curricular coordination.

FRESHMAN LEARNING COMMUNITIES AT INDIANA UNIVERSITY PURDUE UNIVERSITY-INDIANAPOLIS. IUPUI is a large open admissions campus with many autonomous professional schools with their own distinctive cultures. For the past fifteen years, IUPUI has been working to become a model for urban education, focusing on strengthening retention.

Like many freshman experience classes, IUPUI's first-year seminars are one- or two-credit classes that provide students with an introduction to college learning and university resources and a small supportive environment for practicing communications and thinking skills in an academic context. Unlike many, however, these seminars are planned and executed by an instructional *team,* including a faculty member and a student peer mentor assisted by an academic adviser and a librarian, who shape their syllabus and pedagogy.

About half of the 109 freshman seminars are linked to courses in the disciplines and the faculty member of the linked class is on the seminar's instructional team. The teaching teams adhere to a "template" of agreed-upon learning outcomes and pedagogical strategies for the seminar. They also use an expectation-setting contract, "A Partnership for Academic Excellence," signed by each student, which lays out mutual understandings for the first-year experience. Besides these common elements, however, each team shapes its own syllabus.

These seminars have improved student retention and gained such widespread acceptance that they now serve three-quarters of the entering class (Indiana University Purdue University-Indianapolis, *Restructuring for Urban Student Success Self-Study Report,* 1999). In collaborating to create the first-year seminar, faculty and staff members and the students gain new understandings about one another's roles, an increased knowledge of campus resources, new interdisciplinary perspectives, and an enhanced sense of collegiality.

FRESHMAN SEMINARS AT WASHINGTON STATE UNIVERSITY. At the other end of the spectrum, Washington State University's freshman class is almost entirely residential. For over a decade, collaborative teams of faculty and student affairs professionals have worked to strengthen the academic culture for freshmen and give more coherence to their first year at the university. Washington State is also a leader in electronic technology and distance learning. Its freshman seminars have grown out of these strengths.

The seminars at this institution are elective, two-credit classes. Each of the thirty-five sections, reaching about 20 percent of the freshman class, is attached to a large general education course, most often the university's required general education class in world civilizations, but also to other introductory courses such as political science, biological science, communications, sociology, anthropology, and geology. Some of these are medium enrollment classes (eighty to one hundred students), but others are much larger (two hundred to four hundred students). In the seminar, about fifteen students meet in one of three classrooms specially designed for technology use and collaborative learning, and they receive and submit weekly homework assignments on-line. The principal teachers of these seminars are student peer facilitators, more advanced students who receive extensive training.

Research has been the focus of WSU's freshman seminar programs, and this has been important in maintaining faculty interest, involvement, and support. It has also been a robust strategy in the classroom. As the students become familiar with library and Internet research skills, they are pushed to formulate questions appropriate to the discipline or the content of the course they are taking together. Karen Kniep, a student peer facilitator, comments, "We encourage the students to identify a researchable question related to the shared class. We try to get them to stay away from the 'book report' sort of research of the type they might have done in high school. We also ask them to communicate why this question would matter to somebody. My freshman seminar students who are linked to an evolution class are examining the evolution of birds, whether they evolved from dinosaurs. In doing this kind of research, we also want students to see the Internet as a tool for their research, along with the library resources. And we want the students to realize that being able to use something is different from understanding *why* you are using it" (Karen Kniep, personal communication with the authors, November 1999).

A team of resource people support the students' efforts. Assisting every class session is a "Hypernaut"—an advanced student who has been trained to assist learning in the electronic environment. The faculty member of the linked class occasionally visits the seminar, offering ideas to the peer facilitator and the seminar students, and providing feedback on the research questions the students pose. A modest stipend is provided for this faculty commitment. Once the students begin to focus their questions, a university reference librarian assigned to the seminar gives them an orientation on the university's print and database resources. The librarian makes subsequent visits to the seminar later in the semester to continue to be a resource to the students and to review the final products. This iterative relationship to the seminar is valuable, says Allison Walker, a reference librarian who is involved with the seminars. "We are the ones who usually are banging at the doors of the departments to include the library in their curricular planning, but in this instance the freshman seminars program came to us! So often in our work, we meet a class just once to provide a library orientation, but we don't get to see how the end products turned out. In this instance we get to know the students and we work with them in the beginning of their research effort, in the middle, and again at the end" (Allison Walker, personal communication with the authors, October 1999).

At the end of the semester, there is a large poster session and multimedia fair at which the student teams present their work. This event draws an audience of several hundred: students, faculty and staff, the university leadership, and local media. Washington State's evaluation of the seminars indicates they work well for the new students. Students at every academic preparedness level who enroll in the seminars achieve higher cumulative grade point averages than comparable students (Henscheid, 1999).

The IUPUI and WSU freshman seminar programs embody many of the elements that Alexander Astin and others have cited as critical in promoting student learning: setting high expectations for freshmen, building on the power of peers, developing collaborative relationships between faculty and staff, providing a clear structure but also considerable flexibility, and designing a program that is a good fit with the mission and structure of the institution.

Freshman Interest Groups

In the past decade, Freshman Interest Groups (or FIGs) have emerged as an imaginative and cost-effective "cohort in a large class" learning community approach in large university settings (see Chapter Three for more on this). This simple approach does not attempt explicit curricular connections between courses, but it does provide beginning students with a small, knowable student cohort and a coherent cluster of general education courses. More than other learning community designs, FIGs consistently place undergraduate peer instructors in the primary leadership role, thus tapping into an often-overlooked source of expertise and mentoring.

The Freshman Interest Group idea originated in 1982 with Jack Bennett at the University of Oregon. Originally from Australia, Bennett's first teaching experience there in the 1960s was in the "School of the Air," a two-way radio-based educational delivery system for K–7 students living on remote cattle stations hundreds of miles from each other. He reflects:

> From the beginning I had a sense that learning happens best in community, and the only community we had back then were these voices on the radio traveling across the miles. So once a year, I would bring the students together in a camp setting so they could meet each other and develop a sense of community. Coming to the University of Oregon, it immediately struck me how needed community was here, too. The freshman experience was so fragmented and impersonal. There were very few intentional community-building opportunities in classes. I was also struck by how repetitively our academic advising staff was recommending the *same* constellations of courses to incoming freshmen, whether they had a chosen major or were undecided. [Jack Bennett, personal communication with the authors, October 1999]

Building on his perception of student needs for community and the advising reality at the university, Bennett conceived of a structure in which groups of fifteen to twenty students would enroll in three courses. These courses would create a logical port of entry to a specific major or a coherent set of general education courses linked to a common theme, such as the arts, human behavior, or international issues. One course in the mix would be a small enrollment class, frequently English composition, including only the FIG group, while the others would be the larger enrollment, introductory courses typically taken by lower-division students. The FIG group would be kept together in quiz or discussion sections of the large classes as well. In addition, the student groups would meet at least once a week in a special FIG gathering, convened by an undergraduate peer adviser. The faculty members would be invited to have a freshman interest group in their classes but would not be expected to teach their classes differently. The primary goals would be community building and curricular coherence. FIGs would create small groups of students with similar academic interests taking a common and sensible constellation of courses while at the same time getting adjusted to university life with each other's support and that of a more advanced student.

In the decades since, the Freshman Interest Group idea has spread to large numbers of research and comprehensive universities, often reaching half or more of all entering freshmen (O'Connor and others, 2003). To serve students who are decided about their major as well as those who are not, most universities create a pattern of FIG offerings similar to the University of Oregon's original mix: some FIGs revolve around a general education interest area, and others provide courses clearly identified as preparatory to a specific major. In some institutions, schools or departments plan which courses to link together as FIGs whereas other institutions have an all-college unit, often called University Studies or the College of Undergraduate Education, that does this. FIGs at the University of Washington include the pre-med program, which includes chemistry, calculus, ethnic studies, and the FIG seminar, and "Global Preservation," which includes English composition, environmental sciences, geography, and the FIG seminar. (Other examples are shown in Exhibit 3.1; see Chapter Three.)

Different universities have modified the FIG structure to take advantage of local opportunities—and local creativity as well. Although the freshman seminar component is not always a credit-bearing course, some institutions, such as University of Washington, have made it into a one-credit course called "General Studies 199: University Resources, Information, and Technology." The director of the entering student program acts as faculty-of-record. Over three-quarters of the FIGs at University of Oregon (where the peer-led seminars are not credit-bearing) have added a one-credit University Experience course taught by one of the faculty members of the FIG courses. At the University of Missouri-Columbia, University of Texas-Austin, and Illinois State University, the FIG seminar is cofacilitated by the peer adviser and a faculty member or a student affairs professional, but the seminar's activities remain the undergraduate peer adviser's responsibility. The Universities of Missouri-Columbia and Indiana have deepened the co-curricular dimension by situating the FIG programs and the student cohorts in residence halls along with their peer adviser. These programs have served students well and deepened collaborative relationships between academics and student affairs (Schroeder and Hurst, 1996).

Because the FIG groups are generally subsets of larger classes, faculty members whose classes contain FIG students usually are not asked to work collaboratively to create connections between their classes. However, some professors report that they look for ways to illuminate the theme or emphasis of the FIG, and nearly all faculty members make some effort to meet their FIG students. Sometimes, though, curricular connections are fostered explicitly. The University of Washington embeds another learning community design, its linked interdisciplinary writing courses, in about one-quarter of its FIGs. Here, the writing class in the course constellation is linked to one of the large general education classes. Not surprisingly, students in these programs find this kind of FIG the most academically engaging (Goodsell, 1993).

As a general rule, the student-led FIG seminar and its associated activities become the key place for building community. Therefore, the recruitment and training of FIG peer advisers is crucial. Most FIG programs require their peer instructors to take a credit-bearing training course in the spring before their fall leadership work begins. When the FIGs are running, they meet weekly with supervisors to share news and address difficulties.

FIG seminar activities vary greatly but usually the seminars are required to address some basic freshman orientation topics such as campus resources, e-mail and use of electronic technology, advising procedures, and resources. Beyond that, peer leaders are generally given latitude to develop their own syllabi. The students might build informal and formal study groups, work on time management, study strategies and test preparation, learn about career paths, engage in community service projects, participate in campus events or field trips, enjoy pizza parties or potluck dinners, or plan and deliver a creative production. Perhaps most important, the FIG seminar provides a space where beginning students can reflect together in writing and discussion on their coursework and their experiences adjusting to university life.

Evaluations of FIG programs at the University of Washington indicate that this learning community approach is effective for student retention, academic performance, and progress to degree (Tokuno and Campbell, 1992; Tokuno, 1993; Tinto and Goodsell, 1993a, 1993b; Goodsell, 1993). Faculty members report that their FIG students seem the most academically engaged and seem to participate in more lively discussions. There is also the occasional downside of freshman togetherness: some faculty (about 30 percent) note that they have had some difficulty with "high school behavior" on the part of their FIG students (Lowell, 1997).

Qualitative studies of FIGs (Goodsell, 1993; Tinto and Goodsell, 1993a, 1993b; Gordon and others, 1999) reveal that students appreciate the social connections made possible by the Freshman Interest Group structure and act to extend them. As Anne Goodsell reports, the social network developed in the FIG creates a base around which other academic and social support mechanisms begin to develop: study groups form, there are reduced feelings of anonymity in a large university setting, students get into the habit of attending class together and have a decreased tendency to skip classes, and they have a group of peers with whom to socialize and reflect on the freshman experience (Goodsell, 1993).

The University of Missouri's FIG program, which is mostly based in residence halls, served about 25 percent of its freshman class in 1999. It has similarly generated highly positive responses from students and significantly increased student retention (Pike, 1996). A 1997 University of Missouri survey revealed that FIG students were generally more engaged in both the academic and residential communities than their non-FIG student peers, but the most striking difference between FIG and non-FIG students was that FIG students reported how regularly they got together in the dorms for study sessions (Johnson, 1998). A 1998 freshman survey conducted at University of Washington (Lowell, Jundt, and Johnson, 1999) similarly revealed that FIG students reported a higher sense of "belonging to the university community" and met more frequently to study with other students from both inside and outside their classes.

FIG programs also provide a valuable leadership opportunity for undergraduates in large universities. As one program director put it,

> In our exit interviews with our FIG peer instructors, we've learned that this leadership experience has been invaluable to them in terms of skill building and confidence building. The peer instructors' eyes are opened to the work it takes to be a teacher with a plan for every class, and to the responsibility of having a class of your own. The experience also stimulates their thinking about their own education, and leads them

to ask some of those bigger questions they are asking their FIG students, about what it means to be here. [Michaelann Jundt, personal
communication with the authors, October 1999]

Freshman seminars and Freshman Interest Groups have become
widespread in higher education. These modest learning communities,
which are easily adapted to the existing course structure, can promote
the community building and student engagement that we know are
important to student success. They can also bring perspective, coherence, and sound planning to a bewildering array of general education
offerings. Numerous studies indicate that these types of learning communities are effective in improving student retention, student satisfaction, and student motivation (Taylor, Moore, MacGregor, and Lindblad,
2003).

Learning Communities as Intentional General Education Pathways

Although many institutions situate learning communities in freshman seminars or the freshman interest group model, a number use more robust
structures for course integration, making them substantial general education initiatives. At the University of Maryland, for example, the College
Park Scholars Program offers twelve thematic interdisciplinary learning
community clusters for academically talented students wishing to pursue
an alternative general education pathway. Other institutions like IUPUI and
Arizona State University have recently developed thematic integrated learning communities in addition to their extensive freshman seminar and freshman interest group programs. Indeed, it is common for large institutions
to offer a variety of learning community opportunities, often organized
around quite different curricular structures.

Most of these more integrated learning community general education
initiatives are first semester programs, focusing on acculturating new students to college and providing a sensible configuration of general education courses. The English composition course is often a building block for
the course linkages because it has a small enrollment and provides a good
arena for community building as well as a platform for linking skill with
content courses to deepen student engagement and understanding.

Some institutions have gone even further to offer students the opportunity to participate in several learning communities during their freshman year, or at different points in their college career. Institutions using
these more ambitious approaches usually have hybrid general education
programs that require students to take learning community programs

along with specified general education courses, usually from a limited distribution list. Maintaining student enrollment in the same learning community over several terms or years has been difficult in the absence of a learning community requirement in general education.

Learning communities that extend beyond a single term have many advantages. Simply because they involve more of the student's total courseload, they provide more opportunities for promoting intellectual development, skill development, curriculum coherence, and breadth of education. Yearlong programs can work with natural transition points in a student's intellectual development and academic career. They provide extensive time for building community and the sustained practice of complex skills and abilities. Although multiterm programs certainly require more complex negotiations to secure faculty involvement and agreement, the process of developing an ambitious general education program together can revitalize the faculty culture and the institution. Where they have been created, they have deepened the experience of both students and faculty.

Exemplary multiterm general education learning community programs are offered by the following schools:

o LaGuardia Community College

o Skagit Valley College

o North Seattle and Seattle Central Community Colleges

o University of Northern Colorado

o Texas A&M-Corpus Christi

o California State University-Hayward

o St. Lawrence University

o University of Nebraska-Omaha Goodrich Program

o Portland State University

o New Century College, George Mason University

o Hutchins School of Liberal Studies, Sonoma State University

o Wagner College

o The Evergreen State College

Although this list is not comprehensive, these programs affect substantial numbers of students, have provided considerable evidence of their effectiveness, and have strong administrative support systems. They also represent a diverse array of colleges and universities, varying in size, mission, and student audiences, demonstrating how learning communities can be built into general education. Many of these programs include a whole range of the general education innovations outlined previously (see Exhibit 5.1): various pedagogies of engagement, service learning, assessment, and across-the-curriculum skill development efforts. These institutions, described in more detail in subsequent sections of this chapter, represent a new level of sophistication in thinking about what general education can be in the twenty-first century.

General Education Learning Communities at Community Colleges

Because half of the nation's students now begin college in a two-year institution, community colleges are a crucial arena for general education and improving student achievement in the freshman year. Many observers argue that community colleges need to find new ways to think about general education (Raisman, 1991–92; Raisman, 1993a, 1993b; Eaton, 1993). Neal Raisman (1993a, 1993b) contends that the general education mission and curriculum in many community colleges suffers from administrative inattention and lack of assessment. His analysis indicates that general education offerings are very thin, with classes in mathematics and composition dominating. General education programs do face special challenges in community colleges because of their broad mission and student population (Eaton, 1993; Raisman, 1991–92). Forging relevant connections to the many students pursuing occupational programs and those in developmental education is one set of challenges. There are also many questions about the role of general education for students who are not seeking degrees; most notions of general education in two-year colleges assume that students are degree-seeking, but many are not. Eaton notes that there is a cultural barrier as well: the cultural commitment to maximal student choice can stand in the way of more prescriptive notions of general education. Raisman (1991–92) argues that community colleges need to recognize the difference between general education and liberal education as a first step in clarifying their intentions in these areas. Both general education and liberal education competencies are clearly important for *all* students, and ways need to be found to embed these outcomes more broadly in the curriculum (Jacobs, 1993; Edmonds, 1993). Learning communities have emerged as one avenue for accomplishing this (Fogarty, Dunlap, and others, 2003).

As we saw in Chapter Two, LaGuardia Community College was a pioneer in the learning community movement, starting a liberal arts cluster program in the 1970s for students pursuing the transfer degree.

This program continues today, along with many other learning community programs aimed at different student needs and interests.

Community college learning community curricular designs vary widely. Some emphasize the academic transfer population, others aim to bring general education and vocational education closer together. Many programs focus on underprepared learners and bridging the chasm between remedial education and general education, an issue discussed in detail in Chapter Six. Some of the most ambitious contemporary general education efforts are located in Washington State, where learning communities proliferated in the 1980s.

SKAGIT VALLEY COLLEGE. Skagit Valley College has one of the most extensive learning community programs. The college offers sixty learning communities a year at its two campuses and two remote centers. Located an hour north of Seattle, Skagit enrolls about two-thirds of its six thousand students in its transfer degree program. Since 1993, students who seek the transfer degree have been required to take three learning community combinations. Seeking to meet its general education goals of creating curricular coherence and reinforcing basic skills in the context of academic study, the college determined that learning communities provided a "structural" solution to counter the fragmentation in the requirements of the statewide direct transfer agreement with four-year universities.

The school started learning communities in the late 1980s. Preliminary assessments revealed that they fostered the general education abilities most difficult to gain through a "smorgasbord" program: using a variety of analytical skills to solve complex problems, analyzing and using multiple and diverse perspectives, understanding the interconnectedness of fields of study, and connecting academic study to personal and social contexts. The college's assessments indicated that these students not only developed a strong sense of the interrelationships of fields of study and the value of diverse points of view but also connected their learning to the communities in which they lived, both local and national. Because their papers, projects, and exams drew from more than one discipline, students had the chance to develop and use more complex analytical abilities. Learning communities also had the advantage of not further restricting "elective" credits or adding credits to the degree. In sum, Skagit Valley found that learning communities helped it accomplish its general education goals.

Currently, Skagit Valley College requires students to take three learning community combinations of either linked classes or team-taught classes. They are required to take at least one of their two college-level composition courses in a learning community. After that, they can select from a wide variety of offerings. A second required learning community must be selected from those that combine courses from two different areas, for instance, "Antigone to Anti-matter" (mixing dramatic literature and physics) or "Beyond Buckwheat" (mixing film and ethnic studies). For the third learning community combination, students can choose a second composition-based class, a second that combines two different distribution areas, or a third that combines two classes in basic college-level skills, such as reading or library science (Fogarty, Dunlap, and others, 2003).

SEATTLE CENTRAL AND NORTH SEATTLE COMMUNITY COLLEGES. Seattle Central and North Seattle Community Colleges, which introduced learning communities in 1985, are both long-standing leaders in learning community work. As indicated in Chapter Two, Seattle Central's partnership with Evergreen was the triggering incident for the establishment of the Washington Center. Both institutions rely heavily on team-taught, highly integrated learning community models. Seattle Central was one of the institutions Vince Tinto studied in his important research on learning communities in the early 1990s, and it was recognized as community college of the year by *Time* magazine in 2001.

Both Seattle Central and North Seattle Community College currently require students to take ten credits in integrated study through linked courses or coordinated studies programs. A variety of learning communities are available each quarter that fulfill both the integrated studies requirement and other general education distribution requirements.

North Seattle adopted a general education, outcomes-based associate degree in 1995 that requires students to participate in a learning community focused on "discovering the interdisciplinary nature of knowledge" and "learning how to explore primary sources and other good books." Most learning communities are team-taught, theme-based, ten- to fifteen-credit-hour interdisciplinary programs. They aim to transcend the narrowness of disciplinary courses, broaden students' perspectives, nurture their love of learning, and develop basic academic skills. Both colleges are explicit about the ways in which learning communities differ from traditional courses. Seminars are a key feature of the program, student participation is stressed, expectations for collaboration are high, and self-reflection is encouraged.

North Seattle and Seattle Central's learning community programs vary each year, giving the curriculum vitality and a fresh perspective, but North Seattle has found it useful to repeat a few programs every year. A

"Beginnings" program, aimed at entering students, is offered each fall. The fall 2002 version, titled "Beginnings: The Shaping of Cultures, Myths, and Identities," combined perspectives from history, communication, literature, and women's studies. It encouraged students to examine their own experiences while looking at broader issues of origins, values, and identities (especially relating to gender, race, and class) and ways that these have been shaped by history and myths. A second regularly offered program, "Ways of Knowing: How to Choose What to Believe," explores classic epistemological questions from different disciplinary perspectives, including philosophy and science. Often the themes of the programs reflect pressing current issues, such as "Choices That Can Kill You: Ethics, the Environment, and Threats to Our Health." Diversity themes are strongly present in the curriculum at both North Seattle and Seattle Central.

Over the years, students have consistently reported that their learning communities stand out as peak educational experiences. They praise the role of the programs in building their knowledge, academic skills, confidence, motivation, and commitment and interest in civic engagement. They report that certain elements make learning communities successful: a culture that builds trust and encourages students to get to know one another, high expectations and challenging assignments, interdisciplinary themes, and collaborative activities. In addition, students praise longer-than-usual class periods, the emphasis on writing and critical thinking, seminars, and instruction by multiple professors who are both experts in their fields and co-learners on a team (Harnish, 2002). Long-term assessment results are highly positive with degree completion rates significantly higher for learning community students (Wilkie, 1990; Moore and Kerlin, 1994). In both institutions learning communities have become a significant convergence zone for a variety of innovative efforts in service learning, cultural pluralism, assessment, global understanding, and infusing general education into vocational programs.

General Education Learning Communities at Baccalaureate Institutions

In recent years, the course-cluster approach to freshman learning communities has sprung up on a number of campuses, particularly midsize baccalaureate institutions. At Temple University, a large percentage of the freshman class (upwards of 60 percent) is enrolled in course clusters. Some institutions, such as Ball State University, California State University-Hayward, and Texas A&M-Corpus Christi enroll their entire freshman classes in these types of learning community programs. Cal State Hayward is an example of an institution that has creatively addressed the general education needs of both underprepared and college-ready students through learning communities. (This effort is described in detail in Chapter Six.) Course clusters can address multiple issues in general education, including creating a more coherent and challenging curriculum, providing a context for skills development, providing breadth in students' education, community building, and facilitating the successful adjustment to college.

Freshman cluster planners face some big challenges when they think through the issues of course choices, enrollment and staffing, and support for faculty to undertake curriculum planning. The political economy of most medium- to large-enrollment campuses dictates that many freshman-level courses are large and lecture-centered—and therefore do not easily build community. Moreover, large, lower-division general education courses traditionally enroll a mix of beginning and more advanced students. The teachers of these courses usually prefer a broad student mix because more mature students set the tone; they are understandably reticent about teaching "just freshmen." In addition, the learning community cluster idea assumes the creation and development of teaching *teams*. Whereas the Freshman Interest Groups and freshman seminar learning community approaches described earlier make little or no coordinating demands on the faculty members teaching the larger classes, cluster programs *by design* require a team of teachers to be the co-creators of a learning experience that fosters both social and academic connections. A cluster team could well be composed of teachers of quite different role and status and quite varied teaching experience, from junior or senior members of the faculty, to part-time or contract faculty, to graduate teaching assistants.

Several issues come into play when planning for clustered courses: choosing courses for clusters that provide environments conducive to collaborative learning and community building; deciding whether all the clustered classes will have "pure cohorts" of freshmen; and developing and sustaining effective teaching teams across status boundaries as well as departmental ones. Some cluster programs have moved to realign and reduce class enrollments in the courses linked in learning communities so that freshmen can take courses as pure cohorts and so that "freshman-friendly" faculty can teach these smaller classes. Other programs have established clusters that are nested in the regular enrollment patterns of lower-division courses. Whichever design is undertaken, it is critically important to think through where and how the social and curricular connections will be developed, and what kind of ongoing mechanisms for curriculum planning will enable teaching teams to work collaboratively on the courses their students will share.

UNIVERSITY OF NORTHERN COLORADO. The University of Northern Colorado's learning community initiative is an impressive example of starting small, slowly expanding, and tailoring new programs to meet specific student needs and interests. Learning communities began there in 1992, with a program simply called "Cluster." The intention was to create course clusters around interdisciplinary themes, each one based in a college composition class. Today, the twenty-five or so students in these composition classes are enrolled in two to three larger general education classes (which range from nine to eleven credits) that speak to a theme, such as "Mind and Body Connection" (clustering courses in composition, principles of psychology, biology, and a biology lab) and "American Studies" (clustering history, geography, and English). The social and intellectual connections of each cluster develop in two settings: the composition class and three "cluster meetings" or "seminar receptions," which take place at designated times during the semester. The composition class instructor builds reading and writing assignments around the cluster theme and works with faculty colleagues to develop an integrative assignment to culminate the semester. The cluster students and faculty come together for the cluster receptions, social and academic events, and a discussion of an issue stimulated by the cluster theme. The cluster faculty team join in collaborative planning for these evening symposia, sometimes with the students' help as well. Because the faculty are all volunteers for cluster program teaching, the depth of their involvement is understandably variable. Each fall, about a dozen cluster offerings reach about 200 to 250 students.

In 1993, the university added "Advantage," an alternative "mini-cluster" program, to provide a seven-credit learning community experience for students seeking more personal attention and support and for those needing more scheduling flexibility. The courses in this cluster include a base course in college composition, speech, or math; a new student seminar (usually taught by the base course teacher); and a general education class in a discipline. Each community is anchored by a one-credit seminar taught by the instructor of the base course, who also provides extra conference time for his or her students; this individual assumes responsibility for creating the social and intellectual glue of the program. A distinctive feature of this new student seminar, which is called "Undergraduate Studies and the Liberal Arts," is a requirement that the students begin to develop a four-year graduation plan. Advantage communities run in both fall and spring semesters and reach some two hundred to three hundred students each term.

As word spread about student success with these first learning community programs, new, more narrowly focused learning community offerings were developed for students interested in pre-professional majors. "Ascent" was developed for those interested in the health professions or computer sciences. Ascent prehealth students enroll in the fall semester in a new student seminar, a college composition class, and introductory biology and chemistry laboratory science classes. Ascent computer science students take a new student seminar and two programming classes, plus an appropriate level of mathematics. The sciences and computer sciences are supported by Supplemental Instruction. Both Ascent programs provide continued classes to their students throughout the sophomore year. Another more narrowly focused learning community offering is "Class Act," a year of coursework (about nine to ten credits each semester) for entering elementary education teacher candidates, with additional offerings in the sophomore year. In each of these programs, the faculty or staff members teaching courses in which the learning community is a pure group assume the critical responsibilities of building community and academic connections among courses. There is a range of collaboration among the faculty members teaching the linked classes, from loose linkages to fairly tight bonds.

From the outset, the learning community leadership group worked closely with the Institutional Research and Planning Office to study the learning communities and track student progress during and after their learning community experience. This information has been consistently used to make decisions and improve the program. A recent ten-year study provides a thorough analysis of the impact of learning communities as well as an account of a utilization focus in the assessment effort (Endicott, Suhr, McMorrow, and Doherty, 2004). The study reveals patterns of higher rates of persistence, higher graduation rates, higher GPAs, and lower rates of suspension and discontinuance for the learning community students compared with non-learning-community students with similar admissions profiles. The results have been particularly impressive for students at the lowest end of the admissions profile (Endicott, Suhr, McMorrow, and Doherty, 2004). Surveys of students and faculty and annual program reviews are consistently administered to understand student attitudes toward learning communities. Students repeatedly stress the benefits of making friends, getting needed classes and good schedules, getting to know professors, being helped with advising and curriculum planning, and getting the "big picture" through interdisciplinary study (Endicott, Suhr, McMorrow, and Doherty, 2004).

There have been qualitative indicators of student engagement as well. The late cluster coordinator Becky Edgerton once commented, "Over the years, the faculty of the cluster classes have repeatedly told me that the cluster students tend to sit together, and that these students always come to class and do the work. They are not necessarily the smarter students, but the faculty's perception is that they are more dedicated. That might be who they were to begin with, but I suspect the learning community helps to create that expectation as well" (Becky Edgerton, personal communication with the authors, November 1998). Phyllis Endicott, director of the Arts and Sciences Advising Center, adds, "Faculty regularly report that the learning community classes are more talkative; they participate in class more actively and quickly. Some of our faculty who use collaborative learning note that learning community students gravitate to it much more readily" (Phyllis Endicott, personal communication with the authors, May 2001).

The different Northern Colorado learning communities now enroll about a third of the freshman class. Each program has some unique features, but all share certain characteristics that make the overall program coherent and strong: careful faculty selection and training, strong adviser connections, and immediate connections to other university support services such as libraries, computer labs, and the career center through the freshman seminar component of the program (Endicott, Suhr, McMorrow, and Doherty, 2004). The overall program reflects good working relationships between the academic advising center and the faculty, with continuous attention to student recruitment and faculty recruitment. The learning community leadership team consistently works to build the community of teachers involved with the individual programs through orientation sessions, brown bag lunches, and special annual receptions.

TEXAS A&M UNIVERSITY-CORPUS CHRISTI. Texas A&M University-Corpus Christi is an example of a large institution successfully mounting learning communities within the constraints of a statewide core curriculum and the Texas Common Course Numbering System. To facilitate transfer and efficiency in the higher education system, an increasing number of states, including Texas, have developed statewide core curricula. Institutions often view this move with great alarm, seeing it as an incursion into their autonomy and a constraint on their efforts to be distinctive, but most state guidelines are actually quite broad and hospitable to learning communities.

In the early 1990s Texas A&M-Corpus Christi, historically an upper-division and graduate school, made the decision to "grow downward" and accept lower-division students. The school also decided students should experience their first year in a learning community setting. Because of financial constraints, it was agreed early on that the learning community would have to include large classes.

The Texas program has gone through substantial change since it was initially established, evolving from a complex model to a simpler one as enrollment has increased. Where the original program linked four courses, the current effort, the First-Year (FY) Learning Communities program, usually includes three courses, most often First-Year Writing, First-Year Seminar, and one large lecture course. In fall 2002 more than eleven hundred freshmen enrolled in nine learning communities. The teachers of the FY writing courses, a mix of tenured faculty members, adjunct instructors, and graduate students, focus on writing, research, and critical reading in the context of the learning community's focus. Students complete at least one major research writing project that counts in all courses and that they work on in seminar and composition. The FY seminar component of the learning community shifts the emphasis of typical "University 101" courses, focusing primarily on helping students develop critical thinking skills and information literacy in the context of the lecture course content, experience deep learning, and appreciate and respect the challenges of learning in interdisciplinary settings. Throughout the two-semester sequence, seminar students also engage in career exploration and ongoing self-reflection. In both the FY writing and FY seminar, teachers develop active learning, student-centered environments, using informal writing and active discussion as a way to engage students in their learning experiences. What strengthens the connections in the learning community is that each freshman seminar instructor *also* serves as a graduate teaching assistant in one of the learning community lecture classes, attending the lecture, grading papers and tests, and providing feedback to the lecturer. Learning communities also include an optional civic engagement–service learning project that students can choose to complete instead of the more traditional project assignment. The university library plays a key role here, creating a Web site where students can become acquainted with both intentions and examples of service learning, and building their library orientation around finding and evaluating resources related to service learning.

This type of cluster design, including upwards of eight and as many as fourteen individuals (faculty, instructors, and graduate students) on each team, requires a near-heroic commitment to planning and coordination. To prepare to teach in the program, the graduate students and new adjunct faculty teaching the writing courses and the freshmen seminars participate in a required summer session course taught by the directors of First-Year Writing and the First-Year Seminar Programs. In addition, these individuals join the lecture faculty members and the English professors for an intensive, two-day or three-day Summer Teaching Institute to build their teaching teams, share curricula ideas, and establish modes of communication. Throughout the semester, the various teams continue to meet on-line and face-to-face to share news and make modifications. As a result, students experience an interwoven core curriculum in their first year.

The Texas A&M-Corpus Christi learning community program represents a significant attempt to provide, with minimal resources, a learning community experience for all full-time enrolled first-year students and to create some degree of synergistic learning between required core curriculum classes. Also remarkable is the program's commitment, from the outset, to train and support graduate students and adjunct instructors to teach in the learning community. Still, the program faces challenges: continued expansion of the university's entering student population will inevitably force expansion, and the increasing number of FY students who bring college credit makes the linking more and more challenging. At the same time, the first generation of involved faculty are moving aside to make room for newer faculty, many of them hired with the expectation that they will be part of the LC initiative.

General Education Learning Communities Serving Special Populations in Large Institutions

Some general education–focused learning communities are built around special populations. The Goodrich Scholarship Program at the University of Nebraska-Omaha was established in 1972 by the state legislature and named for a prominent senator who sponsored the bill. A nonresidential learning community at an urban, mostly commuter institution, the Goodrich Program is a specialized curriculum in general education, a financial aid program, and a comprehensive program of academic support, counseling, and related student services at the same time. Most of these courses satisfy the general education requirements of the different schools in the University of Nebraska-Omaha, where the students will later complete their major.

There are about 330 Goodrich students at UNO at any one time. The program enrolls seventy-six new students each year, who take five core courses together in their freshman and sophomore years. Approximately 60 percent of the students are from underrepresented populations. All of the students meet federal qualifications for financial aid. Those admitted to the program are given tuition waivers. The program has six faculty, two support staff, and a handful of graduate assistants. The diverse core faculty, in tenure-track positions in the Goodrich Program, also teach one quarter time in the appropriate academic department. Although dual allegiances have often undermined innovative programs elsewhere, this arrangement seems to be viable and mutually beneficial at UNO.

The Goodrich Program assumes that students with financial need will succeed academically if they are exposed from the start to rigorous academic stimulation, complemented by integrated and accessible support services (counseling, advising, and so on) that foster confidence in themselves and their ability to succeed. The program is built to encourage high interaction among students, faculty, and support staff. The students form a close-knit support group, which, as we have seen, is a key element in student success. Though not team-taught, the core courses are closely coordinated with lots of discussion among the faculty. A writing program runs across all five courses, and there is consistent assessment of the writing using the criterion on the English placement exam students take when they apply to UNO. The Goodrich program has graduated many students who went on to assume important leadership positions in city government and the professions. It has won a number of awards for retention, which has averaged over 81 percent from the freshman to the sophomore year, and its graduation rate is 15 percent higher than the university's as a whole (Jerry Cedarblom, personal communication with the authors, December 2003).

General Education Learning Community Programs That Span Four Years

As Jerry Gaff noted in his previously cited study of general education trends (1992), there is increasing recognition that general education should not be relegated to the first year in college alone. Many of the skills required in general education need sustained practice and should be an integral part of the work in the major. Institutions with large numbers of transfer students often also pursue general education in the upper division because they are interested in leaving their stamp on these more mobile student populations. The kind of interdisciplinary perspective and breadth that general education attempts to foster may become more meaningful as a student progresses. Recognizing this, a number of institutions have developed multi-year learning community programs that infuse general and liberal education ideals into the students' entire undergraduate academic career.

One of the most compelling four-year programs is located at Portland State University (PSU). A largely commuter institution, Portland State has been a leading example of how an urban university can develop close ties to its community through an innovative undergraduate program. Four learning goals guide the learning community program, called "University Studies," that extends across the four years of college: inquiry and critical thinking, communication, the diversity of human experience, and social responsibility and ethical issues. Students articulate and document their achievements in electronic portfolios. Community-based learning experiences are a cornerstone of the program and are woven throughout it. The heavy emphasis on community-based learning resonates with Portland State's self-described motto as an engaged urban university: "Let knowledge serve the city."

"University Studies" is a signature four-year general education program for Portland State and an unusual example of a horizontal or sequential learning community that is highly effective because the design is grounded in learning outcomes and is required of all freshmen. As founders Michael Reardon and Judith Ramaley point out, the program also eliminated the inefficiencies of the previous general education program, which was based on the distribution system (Reardon and Ramaley, 1997).

The general education program begins with yearlong freshman inquiry courses that are thematic team-taught courses supported by student peer mentors. Themes include "The Power of Place: The Columbia Basin: Watershed of the Great Northwest" and "Engaging the Cyborg Millennium." Sophomore inquiry courses are offered in the second year, giving the substantial number of transfer students a transitional learning community experience.

All students also engage in a senior capstone course that provides experience working in teams on community-based projects. In "Radical Elders," for example, students are paired with senior citizens who were or are still activists. They do twenty hours of interviews that are then stored in the Oregon Historical Society for future research. That class ends with a public meeting at which both the students and their senior activist partners talk about the experience and their learning (Patton, Jenks, and Labissiere, 2003).

PSU has invested heavily in faculty development and built critical support systems to coordinate the community service components of the program. Its program, like many of the others featured in this chapter, is a highly sophisticated endeavor that has self-consciously evolved, using various forms of assessment to guide its decisions. The program draws on various best practices in the literature on student learning while energetically learning from other similar institutions such as IUPUI, George Mason, and Temple University.

Wagner College offers another example of a multi-year general education program in which learning communities play a prominent role. This new program was heavily influenced by the St. Lawrence effort when Richard Guarasci, who had taught and been an administrator at St. Lawrence, became Wagner's provost and then president. At Wagner the general education program is called the "Wagner Plan for the Practical Liberal Arts." With 1,750 full-time, traditional age, residential students, Wagner is a liberal arts college located in New York City.

The Wagner Plan relies on required learning communities coupled with experiential and community-based learning, intercultural education, and writing, research, and computer competencies. It includes three learning communities—a First-Year Program, an Intermediate (Sophomore-Junior) Program, and a Senior Program—accompanied by traditional liberal arts breadth requirements and conventional majors. Academic advisement and co-curricular learning are also important aspects of the program. Faculty plan the learning communities as a group, but a few courses are team-taught. Monthly meetings of learning community faculty, which now include nearly all Wagner faculty, provide opportunities for regular program review and continued development. A two-day learning community retreat closes out the academic year.

Dean of Enrollment and Advising Ann Goodsell Love reports that "learning communities help students who come in with a profession in mind to see the purpose of the liberal arts courses because they see courses, such as economics, in an integrated way, not just in a vacuum. Undecided students gain a much larger sense of the possibilities available across majors. For faculty, it has been tremendous, a real breaching of the walls and silos of the campus. They've come to know many other colleagues across departments and gained so much from teaching-focused collegial interactions" (Goodsell Love, quoted in Smith, 2003, p. 16).

Experiential learning is a key aspect of Wagner's learning communities, with students usually spending three hours per week at a designated field site. The field sites are carefully linked to one of the three LC courses, the Reflective Tutorial (RFT). The faculty member who teaches the RFT is also the first-year faculty adviser for all students in the RFT.

The first-year program offers more than twenty learning community clusters built on different themes but in the same pedagogical model. The common goals are designed by an FYP faculty of forty-two full-time members and academic administrators in the writing center, library, and student affairs. One example is entitled "Living on Spaceship Earth." This learning community combines introductory courses in environmental biology and microeconomics around the theme of environmental concerns. Every department on campus participates in the FYP LC program, which is supported by an office of experiential learning.

During the second and third years of the Wagner program, students select an intermediate learning community that combines two courses in different fields and prepares them for greater understanding of their chosen discipline. Within the major, the senior learning community consists of a substantive course that explores issues in the field of study linked to a field-based internship or applied learning component such as a significant research project and the RFT. In business, for example, all seniors enroll in a capstone course integrating their previous coursework. The accompanying RFT requires at least one hundred hours of practicum placed in a project or nonprofit organization, usually in Manhattan. All departments and majors follow this senior program protocol (Guarasci, 2003b).

Living-Learning Communities

In the past decade there has been a resurgence of interest in living-learning communities. An important focus of many of the innovative programs of the 1960s and 1970s, interest in living-learning communities declined in subsequent decades with the advent of a more permissive educational environment and widespread abandonment of the *in loco parentis* attitude toward students' residential life. As a result, what could be a rich venue for learning became mostly a real estate operation, as one university president put it. Now, more and more campus leaders are recognizing that students on residential campuses can benefit from intentional living-learning communities. Although many of these communities operate largely as common housing for students with shared academic interests and have minimal connection to faculty and the curriculum, some notable exceptions provide a very strong base for general education. St. Lawrence University offers one of the oldest programs in the United States.

St. Lawrence University students have opportunities to pursue their studies through several types of learning communities, which include the First-Year Program, where all new students live in residential colleges built around interdisciplinary, team-taught courses, as well as two upper-division learning communities: the Intercultural House and the Adirondack Semester.

The First-Year Program (FYP) was designed in the mid-1980s in response to faculty dissatisfaction with several aspects of campus culture. Academic life was perceived as secondary to students' social activities. There was an unhealthy bifurcation between the classroom and the dorm room and the most intellectual students felt marginalized and unhappy. Other problems included passivity toward learning on the part of students, an inadequate composition program, lack of integration in student learning, and superficial, mechanical academic advising.

The FYP is a team-taught, interdisciplinary course that emphasizes the development of communication and critical thinking skills. Faculty apply to teach an FYP course, which they develop around specific guidelines reflecting the FYP philosophy and goals. Recent course titles include the Evolution of the American Family, Images of Africa, Cultural Construction of Our Communities, and Reading Contemporary Media. The work done in the FYP has been the cornerstone of the campus writing-across-the-curriculum efforts. FYP classrooms use pedagogies that expect students to take responsibility for their own learning. Each seminar leader serves as the academic adviser for the students in that seminar.

The thirty to forty-five students enrolled in each learning community course live together in a stand-alone residence hall or wing of a larger building, which is called a "college." Importantly, the student life staff and faculty meet regularly to discuss issues in both the classroom and the residence hall.

The St. Lawrence program is sustained by clear goals, explicit standards for learning community courses, ongoing assessment efforts to ensure that the program's goals align with the syllabi of instructors, and extensive faculty development. The institution has created numerous public venues to share goals and information, ranging from its Web site to pedagogy workshops, to faculty orientation sessions, and also has standing support systems such as the Center for Teaching and Learning.

Evidence of the FYP's effectiveness can be seen in data from the *National Survey of Student Engagement* (2001). Internal statistical and anecdotal evidence suggests similar longitudinal improvements since the creation of the FYP. Faculty also report increases in the amount and quality of class participation. Annual reviews are conducted of randomly selected student writing portfolios to assess the range and effectiveness of the communication skills component. Those assessments show demonstrable improvement in writing skills over time (Cornwell and Stoddard, 2003; Grant Cornwell, personal communication with the authors, October 2002).

Alternative Colleges in Large Traditional Institutions

As we saw in Chapter Two, the early effort in the progressive era to establish an alternative college in a large research university at the University of Wisconsin was unable to sustain itself. This has been a pattern that has since been repeated many times, with a few exceptions such as Lyman Briggs Natural Resources College at Michigan State, the University of Michigan's Residential College in Literature, Science, and the Arts, and Western Washington University's Fairhaven College. A number of the surviving programs were established as small, alternative general education pathways rather than degree-granting programs, such as the Arts One program at the University of British Columbia and the Integrated Studies Program at the University of North Dakota; these required fewer resources and posed less of a challenge to the overall institutional structures.

Established in 1970, the Hutchins School at Sonoma State University is one of the longest-lasting learning community programs in a traditional institution. It offers an alternative general education pathway and a major leading to a bachelor of arts in liberal studies. It enrolls about 420 students, with about one-third of them in the lower-division program. Established more than thirty years ago, the Hutchins program is a spiritual descendant of the philosophy of Robert Hutchins and Mortimer Adler with an interdisciplinary base, but as Les Adler points out in his account of the program, the curriculum reflects the evolving interests of the faculty as well (Adler, 2001). He describes the evolution of the program over time as one of developing a "new and more comprehensive holistic form of learning" (Adler, 2001, p. 155). The building blocks of the program are four sequential twelve-unit lower-division integrated coordinated studies programs titled "The Human Enigma," "In Search of Self," "Exploring the Unknown," and "Challenge and Response in the Modern World." Though the titles are maintained, the interdisciplinary programs are redesigned each year by the cadre of five or six professors who teach them. The curriculum is writing-intensive with heavy reliance on primary texts, and the undergraduate seminar is the central feature of the program structure.

New Century College at George Mason University offers another example of how learning communities can develop in a large traditional university. New Century offers several degree programs (the B.A. or B.S. in integrated studies, the B.A. in interdisciplinary studies, and the B.A. in individualized study) as well as an alternative general education pathway organized around learning communities. Various forms of experiential learning (internships, study abroad, service learning, field studies, and so on) are used at New Century College, whose motto is "Connecting the classroom to the world" (Oates, 2001; Oates and Leavitt, 2003).

The first-year curriculum is a yearlong learning community that meets many of the university's general education requirements. It is divided into four eight-credit team-taught learning communities that run for six or eight weeks each: "Community of Learners," "The Natural World," "The Social World," and "Self as Citizen." Lengthy interim sessions between the units allow students time to undertake various types of experiential learning. New Century's program is competency-based in nine areas: communications, valuing, effective citizenship, critical thinking, group interaction, aesthetic response, information technology, global perspective, and problem solving. The pedagogical approach is based on collaboration, active learning, and developing various skills and competencies across the curriculum and in context. Experiential learning is a substantial part of a student's academic work. Portfolios, which are evaluated at the end of the freshman year, are used to gather evidence to demonstrate mastery of competencies. A "transformative" project is required at the end of the freshman year that applies across the four units.

Institutions Organized Around Learning Communities

At the other end of the spectrum from subcolleges and programs are a few colleges that are organized entirely around the concept of learning communities. In Chapter Two we briefly discussed Colorado College and Cornell College as examples of institutions organized around one notion of learning communities, the block plan. The Evergreen State College is the most prominent example of an entire institution organized around the concept of learning communities. With more than four thousand students, it is an unusually large-scale innovation.

Established as a nontraditional college in 1971, The Evergreen State College has its entire curriculum organized around team-taught interdisciplinary learning communities called coordinated studies programs. These constitute a full load for both faculty and students. As Chapter Two indicated, Evergreen traces its lineage to Meiklejohn's Experimental College. The college articulates its educational philosophy around what it calls the five foci of an Evergreen education: personal engagement, interdisciplinary learning, collaboration, connecting theory and practice, and learning across significant differences. The organizational structure, policies, and practices put this philosophy into practice through narrative evaluations, seminar-based education, team teaching, various forms of active learning, extensive opportunities for fieldwork, undergraduate research, internships, project work, and a commitment to diversity.

Evergreen's coordinated studies programs allow for great coherence, depth, and community building by capturing the participants' undivided attention for as long as a year. Both advanced study and the first-year curriculum are organized in this manner but general education permeates the entire curriculum, which emphasizes breadth and developing a variety of skills in context. In addition to several programs explicitly labeled "multilevel," nine or ten core programs are aimed at freshmen each year. More than half of Evergreen's curriculum is reinvented each year. Typical core program titles are "Great Books," "Paradox of Progress," "Making of Modern America," "Patterns Across Space and Time," and "The Citizen Artist: Activism Through Art." Each of these core programs is designed and taught by a team of three or four faculty members, supported by a student affairs professional with the title "core connecter." The freshman programs also pay particular attention to the needs of new students, especially those entering a nontraditional college with unusual practices such as narrative evaluations, seminars, and working in groups.

Skills such as writing, speaking, doing research, working in groups, critical thinking, and information fluency are learned in context as the students explore the program's themes. The habits of reflective practice are cultivated in numerous ways, through student self-evaluations that are part of the college transcript, twice-weekly seminars, classroom assessment techniques, and the student decision making that is required in this college that has no requirements.

Numerous studies indicate that Evergreen's approach is educationally effective, may be scaled to the cost expectations of a public institution, and is efficient. Evergreen was one of the only public baccalaureate colleges to demonstrate substantial general education outcomes in Alexander Astin's classic study, *What Matters in College?* (1993b), and the college rates highly on indices such as the *National Survey of Student Engagement* (2001).

Learning Communities and General Education: Rich Arenas for Change

As we have seen in this chapter, learning communities are flourishing in hundreds of institutions as both first-year and as general education initiatives. Many are quite modest in their aims, often being one quarter or one semester programs situated at the student's entry into college. At the other extreme are some highly ambitious programs that extend across the four years of an undergraduate education. In between are learning community programs of all shapes and sizes. Clearly, different approaches are appropriate in different settings, and programs often evolve over time, progressing from modest freshman seminars to more complex learning communities.

We believe that general education and the first year of college are rich arenas for establishing learning communities. Many institutions have parceled out responsibilities for the freshman student among various offices and people, with few opportunities for building the kind of deep relationships that will truly sustain them. Too often there is little recognition among the teaching faculty that this is a critical transition period for students. These transition and acculturation issues need as much attention as the content of the curriculum. Learning communities are often a move toward a more holistic perspective on the freshman year.

We began this chapter with a quotation from Alexander Astin's classic book *What Matters in College?*, which raised the central challenge of "whether we and our faculty colleagues are willing to consider the possibility that the student's 'general education' consists of something more than the content of what is taught and the particular form in which this content is packaged" (Astin, 1993b, p. 428). The learning community programs described here have successfully reached beyond the simplistic content-process debate in general education to forge more complex notions of the goals of general education and at the same time provide a coherent framework for bringing many of the most promising new practices together. Some of the most ambitious learning communities also successfully address general education and liberal education goals.

Assessment results for first-year initiatives and general education learning communities suggest that both are valuable, but the goals of these programs and the dimensions that are assessed differ substantially. A recent synopsis of the available research and institutional assessment reports clearly demonstrates the difference in goals and results (Taylor, Moore, MacGregor, and Lindblad, 2003). First-year initiatives are successful in enhancing student retention, persistence, achievement, and satisfaction. They are also successful in promoting a smooth transition to college for new students. General education initiatives have broader goals for student learning and academic achievement.

Learning communities also have lessons to teach us about the politics of general education reform. Too many campuses report a disappointing pattern of minimal change after laboring for several acrimonious years on general education reform. As noted in the beginning section of this chapter, hard-won efforts often dissipate as campuses struggle with implementation (Ratcliff, Johnson, La Nassa, and Gaff, 2001). While working within the latitude of the current course structure and distribution system, learning communities seem able to create coherent learning environments and new forms of instructional leadership and not upset too many apple carts. In a number of institutions, learning communities have provided a way out of the political impasse that often surrounds general education reform.

In the early days of learning communities, discussed in Chapter Two, both Meiklejohn and Tussman raised the issue of how genuine educational reform can happen. Neither put much faith in committees or large prescriptive processes. Instead, they recommended that small groups of faculty be empowered to create meaningful curricula. Many of the successful learning communities described here do just that. Operating under broad guidelines, increasingly defined in terms of learning outcomes or competencies, campuses are developing learning communities for first-year students that address the need to foster interaction in the classroom, community, and a broader, supportive climate for learning. Although personal engagement is a hallmark of an effective learning environment for students, it also seems to be a necessary condition for faculty and staff members to support educational change. Learning communities allow for this personal engagement.

Leaders of learning community initiatives today have many more resources available to help them than before. Universities are now complex enterprises with many specialized roles and functions. As a result, there are more options and decisions to make about roles and responsibilities in designing the learning environment. At the same time, there is also considerable miscommunication, fragmentation, and duplication of services. Critical questions need to be asked about what kind of community we want to be and what kinds of relationships we can imagine to support student learning. In many institutions, we have a long way to go in building our communities and the common culture.

Many of the learning community programs discussed in this chapter are notable for the manner in which they have promoted collaboration across the institution in the interests of student success and more coherent general education. This is not merely an issue of bringing the vast territory of "faculty" together. It is also about forging instructional teams from student affairs, the library, the computer center, and residence life to provide rich support for these efforts. As we have seen, the exemplary programs discussed in this chapter often involve rethinking key roles, such as advising, and developing new models for working together. This is a promising trend that can be adopted with little disruption on many campuses.

Sustaining general education as a vital and interesting arena is another message in these institutional stories. All of these programs work hard to build an institutional culture that supports learning communities. They have been careful to anchor the learning community effort in the institution's mission, and they have inspired their own members to become part of a community of aspiration that reaches toward higher standards of excellence. Many of these programs are now facing the second-stage reform challenges of leadership succession, going beyond the faculty or student affairs leaders who were early adopters, and scaling up to reach a broader audience. These programs recognize and address these challenges. Many have moved to bring their hiring and reward systems into alignment with the practices and values of their learning community efforts.

General education reform raises myriad difficult policy and organizational issues. In many institutions, general education operates against the grain of the dominant organizational structures, the discipline-based academic departments. This is especially the case if the general education program is interdisciplinary. If these new cross-unit programs are to be sustained, support for them will require the careful invention of new organizational forms and practices. A fundamental question that always has to be raised is whether institutions will redistribute some of their resources toward the freshman year so that a greater proportion of our entering students can succeed. This requires recognizing that access alone is not enough, and that we must restructure the academic workplace. Learning communities are one very promising arena as we strive to meet higher standards and the academic success of all of our students.

6

SUCCESS FOR ALL

LEARNING COMMUNITIES IN BASIC SKILLS AND ENGLISH AS A SECOND LANGUAGE SETTINGS

---

*Preparation for higher learning has not kept pace with access.
Less than one-half of students who enter college directly
from high school complete even a minimally defined college
preparatory program. Once in college, 53 percent of all
students must take remedial courses.*

—*Greater Expectations*, 2002

THE ARRIVAL OF UNDERPREPARED but eager students at the doors of institutions of higher education that began in the 1960s challenged assumptions about who was entitled to a college education. In *Beyond the Open Door* (1971), K. Patricia Cross pointed out that primarily white, working-class students, whose parents had not attended college and who were often poorly prepared academically, were demanding access to higher education: "Once again there is pressure to democratize higher education by bringing it within reach of a broader segment of the population. . . . A new sector of the public is being represented by new students in colleges and universities . . . flocking to a new kind of college dedicated to serving a different clientele" (p. 4).

By the 1990s, the entitlement claimed by students in the 1960s was being challenged by institutions that had tried, with varying degrees of success, to provide a college education. By fall 1995, 78 percent of all institutions of higher education offered at least one remedial reading, writing, or mathematics course and 29 percent of first-time freshmen were enrolled in at least one of these courses (National Center for Education Statistics, 1996). In 1998, among the entering freshmen in the California State University system, 64 percent failed the math placement test and 43 percent failed the verbal. In New York City, 87 percent of the students entering one of the CUNY community colleges failed the math, the reading, or the writing placement tests (Estrich, 1998).

The evolution of learning communities in basic skills and English as a Second Language (ESL) programs must be viewed against this backdrop of change and the controversy over expanding access for more "new students." These learning communities were especially responsive to outside pressures during the last twenty years of the twentieth century. The form and function of learning communities in basic skills and ESL programs have changed as attitudes toward them, regulations affecting them, and budgets supporting them have presented new challenges to be addressed.

The Evolving Nomenclature and Scope of Students Served

Originally, all programs that served underprepared students were characterized as *remedial*. As time went on, *basic skills* and *academic skills* were the terms used, less pejorative versions of *remedial*. The word *developmental* was introduced based on the assumption that one could not "remediate" what had not been taught in the first place. This signaled an acceptance of today's educational and economic realities: the curriculum in inner city and depressed rural areas does not even offer the mathematics or writing courses—not to mention other content courses associated with preparation for college—so common elsewhere in the country. Currently, although nearly 75 percent of high school graduates in the United States attend college, only 47 percent of them have fully completed the college-prep curriculum (*Greater Expectations*, 2002).

Over the years, some parts of the country have all but dropped the term remedial, substituting the terms basic skills, academic skills, and developmental. Others never abandoned the word remedial. Here in this chapter we use all these terms, depending on the program being discussed, its geographic location, and the original source for references, quotes, and other information.

The variety in the titles of these programs is matched by the diversity of the students being served by them. They are a complex mix that includes first-generation college-goers unfamiliar with the culture of the college classroom, with many of them students of color; students whose prior education has not prepared them academically for college; returning adults and displaced workers; students with work and family obligations; students with chaotic personal lives that get in the way of learning; students with documented learning disabilities; and immigrants who come to our shores with anything from a third grade education to an advanced degree and who begin their education in this country in ESL programs.

Thirty years after she wrote *Beyond the Open Door*, K. Patricia Cross surveyed the student landscape of higher education in "Portraits of Students: A Retrospective" (2000). According to Cross, Berkeley "was the poster campus of the 1960s" for student protests (p. 7), and "the City University of New York was the poster campus of the 1970s" for the admission of students despite their "poor academic performance as it was measured in the public schools" (p. 8). These students were quickly followed by a diverse mix that added students of color and immigrants, many of whom did not speak English, and this phenomenon spread throughout the country.

These students often have academic and psychosocial needs that do not respond to traditional, conventional college teaching. Although the rewards of teaching such students are great, the challenges are great as well. As Skip Downing, formerly of Baltimore County Community College, notes: "It was really quite amazing . . . to see how many *outside* obstacles were in their way. . . . These students come to us with high levels of problems in their lives and very low coping skills. And perhaps because of these problems they are not skilled enough in the academic arena. They are like mediocre jugglers who are being given one more ball to handle. It is just too much" (Skip Downing, personal communication with the authors, 2003). In "Diversity, Demographics, and Dollars: Challenges for Higher Education," Mary Marcy agrees with Downing's characterization: "Contemporary students are more ethnically and racially diverse, and come from a wider range of socioeconomic backgrounds, than at any time in history. They face more life pressures and bring with them a greater array of life experiences than our original systems ever imagined" (2002, p. 4).

The influx of new students stresses a system that has not prepared itself well for fiscal constraints. As Marcy notes: "While the diversity and number of students are expected to continue to increase . . . institutions are simultaneously being asked to become more financially efficient and more accountable for educational outcomes." Yet the consequences of success (or failure) are great: "By responding effectively to a diverse student body, higher education can model and contribute to a healthy, diverse American democracy. Responding effectively means designing an educational environment that supports students from traditionally under-represented groups, and challenges all students to achieve both academic success and cultural literacy" (2002, p. 2).

In this chapter, we provide a brief, historical overview of the evolution of developmental education and the impact of adjustments to Title IV financial aid policies on that evolution. We survey the current scene and the contraction of remedial and developmental services among both four-year and community colleges. This contraction, partly in response to attendant costs, has made the intervention of well-conceived learning communities in developmental education even more critical, because, as we shall see, when done effectively, they are cost-efficient and dramatically increase student success. The chapter then presents a case study of an especially robust and sustained learning community, followed by descriptions of successful ventures in reading and writing, mathematics, and ESL. We end with a brief section exploring future challenges.

Historical Background

For the last one hundred years, public colleges and universities have provided access to students eager for a college education. The Morrill Federal Land Grant Act of 1862 guaranteed students who were residents admission at land-grant colleges in those states. The Free Academy, established in New York City in the mid-nineteenth century, evolved into the City College of New York, now one branch among many belonging to the City University of New York. Throughout the twentieth century, public state and city university systems across the country provided a high-quality college education to able students. Access to higher education became part of the democratic ethos. However, the open door was also a revolving door. Admission was competitive. Students either arrived prepared to perform at required levels, or they were gone.

These well-established policies and unchallenged assumptions held sway until the mid-1960s. But as Cross noted in *Beyond the Open Door,* although the democratization of higher education at this time was recognized as a good thing, it also raised new issues: "The gap between new students and traditional higher education is large" (1971, p. 5). In 1971, Cross was hopeful that higher education would rise to the challenge of educating the "new students" for whom "the motivation for college [arises] from the recognition that education is the way to a better job and a better life than that of their parents" (1971, p. 15).

Beyond the Open Door was an optimistic and visionary book from today's vantage point. It called for new approaches to teaching and learning that were more suited to the new students clamoring to enter the hallowed halls of academe. Cross hoped for a new kind of education to meet their needs. "New students, then, will be the losers if we concentrate on access programs that merely assure their entrance . . . into traditional programs of education. Why can't we . . . make new educational programs to fit [the] new students?" (Cross, 1971, p. 158).

Although Cross called for change throughout higher education, she envisioned the emerging community colleges as the primary place where the new students would be served. "Traditional college programs are not prepared to handle the learning needs of these new students to higher education" (1971, p. 11). Cross was not alone in noting the mismatch between these students and the academy; there were concerns that community colleges might not rise to the occasion either. In "The Community Colleges: Issues of the 1970s," Edmund J. Gleazer stated: "I am increasingly impatient with people who ask whether a student is 'college material'. . . . The question we ought to ask is whether the college is . . . student material" (1970, p. 47).

Clearly, higher education did not greet the influx of new students with great enthusiasm. In *Changing the Odds: Open Admissions and the Life Chances of the Disadvantaged,* authors David Lavin and David Hyllegard express the hostility that accompanied the implementation of open admissions programs at the City University of New York: "CUNY had launched a no-win policy: if many of the new students graduated, standards had gone down the drain. If they flunked out, open admissions had failed because it could not eradicate the effects of severe disadvantages that students brought with them to college" (Lavin and Hyllegard, 1996, p. 17). In the mid-1990s, reflecting a national trend, CUNY ended remediation in its four-year colleges.

Thirty years after Cross called on higher education to open the door, and to prepare for all students who would come through that door, she observed: "Open admissions had broad public support but not much enthusiasm in academe. It was accomplished more through the creation of community colleges, designed and dedicated to the new mission, than through change in existing structures and people. . . . Traditional institutions never accepted the changes required for open admissions . . . [while] the rise of community colleges took the pressure off four-year colleges in an era of prosperity. During this time, resources could be marshaled for the huge building projects that established a rate of one new community college a week somewhere in this nation throughout the early 1970s" (2000, p. 12).

As Marcy has pointed out, however, those resources are no longer available: "If colleges and universities hope to have a stable or growing environment and offer relevant educational experiences for an increasingly diverse democracy, then many will need to develop new systems to respond to the new student. Campuses need to . . . alter their educational delivery systems [to respond] to a diverse student body, while reducing overall costs" (2002, p. 6).

Although reform movements in higher education consistently call for change, business continues as usual in much of academe. We hope that the need for remediation will go away, but the students who need these services, and who are providing needed tuition revenues, continue to enter our colleges. We know we must work together to improve the quality of primary and secondary school education if we are going to eliminate the need for remediation in college. But attempts to acknowledge the continuum that is education in this country are rarely greeted with much enthusiasm, and proactive responses are few.

The Impact of Financial Aid Policies

The ambivalence about underprepared college students is reflected in the evolution of financial aid regulations related to these students. As a result, learning communities in basic skills and ESL have been shaped by decisions on the use of financial aid. Title IV financial aid policies, the competencies of graduating high school students, the policies of state higher education systems, and the local practices of particular colleges are often not aligned. As a result, changes in federal and state policies have sometimes left colleges and individual programs scrambling to adjust.

In the background of any discussion of basic skills programs, Title IV looms large. Title IV programs are a series of student aid programs created by the Higher Education Act of 1965. Funds for Title IV programs are appropriated each year by Congress. The basic programs under this rubric are the Pell Grant, Supplemental Educational Opportunity Grant (SEOG), Perkins Loan (formerly the National Direct Student Loan), Federal Work-Study, and federal subsidized and unsubsidized loans (either the Ford Direct or Stafford). Title IV aid is based on the premise that the family—the student, the student's spouse, and the student's parents—have the primary responsibility to pay for higher education expenses to the extent of their ability.

In the early 1980s, the state of New Jersey conducted a massive study of the success patterns of basic skills students. The data showed that regardless of their initial deficiencies, these students mainstreamed successfully as long as they made steady progress through their skills courses. However, those who failed these courses were rarely successful, and repeating them had little impact on their success (Morante, 1982, 1983). The findings of this report were widely reported and corroborated by local studies in other systems and on specific campuses. Clifford Adelman came to a similar conclusion a decade later based on his longitudinal study (1980 to 1993) of a large, national cohort. In *Answers in the Tool Box*, he concluded that "the type and amount of remediation matter in relation to degree completion. Increasingly, state and local policy seeks to constrict—if not eliminate—the amount of remedial work that takes place in four-year colleges. But there is a class of students whose deficiencies in preparation are minor and can be remedied quickly without excessive damage to degree completion rates" (Adelman, 1999, p. 6).

Unfortunately, skills programs often did not acknowledge the data that would eventually be used to modify and adjust the distribution of financial aid to students. For too long, programs allowed and encouraged students to repeat courses several times. Eventually, however, the information about the clear circumstances under which students were successful led to changes in financial aid packaging that ultimately had an impact on the shape and duration of basic skills and ESL programs.

When basic skills and ESL experiences were generously supported by both federal and state funding, students were given extra time without jeopardizing their financial aid. However, regulations governing such programs isolated these students in special courses and programs until they were deemed ready to confront college-level courses. Meanwhile, colleges that did not offer skills programs, or did not fund them sufficiently, were sometimes rather cynical. In the absence of placement tests or policies to the contrary, unprepared students were allowed into upper-level courses (without any supplementary support or resources) in order to boost registrations. Courses began with a sufficient number of students to avoid being cancelled, but as the semester went on the unprepared students either disappeared or failed, a phenomenon that was sometimes hailed as proof that standards were being maintained.

Over time, the problems of underprepared students and the programs that were intended to serve them were revealed and documented:

o There were high failure and dropout rates.

o In basic skills and ESL programs, completion and subsequent time-to-degree became longer as additional courses were added to sequences.

o The cost of programs increased as students repeated skills courses.

o Students performed poorly in college-level courses.

o The practice of using Ph.D. faculty to teach arithmetic and grammar was questioned.

As data about pre-college programs became more widespread, it became clear that these programs were not being monitored sufficiently. Runaway costs jeopardized their long-term viability. For too long, adding more of the same rather than trying new approaches had been the common response to addressing student needs.

In the early nineties, there was a major shift in the allocation of funding to students in need of remediation. Effective fall 1994, Title IV introduced quantitative and qualitative components to determine satisfactory progress. Title IV aid for students taking remedial courses (excluding ESL) was limited to thirty hours (in effect, one year), and the maximum time for degree completion was limited to 150 percent of the time normally required to complete a degree. This translated into a maximum of three years of support at the community college and six years at the four-year college, including the three years completed at the community college, if applicable. These changes reflected national concerns about the preparation of students for college, their performance in college, and the amount of time and money spent before they completed college.

State policies followed suit. For example, in fall 1995 in New York State, time limits were placed on the associate and baccalaureate degrees, and a long-standing program that had allowed students on tuition assistance to spend a nonpenalty year completing remedial courses was eliminated. By 1996, students needed to maintain a C average to be eligible for aid. They also had to have accumulated three "real" (as opposed to basic skills) credits toward the degree by the beginning of their second semester. Because CUNY had stopped awarding credit for basic skills courses by that time, skills students had to pass at least one college-level course during their first semester to remain eligible for state tuition aid.[1]

Future policy decisions are likely either to continue current trends and approaches—that is, limit the amount of time students may spend in remediation—or shift their position and hold the secondary schools responsible for graduating students who are prepared to attend college. In either case, isolated, attenuated remedial programs where students make minimal progress toward the degree will quickly become relics, because neither federal nor state financial aid policies will support them.

Assumptions and Practices That Impede Creative Responses

Often remediation has come down to variations on curricular and social isolation. Discrete remedial and developmental courses are taught by faculty in academic skills programs or departments that separate them from colleagues in traditional college departments. The content is rarely integrated with the content of other skills or college content courses, so students labor through boring "skills and drills" courses with no recognizable link to the personal and career goals that motivated them to attend college.

Federal, state, and local programs with special funding streams, structures, and regulations also isolate these students and faculty from the academic mainstream.[2] Acknowledging the multiple needs of these students, these programs invest heavily in individual tutoring and counseling. Therefore, the programs are often housed in student affairs, further distancing them from the academic faculty and stigmatizing students by removing them from the mainstream. Pervasive isolation results in duplication of effort, lack of coherence, and the general "ghetto-izing" of the students and faculty involved.

This approach also isolates the teaching of skills, such as reading and writing, from each other and from other content. The methodology reflects what used to be the prevailing philosophy (still prevalent at some colleges) that students need to be brought up to level through a focus on discrete deficiency skill areas before they attempt college-level work. This approach too often results in frustrating, boring, and demoralizing teaching and learning experiences for faculty and students alike.

Despite the nagging questions about courses that focus solely on the teaching of isolated skills—reading about what? writing about what?—and valiant efforts by individual instructors to introduce disciplinary, thematic, and systematic content of some sort, early learning communities struggled to survive because too often they depended on the commitment of particular faculty who did not have institutional support or recognition. An article published in 1974 described one such flourishing but doomed effort at Baruch College. It discussed the institutional and political challenges at the time that undermined creative responses to addressing the needs of new students: "Open admissions presents a problem. . . . We need to develop methods and materials that are appropriate for students who have found school up until now pretty boring, who haven't had experiences of academic success. We need to learn better ways of motivating our students out of their passivity in the classrooms, of motivating them to think, to question, and ultimately, to communicate. In order to do this our structures, . . . and methods and materials, may have to bend a little. So may our criteria for hiring and reappointing our staffs. . . . It is going to take all our best strategies . . . to stay afloat as best we can until we agree on our ultimate destination" (Lederman, 1974, p. 37). Despite the commitment of faculty, the coordination of content, and the success of students, the Baruch effort floundered in the face of institutional resistance.

The chilly climate that greeted early learning communities is described in a recent doctoral study that evaluated the success of Parkland College's integrated studies communities. The dissertation begins with a brief historical overview of failed attempts to implement learning communities at Parkland College in Champaign, Illinois, over a twenty-year period, finally ending in the successful implementation of the integrated studies program, described later in this chapter:

> The year is 1977. Five energetic young faculty members at Parkland College are meeting to discuss how to address the needs of underprepared college students. . . . This committee, representing various departments and disciplines across the college, . . . decides to propose a model in which a cohort of students enrolls in four linked classes. Although this has not been tried at Parkland, similar models being tried out on the West Coast are gaining enthusiasts from student, faculty, and administrative ranks.
>
> Jump ahead twenty years to the fall of 1997. Seven energetic faculty members at Parkland College are meeting to discuss how to address the needs of underprepared college students. . . . This seven-member task force is made up of individuals from various departments and disciplines across the campus. . . . They are thinking of proposing a model in which a cohort of students enrolls in four integrated classes, a model that never has been implemented at Parkland.
>
> In fact, the 1977 committee was only the first of many documented attempts to coordinate services for the underprepared student population, attempts which, for some reason or other, rarely seemed to be implemented. [Moore, 2000, p. 4].

The persistent failures in establishing learning communities and their ultimate success at Parkland occurred for reasons familiar to those who work with developmental students in higher education. The failures arose from a lack of enthusiasm for teaching underprepared students, departmental power and turf issues, and an absence of support from the administration. The more recent success at Parkland may be attributed to an administration that understands not only developmental education issues but also general concerns and trends in higher education, chairpeople who have developed more collaborative approaches, and an environment that welcomes thoughtful, well-researched approaches to developmental education.

Resistance to new approaches or the disappearance of approaches whose survival often depends on specific faculty members or external funding is common throughout higher education. Institutional and political resistance to change in academia, particularly among faculty whose experience has taught them that passivity and patience frequently win in the end, have halted many good initiatives. Nevertheless, the changing landscape of higher education, its students, and the demands being made by financial aid regulations have been a creative spur to those who have believed in open admissions and the right of underprepared students to improve their lives through higher education.

As financial aid regulations changed, linking credit accumulation and satisfactory progress toward degree to the receipt of aid, basic skills and ESL courses were integrated with each other and with college content courses more widely. Knowing that students had to move through skills courses and accumulate college credits to remain eligible for various federal and state aid programs, colleges began experimenting with new approaches that reflected new knowledge about how students learn and the importance of active engagement.

Making a virtue of necessity, colleges began carefully differentiating basic skills students through the sophisticated use of placement test information; increasingly, programs were tailored to the students' individual strengths. Poor writers with good reading skills were placed in college-level courses more rapidly than those who lacked both reading and writing skills. Especially among the ESL population, it became clear that a student who had completed calculus or had been a doctor or physical therapist before coming to the United States brought a different level of sophistication to the learning of language than an immigrant who arrived with a third-grade education. Placement and course linkages became more nuanced as a result.

Current Issues in Developmental Education

Ambivalence does not die easily. The debate continues about whether underprepared students belong in higher education at all, and whether higher education is obliged to prepare them. As Cross (2000, p. 8) points out: "Open admissions is now accepted as national policy; in fact, the majority of college students in this country attend open admission colleges. Some, admittedly, are not prepared to do college-level work and the old debate resurfaces. Do colleges . . . have an obligation to prepare students for college-level work, or should they wait until students are prepared before admitting them? What should colleges expect of students, and what should students expect of colleges?" Indeed, the linking of open admissions with remediation has had a negative impact on both: "Developmental education has become the litmus test for open admissions despite the fact that remediation was hardly a new function imposed by open admissions. . . . A national phenomenon with a long history, remediation is . . . fundamental to higher education in the United States (Reitano, 1999, p. 35).

At the 1998 Conference on Replacing Remediation in Higher Education, which was jointly sponsored by the Ford Foundation and the United States Department of Education, Vincent Tinto gave the keynote address, titled "Learning Communities and the Reconstruction of Remedial Education in Higher Education." He noted the pervasive need for developmental education among entering college students and the broad-based response among colleges: "It is estimated that nearly 90 percent of all colleges and universities . . . now offer some type of remedial coursework." But "the view is increasingly being expressed that 'remedial education' has no place in higher education . . . [or that] it should be located in the 'lower levels' . . . in particular in the two-year junior and community college" (Tinto, 1998, pp. 1–2).

Today, over half the college-going students in the United States begin their careers in community colleges. Nevertheless, community colleges appear to be reconsidering their commitment to remediation. Concerned that their own delicate balance between transfer, career, and basic skills programs would be upset now that four-year colleges are distancing themselves from remediation, community colleges seem increasingly reluctant to serve students who are unprepared for college-level work. *High Stakes, High Performance,* a study of remedial education in community colleges by John and Susanne Roueche, highlights good programs and good practice throughout the country but nevertheless concludes by asking a set of questions remarkably similar to those raised by Cross: "Are community colleges willing to identify the at-risk student population as an opportunity and to embrace improved retention and goal achievement as a potential critical revenue stream? . . . Are community colleges committed to being 'democracy's colleges'? Do they believe so strongly that they can make a difference for themselves and for the country's economic well-being that they are willing to take on this urgent national problem and be the vanguard of an extraordinary national effort?" (Roueche and Roueche, 1999, p. 54).

The Roueches are not sanguine about the response: "To date there is little evidence that community colleges have stepped up to the task. . . . Many are listening to strong voices that argue in favor of raising scores on assessment tests in order to reduce the numbers of at-risk students coming to their doors; that money is better spent on programs for more worthy students and for a return to more traditional times; and that it is time to reconsider the open door tradition" (Roueche and Roueche, 1999, p. 55). The Roueches point out that support for remedial education has declined as college budgets have shrunk: "Always controversial, remedial education is a multifaceted issue. . . . Interest in this aspect of the community college's curriculum—what some have called the fulcrum that balances colleges' commitment to excellence with student access and success—has waxed and waned during these years. During the last five years, however, there has been a heightened interest in remedial education. . . . This interest in neither subtle nor mild-mannered; rather it is critical, angry, and hostile" (Roueche and Roueche, 1999, p. vii).

No One to Waste: A Report to Public Decision Makers and Community College Leaders (2000), by Robert H. McCabe, echoes many of the findings and sentiments found in *High Stakes, High Performance* while putting much more emphasis on the economic losses and social cost of such shortsighted policies. McCabe's data show that about half of the students placed in them complete remedial programs and then go on to perform well in their college courses. Because these students enter the workforce, he concludes that remedial education is remarkably cost-effective and beneficial.

The data and the analysis presented by Lavin and Hyllegard, the challenge issued by the Roueches, and McCabe's findings about the economic consequences of the performance of remedial community college students, all support the overall success of open admissions in developing the strengths of "new students." Their conclusions come in response to the avalanche of criticism directed at open admissions and the corresponding rise in remediation. Despite the polemics, remediation *has* succeeded in creating productive citizens capable of meeting increasingly complex employment demands and contributing to the development of a strong economy, but the costs are becoming prohibitive. Approaches that get students into the mainstream effectively and efficiently are needed now more than ever.

As we will discuss in Chapter Eight, recent conversations about higher education have focused on the new knowledge about teaching and learning, the roles and rewards faculty may expect, and the purpose of higher education in general. The rhetoric on student success might be viewed as supporting the commitment to underprepared students. In fact, the attitudes toward basic skills and ESL education are now even less enthusiastic than they have been in the past partly because funding is no longer available to support expensive programs.

Forty years ago, the protests at Berkeley and at the City University of New York heralded the arrival of new student populations. Current policies in both of these states, which severely limit basic skills and ESL education in baccalaureate colleges, are again emblematic of national trends. During the past few years, *Academe Today: The Chronicle of Higher Education Daily Report* (http:chronicle.com/daily) has steadily featured articles about the end of remediation and the installation of various placement and exit tests (Hebel, 2002a, 2002b, 2003; Bartlett, 2003; Selingo, 2002). Contributing to the upheaval caused by all the changes is the continuing mismatch between the skills with which many students graduate from high school and those expected by most colleges and universities.

Despite the research on the efficacy of remedial programs under well-defined circumstances, developmental and remedial education have all but officially disappeared from many four-year colleges. Those programs that exist are buried under fancy names and sleight-of-hand approaches that obscure whatever remedial or developmental work is being offered. Many colleges celebrate "the return of standards" while faculty quietly bemoan the lack of preparation among the students who they now cannot serve in special programs even though these programs have, over the years, amassed an impressive (albeit sometimes costly) record of success.

For both community colleges and four-year colleges, the evolution of financial aid regulations has had a tremendous impact on the shape and number of programs that can be offered. As funding continues to decrease, outreach to high schools for early intervention competes for funding against remedial programs inside colleges, although both will probably be necessary at least for the foreseeable future.

Additional pressures in a time of rising costs and diminishing resources have contributed to the challenges that must be confronted by remedial, developmental, and ESL programs. Among student-centered pedagogies that support the new student populations, learning communities figure prominently as moving forward the democratic agenda of the country. But as Mary Marcy points out, such programs are "conceived of as . . . an addition to, rather than an integral part of, a campus's educational delivery system. . . . For them to be integral to a campus delivery system, the structural organization of the campus would have to change" (Marcy, 2002, p. 9).

Learning Communities in the New Millennium

In this environment of upheaval, challenge, and fiscal constraint, the story of learning communities in basic skills and ESL education must be told and examples of successful learning communities assessed based on the criteria being applied today. As interest, commitment, and resources for basic skills and ESL education dwindle, higher education needs to emulate those models that produce successful students in timely and cost-efficient ways—models that promote access, develop excellence, and do not compromise standards.

Learning communities in basic skills and ESL programs address both the real needs of students and institutional needs and constraints. Although the value of learning communities has been enduring, the need for them now is even more compelling. Learning communities in basic skills and ESL programs transform the revolving door into an open door for both access and excellence. Learning communities create an efficient, enriched, and supportive environment for learning. They should have a prominent place in the "reconstruction" of remedial education because they embody what works.

Based on their research, the Roueches and Robert McCabe offer similar lists of best practices, and there is a good deal of congruity in their observations. Both call for strong institutional commitment to remedial programs, the maintenance of high standards, required testing, careful placement and tracking of students, and mandatory completion of remedial sequences.

The Roueches list the most common and effective approaches to supporting underprepared students. At the head of the list is learning communities; the other practices they list are found in intentional learning communities that offer wide-ranging services to their students:

○ Development of learning communities in the program and collegewide

○ Enhanced faculty, tutor, and staff development activities

○ Increased use of college support services by all students

○ Increased college focus on proper placement in [all] courses

○ Development of comprehensive programs, including a "success" orientation of all degree-seeking students [Roueche and Roueche, 1999, p. 34]

McCabe also recommends the use of learning communities, and includes in his list such common characteristics of well-developed learning communities as highly coordinated programs; an integrated counseling component; tutoring; integration of classroom and laboratory activities; staff training and professional development; and supplemental instruction (McCabe, 2000).

It is against such criteria that we evaluate successful learning communities in developmental education. The programs described in the following pages exemplify the best practices and most creative approaches of these kinds of learning communities.

LaGuardia Community College's New Student House: A Model Basic Skills Learning Community

New Student House reflects the economic and political realities to which developmental education has had to adjust. New Student House (NSH) was a visionary response to the challenge of transforming underprepared students into confident and competent college students, and it has remained true to its original purpose while adapting to an ever-changing landscape. In its original manifestation as a learning community for developmental students and in its second iteration as a learning community serving English as a Second Language students (see the later section in this chapter for a discussion of the ESL/NSH), New Student House has been shaped by the characteristics and needs of its student body.[3]

LaGuardia Community College (CUNY) is one of the most diverse community colleges in the country. At LaGuardia, many students are the children of immigrants or are immigrants themselves. They come from over 140 different countries. They speak over one hundred different languages. Like schools in other port-of-entry cities along the East and West Coasts, LaGuardia is enriched and challenged by an influx of present and future citizens who arrive unable to speak to their instructors or to each other. At LaGuardia, a common denominator must be created, not assumed.

Since the late 1970s, learning communities at LaGuardia have helped initiate students into the academic community, giving them the skills, confidence, and the support they need to rise to the challenges of coursework. During any given semester, over forty different learning communities are offered. Some serve developmental or ESL students, others are requirements for the major or may be used by students to fulfill major course requirements. In all cases, these learning communities contribute to the sense of community so important in a large, urban college where students juggle education with work and family obligations, and where the classroom is often the only space in which academic community may be experienced.

NSH was created for students whose test results placed them in the lowest cohort of reading and writing skills and often the lowest cohort of mathematics as well. Developed during the 1991–92 academic year and piloted in 1992, it initially brought together developmental reading, writing, speech communication courses, and counseling in the freshman seminar for a large cohort of students, some sixty-six to ninety students per semester (depending on grant funds available and the exigencies of the fiscal crisis of the time).

Originally funded by a three-year grant from New York State, the founding team—three faculty members and a counselor—spent a year planning the program. Each participating teacher was released for three hours over two semesters for planning, curriculum development, and project design. NSH faculty worked with a counselor whose student load included only NSH students. He taught the freshman seminars attached to NSH and would periodically attend classes to model good academic behavior for the students and give feedback to faculty. The counselor served as the "point person" for case management, working with faculty to meet the needs of individual students in real time. New Student House generally provided participating faculty with a full workload.

The program was successfully implemented after the planning year. During the third year, the original teaching team committed to training two additional teams so that the population served could be expanded. Within four years, the college was offering three New Student Houses annually, serving 180 to 270 students. In fall 1999 a new NSH for business students, including the class Introduction to Business, was introduced as part of an ongoing response to changes in federal aid guidelines. This added an additional 75 students to the NSH head count.

The thematic link for the original New Student House was a study of relationships; the rich set of readings, activities, and writing assignments reflected the variety of student backgrounds. The curriculum modeled the content and approaches that create "a new kind of community that honors our multiplicity" (Matthews and Lynch, 1997, p. 125). Cultural diversity was explored through a series of readings that included novels, short stories, and articles from a wide assortment of periodicals. Intense involvement on the part of faculty and students comes at a cost, but thoughtful participants also learn valuable lessons about themselves. One of the instructors articulates the evolving nature of the process: "What do I think about it now? After doing it for a few years? The intensity can be draining. Energizing, but over the long haul, it's tough. . . . I'm trying to develop topics and strategies that are less direct and deal with important issues without putting students on the spot . . . a less volatile approach."

As faculty learn how to survive the difficult context and complete the difficult tasks they have set for themselves, they offer their students the opportunity to succeed in college. During the first year of working with students who historically had a dropout rate hovering around 40 percent, New Student House lost one student from the original seventy-five. Subsequently, New Student House students have continued to maintain an impressive record of course completion and retention: 85 percent and above.

Students express appreciation of the theme and the collaborative experiences: "The challenging thing about [NSH] is that the teachers give you a chance to be heard. . . . It feels like a community because there are all kinds of people, different races, different languages spoken and we are all together." The choice of theme was logical and inspired, and the choice of faculty contributed as well to the success of the program. As one faculty member noted: "I've taught in collaborative ways with other faculty where I've not been this successful. I think what made this group successful is that three very flexible instructors were willing to listen to one another and try to come to a true collaboration on how to approach a topic or a theme" (Matthews and Lynch, 1997, 124).

The innovative structure also allows for various kinds of reinforcement: "When students come together in groups of ninety in the theater [the biweekly, joint, three-class meeting], they quickly see what they have been doing in the thirty-person class is very pertinent to the rest of their lives. And that's very beneficial. If I were teaching three [separate] sections of speech, I wouldn't get that kind of link and the immediate student gratification" (Matthews and Lynch, 1997, p. 125). Such a statement speaks to the evolution and growth of confidence in faculty. The team originally resisted the idea of meeting as a whole and approached the prospect gingerly, being apprehensive about how to do it. Learning on the job, they came to see it as an opportunity for creative teaching and large group engagement.

In an in-house publication on collaborative learning, the counselor who taught the freshman seminar contrasted the experiences of students in the New Student House with those who were not part of this learning community: "I realize how few (non-House) students I still see compared to students who are involved in the House. I believe one of the reasons is, for some of these students, the New Student House offered some vague form of stability. . . . Even though the New Student House is only a title for a program that in reality has no identifiable locale on campus, it is quite possible that it provides some sort of temporary shelter from a world of ignorance, poverty and violence" (Matthews and Lynch, 1997, p. 127). Structures such as New Student House are rescue operations, reaching out and providing students with the support they need to become functioning and contributing students and citizens.

NSH is a credit to the dedicated faculty teaching in the program and a model of successful intervention at the college level that prepares under-prepared students and launches them successfully on the rest of their college careers: "Our basic skills students need to feel that what they bring to the table is validated. They often come with so much negative baggage, that their first college experience will either turn them on to higher education or send them packing. . . . What we are doing in NSH is essentially preparing students for college courses as well as preparing them for their responsible place as part of the larger communities. . . . NSH is really about educating responsible, critical thinking citizens of the world."

One member of the original team and a trainer of subsequent teams reflected on the elements that allow faculty to work together to create a sense of community and a supportive learning environment for their students: "As faculty, we are trying to have the students experience subject matter in a deeper, richer way while they are working to improve basic college skills. The goal for a learning community such as NSH is to create a learning atmosphere for students where ideas can be dealt with in substantive, creative and challenging ways."

And students get it as well: "What stands out about this program in contrast to other classes I have taken is that the professors believe in their students and want them to do well. The program was challenging because it required me to speak out more [and] it made me more open-minded."

For developmental students, the conscious creation of community in the midst of such diversity provides a necessary support system: "The distinctive [thing] about this [class is] that the teachers and students all work together; we all know each other. We learned teamwork by going to class together and doing group work together." Students believe that NSH "feels like a community because we are all looking out for each other's well-being and we see each other every day for about four to five hours." One young woman "felt I would not be able to handle college, but so far I am doing well." Appreciative of "the wonderful staff and students," she felt NSH was "well worth it" and prepared her to continue her education.

An English instructor underscores the benefit of teaching in an environment that honors diversity and values its potential for creating community: "I think it's a real advantage in an urban community college setting to have people of so many backgrounds represented. It makes it pretty much impossible for one group to dominate or intimidate another. In class, we have students who speak ten different languages at home. That's a lot of ways to say good morning"(Matthews and Lynch, 1997, p. 135). And a lot of different backgrounds, perspectives, and contrasting attitudes to enrich learning. Good planning, dedicated faculty, and a smart design that includes real and challenging content virtually guarantee a successful academic experience to even the most poorly prepared students. Learning communities that nurture and support this diversity in a rich academic community serve their students well.

In "Learning Communities and the Reconstruction of Remedial Education in Higher Education," Vincent Tinto (1998) cited New Student House (NSH) at LaGuardia Community College as one of the few learning communities for developmental students that had been studied to show their comparative effectiveness in promoting student success; it had been one subject of the only detailed study of developmental learning communities at that time (Tinto, Goodsell, and Russo, 1994).

Tinto's research on New Student House supports the observations of the faculty involved in the project. He asked two questions: "Does the program make a difference? If it does, how does it do so?" (Tinto, 1998, p. 8). Tinto identified two experiences that supported student success: supportive peer groups, and shared learning-studying together that result in involvement, learning, and persistence. NSH students had higher peer group and learning activity scores than non-NSH peers in the control group. They passed their developmental courses at a higher rate than the comparison group, and their grades were higher as well. Their persistence rate from fall to fall was 7 percent higher than the comparison group, although that group experienced similar pedagogical approaches (such as collaborative learning) in their classes. NSH students performed better because they experienced a richer, more integrated educational experience.

Tinto noted that NSH "combines the work of both faculty and student affairs staff. . . . A trained counselor . . . keeps students in line by serving both as a course facilitator and a student counselor. . . . The very structure of the program promotes collaboration between academic and student affairs sides of the house" (Tinto, 1998, p. 7). NSH thus exemplifies best practice as defined by the Roueches: "Remedial education has evolved from detached efforts to rectify individual skills deficiencies to more complex, organized efforts to develop the cognitive and affective talents that describe the whole student" (Roueche and Roueche, 1999, p. viii). NSH addresses the important finding among academic researchers that "the more students are involved in the social and academic life of an institution, the more likely they are to learn and persist . . . in ways that are meaningful to all . . . students, and to commuting as well as residential campuses" (Tinto, 1998, p. 2).

By the mid-1990s, the City University and its developmental and remedial programs were under siege by both its own board of trustees and state and national changes in financial aid policies. Yet, despite a dizzyingly rapid series of policy changes, New Student House has survived and even expanded. Its early beginnings, a model of thoughtful collaboration by faculty to create structures and content that support student achievement, gave it a strong and secure foundation on which to build. As university, state, and federal regulations changed, New Student House substituted a variety of full credit courses for the original partial credit developmental speech communication course so as not to jeopardize eligibility for financial aid.

The lesson learned here and in so many of the programs described in this chapter is that the *intentional* linking, as co-requisites, of developmental or remedial courses with college content courses for which they are prerequisites works very well in many different circumstances. The evolution of New Student House is a prime example of developmental and (as we shall see) ESL education reformed as the world around it changes, and in turn, reforming what we know about how to foster student success. Although some of these efforts began with special funding and need some additional funding to support faculty development, many offer neither stipends nor reassigned time to faculty; instead, in the words of one of our colleagues, a director of learning communities, "We simply sell it to our colleagues as the most rewarding teaching any of us have ever done."

Reading and Writing in Basic Skills Learning Communities

The most common examples of developmental learning communities are those that link reading and writing with each other and with content courses. Like New Student House, they frequently integrate support services as well. The best embody the good practices cited by the Roueches and Robert McCabe. Examples of such creative combinations are abundant. This section will highlight a few that have demonstrated consistent evidence of success.

GROSSMONT COMMUNITY COLLEGE. Project Success at Grossmont Community College in San Diego is a long-standing collaborative learning program. It began in 1985 with one linked developmental course and has since become institutionalized and expanded beyond its original developmental focus. The "transfer strand" links required general education courses with introductory courses in academic fields: humanities, psychology, history, speech, philosophy, or art history. Project Success also recently added an honors component. Today it is one of the largest and longest-running learning community efforts in the United States, with twenty-five to twenty-seven linked classes running each semester. It serves twelve hundred to fifteen hundred students annually, six hundred of them developmental students.

Like most successful developmental learning community programs, Project Success learning communities are offered to a range of students at different levels of achievement.

Project Success learning communities at the developmental level (the "fundamental strand") link basic writing and reading courses to improve vocabulary, language and communication skills, reading and study techniques, and paragraph and essay development. Students read substantive nonfiction works, such as *The Color of Water, Night, Warriors Don't Cry,* and *It is Not About the Bike,* chosen because they support the exploration of the themes of journeys and courage that pervade the courses.

A study completed in 1995 by the Office of Institutional Research and Planning found that Project Success students completed more semester units and had a higher GPA, a higher success rate, and a lower withdrawal rate than the control group. In addition, when enrolled in the next highest level of English after they had completed the remedial English course, Project Success students showed a persistence rate that was 12 percent higher than those who were not in the program. A second assessment study in 2000 corroborated these findings and indicated greater persistence and higher retention for Project Success students than their peers. These data help address the misgivings of the skeptical. One of our colleagues stated: "At first, some of our colleagues thought our students were more successful because we were lowering our standards. What we were actually doing was getting to know them as students."

Over the years, Grossmont has reached out to counselors, peer mentors, and faculty and incorporated formal and informal faculty development opportunities. Instructors are in close contact with each other during the semester and integrate the content and assignments of their courses. Care is taken to establish community in a number of ways. Each semester, for example, the college has a theater night and buys out an entire performance so that all Project Success students may attend. Because the courses are part of the normal teaching load, they are value-added with virtually no cost added. The only real cost is some release time for the coordinator.

PARKLAND COLLEGE. Integrated studies communities (ISC) at Parkland College, mentioned earlier in the chapter, began in 1998 after the success of developmental learning communities began to get wide coverage throughout higher education. Parkland's catchment area includes fifty-five urban and rural communities in Illinois, some low-income, and many of its students are academically unprepared. Begun initially to serve the lowest level of students, those with seventh- to ninth-grade reading levels, ISC was extended to students who entered with tenth- through twelfth-grade reading levels and added a college-level, transferable course for which these students would not ordinarily be eligible. Today, students are placed in the programs based on careful assessment of their abilities. ISC offerings include combinations of developmental reading and writing courses with college-level courses, which are taught by full-time and part-time faculty. These coordinated programs involve team teaching and extensive cooperation and integration. The thoughtful coordination of developmental and college-level courses here, as in many of the learning communities cited in this chapter, promotes success for these students.

Assessment results are consistent with successful developmental learning communities around the country. These include higher rates of persistence, increased sense of connection with the college, more collaborative interaction with peers and faculty, and increased levels of intellectual engagement and depth of understanding than in control groups. Faculty report professional growth and the growth of an interdisciplinary perspective. ISC has been so successful at Parkland that it has spurred the growth of learning communities beyond the developmental. The college now boasts linked and team-taught courses across disciplines and in honors. However, Parkland's team-teaching model is expensive, and the faculty-student ratio is too low to support any real expansion of the developmental learning communities. The school is now exploring less costly alternatives. Generally, to continue or expand such programs, the program directors need to work with the administration to develop local guidelines for cost-efficient, sustainable programs and then work within them.

METROPOLITAN COMMUNITY COLLEGE. Metropolitan Community College (MCC) in Omaha, Nebraska, hosts the AIM program, a one-quarter linkage of developmental courses in reading, English, and math joined to a success strategies class titled Academic Foundations that is taught by a counselor. The faculty is paid for one extra planning hour, "and are expected to meet weekly to discuss the class and the students. The counselor generally is the convener of this meeting." Faculty at MCC believe that their close and frequent communication with each other about their courses and their students is essential, but the addition of a counselor is the key to student success. As a colleague told us: "We have always run student services efficiently, with students able to come in and meet with any available counselor or adviser, but often they did not see the same person twice in a row. To provide more continuity, we have assigned a single counselor to the learning community cohort, so he or she is there for the students for the entire quarter and often afterwards." Indeed, based on the success of AIM, the student services department recently restructured so that all developmental students are assigned a particular counselor. More than five years old, this program was recently enhanced with funding from a Title III grant. It has expanded with continuing success, and its impressive completion and retention rates mirror those of the other learning communities cited in this chapter (see Raftery and Van Wagoner, 2002).

CALIFORNIA STATE UNIVERSITY-HAYWARD. California State University-Hayward has an ambitious general education learning community initiative for all its first-year students. These learning communities serve both mainstream and developmental students, who constitute 55 to 60 percent of the incoming class; in 2002, that meant 400 students out of 750. Entering students choose from a wide variety of social sciences, natural sciences, and humanities clusters, all of which contain college-level or developmental English or speech courses, an information literacy course, and a course in the discipline. As with most large learning community initiatives, curricular coordination varies widely: at one extreme students merely travel together as part of an administrative block of courses; at the other, faculty create joint syllabi and closely coordinate their work. At its best, close coordination yields stellar results. For example, in 2002 an "Ancient World Cluster Conference" was put together by developmental and freshman composition students taking different tracks of one cluster. Offered to the entire college community, the daylong conference featured speakers Chris Phillips, author of *Socrates Café,* and Thomas Cleary, a well-known translator of ancient texts, as well as many student panels.

At Hayward the composition program views the clusters as an opportunity to serve students better. Composition instructors, primarily graduate students or graduates of Hayward's master's program in composition, take seminars on the theory and practice of composition, the teaching of remedial writing, and pedagogy. A variety of faculty development interventions include a practicum in which they "shadow" an experienced teacher. Once they begin, the teachers attend three to four professional development meetings each quarter. Composition instructors hold office hours in the same room, a logistical decision that facilitates ongoing communication and peer learning. These young faculty attribute their success to their intentional training, close supervision, and the support they receive; their group solidarity compensates for the uneven quality of cooperation they receive from the subject faculty with whom they share students.

Developmental students at Hayward are neither stigmatized nor isolated. They are mainstreamed immediately because their remedial writing classes are linked with college-level general education courses. As much as possible, students stay with the same composition teacher for as many quarters as they need to pass college-level composition. When this is not possible, continuity is maintained through the thematic nature of the courses they follow.

The results are impressive. A four-year study of the 1998 to 2002 cluster program stated that it "has successfully supported and enhanced the development of students' academic skills, provided a broad foundation for lower-division students, [and] supported the development of collateral skills in problem solving, working with others, awareness of diversity issues, and their ability to synthesize information. [Students] report significant gains in the skills to assist them in a life of learning" (General Education Program History, p. 10). The extensive data collected support the conclusions that the students in these learning communities complete their general education coursework and other requirements and have good retention rates that have risen annually. In addition, since this program began, the overall student pass rate on the required CSU writing exam has increased dramatically.

DE ANZA COMMUNITY COLLEGE. De Anza Community College in Northern California's Silicon Valley has used its demonstrable success with a wide array of learning communities—including efforts to serve underprepared and underrepresented students—to develop, with support from the Packard Foundation, a regional learning community consortium of twelve community colleges from the four Silicon Valley counties. All these colleges are developing learning communities for underprepared students. The group shares information, experiences, professional development retreats for faculty and staff, and assessment results, and provides informal support for all participants. The model of reaching beyond the walls of individual institutions to pool resources for professional development and enrichment would work well at colleges and universities throughout the country.

In sum, whether they link developmental reading, writing, or speech courses with each other or link them with college-level courses, developmental learning communities have been consistently successful at a remarkable number of diverse campuses, as the preceding examples illustrate. Because learning communities allow faculty to learn together as colleagues in a shared intellectual and pedagogical venture, they offer a context to refine their scholarly and teaching skills. At their best, they are part of comprehensive programs that include counselors, tutors, and other college staff, and they enhance learning through coordination of skills, content, and themes. They address the complex lives of their students but do not compromise on standards. Students have managed to enter the mainstream in the increasingly limited time offered to them. Students thrive because these learning communities offer an alternative to fragmented lives—integrated and reinforcing learning experiences.

Mathematics and Science in Basic Skills Learning Communities

As noted in Chapter One, mathematics and science education is at a crisis point in the United States. Indeed, concern over the teaching of mathematics and science extends beyond the remedial realm into the mainstream college. In "Tracking the Process of Change in U.S. Undergraduate Education in Science, Mathematics, Engineering, and Technology" (2001), Elaine Seymour, coauthor of *Talking About Leaving: Why Undergraduates Leave the Sciences* (1997), suggests why there needs to be a shift from "science-for-the-few" to "science-for-all":

> Competitive global market realities require that all educated citizens become science-and-math-literate. At an individual level, this will increasingly be required in order to achieve a good standard of living. The wider implications are both societal and moral: [one expert] argues that science, mathematics, engineering, and technology (SMET) faculty have the collective power and opportunity to change the conditions that have created a permanent and growing underclass in U.S. society, one cause of whose limited job options is lack of scientific, mathematical, or computing skills. [Seymour, 2001, p. 84]

The National Science Foundation and several other foundations have funded a variety of initiatives to strengthen the teaching of SMET. The quantitative reasoning movement attempts to prepare students to estimate, read graphs, and calculate percentages, for example, in classes other than mathematics. The calculus reform movement, other math reform efforts, the chemistry reform movement known as Chemlinks, and related reform efforts in engineering and the biological and health sciences are all heavily funded by the National Science Foundation. They share a commitment to changing how math and science are taught at the college level and to relating the study of the two to each other, to other disciplines, to K–12 practices, and to real life.

Not unexpectedly, even more students require remedial or developmental intervention in math than in reading and writing. Where 37.7 percent of remedial education students are deficient in reading and 47.7 percent are deficient in writing, 62 percent are deficient in mathematics (McCabe, 2000). Nationally, mathematics is the "greatest hurdle" (McCabe, 2000, p. 40) faced by developmental students. Yet this is true at a time when "numeracy is the currency of modern life. . . . And as its importance and scope have expanded, so have the economic and social consequences of innumeracy" (Steen, 1997, p. xviii).

The need for learning communities that support the learning of mathematics is great, but the relative scarcity of such programs reflects the more general resistance of these faculty to working with their colleagues in learning community settings. It also reflects the inability of social science and humanities faculty members to imagine how mathematics could be linked effectively to their courses. Neither group has exhibited the vision necessary to move forward constructively (and together): "This idea of turning content on its head to fit the subject to the audience is the real uncharted territory of mathematical education. . . . It will take people with deep understanding of content and a willingness to perceive the possible advantages of breaking out of the box of content and the linear approach. Until this happens, our own academic community will be our own worst enemy in this discussion" (Malcom, 1997, p. 35). Furthermore, until this happens, the potential of learning communities to transform traditional gateway courses into springboards for students to professions otherwise closed to them will not be realized.

The issue of appropriate terminology becomes most apparent in mathematics. College basic skills courses in mathematics are often not remedial because students have never taken, much less failed, the kinds of courses they needed to prepare them for further study in mathematics. High schools routinely track students into inferior courses and limit future options from an early age. As Adelman (1999) points out, "Of all precollege curricula, the highest level of mathematics one studies in secondary school has the strongest continuing influence on bachelor's degree completion" (p. vii). Too many students arrive at college never having taken algebra or any of the subsequent mathematics courses that build on this

eighth- or ninth-grade class, and they also often come with minimal exposure to science courses in general and science courses with laboratory experiences in particular. Even students who have successfully completed
higher-level high school math courses are often unable to carry over and
apply their skills in other courses, science in particular. What Shirley
Malcom observes about mathematics can be just as easily applied to
science: "Mathematics is everywhere: we should offer students the opportunity to study what they know, what they love, what they care about,
what interests them, and then find the mathematics in it" (Malcom, 1997,
p. 31). But providing both initial and sustained exposure to mathematics
and science, as well as the chance to apply what has been learned, are
continuing challenges in all levels of education in the United States.

The poor performance of American students in mathematics and
science is well known, well documented, and the subject of myriad news-
paper and television reports. The Trends in International Mathematics
and Science Study (TIMSS) survey, first conducted in 1995, revealed that
while "U.S. fourth-graders performed well in both mathematics and science in comparison to students in other nations, U.S eighth-grade students
performed near the international average in both mathematics and science,
and U.S. twelfth-graders scored below the international average and
among the lowest of the TIMSS nations in mathematics and science." A
1999 study (TIMSS-R) confirmed that American high school students lag
far behind students in other developed countries. Videos of classroom performance generated as part of TIMSS are especially telling. The rush to
cover content superficially in classrooms here contrasts starkly with the
thoughtful, focused approaches taken to carefully chosen topics in other
countries. Whatever the cause, the result is a massive loss of students
majoring in the SMET disciplines and a lack of scientific literacy and
quantitative reasoning among those who are not majors in these fields. In
this context, remedial and developmental programs are especially critical.

UNIVERSITY OF TEXAS-EL PASO. The most important and compelling
effort to reach out to low-performing students who aspire to careers in
science and math-related fields is the CircLES (Circles of Learning for
Entering Students) program at the University of Texas-El Paso (UTEP).
CircLES is a stellar example of how math and science learning may be
successfully integrated into developmental learning communities and prepare students who are traditionally "written off" to pursue majors in
mathematics and the sciences. Like the general education program at Cal
State Hayward, CircLES is an institutional ramp-up of programs for first-
year college students, both those who enter on level and those in need of

developmental work. Both the Hayward and UTEP programs offer all their entering students the same types of learning communities with different combinations of courses.

UTEP is a research institution with the dual mission of open access to serve its community. The CircLES program is one example of the Model Institutions for Excellence (MIE) initiative, an eleven-year, $26.5-million project sponsored by the National Science Foundation at UTEP. In 1995, six minority-serving colleges and universities were selected as MIE institutions to develop and implement new models in undergraduate education that increase the quality and quantity of underrepresented populations in the fields of science, technology, engineering, and mathematics. UTEP was one of them.

The CircLES program began as an effort to give entering pre-science and pre-engineering students an "academic home," help with the transition from high school to college, and a connection to the Colleges of Science and Engineering early in their college career. The goal was to increase their first-year persistence rate. Sixty students chose to participate in the pilot in 1997. At the urging of the MIE advisory board, the program was scaled up in 1998 with the intention of including all first-time, full-time students. It was during this ramp-up that students who needed remedial math courses (about 38 percent of entering science-engineering students at UTEP, or some 250 to 275 students annually) participated in the program.

Currently, the science and engineering learning community course clusters include a science- or engineering-oriented first-year seminar, a mathematics course, and an English course. To help these students make the transition from high school to university, the CircLES program implemented a mandatory weeklong summer orientation for entering students and offered proactive advising and mentoring. The summer program continues as originally conceived, but the structure of the learning communities has changed to align better with institutional and academic requirements. Curricular integration and pedagogical interventions, dependent as they are on the willingness of individual faculty to experiment with their teaching and cooperate with their colleagues, are uneven, as is the case in most large learning community initiatives. Nevertheless, since 1998 the retention rates of first-time, full-time students in science and engineering are significantly higher than students in a comparison group.

University 1301 (the seminar in critical inquiry) is a three-credit-hour course required of all entering students. Each seminar revolves around an engineering or science content theme, so there is a glimpse of a discipline; engineering faculty teach engineering students, science faculty teach the sciences.

The faculty are chosen to teach the seminar based on submitted proposals. They commit to a faculty development process during which they learn about the goals of the seminar, discuss and compare previous seminar syllabi, and consider ways to insert the learning outcomes into their own syllabi. The faculty development process includes a heavy emphasis on cooperative learning and uses the resources available through a teaching and learning center that was established with MIE funds. Faculty development also addresses an issue that is endemic not only with developmental students but with all first-year students: according to one of our colleagues, faculty "are really afraid when they have to deal with incoming students because they know how difficult it is. They resist all the preparation, all the working with students. [They] need tools to work with this population."

As it has evolved, the seminar is now linked with broader faculty professional development efforts associated with the University College, the administrative unit that oversees all services dealing with entering students. This move was part of the effort to institutionalize and sustain the learning communities in science and engineering. Applying one of the most important lessons learned, CircLES constantly adapts to contextual pressures, opportunities, and constraints.

Other crucial elements of CircLES reflect defined best practice in developmental programs. Counselors who are UTEP graduates with degrees in engineering and science are assigned to appropriate clusters. In structured weekly sessions, they train the peer mentors who are assigned to each cluster and also coordinate the summer orientation sessions for the new students. The summer program is especially important, because it includes a mathematics review. In summer 2002, almost 40 percent of the entering science and engineering students who initially placed into developmental math moved into pre-calculus or calculus after the review, and another 37 percent moved from an initial placement into pre-calculus to Calculus I for the fall semester. Such a simple idea—a review of mathematics before taking a test—with such great consequences: aspiring science and engineering students are able to enroll in disciplinary courses much faster than formerly. The results of CircLES are impressive. Before CircLES, the one-year retention rate for SMET students among the 1997 baseline group was 56 percent. In 1998, among the CircLES group, it was 68 percent. After four years, 27 percent of the 1997 cohort was still at UTEP, while 39 percent of the 1998 CircLES group had been retained. Since the scale-up of the program, the first-year retention rate has increased over five years to approximately 80 percent. When the findings are disaggregated, the greatest gains are among the developmental students. This might be because developmental CircLES students spend an entire year in the program instead of one semester and thus reap greater benefits. In any case, "students who enter the university at the developmental mathematics level and who participated in the CircLES program have significantly higher one-year retention rates than the retention rates of developmental mathematics students in the baseline group" (Della-Piana and others, 2003, p. 14).

Two smaller long-standing learning communities at community colleges also suggest the potential of such intentional pairings. The following paragraphs describe one that pairs developmental math and chemistry courses in preparation for a college-level chemistry course, and another that pairs a college biology course with either a developmental study skills course or a transfer-level study skills course.

EDMONDS COMMUNITY COLLEGE. At Edmonds Community College, the CheMath learning community links a remedial math course with a precollege–level chemistry course. Before CheMath, students were required to complete the math course (if their placement test scores were low enough to require them to take the course) as a prerequisite for the college-level course Chemistry 131. The question posed about student outcomes from an eight-year study of this learning community was this: "Is there a significant difference between students in the [CheMath] program and those who merely take the same remedial math courses without the concurrent chemistry course?"

The answer was yes. At-risk students who took CheMath did significantly better in Chemistry 131 than those who had completed remedial math as a stand-alone course. The initial study involved 539 students enrolled in Chemistry 131, 139 of whom were characterized as being at risk based on their placement scores. Of these, 62 were graduates of CheMath whereas 77 had completed a stand-alone remedial math course. Among the at-risk group, the CheMath students, based on their placement scores, were at greater risk of failure than the at-risk control group. Nevertheless, "the completion rates and average GPA for at-risk students in [CheMath], despite generally lower placement scores, were higher than those of other at-risk students" (Edmonds Community College, 2001, p. 4). The promise of the syllabus that "studying mathematics and chemistry together will enable you to see the relationship between the two and will enhance your understanding of both subjects," was delivered. Currently, approximately 100 students take CheMath each year, recruited either through word-of-mouth, outreach to lower-level mathematics courses, or failure to pass the placement test for general chemistry. This latter group must take CheMath in order to take general chemistry.

SPOKANE FALLS COMMUNITY COLLEGE. Since the late 1980s and until recently, when one of the partners retired, Spokane Falls Community College paired a developmental study skills course with an introductory college-level biology course in the belief that "if we could teach the students *how* to learn the biology, and not just the biology, they could take this approach to other classes . . . a teach-a-person-to-fish approach ("Teach a Person to Fish," 1994, p. 8). The results of the initial experiment convinced the teaching faculty that they had done something important: although there were fewer As in the paired biology, there were an equal number of Bs, many more Cs and Ds, and far fewer F grades or withdrawals. Even more important, the faculty team discovered that some of the traditional study strategies taught in generic study skills classes "weren't effective or efficient for learning biology." As a result, the content of the study skills course was changed to reflect the reality that had been revealed. They also noted the enriched experience students were having because of the related reading and writing they were doing in the study skills course.

The College Reading and Study Skills course was initially developed in the 1980s as part of a Title III grant. A subsequent seed grant from the Washington Center supported the faculty members to work together and develop a more integrated approach. Once again, the results showed that the teaching of skills in a meaningful context made more sense to both faculty and students than isolating the teaching of skills from the content to which it needed to be applied. Currently, the majority of developmental-level skills courses are paired with introductory courses throughout the curriculum.

In summary, poor grades in math and science are well-known predictors of general failure. Although good examples of learning communities for developmental students in math and science are far fewer than in reading and writing, the robust results from the initiatives described in the preceding paragraphs suggest the real potential of such approaches. As the teaching of math and science evolves, the development of well-conceived learning communities to support all levels of students should be part of the mix.

English as a Second Language in Basic Skills Learning Communities

Waves of immigration created the circumstances that led to the development of a formal discipline dedicated to the teaching of English as a Second Language. However, whether second language learners should even be admitted to college before mastering English has been a source of debate over the years. Perhaps as a reflection of this debate, the position or place of ESL courses also has been the source of some controversy. Although ESL faculty claim that their students should be viewed in the same way we view native students who are studying a foreign language, ESL courses have frequently been treated as basic skills courses because there is no consensus about the presence of non-English speakers collecting credits on an English-speaking campus.

There are two additional reasons for giving ESL basic skills status. In the beginning, ESL faculty resisted distinguishing between those ESL students who arrived in their classrooms with substantial (frequently professional) educations and those who had not been well educated in their native countries; this initial refusal undermined claims that ESL was a college-level initiative. Second, the rich funding that supported ESL programs was linked to the initially rich funding for basic skills courses, and as that funding diminished, ESL programs faced the same challenges. They too had to address attenuated programs, heavy commitment of hours by students and faculty, and time-to-degree and cost issues as financial aid regulations got stricter. In the context of ESL, learning communities offer students the credits they need to continue to be eligible for various kinds of financial aid throughout their college careers.

Holistic approaches to language learning are a basic tenet of the English as a Second Language pedagogy. Reading, writing, and oral skills have always been taught simultaneously, and the success of early attempts to link ESL and content courses—such as the learning communities at Seattle Central Community College in the mid-1980s that linked ESL classes to both vocational and transfer courses—attests to the value of such an approach. Often more sensitive to the varied backgrounds, educational levels, and varying proficiencies that ESL students brought to their classrooms, these instructors tend to be creative and flexible in their approaches.

KINGSBOROUGH COMMUNITY COLLEGE. One of the most successful and sustained ESL learning communities is the Intensive English Program (IEP) at Kingsborough Community College (CUNY), which serves approximately 250 entering students annually. Described in detail in "Making Writing Count in an ESL Learning Community" (Babbitt, 2001) and based on the scholarship that demonstrated the positive academic and social outcomes of learning communities, this program is a model of cooperation, integration, and exemplary practice.

IEP is a first-semester experience for ESL students. It consists of "an eight-hour noncredit ESL class; two three-credit courses in other academic disciplines; two one-credit student development (SD) courses; and four hours of tutoring, for a total of eight college credits and twenty contact hours" (Babbitt, 2001, p. 50). The credit courses for the lowest level of ESL students include two speech courses; in the upper-level blocks, there is one speech course and either a sociology, psychology, or American history course. The ambitious goals of the IEP are as follows:

o Accelerate ESL students' acquisition of academic written and spoken English.

o Allow ESL students to take, and to prepare them to succeed in, credit-bearing courses in their first semester and beyond.

o Significantly improve the retention and graduation rates of ESL students.

o Encourage and facilitate ESL students' integration into all aspects of college life by providing a solid grounding in the college academic-social community. [Babbitt, 2001, p. 50]

IEP begins with outreach into academic departments for faculty who enjoy working collaboratively with colleagues and are amenable to adding writing assignments of various kinds and lengths to their syllabi. Once identified, faculty from both the ESL and content courses participate in faculty development activities that have two goals: "providing the teachers (and tutors, if possible) with the necessary time to discuss and thoughtfully plan how they will coordinate and interrelate course materials and . . . acquainting faculty members with different pedagogical techniques" (Babbitt, 2001, p. 52). They also identify relevant extracurricular activities, both on and off campus, for student participation and further integration into the life of the college. Counselors who teach the student development courses are an integral part of the team, an early warning system, and a resource. Tutors attend parts of all the classes in a particular block to familiarize themselves with content and to give help, with small group activities, for example. They often attend meetings, workshops, and field trips as well. Instead of being isolated in a skills center, the tutors in IEP are an integral part of this program. "Making Writing Count in an ESL Learning Community" describes in detail the myriad ways in which writing becomes a seamless part of the fabric of the learning community, including "free writing, dialogic journal writing, point-of-view writing, essay writing with several revised drafts, academic project writing, rewriting of lecture and discussion notes, . . . and reflective writing" (Babbitt, 2001, p. 54).

The results are encouraging. What began originally in 1995 as an optional program for ESL students became a mandatory program in fall

1998 for first-semester ESL students because the success rate among IEP students was so much greater than for the others. Data revealed that over 80 percent of the students taking the IEP advanced to the next level with significantly over 50 percent skipping a level. A smaller study of one section comparing IEP ESL students with non-IEP ESL students revealed that almost twice as many of the former passed the content course and that the failure rate among the non-IEP students was four times greater. Once the program became mandatory, the difference in pass rates dropped, with the lowest level of ESL having almost similar rates. However, the pass rates for the two upper-level ESL courses continue to reveal a significant difference between students in the IEP and those in the non-intensive ESL courses. IEP students pass at rates from 14 percent to 27 percent higher than those who are not in the program (memo from Babbitt to Dr. Morton Euhr, Grants Officer, 1/10/2001 re: Intensive ESL Program Perkins Report for Fall, 2000). The structure accounts for the success of IEP:

> The framing of the IEP curriculum in a strong content-based, inter-disciplinary, and collaborative structure with a whole-language fluency-first base fosters the creation of cohesive academic-social learning communities among students in the same block of classes. Our focus on having students develop an analytical thinking and writing base addresses our need to prepare students for the academic mainstream. The strong social network students form also prepares them for the challenges of college life. By developing this essential academic base in their first semester, students begin immediately to tackle the demands of college courses. . . . [They] participate actively, work together, and are listened to and valued by their peers. The learning community empowers students to develop reading, writing, and critical thinking skills through the academic writing they do. The academic-social bonds that students form in the program during their crucial first semester in college seem to facilitate their integration into the larger college community and to lay the foundation for a successful college career. [Babbitt, 2001, p. 60]

LAGUARDIA COMMUNITY COLLEGE. At LaGuardia Community College, faculty extended the New Student House (NSH; see the earlier section on this subject) and created an ESL/NSH. During the spring of 1996 faculty selected the theme—Immigrants in the United States—textbooks, and other materials, and developed a joint syllabus of major weekly activities. ESL/NSH was first offered that fall.

The ESL/NSH brought together as many as six faculty and a counselor, who taught the freshman seminar, into one cluster. Exploring the immigrant experience was a natural and logical approach. No doubt, many ESL courses (stand-alone as well as those in learning communities) organize curricula around this rich theme, which allows students to compare their experiences with those that they read about.

But the ESL/NSH students had a special advantage over their peers and were able to perform at a much higher level—the "more, better" syndrome. Because ESL/NSH combined an ESL course with additional reading and oral communications courses, the faculty used a textbook and assigned readings that otherwise would have been too difficult and probably too time-intensive (the text was *America Now* and assigned readings were from *The New York Times*). Because ESL/NSH students studied the same readings in *all* courses at the same time, they were able to engage in more concentrated and in-depth analysis of theme-related issues than other courses that might be exploring a similar theme. Ideas about a specific topic, relevant vocabulary, grammar, and sound symbol correspondence reinforced in the three courses provided essential tools for language use and facilitated expression of ideas in writing.

The faculty members in ESL/NSH depended on mutual reinforcement to make difficult materials accessible to their students and also to push their students to higher levels of reading, writing, speaking, and listening than they would have been able to do alone. This, in turn, allowed for the assignment of more complex work. Mutual reinforcement also extended to students in academic difficulty who were routinely scheduled for joint conferences with all their teachers, and the participating counselor, to discuss strategies for improvement and the importance of concentrated effort. This intervention, along with the special advantages already noted, worked well. At the end of the first semester, 77 percent of the students moved on to a higher-level course. Of these, an impressive 24 percent skipped the final ESL level. Ten students entered directly into the non-ESL developmental English course; two students skipped two levels to enter the regular freshman composition course. In contrast, the stand-alone ESL course at this level moved along 50 percent of its students each semester. Since that first semester, the impressive student success data have held steady. The pass rate of the ESL/NSH consistently is more than 25 percent higher than that of students in traditional ESL courses, although themes and courses have changed in response to financial aid regulations. ESL/NSH now serves fifty to seventy students each semester.

Another early learning community at LaGuardia Community College placed ESL students with high math scores in one ESL course linked to two introductory computer courses: one was for students interested in majoring in computer science, the other for students who wished to become computer technicians. Prerequisites in reading and writing for these courses were waived to see if an intensive content-based ESL course taught in conjunction with the content course itself would improve English reading, writing, listening, and speaking skills while providing the supportive environment necessary for students to pass the content course as well. The ESL instructor used material from the texts of the computer courses and designed her course around the vocabulary and concepts being taught in the computer courses. Both of the introductory computer courses included non-ESL students as well. The ESL students consistently outperformed the native students, no doubt because they were spending so much additional time focusing on the content of the computer courses, and they made impressive gains in English language skills as well. Currently, LaGuardia offers many ESL courses linked to a variety of content courses. A forthcoming study will present data that support the results of the early learning community: students in ESL-content pairs consistently outperform students taking these courses in stand-alone versions.

Learning communities in ESL programs accelerate student progress and mainstreaming. They contextualize language learning and give adult students the opportunity to interact with a new language in a rich and nuanced way. Those that explore shared experiences or are linked to courses in professional or vocational programs address the interests and aspirations of their students. As in other learning communities designed for students with special needs, the presence of a broad and integrated faculty–student affairs support system contributes to the success of these educational experiences.

Challenges to Come

We enter the twenty-first century facing a more complex set of challenges than in the past. As math reformer Lynn Steen puts it: "Literacy is no longer just a matter of words, sentences, and paragraphs but also of data, measurements, graphs, and inferences. Pattern and number lurk behind words and sentences, in machines and computers, in organizations and networks. Literacy is about reading and reasoning, writing and calculating; it is about solving problems and using technology; it is about practices as well as knowledge, procedures as well as concepts" (Steen, 1997, p. xxvii). Whatever the language we wish to use to describe efforts to improve literacy—remedial, developmental, compensatory, academic skills—it is harder now than ever to conceive of a time when students whose literacy in one area or another will not need to be brought up to a functional level. Although we may hope that secondary education will rise to the challenge and link high-stakes testing with high-quality teaching and learning, a continuing need for developmental education at the college level is likely, especially given the range of students who are served by these programs. At stake is the future of a country that can no longer afford to close doors and limit opportunities. If we doom so many to second-class citizenship because they lack basic skills, we risk condemning all of us to second-class citizenship in the global economy.

Throughout this book, we refer to articles and books that suggest how much more we know today about how to educate for the new, expansive literacy and how the best kind of assessments should reflect and support what we know (see, for example, Marchese, 1997; Tagg, 2003; *National Survey of Student Engagement,* 2001). Colleges and universities have been challenged to practice what their own scholarship has revealed about best practice. And real practice suggests how far we have come—and still have to go—in redefining and applying what we have learned. Developmental learning, like all learning, occurs best in contexts that intentionally create and support the best conditions for learning. Learning communities can provide that context, and sufficient examples of successful models exist to stimulate replication. Will higher education commit to the task? (Matthews, Smith, MacGregor, and Gabelnick, 1997)

The challenge for higher education is great; the challenge for developmental education is even greater. As many four-year colleges back away from offering developmental education and raise the admissions bar either to eliminate or to mask the need for such courses, will community colleges step up to meet the need? K. Patricia Cross was indeed prescient in her 1971 work *Beyond the Open Door* when she characterized most four-year colleges as having neither the flexibility nor the vision to embrace the new student, looking instead to community colleges to reach out and address these students' needs. The Roueches' more recent *High Stakes, High Performance* (1999) suggests, however, that community colleges are finding the task too costly. Both senior and community colleges face similar challenges: educating underprepared students who either do not have the appropriate background or have the background but lack the carryover and application skills that will enable them to succeed. Examples of fine developmental education programs in both community and four-year colleges underscore the good work being done throughout higher education to address the needs and ensure the success of all students. Comprehensive and substantive programs exist at both community colleges such as Grossmont and LaGuardia and four-year colleges such as California State University-Hayward and the University of Texas-El Paso. Many more programs are small efforts.

Whether this good work will be more widely acknowledged, supported, and brought up to scale remains to be seen.[4]

In *Honored But Invisible: An Inside Look at Teaching in Community Colleges,* Norton Grubb (Grubb and Associates, 1999) observes that the best teaching faculty create "communities of practice" in a desert that neither encourages nor nurtures such practice. The best faculty seek out others: "Effective instructors were almost universally linked with other faculty, often in learning communities, while really bad teachers were generally alienated from their peers." Faculty who teach in "meaning-centered and constructivist ways tend to see learning as a social enterprise" and gravitate toward each other and to learning communities. For Grubb, "The isolation of instructors in community colleges . . . contributes to the invisibility of teaching. . . . There are few discussions about instruction, no forums where . . . pedagogical problems . . . can be debated and resolved, and no ways to bring problems to the attention of administrators. In an institution where learning from peers is one of the few ways of improving teaching, isolation means that new instructors, or experienced instructors who come across a new challenge . . . have nowhere to turn for help" (p. 55). The same may be said of teaching in most four-year colleges and universities, where the privileging of scholarship as the road to tenure and promotion exacerbates the situation even more. The exceptions are generally those colleges and universities with robust teaching centers that promote lively discussions around practice and with reward systems that acknowledge that practice. Grubb's work underscores the importance of rebuilding faculty community, a subject that we explore in Chapter Eight.

As Grubb points out, many community colleges offer learning communities in remedial education, and "the combinations are endless and inventive" (Grubb and Associates, 1999, p. 203). Furthermore, linking skills courses of all kinds with introductory courses in the major solves the problems of content and motivation: "In conventional remediation, students enter a college for academic or vocational purposes [but] find themselves doing sentence completion exercises, arithmetic drills, and three-paragraph essays on contrived topics, and dropout rates from these courses are alarmingly high," while students fortunate enough to have been placed in or who have chosen developmental learning communities enjoy higher "course completion rates and subsequent enrollment" (p. 204). The data support the effectiveness of learning communities that link skills with each other or with college-level courses of interest to students.

For Grubb, "The benefits of such learning communities are enormous. The obvious question is why they seem so rare—why, for example, they have not superseded the tutorial labs and dreary skills-oriented classes that we observed so often" (p. 204). Grubb's answer, an indictment of business as usual, is worth noting: the principal reason is that "they require institutional commitment, and sometimes resources. . . . The commitment to learning communities as a normal approach to developmental education rather than an exceptional experiment is rare . . . testimony to enrollment-driven funding, conventional practice, and sheer inattention to the institutional requirements for improving teaching" (Grubb and Associates, 1999, p. 205).

The invisibility and isolation of teaching are especially fatal for students whose prior educational experiences have been fragmentary and who desperately need to see connections and become engaged in a comprehensive learning process. If colleges and universities find that learning communities are helping them educate and mainstream developmental, remedial, and ESL students in a timely and cost-effective way, then learning communities help solve the dilemma posed when remedial and developmental programs are seen as deflecting resources from other essential goals.

It is no accident that this chapter ends with the commentaries of individuals who have long been associated with community colleges. At this point, many four-year colleges are walking away from developmental, remedial, and in some cases, ESL education, unless they serve special populations as part of their mandate or as a function of their geographic location. In a sense we have come full circle, to the time before open admissions, with one important difference: hundreds of community colleges throughout the country, where currently over half of the freshman class begins its college career, are essentially open admissions institutions.

Instead of leveling the playing field for all students, we seem to be plowing many under so that others may advance. The documented success of learning communities in developmental, remedial, and ESL education offers one beacon of hope that higher education will be able to reach out and serve disadvantaged populations and help them realize their potential and the promise of higher education. The programs discussed here, the work of committed faculty who generally enjoy the support of enlightened administrations, suggest the potential of these thoughtful approaches.

We need to pay attention to what works. The AAC&U report *Greater Expectations: A New Vision for Learning as a Nation Goes to College* suggests how critical the successful completion of a college education has become: "The unprecedented expansion of college enrollments creates an extraordinary opportunity to prepare the informed citizens and competent employees needed for the new knowledge-based society. . . . Universal readiness for and success in obtaining a college education of high quality are democratic values, moral imperatives, and economic necessities. The country deserves no less" (*Greater Expectations,* 2002, p. 1).

The current political and economic climate, the confluence of various policies on remediation and developmental education, and the ongoing concerns about the cost of higher education put additional pressure on developmental, remedial, and ESL programs to accomplish their work. Now more than ever, we must join access with excellence. In this context, learning communities are a proven innovation and a reforming of traditional approaches.

PART FOUR

INITIATING AND STRENGTHENING LEARNING COMMUNITIES

INFORMATION AND FEEDBACK

USING ASSESSMENT TO STRENGTHEN
AND SUSTAIN LEARNING COMMUNITIES

*If change is going to be effective, reformers need to develop
a constant information-and-feedback process.*

—William Tierney

*Could we create a learning culture where students and teachers
would have a shared expectation that finding out what makes
sense and what doesn't is a joint and worthwhile project,
essential to taking the next steps in learning?*

—Lorrie Shepard

ASSESSMENT AND ACCOUNTABILITY are becoming permanent features of the higher education landscape. For the past twenty years, higher
education coordinating boards, legislators, and accrediting associations
have been asking colleges and universities to define and document measurable progress toward their educational goals more clearly. What began
in the 1980s as a focus on broad performance indicators of institutional
quality and efficiency has moved more recently to an emphasis on student
learning and educational effectiveness. The calls for accountability are

increasing as the costs of a college education escalate, public funding for higher education declines, accrediting bodies ask institutions to be more explicit about the quality of their students' learning, and the federal government pushes "high-stakes testing" up the ladder from K–12 education to colleges and universities.

In these same two decades, learning community initiatives have developed and spread. The assessment of learning community programs has evolved along with assessment in higher education in general and has faced the same promise and problems. It should come as no surprise to learning community leaders that their initiatives will be scrutinized. Learning communities are not only "the new kid on the block" but often a big and highly visible new kid, with their ambitious goals and an agenda that includes improving student learning and reforming curricular structures, pedagogies, and institutional relationships. Moreover, learning community programs are situated in the very places where institutional assessment most often focuses: the freshman year, the general education curriculum, the underprepared student. And perhaps most importantly, robust learning community initiatives require investments—of individuals' time and energy and of institutions' monetary resources. To justify these investments, learning community programs must prove that they are living up to their aspirations: evidence of program effectiveness is essential.

Learning community programs are also dynamic, evolving innovations. To realize their full potential, these innovations must include ongoing self-reflection and feedback. *In this chapter, we argue that assessment should not be an afterthought tacked on an educational program; instead, it should be an integral part of the process used to develop and sustain the entire educational enterprise.* For learning community initiatives to become lasting reforms, they must incorporate both the "proving" and the "improving" aspects of assessment work as fundamental practices. Successful learning community assessment should involve explicit cycles of planning, inquiry, and reflection, especially at the classroom level where teachers and learners do their work. Carried out consistently, systematic classroom assessment practices can strengthen learning community programs and generate evidence of their efficacy. Learning community assessment should also inform and advance larger institutional assessment endeavors. In this chapter, we begin by discussing the multiplicity of fields that assessment work comprises, and the institutional assessment context in which most learning community initiatives are situated. We then present an assessment cycle that is highly useful for framing assessment. We describe strategies for making this assessment cycle explicit, public, and collaborative—both in individual learning community classrooms and for learning community program assessment as a whole.

The Varied Purposes and Practices of Assessment

What we call *assessment,* although a phenomenon barely two decades old in higher education, has grown into a rich, multidimensional field. The term itself is used in many educational contexts and for sometimes conflicting purposes. As a result, it has varied connotations. We will briefly discuss several trends and strands in this work because they all contribute to assessment conversations, practices, and scholarship. Learning community assessment is influenced by these strands as well, as we will explore further in this chapter.

Assessment to Satisfy Accountability Requirements

Calls for greater public accountability from higher education have been growing for twenty years. These mandates arose in the early 1980s, partly in response to several national reports, especially *A Nation at Risk* (U.S. Department of Education, 1983), which criticized the performance of both K–12 and higher education, and partly because state budgets, after twenty years of generously funding the rapid growth of higher education, were severely strained. Legislatures and state higher education boards pressed public campuses to document and strengthen their quality and efficiency. Accreditation associations soon followed, asking institutions to articulate goals for student learning, document student progress, and assess alumni and employer satisfaction. Deeper and more public commitments to these tasks were to create a "culture of evidence" on campuses. At first, state policy leaders rushed to the apparent convenience of off-the-shelf tests of student competence, but a groundswell of resistance among institutions soon gave way, in most states, to the encouragement of locally designed assessment activities.

Virtually all states and accrediting associations now require colleges and universities to undertake assessment. Some states, such as Washington, Missouri, and Virginia, have invested in assessment, providing campuses with budgetary support to develop assessment plans and programs, while other states have left institutions on their own to build assessment programs with internal resources (El-Khawas, 1995; Ewell, 2002a, 2002b). Yet although many assessment endeavors engage hardworking committees and generate important data about students and their needs and progress, a 1999 national survey offers the disappointing news that this information is generally neither well disseminated in institutions nor acted upon (National Center for Postsecondary Improvement, 1999).

More recently, accountability expectations have increased. The standards of effectiveness and efficiency are becoming higher, and institutional assessment results are expected to become more public (Ewell, 2002a). Accrediting bodies are asking that campus accreditation information document *student learning and achievement* and demonstrate explicit institutional processes for acting on information about educational effectiveness. The National Center for Public Policy in Higher Education has published two national "report cards" rating each of the fifty states on various measures of effectiveness; both reports gave every state an "incomplete" in "student learning" because of the lack of common benchmarks for student learning that would allow for useful state-by-state comparisons (National Center for Public Policy and Higher Education, 2002).

Although some states, such as Florida and Texas, have had statewide tests of students' academic skills for many years, talk of national standards and a national test is again on the horizon, this time led by business, governors, higher education policy leaders, and the U.S. Department of Education (Callan and Finney, 2002; Ewell, 2002b). The state governments' rationale is that more precise information about the educational attainment of their residents could help them make more informed decisions about their investments in higher education. The federal rationale is to move national standards, accountability, and testing from the public school arena into postsecondary education. These discussions now emphasize "educational capital," and the idea that states can quantify this capital based on student performance on a variety of national achievement tests. Such talk has led to concern about the narrow, reductive nature of national tests and pressures to teach to them, as well as concern about a loss of campus autonomy and the thorny problems of publicizing results (Shavelson and Huang, 2003; Allen and Bresciani, 2003).

Strands of Inquiry and Practice in Assessment

Below this political swirl of calls for accountability, assessment encompasses a rich array of practices informed by multiple fields. Some strategies for program evaluation stimulate the ongoing improvement of educational initiatives, rather than simply judge them. Others are influenced by new knowledge about the nature of student learning and development and ways to deepen it. We briefly summarize six major strands of inquiry and practice that shape assessment work.

PROGRAM EVALUATION. The concept of program evaluation in order to foster organizational improvement has grown rapidly in recent decades and many of these practices have had substantial influence on assessment theory and practice; indeed, the influence of evaluation practice has been so great that the terms *evaluation* and *assessment* are often used interchangeably. Stimulated in the 1960s and 1970s by the expansion of federally funded social and educational programs with evaluation expectations, program evaluation encompasses diverse strands and schools of practice. Several trends have influenced evaluation of educational reforms. Qualitative data (and methodologies for gathering them) have gained much wider acceptance alongside quantitative measures of results. Throughout program planning and implementation, there has been a strong emphasis on improvement-oriented (or formative) evaluation methods alongside judgment-oriented (or summative evaluations) that come at an end point. Involving different stakeholder groups, especially the program participants themselves, is increasingly seen as important in helping to frame evaluation, generate information about a program's progress and problems, and then take action based on this information (Argyris, Putnam, and Smith, 1985; Chilemsky and Shadish, 1997; Guba and Lincoln, 1981; Scriven, 1996; Stake, 1995; Patton, 1997; Whyte, 1991; Russ-Eft and Preskill, 2001).

STUDENT LEARNING. Moving from the organizational to the classroom level, a rapidly expanding research-based literature is leading to a more complex understanding of human learning. Increasingly we believe that learning is an active, constructive process of making sense and meaning. It is stimulated by practice, encounters with complex problems, and interactions with other people, and it is developed through self-monitoring and reflection (Vygotsky, 1978; Bruner, 1990; Bruffee, 1993; Bransford, Brown, and Cocking, 1999; Entwistle, 2000; Shepard, 2000; Wiske, 1998; Ramsden, 1992; Candy, 1991).

STUDENT DEVELOPMENT. Paralleling the study of student learning is research on the social, intellectual, and ethical development of students in college as well as key factors that promote or inhibit it. The research identifies reinforcing themes, such as the importance of the social environment that students encounter in college, especially involving their peers, in both their classroom and out-of-class experiences, as well as the value of inclusive learning environments that foster more complex and self-authored levels of meaning-making (Perry, 1970; Belenky, Clinchy, Goldberger, and

Tarule, 1986; Tinto, 1987; Chickering and Reisser, 1993; Astin, 1992; Pascarella and Terenzini, 1991; Kegan, 1982, 1994, Gardiner, 1994; Parks, 2000; Baxter Magolda, 1992, 2001; Smith and Associates, 1997).

LEARNING OUTCOMES ASSESSMENT. The past thirty years has seen the emergence of a body of teaching practice that delineates student learning outcomes and creates assessment occasions that demonstrate them; this work has been significantly shaped by the groundbreaking work at Alverno College. Leaders in this arena argue that the first critical aspect of outcomes assessment is to make complex abilities and the nature of competence more transparent and meaningful to students. The second aspect is to ask students to demonstrate what they know and can do through a variety of performance tasks. The third and final essential element of this type of assessment is observation and feedback: providing students with qualitative information about their work that relates to explicitly stated criteria, and asking them to engage in self-assessment as well (Alverno College Faculty, 1994; Huba and Freed, 2000; Wiggins, 1998).

CLASSROOM ASSESSMENT. Although formal feedback from teachers to students is an essential feature of classroom teaching, *informal* feedback from students to teachers can also be important in shaping the learning environment. The valuable role students can play in providing teachers with information on their learning first gained notice in the late 1980s, when K. Patricia Cross and Thomas Angelo published the first edition of their handbook, *Classroom Assessment Techniques* (1988). Of the rich collection presented, the "one-minute paper" is the most well-known and emblematic of this approach. This simple, easily adopted technique was a breakthrough. Instead of receiving feedback on the class at the end of term on routinized course evaluation surveys that are not often taken seriously by students, faculty members could now easily and informally obtain qualitative feedback right at the moment when they could respond and make adjustments. In turn, students could be asked to reflect more frequently and systematically on their learning progress and questions. Cross and Angelo further refined their collection of formal and informal classroom assessment techniques in a larger handbook in 1993 (Angelo and Cross, 1993).

CLASSROOM RESEARCH AND THE SCHOLARSHIP OF TEACHING AND LEARNING. The 1990s also saw more formal inquiry into the nature of student learning in relationship to teaching practice take shape, and this promises to grow as a national movement. Ernest Boyer's *Scholarship Reconsidered: Priorities of the Professoriate* (1990) advanced a compelling argument for enlarging the focus of academic research and scholarship to include systematic inquiry into the teaching of one's discipline and the resulting student learning. Efforts to "examine not only teacher practice but the character and depth of student learning that results (or does not) from that practice" (Hutchings and Shulman, 1999, p. 13) are only just now developing. How these activities will ultimately play out and what contributions this work might make to teaching and assessment practices are still open questions. Nevertheless, good advice about classroom research practice is emerging (Cross and Steadman, 1996; Wiske, 1998). The Carnegie Academy for the Scholarship of Teaching and Learning, together with the American Association of Higher Education, are leading a major national project on this strand of inquiry.

Assessment as Catalyst for Continuous Improvement

What we call assessment, then, draws on all these bodies of research and practice, each one of them multifaceted and still evolving, with distinctive purposes, intellectual foundations, and specialized vocabularies and professional communities. The essential focus of assessment is on students and their learning in all its complexity and thus on the importance of inquiring about that learning, discovering whether our strategies and results mesh with our aspirations and goals, and most important of all, acting on our new knowledge in order to achieve more effective practices. Higher education, whose historic *raison d'être* has been to cast an empirical and critical eye on everything else in the world, is now moving (or being forced to move) to cast a critical eye upon itself, on its own effectiveness in teaching and student learning, at the classroom, program, and institutional levels. Based on all these bodies of research and practice, campuses are beginning to move away from customary routines of instruction and intuition-about-what-works toward a place where practice is informed by data, dialogue, and conscientious reflection.

The Assessment Context on Campus

Learning community assessment has evolved in tandem with these trends and it encompasses, to one degree or another, all these strands of practice. The high visibility of many learning community programs and the campuswide pressures for fiscal efficiency and external accountability have combined in recent years to put these initiatives (and indeed, all reform initiatives) under considerable scrutiny. Although these pressures present challenges to learning community programs, they also present opportunities. The challenges stem from the reality that on any individual campus, assessment work occurs in a complicated and often contradictory institutional and political context. The opportunities, as we shall see, spring from the collaborative possibilities for teachers in learning communities to undertake assessment in a more integrated fashion.

Although assessment mandates have been expanding for nearly twenty years, actual assessment initiatives too often have remained small, underfunded appendages to campus practice. Most campuses are in "compliance mode," with institutional research offices generating data only to satisfy external mandates. Few campuses have seen these mandates as an opportunity to build institutional curiosity about how well students are learning (Maki, 2002). Most faculty members still resist conversations about assessment, including the kinds of assessment approaches they might find useful, and possibly powerful, in their own classrooms. Much of the terminology of assessment—*student learning outcomes, value-added attainment, quality indicators,* and *proxy measures*—seems alien and mechanistic. Furthermore, external mandates are seen as intrusive on faculty autonomy; faculty feel that these mandates question their competence as teachers and expert evaluators of student work.

Even those who support assessment generally dichotomize this work; classroom assessment is done privately by faculty members, and institutional assessment is seen as the entirely separate, more public work of generating assessment plans or aggregated data to comply with requests from coordinating boards, legislators, or accrediting bodies. This disjunction grows larger with institutional research professionals, often isolated in administrative offices, "crunching numbers" for reports that few faculty members see, much less find useful enough to reflect on.

In this context, most learning community programs are assembled with minimal resources for implementation and assessment. Yet these innovations are pressed to demonstrate credibility almost immediately. Whatever results are generated are of interest to administrators eager to report good news, or skeptics hoping for something less. Like it or not, these new learning community ships are often asked to head into open water and prove seaworthy—in often-turbulent political seas.

Despite all these problems, these reform initiatives present important opportunities for strengthening both learning communities and assessment. At the classroom level, many learning community offerings involve teaching *teams,* who share a student cohort and have a unique chance to design and reflect on the learning activities of the students they see each week. Because they are invested in creating a successful experience for their students, these teams have a fundamental interest in the outcomes of their efforts. Rich professional development is possible here, as teaching teams share learning outcomes and solicit the kinds of formative feedback that strengthen teaching and learning and the community of learners as well.

The assessment of learning community initiatives also offers the opportunity to move forward the assessment agenda of a campus, however small or fragile it might be. Learning community programs have become important sites for assessment of freshman year programs or the general education program, especially when learning community students are compared with the wider student population on campus. Increasingly, those involved with learning community initiatives have begun to collaborate with institutional assessment staff, gauging how well learning community programs meet their goals. In these ways, learning community assessment is becoming a critical venue for making connections between classroom and institutional assessment (Huba, Ellertson, Cook, and Epperson, 2003; Flateby, 2003; Patton, Jenks, and Labissiere, 2003).

The Assessment Cycle

Program development and evaluation ideally revolve around the sequential steps shown in Figure 7.1, which depicts the assessment cycle. Widely known in program evaluation, this cycle is equally appropriate for educational assessment at all levels. Whether the focus is on an

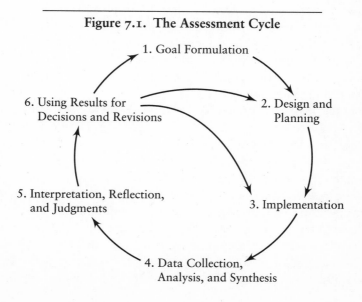

Figure 7.1. The Assessment Cycle

1. Goal Formulation

6. Using Results for Decisions and Revisions

2. Design and Planning

5. Interpretation, Reflection, and Judgments

3. Implementation

4. Data Collection, Analysis, and Synthesis

individual student's learning, a discrete course, a particular learning community offering, or a learning community initiative as a whole, it is a valuable model for framing, understanding, and strengthening our work.

Proceeding in clockwise fashion, assessment begins with Step 1, *goal formulation.* We identify our aspirations for our courses or programs based on our understanding of needs and opportunities. Identifying these needs and opportunities often requires substantial assessment at the outset, because the information we gather about the present reality often shapes the idea for a program. The goals we develop influence Step 2, *design and planning.* At Step 3, *implementation,* we carry out our designs in the actual teaching of a course or delivery of a program, often gathering informal feedback in the process. Step 4 involves *data gathering;* these data might concern student learning or include responses to the learning community on the part of everyone involved with it. During Step 4 we also *analyze and synthesize* this information so that it is useful. Depending on the particular situation, this information might be shared only among teachers and students or the faculty and staff members involved in learning community teaching, or it may be communicated to others who have an interest in the program.

The next two steps in the cycle are especially crucial. Step 5, *interpretation, reflection, and judgment* about our learning community experience and the information that has been distilled from it can lead us to take action, shown in Step 6. Our *decisions and revisions* might relate to any aspect of the program: its goals, design, delivery, and even future assessment work; here, the cycle begins anew. Assessment, then, is not a one-step, terminal undertaking that gets appended at the end of an educational endeavor; rather, it is an integral set of activities that both initiate and thread throughout the entire educational enterprise, included in all the ongoing steps of setting goals, planning and designing, implementing, reflecting, and modifying.

This cycle may seem straightforward and logical in the abstract, but its potential is often not realized in practice. First, it is often practiced haphazardly. Learning community assessment and higher education assessment in general are usually not as systematic as this circle of steps implies. Second, because different individuals frequently work on the different parts, the cycle is often not fully closed: information does not consistently inform program goal setting and design, communicate performance, or inform practice. Third, generally too few people are actively engaged in assessment work. Learning community leaders, like other reformers in higher education, often launch programs with limited time and resources and are often so caught up in the logistics and coordination required for program start-up that they give assessment scant attention. Fourth, some educators, who are acculturated to thinking of evaluation as only coming at the end of a program, put off assessment until the program is more fully developed; then the cycle is undertaken in a rushed and often sloppy fashion.

In this book we argue that learning communities are a reform movement. As such, we need to embrace this assessment cycle as fundamental to learning community work. In a recent article on the challenges facing institutional reform, William Tierney argues, "If change is going to be effective, reformers need to develop a constant information-and-feedback process" (2001, p. 24). If we do not take the multiple steps—gathering baseline data, setting goals, planning carefully to meet our goals, gathering evidence, interpreting and disseminating results, and reflecting and taking action, reformers like ourselves can neither learn from our own practice nor solidify our initiatives in our institutions. Assessment practices enable us to do just this, so as initiators of a reform movement we must embrace them in ways that make our intentions and our results— and this entire assessment cycle—more public.

Furthermore, our assessment work needs to be broadly collaborative. Theorists in the fields of evaluation and organizational learning argue that any program development and evaluation work becomes most valuable to the organization when each of these steps involves key players in inquiry and dialogue, goal setting and reflection, and a willingness to work through differences (Cousins and Earl, 1992; Argyris and Schön, 1996; Senge, 1990). Our experience working with learning community assessment on dozens of campuses bears this out. When learning community assessment has involved teams and creatively engaged multiple stakeholders, and when everyone involved sees assessment as part of their work, the learning community assessment is more robust and the overall initiative is more successful.

Assessment in Learning Community Classrooms

At the heart of assessment on any campus is the assessment that happens in classrooms. It is here that the constant information-and-feedback process that William Tierney advocates is the most immediate and has the greatest potential to strengthen teaching and learning. As learning communities act to reform curricula, they also have the potential to reform assessment in two important ways. First, learning community teaching teams work collaboratively not only to create a connected curriculum but also to coordinate their assessment practices. They can set common expectations across classes to reinforce certain outcomes for student learn-ing. In the more integrated learning communities, teaching teams can design common academic assignments and provide collective feedback on student work. Second and equally important, learning community students share responsibility for the success of the learning community. Their reflec-tions on their learning and their feedback on the state of the learning com-munity are crucial to the success of these programs. When these kinds of intentional, reciprocal assessment environments are developed, the endeavor can be highly worthwhile for faculty and students alike, strength-ening both learning and community. The work that both teachers and stu-dents produce can inform and enrich institutional assessment as well. We will discuss in turn each of these dimensions of classroom assessment.

Collaborative Design of Curriculum and Assessment: Setting Common Expectations

When they teach their individual classes, most faculty members intuitively move through some version of the assessment cycle as they consider their teaching goals and course designs and reflect on how students seem to be learning. Yet their planning-teaching-and-revising process is usually a pri-vate, tacit affair. When faculty members (and student affairs staff, or librarians, or even students) join learning community teaching teams, the necessity for collaborative planning presents a singular opportunity for this assessment cycle to become more public, explicit, and intentional.

Collaborative curriculum planning requires investments of time and energy. Support and professional development for faculty and staff are essential, especially for those new to learning community teaching. As learning community programs have been initiated, curriculum plan-ning institutes or off-campus retreats are often held to provide teaching teams with concentrated time for planning. At many institutions, these retreats have become annual events. These kinds of focused planning occasions offer uninterrupted time for planning and team building, critical ingredients in learning community effectiveness. In an eight-hour block of time, teaching teams can make significant progress in planning a semester-long learning community. At their best, these events are highly stimulating, fostering a spirit of experimentation and risk taking.

In these curriculum planning settings, teaching teams are asked to sit-uate their curriculum planning in Step 1 of the assessment cycle, goal for-mulation, and to see this step as indispensable. Teams may be asked to work with a planning heuristic such as the one presented in Exhibit 7.1. (A more extended rationale for this curriculum planning approach and

Exhibit 7.1. A Heuristic for Learning Community Curriculum Planning

Suggested materials for this activity: Post-its (sticky notes,), 2 × 2 inches or 3 × 5 inches, in various colors. Sheets of flip chart paper and marking pens. Syllabi you have previously used of courses that will now be part of the learning community offering. A list of the overarching intentions or learning outcomes for the entire learning community initiative on your campus—if they exist and if you know them.

1. Start by working individually, setting your syllabi aside at first. Call to mind the knowledge, abilities, and perspectives you are most passionate about enabling your students to gain in your course or discipline. More importantly, consider what genuine, enduring understandings you hope will result from your course. Generate all you can in a few minutes, and write *each* outcome on a separate note. (This activity works best when each person on the learning community teaching team uses a different color note.) Then, prioritize. First, identify what are the most enduring understandings you want students to gain from your course; second, determine what is important for them to know and be able to do; and third, determine what is simply worth their being familiar with. Consider next your larger aspirations for this learning community: What additional outcomes do you hope the learning community experience will allow the students to achieve, beyond the content knowledge, abilities, sensibilities, or perspectives they will gain in your individual course? Write down each of these on individual notes as well.

2. Next, move together with your teaching partners. Describe the aspirations and goals for student understanding and for the learning community you've jotted down as you lay out your sticky notes on a table or paste them onto flip chart sheets. Be sure to add more notes that list general institutional goals or outcomes for the entire learning community initiative, if you know them.

3. Build connections. Working together, arrange and rearrange your notes on the flip chart paper, drawing out key ideas and meaningful connections. Using this material, identify one or more provocative questions that might engage students' interest and help focus the inquiry and learning in your learning community. Here are a few examples:

> How do photography, television, film, and video affect how we feel and act?
>
> How might we minimize the impact of corporate greed and fraud?
>
> What does it mean to be an American in our highly diverse and multicultural society?
>
> Whose responsibility is the cleanup of toxic waste?

Write these provocative questions on individual notes also.

(Continued)

Exhibit 7.1. A Heuristic for Learning Community
Curriculum Planning (*Continued*)

4. Invent one or more integrative learning activities (including, if appropriate, out-of-class experiences) that would speak to your question or questions and foster the understandings or outcomes you have laid out.

5. Based on the questions and activities you have developed, now create ideas for assessment occasions that would ask students to demonstrate what they know and can do and demonstrate their overarching understanding of the courses in the learning community and their overall experience. Each person on the teaching team should be specific about what he or she believes constitutes evidence of understanding for each assessment occasion. Develop appropriate criteria to judge student work.

6. Finally, reconstruct your syllabi or construct a joint syllabus, incorporating the goals for understanding, provocative questions, learning activities, and assessments that you have jointly developed.

another version of this heuristic is presented in Malnarich and Lardner, 2002.) This heuristic invites what is variously called a "designing down" or "designing backward" approach, in that teachers are asked to imagine ideal end points for student learning and then work backward from there to design appropriate learning experiences and assessments (Wiggins and McTighe, 1998; Huba and Freed, 2000; Fink, 2003). A key feature of this approach is to ask faculty members at the outset to set aside the syllabi of their individual courses. Too often, when faculty members start working in a "my syllabus versus your syllabus" mode, planning conversations can devolve into negotiations over coverage—and all kinds of synergistic possibilities may be missed. With this alternative process, faculty members are asked to begin by articulating their goals for *student learning* in each of their classes and their *desired results* for the learning community as a whole. The idea here is *not* to set aside faculty members' important intentions for student learning but rather to *articulate* those intentions and sharpen them and then collaboratively invent ways to reach them through the learning community structure.

This heuristic stresses three important elements that are often overlooked in conventional, coverage-oriented syllabus design: intentions for student understanding, provocative questions, and assessment occasions that focus on demonstrating that understanding. Developing learning communities around these elements can spark deeper connections and synergy among classes, providing a more integrated learning experience for students.

ENDURING UNDERSTANDING. Today, researchers and educational leaders are exploring dimensions of student understanding and working with teachers on ways to foster it (Wiske, 1998; Wiggins and McTighe, 1998; Mentkowski and Associates, 2000). Teachers engage in a process of inquiry about what, for them, constitutes real and "enduring understanding"; what evidence they would accept as demonstrations of that understanding; and how best to communicate these intentions and shape students' learning experiences to build those capabilities (Wiske, 1998). In their highly accessible handbook on curriculum development for schoolteachers, *Understanding by Design* (1998), Grant Wiggins and Jay McTighe present a provocative discussion of student understanding and highlight issues that are equally appropriate for a higher education audience. They also provide extensive advice about assessment strategies that emphasize understanding.

Wiggins and McTighe challenge teachers to clarify their highest priorities for student learning and understanding. Figure 7.2 aims to stimulate teacher thinking and priority setting. In the figure, the space inside the largest ring represents the vast amount of content and abilities that might be developed in a course. Inside that space, teachers are encouraged to identify the information students should encounter. Next, in the middle ring, teachers identify the most essential knowledge and skills the course must teach. These are elements teachers would not want to give up under any circumstances. Finally, in the smallest inner ring, teachers identify what for them would constitute the *most enduring* understanding, the essential hallmarks of learning in their course. It is this understanding,

Figure 7.2. Establishing Curricular Priorities

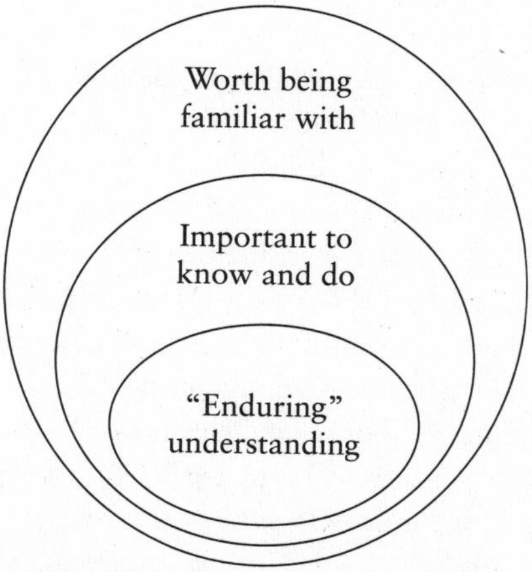

Worth being familiar with

Important to know and do

"Enduring" understanding

Source: Wiggins and McTighe, 1998, p. 10. Copyright 1998 Pearson Education, Inc. Used with permission.

Wiggins and McTighe contend, "that we want students to 'get inside of' and retain after they've forgotten many of the details" (p. 10). For these authors, what is worth understanding usually represents a "big idea" having enduring value beyond the classroom or the course. It usually resides at the heart of the discipline. What is worth understanding is often complex or counterintuitive enough to require serious investigation, and therefore can offer real potential for engaging students. In learning community planning settings, sharing teaching priorities in this fashion can stimulate a new way to share curricular ideas. It can put teachers' goals squarely on the table, and efficiently focus curricular planning toward possible points of intersection.

PROVOCATIVE QUESTIONS. Wiggins and McTighe make a convincing argument for organizing a curriculum around *questions* "rather than simply teaching students the 'expert' answers found in textbooks" (1998, p. 27). Provocative or "essential questions," as they put it, not only draw in learners and give meaning to knowledge and skills to be learned but also sharpen and concentrate the *scope and direction* of inquiry: teachers and students know why they are exploring certain concepts or practicing certain skills because they are foundational in addressing the question at hand. Many learning communities organized around interdisciplinary themes are framed around provocative questions, which serve as the critical connective tissue among the courses. There should be no obvious right answers to these questions. The idea is to engage students, to stimulate inquiry around more questions and ideas. Most importantly, these questions can invite the creation of assessment occasions, in which students can formulate answers of their own.

ASSESSMENT OCCASIONS. Assessment occasions can be arenas for both the development and demonstration of understanding. The notion of demonstrating understanding itself implies deeper learning and some kind of performance in a context.[1] Understanding is not just having knowledge or ability but being able to use it in meaningful ways. Because they link disciplines, explore interdisciplinary questions, and often link classroom and community, learning communities can present stimulating contexts for students to bring together knowledge and skills, synthesize ideas, and demonstrate competence. These are the types of occasions when, as Harvard School of Education's David Perkins puts it, "We ask learners not just to know, but to think with what they know. . . . To gauge a student's understanding, ask the person to do something that puts the understanding to work—explaining, solving a problem, building an argument, constructing a product" (1998, p. 41).

A second and equally important aspect of planning for student assessment occurs as teachers move into conversations about Steps 4 and 5 in the assessment cycle—data gathering, analysis, interpretation, and judgments about student work. It is here that faculty are collaborating on soliciting and evaluating evidence of student learning, and providing students with feedback. Planning conversations should address team members' notions of student competence relative to the goals they set out for the learning community. Critical to the design of assessment occasions is the articulation of criteria for what constitutes excellent, good, acceptable, or unacceptable work and the building of agreements about who will grade what aspect of students' work. Along with the *Understanding by Design* handbook, there are numbers of other helpful resources on student learning outcomes assessment, the development of criteria for evaluating student work, and strategies for making student evaluation meaningful (Walvoord and Anderson, 1998; Huba and Freed, 2000; Wiggins, 1998; Fink, 2003).

Examples of Learning Community Assessments

The following are three examples of learning community assessments that were well rooted in the faculty teams' goals for student understanding and stimulated by provocative questions. In each of these instances, the faculty team clarified their student learning outcomes, created learning activities to develop them, and then invented performance occasions that would bring together the students' knowledge, abilities, and creativity. Although one of these assessments was a culminating end-of-term event, the others were more modest in scale. Yet all three align learning goals with expectations of competence in a stimulating performance setting.

EXAM ON NEW URBANISM AT BELLEVUE COMMUNITY COLLEGE. In a program entitled "The Power of Place," involving English composition and an American studies course in humanities, students were asked to explore the relationships between historical and contemporary Americans in their landscapes and to develop writing skills in that context. Important readings included Gallagher's *The Power of Place* (1994) and Kunstler's *Home from Nowhere* (1996). For an exam, the teachers wanted their students to apply the abstract concepts of "new urbanist design" to a familiar urban landscape. They also wanted the students to demonstrate the writing abilities they had honed over the term, justifying assertions with evidence in logically developed essays with appropriate grammar and syntax. The exam began with a short field trip to a nearby shopping district where rapid growth has stimulated community improvement and gentrification. The exam question was: "In what ways, if any, does Red-mond Town Center put the theories of new urbanist design into practice, and in what ways, if any, does it fail to do so? While you are here, take notes for the essay question. We will meet at the agreed-upon time to return to our classroom to write the essay" (J. Seeman and R. Jeffers, personal communication, May 2002).

DEBATES AND ESSAYS ON ART AND CENSORSHIP AT LAGUARDIA COMMUNITY COLLEGE. At LaGuardia Community College in New York City, the "Freedom and Communication" learning cluster took advantage of a controversy over censorship in the arts to engage students in thinking about censorship and the nature of art itself. In their course cluster that included English composition, the research paper, oral communication, and philosophy, the faculty team wanted students to study a controversy and examine how their positions might change through synthesizing infor-mation before, during, and after actually encountering the object of controversy firsthand. In 1999, then-mayor Rudolf Giuliani was threaten-ing to close the Brooklyn Museum because its art exhibit, "Sensation," was extremely offensive and distasteful to some. In the oral communication class, students studied First Amendment rights and issues involved in the funding of public cultural institutions. The English instructor provided historical background on censorship of the arts in America, and the philosophy instructor introduced philosophical ideas about art. The class then visited the exhibit and interviewed visitors as well as museum staff. Through a series of assignments involving discussion, debates, and essays, the students worked to form their opinions about the art itself, the role of public muse-ums, First Amendment issues, and the controversy raging in the New York City press. Their investigations and debates in class over these issues even-tually led to group research essays and presentations on art and censorship. A final assignment asked students to write a reflection on how their personal views had changed through study of this complex issue (W. Koolsbergen and P. van Slyck, personal communication, September 2002).

PROBLEM-BASED LEARNING AT THE EVERGREEN STATE COLLEGE. A yearlong coordinated studies program for Evergreen freshmen explored the theme "The Olympic Peninsula: Timber, Salmon, and Energy." The students and their faculty studied these three intertwined resource issues in the Pacific Northwest. In the fall quarter students explored stream ecology and salmon issues, in the winter they studied forest ecology and timber issues, and in the spring they focused on energy, particularly hydropower. For the culminating project, the faculty team wanted the students to apply their knowledge and abilities to a complex resource issue and to make sense of competing agendas and the interests of various stakeholders. They chose an issue that has evaded resolution on the Olympic Peninsula for years, and whose primary protagonists (an electric utility and an Indian nation) had recently been locked in a contentious lawsuit. The faculty team presented the students with these questions: "Should the Lake Cushman hydroelectric dams be taken down as a strategy to save endangered salmon? If so, what are the other alternatives for power generation for Tacoma City Light, the utility that owns the dams? If not, what are the other alternatives for restoring salmon habitat on the Skokomish River?" The faculty team purposefully built a mutuality into this question, so that students could not take a stand on one side of this debate without speaking to the needs and interests of the other. At first, students spent considerable time figuring out what they did know and what they did not, and what they needed to learn to take an informed stand on this issue. Then they divided into small research teams to gather information and report back to the whole community. The teams researched how hydroelectric power is generated, what taking down a dam actually involves, what that would do to in-stream flows and salmon habitat, what state, federal, and tribal policies might come into play, and what alternative energy sources were viable. At the term's end, using the knowledge the whole community had acquired over several weeks of work, each student wrote an individual paper in response to the question (R. S. Cole and S. Anthony, personal communication, May 2003).

As these examples show, when teaching teams design learning experiences around common intentions for student learning and develop interesting assessment occasions to illuminate them, learning outcomes can come alive and have meaning. Too often on campuses, the articulation of learning outcomes is merely an abstract exercise carried out in committee, summarized as a list in a report, and sent to external bodies. In learning community programs, learning outcomes can become tangible and provocative for teaching teams because they have actual students and an actual curriculum for which they are taking collective responsibility. Articulating and assessing for learning outcomes are precisely what accrediting bodies are pushing campuses to do in a more systematic fashion; learning communities can become important sites for developing faculty interest and competence in these practices.

Undeniably, it is demanding to describe student understanding and to engage in collaborative design of curriculum and assessments. It involves making our teaching public, taking risks, and thinking in new ways. Most of us are new to this. We have learned our craft privately, in our individual classrooms. Most of us were trained to demonstrate a sophisticated understanding of our discipline and expand on it through research, not to articulate what beginning understandings of our discipline should look like—much less design ways to elicit student demonstrations of this understanding.

In addition, over the past two decades, conceptions of student learning and alternative ways to foster and evaluate it have broadened significantly, with profound implications for both teaching and assessment practice. This is why faculty and staff development that focuses on fostering student learning and understanding and on creating and evaluating student learning performances are so fundamentally important to learning community planning. It has consistently been our experience that when learning community teaching teams are supported with blocks of time to work together on these matters, they make great progress and find this work intensely generative. And the depth and quality of their learning communities show it. As Karen Barrett, associate dean at University of Hartford, reflected, "In retrospect, we think the faculty development and collaborative faculty planning for our learning communities was crucial. The more time certain faculty teams spent in collaborative planning for their learning community, the more successful that learning community was, by every indicator: perceived student learning, actual student learning, and the students' sense of the social benefits as well" (Karen Barrett, personal communication with the authors, October 2002).

Formative In-Class Assessments: Including Student Feedback

Required demonstrations of student learning—through quizzes, tests, performances, papers, lab reports, and so forth—provide teachers with valuable feedback about student understanding. Teachers often work intuitively through Steps 5 and 6 of the assessment cycle, using evidence about student learning to revise their courses. However, information about students' learning and thinking need not emerge only from these formal assessments. In ongoing ways, teachers can—and should—ask students for informal feedback on their learning progress and on the overall state of the learning community. This information can affirm that the program is on course or pinpoint areas for improvement.

It is important to recognize that learning communities are complex social systems. Several teachers and students are engaged in learning collaboratively, and sometimes, living together in a residence hall. These social arrangements are quite different from individual, isolated class-rooms. In learning communities, both curriculum and community evolve dynamically over the weeks of the term with the inevitable highs and lows of group formation and development, and the waxing and waning tensions in the community's work and life together in and out of class. As writing teacher Susan Wyche-Smith (1995) points out, the task of teaching is not to avoid the predictable flat or difficult moments in collaborative learning environments but rather to anticipate and respond to them in ways that are productive and educational.

Therefore, paying attention to students, their learning, and the community overall must become essential practice for faculty and students. Discovering how the community is evolving can stimulate everyone to improve—to make midcourse corrections, to recommit to agreed-upon norms, to strengthen everyone's ability to work interdependently. Everyone, teachers and students alike, should feel mutually responsible for the learning community's success. Regularly attending to this through formative in-class assessments makes this mutual commitment more tangible. As they take note of what and how students are learning, teachers demonstrate their commitment to be responsive to student voices. Asked to undertake honest self-reflection on their learning and the community's well-being, students have to pay closer attention to these matters. The entire community commits itself, then, to building trust and collaboration around cycles of reflection and feedback. Therefore, preparation for learning community teaching should build the capacity of faculty and staff members to undertake formative assessment strategies. Thomas Angelo and K. Patricia Cross's compendium *Classroom Assessment Techniques* (1993) is a rich source of ideas for in-class assessments; many learning community program faculty consider this handbook indispensable. Of the many formative assessments used in learning communities, we describe six here. Some focus entirely on students' learning of academic content or skills, whereas others aim to surface issues of group process and the quality of community in the program.

ASSESSMENTS OF PRIOR KNOWLEDGE. This strategy is essential at the beginning of any instructional encounter; it probes students' knowledge through individual writing and small group discussions. Given students' diverse educational backgrounds and life experiences and the vastness of information technology, it is foolish to assume the level of knowledge and understanding students bring to our subject matter. The information gleaned in these assessments helps teachers discover the nature of students' knowledge and their opinions as well. Most importantly, it helps teachers recognize where to build on what students already know and how to deal with misconceptions. In interdisciplinary learning communities at North Seattle Community College, one of the first classes is often designed around a "What do you already know about. . . ?" exercise that urges students to engage with the program theme and identify what background knowledge and initial ideas they have. For example, in the "The Fall of Empires" program taught in the early 1990s just after the collapse of the Soviet Union, working individually first and then in groups, students described what they knew about the Roman Empire and about the former Soviet Union and Russia. A final question—one that would become an essential question for the learning community—was, "What characterizes a society in decline?" These kinds of opening discussions not only provide a sense of the students' background knowledge but can often generate a set of important, intriguing, and *real* questions that can be developed and explored throughout the term (Smilkstein, 1995).

ONE-MINUTE PAPERS. Mentioned earlier in this chapter, these short in-class feedback memos are probably the most widely disseminated classroom assessment technique. Teachers ask students to spend the last couple of minutes of class answering the following questions: (1) What was the most important idea you learned today? (2) What questions remain uppermost in your mind as we conclude this class session? Students often write this feedback on index cards or half-sheets of paper (for ease of reading) and turn them in anonymously. This simple strategy provides teachers with useful and immediate information on what stood out for the class as important learning and what was confusing and might need clearing up. If given regularly, one-minute papers also can build students' capacity to pay attention to their learning and engage in metacognitive "thinking about thinking" activities.

"INKSHEDDING." A longer variation on the minute paper, *inkshedding* (a seventeenth-century phrase) is a strategy for eliciting anonymous student responses to a specific or open-ended question. As developed by James Reither and his colleagues at St. Thomas University in Canada, and described by Susan Wyche-Smith (1995), inkshedding has three identifying characteristics: the writing is done quickly in five minutes or less; the responses are disseminated to the entire class in some form, oral or written; and the responses are anonymous (although some students may elect to sign their names). Prompting questions are variable, depending on what teachers want to know from students. As Susan Wyche-Smith puts it, "No hard-and-fast rules exist. I use inkshedding when I think it is most needed: when I feel out of touch with students, when discussions bog down, when conflicting views threaten class community, or when I want every student to have a voice on a decision without feeling pressure from the other students or me to decide in a certain way" (Wyche-Smith, 1995, p. 2). How inkshedding is done also is variable. In some classes, the student writing is redistributed and read orally. In others, student teams type up entries for paper or electronic distribution. In larger classes, teachers rotate the inkshedding and writing-up tasks among smaller student groups. What is important is student access to one another's responses, so that everyone in the community can learn what fellow students are thinking and feeling, and if needed can act on this knowledge in constructive ways.

SMALL GROUP INSTRUCTIONAL DIAGNOSIS. Known variously as small group instructional diagnosis (SGID) or student group instructional feedback (SGIF), this structured interview process is usually undertaken just once a term (Clark and Bekey, 1979; White, 1991) to give teachers concentrated feedback on how the course or program is going. On a designated day, a facilitator (not a member of the learning community teaching team but someone familiar with it and its goals) leads the class and solicits feedback while the teachers are absent from the room. The faculty team and the visiting facilitator make clear to the students in advance that this feedback is voluntary, confidential, and anonymous. The facilitator asks the students to form small groups and asks, "What is helping your learning in the program? Also, what improvements would you like to see, and how would you suggest they may be made?" After discussing these questions, the student groups report out to the facilitator who captures perceptions and suggestions on a flip chart. Working with the class, the facilitator then reviews and clarifies the points on the list and asks for a show of hands to identify how many students agree with each statement. This last step is essential because different perspectives often surface; it is critically important for the teachers, and the class as well, to know, for example, that only five students out of a class of fifty think the reading load was too heavy, or that the entire class agrees that the service learning projects, although very time consuming, were an essential part of their learning in the class.

In discrete classes, the SGID generally focuses on the quality of instruction by *one person* and what he or she can do to improve the class. In learning communities, however, the focus of the SGID is broader. Students are asked to reflect on *multiple instructors and the community as a whole*, and what *everyone*—students included—can do to strengthen the learning environment. Soon after the class meeting, the facilitator meets with the teaching team to review and discuss the student feedback and to consider what, if any, midcourse corrections should be made. An important final step occurs when the faculty team members speak with the class about their response to the SGID feedback and discuss possible changes or next steps.

Compiled over time, SGID information can be useful. At De Anza College, the director of professional development is the principal SGID facilitator in both discrete classes and learning communities. As a faculty development leader, he is in a unique role to carry information beyond single classes. Over several years, he has compiled the anonymous feedback that learning community students have provided, noting what, in general, they value particularly in the programs and what they find challenging. He presents these findings in orientation sessions for faculty members and counselors who are joining learning community teaching teams for the first time. This is an impressive example of closing the assessment loop, using formative data for program improvement and faculty development at the same time.

PROCESS EVALUATION. A less formal, shorter, and more public version of the SGID is the plus/minus/delta $(+/-/\Delta)$ exercise that was invented decades ago as a short process improvement technique in collaborative groups (Coover and others, 1978). At the conclusion of a section of a program, or even as a biweekly "check-in," the entire community gathers for a house meeting and all participants are asked to engage in a brief reporting of the pluses (what has gone well this week), the minuses (what has not gone so well), and the deltas (what changes might be made to strengthen learning and the community). Facilitators, variously members of the teaching team or some students, capture this information quickly on flip charts without any discussion at first. Once all the opinions have been generated, the group can decide whether and how to discuss the suggested improvements more extensively. This exercise works powerfully when there is a high degree of trust in the community and student maturity about talking through issues in full view of their teachers. Like the SGID strategy, this exercise also works to situate responsibility for improvement with everyone, students and teachers alike.

STUDENT SELF-ASSESSMENT. Finally, many learning communities involve students in self-reflection and in writing formal self-assessments of their learning. As mentioned in Chapter Four, reflection and self-assessment are core practices of learning community pedagogy. In engaging students in self-assessment, faculty members are not asking students to give themselves grades. Rather, they are developing their abilities to make judgments about their own work, using the same criteria that the faculty members are using (Loacker, 2000). Self-assessment exercises can also ask students to describe their learning in more open-ended, qualitative ways, identifying how it is meaningful, and connecting this learning to other learning they have done or to larger considerations about the future. Student self-assessments are not anonymous, and they may be graded or not, depending on the faculty members' purposes for the reflective work.

Sustained reflection on their learning is unfamiliar to most students, but like any skill, self-assessment develops and deepens with practice and feedback (Mentkowski and Associates, 2000; MacGregor, 1993). Self-reflective writing can begin the first day of class with students reflecting on the reasons they enrolled in the learning community, their expectations for the experience, and their questions at the start. As the program progresses, many faculty members engage students with short reflective writing assignments or ongoing journal work to build their capacity for self-reflection. Student self-assessments can also take the form of "post-writes," self-evaluative afterthoughts accompanying a paper, lab report, or other work, which describe the processes and challenges associated with producing that work. Self-assessments can also be formal writing that bridges theory and practice, linking classroom content with service learning, or preparation for a practicum with the fieldwork itself (Eaton and Patton, 2003). Self-assessments can also take the shape of essays that present and reflect on a portfolio of work presented at the end of the term. Or they can be more global reflections in which students comment on the entire learning community experience and consider what will be taken forward from it.

The reflective talking and writing students undertake can be valuable for deepening their engagement and development in any educational setting, but it can be particularly important in learning communities where students are asked to draw connections among ideas, consider multiple perspectives, and work interdependently with others. Written student self-assessments can also can become important evidence for wider assessment work (Moore and Hunter, 1993).

In her presidential address to the American Educational Research Association, "The Role of Assessment in a Learning Culture," Lorrie Shepard explored "the kind of assessment that can be used as part of instruction to support and enhance learning" (2000, p. 10). She laid down this challenge: "Could we create a learning culture where students and teachers would have a shared expectation that finding out what makes sense and what doesn't is a joint and worthwhile project, essential to taking the next steps in learning?" (p. 10). Shepard asks teachers to make it common practice to close the assessment cycle systematically by regularly gathering and using information about student learning. What students say in these in-class, formative assessment activities—about what has been most meaningful, about what connections they are making and what questions they are now asking, about what has worked well for them or what has been confusing or challenging—provides teachers with an invaluable window on student learning and development and gives them practical information for taking their next steps. Equally important, when these kinds of activities occur frequently and consistently, when teachers and students regularly pay attention to their own and one another's learning, Shepard's ideal of a "learning culture" comes within our reach.

Assessment of Learning Community Programs

We have argued that making the assessment cycle (see again Figure 7.1) collaborative, explicit, and complete can bring focus to learning curriculum planning and strengthen classroom teaching. Similarly, systematically going through this cycle can strengthen learning community program assessment as well. In this section of the chapter, we argue for the necessity of embracing both agendas: proving and improving learning communities. Then we explore some distinctions between assessment and research. Next, we suggest a set of planning questions for embedding assessment activities in the full range of learning community program implementations. Finally, we discuss the current state of learning community assessment and offer suggestions for how to make it more robust.

Proving and Improving Learning Communities

Like any ambitious reform initiative, learning community programs must embrace the two major strands of program assessment simultaneously— that of *improving* programs as they develop and that of *proving* that they are worth undertaking at all. Learning communities represent "new work" on a campus: new ways of structuring coursework; new commitments to community, diversity, active learning, curricular integration, and reflection; new working relationships that cross departmental lines and sometimes involve community partners as well. What makes learning communities stimulating for faculty and staff members is this newness and the spirit of experimentation that can be sparked as a result. Precisely because these initiatives represent emerging work, it is important to let them *be* new, to encourage invention and creativity. Nevertheless, it is equally important to gather feedback and reflect on these endeavors so they can be improved *as they develop.*

At the same time, learning community initiatives face the institutional scrutiny that confronts any reform initiative. They are under pressure to prove themselves, to justify the investments of resources and human energy required to establish them. For many learning community leaders this pressure feels burdensome, yet the reality is that no reform will be sustained if it does not demonstrably address institutional needs.

The work of both improving and proving learning communities, then, necessitates constant information-and-feedback processes. These processes are demanding enough to require a team effort. The assessment team should be constituted as a supporting task force to the learning community leadership group. The assessment coordinator should be someone other than the learning community program leader, not only to divide up the work but also to keep the roles of program implementation and assessment appropriately separate. Preferably, assessment teams are made up of individuals with program evaluation and assessment expertise and members of teaching teams. Occasionally, graduate or undergraduate students also serve on these teams.

Program Assessment and Evaluation Versus Research

Some clarification of the three terms *assessment, evaluation,* and *research* is appropriate. As the field of program assessment has evolved over the past two decades, it has incorporated many of the principles and practices of the larger field of program evaluation, and the terms *program assessment* and *program evaluation* are often used together or interchangeably. Like program evaluation, program assessment focuses on a particular organizational context and aims to provide information for both decision making and improvement. Like program evaluation, program assessment has the dual purposes of gathering formative information throughout the process to inform the program and strengthen it, and producing summative information at the end to develop more comprehensive judgments about the program, and in some cases, disseminate those judgments to external audiences.

In many program assessment-evaluation undertakings in higher education, the term *research* frequently appears, and it too is often used interchangeably with the terms program assessment and program evaluation. To muddy matters further, the units that gather assessment data are often called "Offices of Institutional Research." Muddier still, a participatory approach to formative program evaluation has emerged in the last twenty years, with the name *action research*. Although some practices of educational program assessment-evaluation overlap with those of educational research, there are important distinctions. Many textbooks on evaluation in organizations stress these differences; they reason that although program evaluation-assessment and research employ similar methods of data collection and analysis, these two endeavors "are initiated for different purposes; they respond to different kinds of . . . questions and needs; and they communicate and report their findings in different ways and to different groups" (Russ-Eft and Preskill, 2001, p. 9).

Because the information-gathering strategies in program assessment and evaluation are similar to those used in social science research, misunderstandings abound over the methodologies, purposes, and limitations of these efforts. Exhibit 7.2 offers some distinctions between program assessment and research as they relate to higher education reform initiatives.

To be sure, formal learning community research is important work, and its findings have made significant contributions to learning community theory and practice. In the early 1990s under the auspices of the National Center on Postsecondary Teaching, Learning, and Assessment, Vincent Tinto and his students at Syracuse University conducted parallel studies of learning community programs at three different institutions (Tinto, Goodsell-Love, and Russo, 1993); their widely disseminated findings elaborated a theory of student retention and prompted many new learning community initiatives. With support from the Lumina Foundation, Tinto is now undertaking a new research effort focusing on learning communities for underprepared students. As of 2003, over thirty doctoral dissertations or major studies have examined the effects of learning communities at single institutions, and several other studies have examined learning community outcomes across multiple institutions (Taylor, Moore, MacGregor, and Lindblad, 2003). This research has been important and informative.

Yet as Upcraft and Schuh argue in "Assessment Versus Research: Why We Should Care About the Difference" (2002), programs cannot always be assessed with the fine detail of research studies because of limitations on resources and time and the pressures of planning calendars and campus politics. What determines the focus of program assessment is usually not a researcher's hypothesis, but previously agreed-upon questions that need to be answered in order to make decisions about the program during a certain window of time. Assessment is much more embedded in ever-changing campus politics than research is, and the information that assessment generates should have much more immediacy in informing and strengthening local practices.

Exhibit 7.2. Distinctions Between Assessment and Research in Educational Initiatives

	Assessment	Research
Purpose	Provide information to guide decision making in a particular context, strengthen programs, and stimulate improvement.	Develop theories and new knowledge. Inform practice in general.
Audiences	Multiple audiences, mostly internal ones on campus: key decision makers and other stakeholders and teachers and student affairs professionals involved in the delivery of the program, occasionally external stakeholders such as state-level higher education boards or accrediting bodies.	Other researchers, and scholars, practitioners and leaders interested in research results.
Planning and design	Nested in program planning and goals, and specific purpose of the assessment activity. Pays close attention to audience, stakeholders, and communities of practice on the campus.	Nested in literature review, existing research, and hypotheses or research questions.
Identification of questions	Often done collaboratively, with attention to or in response to institutional stakeholders' priorities.	Often done by the researchers on their own and in building upon previous research; may involve stakeholders' questions or issues.
Data collection and analysis	Quantitative and qualitative data-gathering methods, with both externally or internally developed protocols.	Quantitative and qualitative data-gathering methods with both externally or internally developed protocols.
Reliability and validity	Attempts to be objective and credible within constraints of time, resources, and expertise. Is rooted in campus values and politics; generalizability of findings is not the primary goal.	Attempts to be objective and value-free; seeks to establish findings that are generalizable.

(Continued)

Exhibit 7.2. Distinctions Between Assessment and Research in Educational Initiatives (*Continued*)

	Assessment	Research
Timetables	Often driven by the academic calendar, curricular planning schedules, budgeting deadlines, or reporting deadlines based on funding-grant expectations or accreditation timetables.	May or may not face time or resource constraints.
Recommendations	Implications-recommendations are campus-specific, with the aim to inform and improve educational programs; they are communicated to key decision makers and other stakeholders in a position to act on them.	Implications-recommendations usually focus on research problems or lines of inquiry for future research; occasionally make generalizable recommendations for practice.
Formal dissemination of information	Primarily for internal use; reports to stakeholders on the campus via paper reports or campus Web sites; may be communicated externally to accrediting bodies or shared in professional networks.	Dissemination distribution networks; findings may be published in journals or books or reported at conferences on research or practice.

Source: Adapted in part from a similar chart in Russ-Eft and Preskill, 2001, pp. 8–9. Adapted by permission of Basic Books, a member of Perseus Books, L.L.C.

Acknowledging that learning communities are complex interventions, we do our best to identify our hoped-for outcomes and to gather and interpret the most credible information we can to inform our practices. Yet assessment methodology and findings are often dismissed, questioned, or attacked on some campuses on the grounds that the assessment did not fully adhere to certain research methods, statistical protocols, or a robust enough experimental design. Upcraft and Schuh advise that assessment investigators be clear about their intentions and their methods for the assessment program and that they be candid about the overall limitations of their efforts, including those of time and resources. We also suggest that collaboration from the outset with the institutional research and assessment office can give credibility to learning community assessment and save time and resources as well.

Embedding Assessment in Learning Community Planning and Implementation

Much of the work of program assessment involves developing, capturing, and disseminating different kinds of information over the assessment cycle. Ideally, learning community assessment should generate information to inform planning at the start, illuminate practice and stimulate improvements throughout, and then, at the end, give a picture of results that can inform decision making. In Exhibit 7.3, we suggest a set of questions for the learning community program assessment team to work through as they develop their assessment plan and carry it out. We will comment briefly on each of these sets of questions.

SURVEYING THE LANDSCAPE AND LINKING TO ONGOING ACTIVITIES. Assessment work should begin during the program development stage with goal formation and planning (Steps 1 and 2 of the assessment cycle; see again Figure 7.1). Forging alliances with campus assessment personnel, the assessment team should learn what assessment work is under way and ask what existing data can inform learning community planning. Data from admissions, rates of retention, entry to certain majors, graduation rates, and student satisfaction surveys can guide the development of goals, choices about curricular structure and courses, and choices about pedagogical practices as well. Critical areas are often first-term adjustment needs and developmental opportunities, "high-risk courses" (those with consistently high rates of withdrawal and failure), key gateway or prerequisite courses, and developmental courses. If the learning community program is already under way when the assessment is initiated, it is still worthwhile to address these questions and assemble baseline information.

DESCRIBING THE PROGRAM'S INTENTIONS AND DESIGN. Assessment can make a crucial contribution to the learning community initiative at the outset by helping the planners clarify their goals, their intended student audiences, and their overall rationale for program design. As indicated in Figure 3.1, "Ascending Steps of Learning Community Goals" (see Chapter Three), goals for learning community programs can be extensive. Goal-setting conversations are essential and valuable, as program leaders and key decision makers clarify their often-divergent intentions for the initiative.

Goals and intentions are an obvious starting place, but equally important are understandings about the student audience, the nature of investment in the program, and the curricular and pedagogical environment to be created.

Exhibit 7.3. Planning Questions for Learning Community Assessment

Surveying the Landscape and Linking to Ongoing Activities

1. What is the state of institutional assessment on our campus, and how might we forge productive alliances with ongoing assessment activities?
2. What information might already be available through ongoing institutional research or assessment activities, and how might we obtain it?
3. What institutional data about student or curricular needs can help inform learning community design?

Describing Program Intentions and Design

4. What are the goals for the learning community initiative—for students, for those on the teaching teams, for the curriculum and the institution?
5. Who is the student audience the program aims to reach and what is the rationale for targeting that audience?
6. What kind of curricular and pedagogical environments should the learning community have?
7. What kind of collective understanding and responsibility are there for these goals among the teaching teams and others who support the learning community initiative? Is this does not exist, how can we foster it?
8. What specific investments is the institution now making in the learning community program?

Clarifying What Evidence Is Needed

9. What describable or measurable outcomes would be most appropriate for determining how well the program is reaching our goals—including outcomes for students, teaching teams, curriculum, institution, and community-industry partners, if any?
10. Besides ourselves and key learning community leaders, who are the other stakeholders who should receive information about the initiative and its results? What matters to them, and what will count as evidence?
11. What types of information (from teaching teams, from others who support the learning community program, and from the students themselves) would be most useful to help us understand and strengthen the program?
12. What information might be available from assessment activity in the learning communities themselves? How might we build relationships with teaching teams so that we can obtain such information?

Agreeing on Time Lines and Responsibilities

13. What are the most cost-effective and time-effective strategies for gathering this evidence?
14. What is a realistic time line?
15. Who will be responsible for gathering evidence? Who will be involved in analysis?
16. Do we have the right team to carry out this assessment activity, both to establish credibility and to shoulder the work? Who else needs to be drawn into this effort to accomplish these tasks?

Exhibit 7.3. (*Continued*)

Communicating and Using Results

17. What assessment results need to be communicated to whom, and when?
18. How and when should learning community program leaders and teachers share and reflect on assessment results in order to strengthen the initiative?
19. How and where should we archive the history of the initiative and the assessment results?

The assessment team should build a record of Steps 1, 2, and 3 of the assessment cycle (see again Figure 7.1) so that audiences of assessment reports will have a detailed picture of the learning community program.

In his comprehensive book on assessment, Alexander Astin advocates the use of an inputs-environment-outputs (or I-E-O) framework as a strategy for fully describing and assessing an educational program intervention (Astin, 1991). Astin represents his I-E-O model with the triangle shown in Figure 7.3. To provide a complete story of educational interventions, Astin argues, we first need to describe who the inputs (the students) are as they enter the program. Second, we need to describe the environment of the program: the kinds of curricular, co-curricular, and pedagogical environments we put in place to strengthen student success, student learning, and so forth. And third, we need to portray outputs or program outcomes. For Astin, the story of an educational intervention is only complete when inputs and environment are described so that we can better understand what kind of "value added" has come from our program. The purpose of the model is "to allow us to correct or adjust for such input differences in order to get a less biased estimate of the comparative effects of different environments on outputs," using various forms of statistical analyses (1991, p. 17).

Figure 7.3. Astin's Inputs-Environment-Outputs Framework

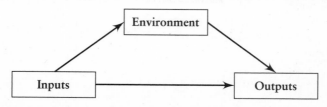

Source: Astin, 1991, p. 18. Reproduced with permission of Greenwood Publishing Group, Inc., Westport, Connecticut.

Astin's model is useful for building a fuller assessment picture. We suggest some important elaborations on this framework, however, in Figure 7.4. Along with describing student characteristics at the inputs point, we believe it is essential to capture other inputs, such as the program's stated intentions, the composition of teaching teams, and the nature of investments in the program (resources, administrative structure, curricular planning, and faculty and staff development). As Astin suggests, it is also valuable to describe the teaching and learning environment of the learning community offerings: the curricular and co-curricular elements, and the pedagogical practices. Descriptions of program outcomes naturally focus on students, but our intentions for learning communities are also to create stronger communities of practice around teaching and to influence curricula and institutions in positive ways. Learning community assessment should therefore focus on these dimensions as well. Finally, assessments should present conclusions and recommendations based on an analysis of inputs and intentions, environment, and outcomes (we will discuss this further in the following section).

An obvious reason for providing this information is to describe the program itself as fully as possible. Often, those outside the learning community initiative have a limited understanding of the actual curriculum

Figure 7.4. A Learning Community Assessment Framework

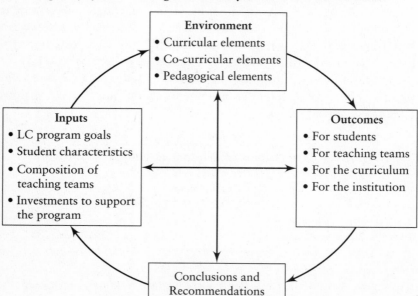

Environment
• Curricular elements
• Co-curricular elements
• Pedagogical elements

Inputs
• LC program goals
• Student characteristics
• Composition of teaching teams
• Investments to support the program

Outcomes
• For students
• For teaching teams
• For the curriculum
• For the institution

Conclusions and Recommendations

and pedagogy of learning communities, or the kinds of investments these programs require. A second, equally important reason for doing this is that learning community programs evolve over time and institutions often experience turnovers in leadership. Thus, it is essential that assessments fully tell the learning community story, with all the elements depicted in Figure 7.4. If these elements are overlooked in assessment reports, it is impossible to know what kind of learning community program was put in place at a particular time or what to conclude about a program's effectiveness or how best to strengthen it.

CLARIFYING WHAT EVIDENCE IS NEEDED. To plan for data gathering, analysis, and synthesis (Step 4 in the assessment cycle), the assessment team must determine what types of evidence will best portray the program's intended outcomes—for students, for involved staff and faculty, and for the institution. They also need to ask what issues are important and what evidence matters most for making decisions about program improvement. Key decision makers at the institution should also be brought into these conversations and consulted about what evidence of program outcome is most important. We cannot stress enough that the indicators of program effectiveness and strategies for gathering that information need to be closely aligned with learning community program goals.

As Figure 3.1 indicates, a variety of outcomes are put forward for these programs. Exhibit 7.4 summarizes strategies and instruments that are commonly used for gathering evidence related to these goals. Obviously, learning community assessors have an extensive array of quantitative and qualitative strategies from which to choose. In any program evaluation, it is fundamental good practice to use multiple measures and gather a variety of data. Different types of information should be brought together to create a full picture of the learning community students and their teachers, the teaching environments, and their outcomes.

Many learning community programs geared to freshmen use one of the nationally distributed surveys appropriate to first-year college students. Administered at the beginning or end of the first year, these surveys can yield valuable information about student expectations and experiences.[2] All questionnaires have versions appropriate to community college learners, and most are set up so that institutions can add their own, more locally specific questions. Results can reveal useful data about students' attitudes and expectations and about their experiences and degrees of engagement in activities related to successful adjustment and engagement in college. The statistical reliability and validity of these surveys give them credibility, and because many are benchmarked by type of institution, results from

Exhibit 7.4. Strategies Used to Portray Learning Community Outcomes

LC Outcomes for Students

Goals	Types of Evidence
Good participation and enrollment	Student admissions indexes Student performance on intake diagnostic/ placement tests Demographic data (gender, race/ethnicity, age, and other information) College Student Survey (CIRP) College Student Expectations Questionnaire (CSXQ) College Student Inventory (Noel-Levitz) Locally developed beginning-of-program questionnaires that ascertain how students discovered the program, why they enrolled, what their aspirations are for the experience
Good response to the program, increased interaction with peers, faculty, student affairs professionals	Course evaluations; locally designed questionnaires Your First College Year Survey Survey of Student Engagement (NSSE/CCSSE) Student Satisfaction Inventory (Noel-Levitz) College Student Experiences Questionnaire or Community College Student Experiences Questionnaire (CSEQ, CCSEQ) In-class observations by third-party evaluators Focus group and individual interviews, student self-assessments, end of-program reflective conversations
Better retention, progress to degree	Institutional data on course completion, persistence to subsequent terms or years Credit attempted in subsequent terms Completion of general education requirements; transcript analysis Matriculation to advanced work or major by underprepared students or underrepresented groups of students Increased tuition income resulting from higher retention Higher rates of transfer from two- to four-year institutions Graduation rates
Achievement and demonstration of learning outcomes	GPA in learning community courses or grades in certain courses; reduced rates of withdrawal and failure in learning community classes Grade distribution patterns, especially for more at-risk students

Exhibit 7.4. (*Continued*)

Goals	Types of Evidence
	GPA in subsequent terms, or grades in subsequent related coursework
	Successful entry to and success in certain majors
	Pass rates and success on writing or mathematics proficiency tests; other standardized tests, institutional proficiency exams, licensing exams for professions
	Student/course/program portfolios of student work
	Student self-evaluations
Diversity and citizenship understandings and skills, leadership skills, new or affirmed values aspirations, commitment	Locally developed questionnaires
	Focus group or individual interviews, end-of-program reflective conversations
	In-class observations by third-party evaluators
	Reports of student life or service learning staff on student engagement in student leadership activities, service learning
	Student self-assessments
Academic maturity, self-confidence, motivation	Class attendance patterns, in-class participation
	Consultation with faculty, student affairs units
	In-class observations by third-party evaluators
	Locally developed questionnaires, student self-assessments
	Focus group or individual interviews, end-of-program reflective conversations
Student intellectual development	Learning Environment Preferences Questionnaire
	Measure of Intellectual Development essay (MID)
	Student self-assessments (rated with MID protocol)

LC Outcomes for Faculty Members and Others on Teaching Teams

Goals	Types of Evidence
Good participation	Demographic information
	Questionnaires or interviews that ascertain what drew these individuals to learning community teaching, what their aspirations are
Good response, higher levels of satisfaction, deepened understandings, increased self-confidence, motivation, leadership	Individual and focus group interviews, end-of-program reflective conversations
	Locally designed questionnaires
	Course-program portfolios
	Teaching portfolios or self-evaluations

(*Continued*)

**Exhibit 7.4. Strategies Used to Portray Learning
Community Outcomes (*Continued*)**

Goals	Types of Evidence
Enlarged pedagogical repertoire, widened scholarly interests, new understandings of other disciplines	Individual and focus group interviews, end-of-program reflective conversations Locally designed questionnaires Course-program portfolios Narrative evaluations from students Conference presentations and publications Teaching portfolios or self-evaluations

LC Outcomes for Institutions

Goals	Types of Evidence
Better understanding and general response	Individual and focus group interviews End-of-program reflective conversations Locally designed questionnaires
Better interdepartmental collaboration	Evidence of collaborative structures-efforts (formal and informal) New curricular initiatives
Good fit with institutional goals	Admissions-catalogue-Web site information Learning community program reports, promotional materials Reaccreditation reports and feedback
Improved campus climate	Surveys of students and staff Residence hall occupancy rates Records of incident reports, drinking, and substance abuse Use of study areas and libraries
Strengthened curricular offerings	Revisions to general education programs, freshman year curricular offerings, study in minor or major Course or program portfolios Reaccreditation reports and feedback
Achievement of diversity-related goals	Patterns of achievement, entry to certain majors, and graduation rates and graduate school admission for women and students of color Cultural pluralism emphases in learning community courses, co-curriculum Individual or focus group interviews with students, staff, and faculty Reaccreditation reports and feedback

Exhibit 7.4. (*Continued*)

Goals	Types of Evidence
Increased cost efficiencies	Institutional data on enrollment patterns, student retention, student progress to degree, graduation rates, and comparative costs or resulting cost savings
Supportive reward systems	Hiring, tenure, and promotion policies; teaching awards
	Special stipends or grants for learning community curriculum planning, assessment efforts, or research projects on learning community effects
	Course/program/faculty/student affairs portfolios
	General faculty and staff professional development activities
	Professional development days; planning retreats or summer institutes related to learning community development
Strengthened institutional culture, enhanced institutional reputation, values, aspirations, and commitment	Institutional publications
	Individual or focus group interviews with students, staff and faculty, parents, alumni
	Design or redesign of classroom or residence hall space to support learning community initiative
	Grants and fundraising initiatives using learning communities as strategy
	Reaccreditation reports and feedback

one institution can be compared with data from peer institutions. If any of these surveys is administered to large segments of entering classes, they might provide useful comparative data about students in the learning communities and about students not enrolled in these programs; this information can also be compared to data gathered at institutions.

It is also essential to gather formative information about the experiences of involved students, faculty, and staff—data that can contribute directly to understanding and improving the initiative. As we have already suggested, substantial formative information can be generated naturally in learning communities themselves as part of ongoing processes of teaching, learning, and reflection. In reflective conversations, formal midcourse feedback sessions, written self-assessments, and portfolios of classwork, students provide invaluable windows on their experience and ideas for program improvement. The assessment team should forge relationships with learning community teaching teams to explore how information from in-class assessments can be gleaned and shared in constructive ways.

Some of the most useful information can be drawn from assessment activities that already occur in learning community classrooms. Reflective discussions and focus groups are regular features of learning communities at many institutions; assessment teams can sit in, distilling perceptions of program effectiveness. Small group instructional diagnosis (SGID) data, described earlier, can be mined from several programs for patterns about what works and what does not work for students in learning communities. At the end of a term, some programs hold on-campus or off-campus retreats so students and their teachers can reflect on the whole term. These discussions, often held with assessment team members, can bring a community to a meaningful close while also providing teachers and assessors with significant information that they never would have been able to glean from more content-oriented papers or exams.

Written student self-assessments (also called self-evaluations) are another excellent source of information and are a fixture of many learning community programs. Students are generally asked to write them for in-class purposes, but they also can sign release forms so that these papers can be read anonymously for program assessment. These essays can be evaluated in several ways: scored as writing samples, analyzed for their content, or rated in terms of student intellectual development, using the Measure of Intellectual Development (MID) protocol. The MID, derived from William Perry's scheme of student intellectual development, examines and uses a quantitative scale to rate the ways in which students describe knowledge and the roles of teachers and learners, peers, and evaluation in their classrooms. MID essays are particularly valuable because they engage students in a meaningful reflective writing task while at the same time providing teachers and assessors with both qualitative and quantitative information about student learning and development (Moore and Hunter, 1993; MacGregor, 1987; Avens and Zelley, 1990).

Portfolios of student work are another rich source of evidence about student learning. Dozens of individual learning community programs ask students to create portfolios, but a few institutions, such as New Century College at George Mason University, the Hutchins School of Liberal Studies at Sonoma State University, and Portland State University, have made portfolios a centerpiece both of learning community pedagogy and institutional assessment practices. Portland State's portfolio assessment practices are particularly notable because all first-year students are asked to create a summative portfolio of their year's work in a learning community that relates specifically to the university's general education learning outcomes. Most of the students in the program now create electronic portfolios on personal Web sites. Each summer, teams of faculty read randomly selected portfolios from each Freshman Inquiry program. Using rubrics related to the general education outcomes, these teams score each portfolio and these scores are communicated as feedback to each Freshman Inquiry teaching team. Through these processes, Portland State teachers have important conversations not just about the program's effectiveness but also about first-year students and their learning experiences (Patton, Jenks, and Labissiere, 2003).

All of these embedded assessment strategies capture the students' voices and reveal their experiences and ability to make meaning in these programs—so essential to understanding what affects their learning and development and whether these programs are producing the kind of outcomes they aspire to. These strategies also serve to strengthen learning and community *in* learning community classes while contributing important program assessment evidence as well.

AGREEING ON TIME LINES AND RESPONSIBILITIES. We suggest that the assessment team set realistic priorities for gathering baseline information about the learning community program that describes the inputs-investments, environment, and outcomes elements suggested earlier. Starting small, taking a first-things-first approach, makes obvious sense. Over time, as the assessment team builds capacity and confidence, their activities can be broadened and expanded to more ambitious levels. As mentioned earlier, alliances with existing assessment offices can be advantageous: the learning community assessment team may be able to tap into its expertise and credibility, use existing institutional data, or coordinate with ongoing activities. Also, many assessment teams have profitably engaged students in their work by involving individual students on assessment task forces, or even asking research methods and statistics classes to assist with information gathering and analysis.

COMMUNICATING AND USING RESULTS. Steps 5 and 6 of the assessment cycle—communicating, interpreting, and reflecting on assessment information, and making decisions and revisions as a result—are critical elements of the information-and-feedback process. Assessment activities are not complete if they simply report program outcomes; also needed is a communication strategy *and* a conversation strategy for building awareness and understanding of the initiative and making good use of the results. Here is where many campus assessment projects flag, and learning community assessment is no exception. As educational researcher Patrick Terenzini puts it, "Most assessment programs lack a carefully thought-out dissemination plan for converting findings into information, and getting that information into the hands of people who can act on it. Dissemination plans should receive as much care, attention, and discussion as study designs" (2001, p. 12). We would add that *action plans* should receive care, attention, and discussion as well: assessment results have the most value when they lead to steps that improve the learning community initiative.

Sharing and using assessment results are matters of political strategy. The entire learning community leadership team should think through who the different audiences are for assessment results; whether these individuals are friendly, neutral, or unreceptive to this reform initiative; and how and when results should be presented to assure the ongoing development of the learning community initiative. Formal assessment reports are important, and many learning community initiatives create Web site access to them. Shorter synopses, fact sheets, and executive summaries may be all that busy individuals will take time to read. Often, assessment reports do not get the attention they deserve because they are simply too dense and confusing to wade through; it is a worthwhile investment to make both full reports and synopses readable and visually attractive.

The dissemination of results should be linked to planning for meetings in which they can be discussed and acted on. The assessment team and the learning community leadership group should strategize together about the timing and design of these occasions. These meetings can take a variety of forms, from briefing sessions with campus committees or administrators to annual planning retreats of learning community leadership groups to faculty and staff development activities. Scheduling meetings with key communicators and decision makers to discuss reports can often ensure that they are reviewed.

Finally, learning community programs need an official archive of some kind, an agreed-upon place for key program material. Learning community program archives can serve as a valuable resource center of syllabi, promotional information, records of planning meetings and faculty and staff development activities, assessment reports, and other artifacts that reflect the programs' development. As the teachers and the leaders of the learning community initiative change, and as there is turnover in administrative personnel as well, these resources, and a formal record of the program's history, are valuable to have in one place.

Information and Feedback: Using Assessment to Strengthen and Sustain Learning Communities

Ideally, these questions will stimulate teams to consider the entire assessment cycle and develop strategies for carrying it out in ways appropriate to their campus context. As we reflect on this cycle and the state of learning community assessment, we see several ways that information and feedback can contribute more powerfully to strengthening these reforms. *Put simply, learning community initiatives could benefit from more information and more systematic feedback.* First, assessment reports need to present more detailed information about the *nature* of learning community initiatives, and over time assessment practices should move to focus more on the learning of both students and teachers. Second, assessment results should be used more systematically to strengthen initiatives. To do this, institutions should create more occasions for collaborative reflecting and acting on assessment results.

Creating Fuller Pictures of Learning Community Interventions

Learning community assessment reports are still evolving in their depth and sophistication. A recent study of 118 institutional assessment reports conducted by the National Learning Communities Project concluded that although these reports describe some results, the information they provide about *the nature of learning community interventions* is highly uneven or absent altogether. Using the elements of the learning community assessment framework shown in Figure 7.4 as an ideal, this study found that assessment reports often did not present much information about the inputs—the student population who enrolled in the program. Few reports discussed whether these students were the intended audience in terms of academic preparation or ethnic diversity, or whether they were similar or different from comparison groups. This limited information not only fails to provide useful data for evaluating the programs' recruitment efforts and for designing curriculum and pedagogy but also leaves these assessments vulnerable to the criticism that the learning community's success was a result of a "volunteer effect"—that is, that already motivated students or students who were likely to be successful self-selected into the program (Taylor, Moore, MacGregor, and Lindblad, 2003).

This study also found that although most reports provided some information about the intentions of the learning community initiative, few described the particular curriculum, pedagogy, or classroom assessment strategies established to meet those goals. Fewer still described program investments (faculty and staff development, capital expenditures, or other types of program support)—critical information for decision making. Few studies examined outcomes for teaching teams, whose reflections and ongoing commitment to learning community initiatives are crucial. Nearly all the reports indicated that their learning communities were successful and well received, and in a number of instances, greatly so. Yet at this point, learning community assessment has not identified what practices make a significant difference to students or to their demonstrated learning. In short, we have much more to learn and document about learning community students, curricular designs, pedagogical strategies, costs, and the effects of these programs on those who teach in them.

In addition, the assessment reports reveal that most assessments focus on outcomes related to the lowest steps on the staircase of learning community goals (Figure 3.1). To date, evidence gathering has focused on student course completion and persistence, student achievement as measured by grades, and satisfaction surveys of students and instructional teams. To be sure, the news is very promising: the reports indicate that learning communities generally increase student retention and academic success, and satisfaction levels are high, both among learning community students and their teachers. In learning community assessment, retention, academic success, and satisfaction are necessary indicators of program impact to examine first. Most programs are established to increase retention and achievement, and it is essential to discover whether students and teaching teams find their experience worthwhile. Aggregated data from multiple learning community offerings can provide an important first snapshot of program impact. However, if this is the sole extent of the assessment enterprise, then the reported outcomes have a sketchy quality. These findings do not tell the needed qualitative story of students' and teachers' experiences in learning communities, what specific elements or practices made certain learning communities positive for students and teachers, or what made other ones challenging or disappointing. With some notable exceptions, these reports generally did not describe the quality of student learning that the learning communities stimulated.

These patterns of assessment evidence are not unique to learning communities. Limited aggregated information is typical of assessment reporting at most colleges and universities. A review of assessment studies on another intervention, freshman seminars, indicates that the overwhelming majority of studies investigated effects on student retention, fewer looked at effects on grade point averages, and even fewer focused on other learning objectives or changes in behavior or attitudes (Barefoot, 1993).

Similarly, a recent study by the National Center for Postsecondary Improvement at the University of Michigan found that most institutions' assessment practices "emphasize the use of easily quantifiable indicators of student progress and pay less attention to more complex measures of student development" (National Center for Postsecondary Improvement, 1999, p. 55).

Assessing learning communities in more complex ways requires greater investments of time and resources. This is why ongoing, substantial assessment *teams* are so important to learning community initiatives. These teams should enlist a working group at the outset and recruit or develop capacity in assessment practices. Working with learning community instructional teams, they can generate understandings about learning community goals and decide what matters most to evaluate and what evidence of program results is most useful to gather. These teams can also be the initiators of conversations about reflection and improvement. Building this kind of base, these teams can, over time, move toward deeper and more nuanced forms of assessment.

Using Feedback to Stimulate Improvement

Feedback matters to reform work—significantly. Assessment information has been decisive in solidifying many learning community initiatives and influencing changes in direction. When the assessment program can marshal comprehensive information about learning community inputs and investments, the teaching and learning environment, and the outcomes, conversations about this information are usually lively and thought-provoking. New lines of inquiry and new ideas and goals for the learning community initiative can emerge.

Assessment information has been key to institutionalizing learning community initiatives. For example, in the late 1970s, when LaGuardia Community College discovered that students had consistently high rates of course completion in learning clusters, and at the same time faculty members in English were highly supportive of teaching composition in thematic course clusters, the institution moved to require full-time A.A.-degree students to fulfill their writing requirement in a learning cluster. This requirement has remained in place ever since. At Grossmont College, data about student success and growing faculty interest in developmental reading-writing learning communities led the institution to expand its learning community initiative gradually over a twenty-year period to a point where, today, hundreds of students are enrolled in these combinations every semester and learning communities are a hallmark of

264 LEARNING COMMUNITIES

developmental studies. Northern Colorado State University used data about student retention, achievement, and rates of B.A. completion along with feedback from students and faculty to build support for the expansion of a variety of freshman communities over several years. Northern Colorado also discontinued some learning communities whose results indicated they were working less well (Endicott, Suhr, McMorrow, and Doherty, 2004). Similarly, Iowa State University used data on student retention, persistence, and satisfaction in a fledgling learning community program to make a successful case to institutional leaders for a substantial budget line. This assessment team cemented its argument by translating increased sophomore retention numbers into increased tuition dollars for the university—a powerful currency for arguing for program value (Huba, Ellertson, Cook, and Epperson, 2003).

Qualitative information can also be helpful in affirming and solidifying program direction. As described in Chapter Five, in the early 1990s, St. Lawrence University instituted an ambitious Freshman Year Program located in its residence halls. When the program (by all accounts considered intensely demanding by students, faculty, and staff) had been in place for a few years, its leaders queried upperclassmen about its value: Had it provided an effective introduction to college learning and the St. Lawrence community, and should it be continued? The answer from the students was a resounding yes—providing the institution with a clear validation of its worth (Cornwell, 1996).

Assessment data can also advise important changes in learning community program emphasis or direction. At Texas A&M University, an ambitious first-year engineering community program serving all fifteen hundred entering students, has hundred-student clusters, each taking two or more required courses and having modest interaction with engineers from industry. Student comments in meetings with individual department representatives and their feedback during retention studies clearly indicated a desire for more opportunities to understand engineering practice and careers. Based on this feedback, the College of Engineering created "Industry Night" as a new addition to the learning community, which was well received. Also, the learning community leadership had made a commitment to instituting a high degree of collaborative learning in the learning community classes. Consistent feedback from faculty members indicated that many teachers were frustrated with the need to improve the interpersonal skills of students, which the college thought might be improved with increased focus on diversity. As a result, the program solicited industry representatives for assistance with diversity training workshops both for students and faculty members (Morgan and others, 2002).

Perplexing enrollment data spurred Seattle Central Community College to make substantial improvements to its coordinated studies program. This lively, well-received learning community initiative enjoyed high faculty commitment. Yet a few years into the program, the data indicated that learning community students were predominantly white, a pattern not reflective of the highly diverse student body. The learning community leader, an associate dean of humanities and social sciences, strengthened her resolve to hire more faculty of color to her division and recruit those new instructors immediately into learning community teaching. She encouraged these teams to invent themes that would engage diverse students and encouraged academic advisers to make students of color more aware of the new opportunities. These actions paid off, and the enrollment profiles in Seattle Central's learning communities soon reflected the diversity of the campus as a whole.

Creating More Reflective Occasions

Most essential in assessment is making the time for learning community leaders and practitioners to learn from and employ information and feedback. When convened systematically and in a spirit of improvement, reflective occasions can inform and strengthen all the elements of the initiative. In their trenchant paper on assessment, problem-based learning advocates John Harris and Dennis Sansom contend that true improvement in the educational enterprise depends on teams of people working toward *increased collective understanding* (Harris and Sansom, 2001). They assert that we must work to embed critical self-reflection into our daily work, and in so doing, create "communities of judgment." Educational reform, they say, is less about measuring results and leaving it there and more about forming informal communities of judgment that use both hard data *and* their own intuitive knowledge to understand student learning better and how to facilitate it. We agree. We see tremendous and often untapped potential for communities of judgment—and practice—at multiple levels of the learning community enterprise, to improve not just student learning but all of our learning about deepening these programs. It is this kind of collective learning that organizational theorist Peter Senge argues is so crucial to creating learning organizations (1990).

In learning communities, the teaching teams are the creators of learning experiences for students and they are also the first-line communities of judgment about the results—not merely judging student progress but judging the quality of the whole initiative. In the formal and informal procedures we have described, learning community programs can generate a wealth of information. Yet, learning from this information is challenging. Despite virtually universal acknowledgment of the value of drawing lessons from program results, teaching teams are often too busy, especially at the end of academic terms, to schedule conversations about their experience, to identify what worked well, or to imagine what they might change. Even less frequent are occasions for teaching teams to transmit these insights as good advice to new teaching teams.

Nevertheless, several learning community initiatives have developed activities that create both reflective moments and communities of judgment. Some campuses hold annual learning community institutes or planning retreats that both look back on the previous year's experience and results and look ahead to the future. Others have instituted end-of-term interviews with teaching teams, often convened by the learning community coordinator or members of the assessment task force; these meetings may be attended by other interested parties, such as advising staff, campus leaders, or faculty new to learning communities (Smith and MacGregor, 1991; Bystrom, 1995). Others have used formal program reviews of their learning community program as an occasion for self-study and feedback from an external site visit team (Levine Laufgraben and others, 2004).

Ongoing reflective occasions and program reviews are opportunities that can foster the kind of meaning making that keeps reform initiatives fresh and continuously developing. They can sustain a spirit of experimentation and a larger culture of shared practice, elements we believe are vital to the work of reform. And through these processes, faculty and staff can assume a larger collective responsibility for student learning and for using feedback to deepen their work. Summing up, here is what we recommend for good practice in learning community assessment:

○ Assessment should be established as a cycle of practices that are internally embedded in all learning community program activities: initial planning and goal setting, design of curriculum and classroom practices, overall program implementation, and ongoing improvement activities.

○ Assessment involves information-and-feedback processes that should inform and strengthen learning communities at the classroom and program levels while also providing information about results.

○ The heart of assessment should be in learning community classrooms, in the ways students are evaluated and given feedback and in the ways students are involved in reflecting on their learning and providing feedback to teaching teams.

o At the program level, substantial teams are essential for carrying out robust assessment work.

o The assessment endeavor should recruit partners who have expertise in program assessment and evaluation and can bring that expertise as well as credibility and visibility to the effort.

o Recognizing that learning community programs are complex and variable, assessment reports should describe inputs and investments as well as the curricular and pedagogical environment of the learning community program.

o Learning community assessments should capture basic quantitative information about student retention and academic progress in these programs, but over time they should also describe the student experience and the nature of student learning and development that result.

o Because learning communities depend on collaborative instructional teams, learning community assessment should focus on the experience of these individuals as well.

o Learning community leaders should become more strategic about communicating results, both to legitimize learning communities and to build wider understanding of them.

o Assessment's power and ongoing effectiveness spring from the reflective communities of judgment that develop around educational reform. These communities can be the seedbeds of insight for ongoing understanding and improvement of learning community practices. Assessment teams should create the reflective occasions where those involved in learning communities can come together to learn from their experiences.

o The assessment endeavor is successful to the degree that results are both useful and *used* to strengthen learning community programs and deepen their practices.

8

RECRUITING AND SUPPORTING LEARNING COMMUNITY TEACHERS

Only if the teachers are learners too, and if they are seen to be learners, can they genuinely model deep learning for the apprentice learners in the community.

—John Tagg

HIGHER EDUCATION is in a period of rapid change, and the restructuring of academic life is creating new challenges and opportunities, especially for faculty. In their book *Good Work: When Excellence and Ethics Meet,* Howard Gardner, Mihaly Csikszentmihalyi, and William Damon (2001) explore the conditions that promote good work in contemporary society. They argue that professions are healthiest when the values of the larger culture are in line with those of the field and when the expectations of stakeholders match these values. "When these conditions exist, individual practitioners operate at their best, morale is high, and the professional realm flourishes" (p. 27). They call this condition, which undergirds good work, *authentic alignment,* an ideal that describes the mutual interdependence of work, roles, work culture, and personal values.

In *The Learning Paradigm College,* John Tagg (2003) argues that the persistent problems in higher education over the past thirty years are the result of fundamental misalignments between these areas. As Tagg argues, "At many institutions there is no living community of practice among the faculty that is actively negotiating the meaning of teaching and participating in revising the tools they use and rules that govern them. . . . The reified artifacts that define our roles as teachers—the course outlines, the calendar, the departments and divisions—are fossilized beyond all negotiation. . . . We have made the means the end. We have made the tools of our work the object of our work, and in doing so, have vitiated our own freedom to negotiate meaning" (2003, p. 263).

While Tagg describes an internal malaise within the academy, external factors have certainly contributed to this malaise and therefore to this sense of misalignment. State legislatures, boards of trustees, and business executives have criticized the university's teaching loads and tenure practices, even as they have called for higher retention of students and more engaged teaching practices. Many faculty feel pressured and undervalued.

In contrast, we know from twenty years of interviewing teachers in learning communities that teaching experiences in learning communities are often transformative precisely because they promote good work and respond to many of the demands for change in the academy. They can provide a place for revitalization and realignment of role, culture, and values. The challenge, then, is to figure out how to make this experience more widely available, attractive, and doable with adequate support so that the learning community movement will grow and prosper.

In this chapter we argue that creating effective learning communities for faculty and other learning community teachers is an essential element of expanding and sustaining high-quality learning communities for students. We begin by discussing the current restructuring of academic life and its implications for learning communities. We then go on to describe the ways that institutions recruit and support learning community teachers and build a learning community of teachers who can, as John Tagg puts it, "genuinely model deep learning for the apprentice learners [students] in the community" (2003, p. 263).

The Restructuring of Academic Life

Large-scale faculty retirements and replacements, the changing conditions of employment, and new expectations about the nature of faculty work and productivity are all contributing to what Martin Finkelstein and Jack Schuster refer to as the restructuring of academic life. In some institutions this restructuring is recognized as a major issue and a major opportunity, and careful planning is being undertaken; in others, it is accidental, unwittingly reshaping professional roles and responsibilities. Nevertheless, we are witnessing important changes in demographics, academic appointments, and professional responsibilities.

In the last thirty years, faculty demographics have changed dramatically. In 1999, fully 51 percent of the nation's faculty were over fifty years of age compared with 23 percent in 1969. Sixteen percent were over age sixty and starting to retire in large numbers (Sanderson, Phau, and Herda, 2000). Considerable turnover has already taken place, with one-third of the current faculty hired in the 1990s (Finkelstein, Seal, and Schuster, 1998). This new cohort is more female, more international, and more multicultural, although faculty of color continue to be underrepresented. The newer teachers are also more diverse in their prior work experiences, often coming to full-time faculty positions after years of part-time teaching or from occupations outside the academy. The discipline mix of the faculty is also different: substantially fewer new faculty members are being hired into the liberal arts.

New faculty members are also being hired under different types of academic appointments than their predecessors. The proportion of part-time appointments is nearly double what it was in the 1970s, as cost-conscious institutions opt for economy and flexibility (Finkelstein, Seal, and Schuster, 1998). In addition, more and more full-time faculty members are now being hired off the tenure track. Indeed, the percentage of non-tenure-track full-time faculty appointments swelled from 3.3 percent in 1969 to 52.2 percent in 1997 (Finkelstein and Schuster, 2001). This trend is especially notable in four-year institutions, where a respecialization of academic life is taking place around differentiated roles in teaching, research, and public service.

In terms of the health of the profession and the need to do good work, there are many reasons to be concerned about these trends. Although some worry about academic freedom, the greater threat may well be the difficulty in building an academic community with a strong core of individuals who can carry the task of institution building and sustaining the long view. Of course, institutions vary in how large the activist permanent core needs to be, but any healthy institution needs a core of people with a long-term commitment to it who help build and sustain the community. In many colleges and universities, the community is increasingly fragmented. There are unspoken and unresolved questions about who is in the core, who gets tenure, and how people in different roles are compensated, supported, and included in the faculty culture.

Not surprisingly, there is evidence that the faculty sense of community has diminished. When asked to rate their sense of community on their campus, respondents at all types of institutions reported substantial declines between 1989 and 1997. In 1997, only 27 percent of the nation's faculty rated the sense of campus community as "good" or "excellent." At the same time, their responses suggested where some of their commitment and energy has gone; respondents indicated that their academic discipline is most important to them, followed by their department, and, finally, their college (Huber, 1998).

Despite the demographic changes in the profession, the pedagogical approach of the new cohort of faculty hired in the 1990s does not differ much from the older cohort. The lecture still dominates, and classroom strategies are not much different from what they were before (Finkelstein, Seal, and Schuster, 1998; Outcalt, 2002). Women, a growing proportion of the faculty, stand out as the exception in the Finkelstein, Seal, and Schuster study: they spend more time with students and rely less on lecturing as their primary approach to teaching. The similarities between the pedagogical approaches of the new cohort and the older cohort are surprising in light of the widespread calls for increased active learning over the past twenty years. Perhaps most telling, the Finkelstein, Seal, and Schuster study indicates that the new cohort is even more research-oriented than their senior colleagues.

Changes in faculty roles and reward systems were further explored in a study based on the American Association for Higher Education's 2002–03 national survey of 729 chief academic officers of four-year colleges and universities (O'Meara and Rice, 2004). Building on the work of Ernest Boyer, Lee Shulman, and Gene Rice, the AAHE has led a ten-year effort to encourage colleges and universities to revise campus role and reward systems. The aim is to raise the status of teaching and undergraduate education by broadening the definition of scholarship, linking teaching with scholarship. The results of this national survey, the first comprehensive report on the impact of this work, indicate that a majority of the institutions have indeed embraced broader notions of scholarship and are encouraging and rewarding multiple forms of it. Still, the paradox we have been describing remains. Institutions that made formal changes to their role and reward systems reported higher increases in faculty satisfaction with roles and rewards, faculty involvement in the scholarship of teaching and learning, and greater congruence between faculty priorities and institutional mission. Yet none of these changes have diminished the importance of research. Rather, expectations in this area and in teaching have so increased that they raise concerns about burnout and contribute to a deepening malaise. We raise these issues here because we believe that learning communities represent a hopeful avenue to address this core issue of alignment and can also greatly help in building community, often bringing the different cultures of the academy together in new ways.

Who Teaches in Learning Communities?

If learning communities can help address institutional fragmentation, then it is important to recognize who is teaching in them and who might teach in them in the future. Many different faculty and staff members teach in learning communities, although this varies significantly by institutional type. Although most research universities employ graduate teaching assistants, part-time faculty, and non-tenure-track faculty to teach the freshman courses where learning communities are located, some research universities, such as Georgia State, University of California-Los Angeles, University of Hartford, and Duke University, have made it a priority to involve tenure-track faculty in their first-year programs. Student affairs professionals and undergraduate peer tutors are also often part of these teaching teams, especially in learning communities that involve freshman seminars or residence life. In community colleges and private four-year colleges, tenure-track full-time faculty are more likely to teach first-year students, although community colleges traditionally employ large numbers of part-time faculty and teachers hired on nonpermanent appointments.

Departmental involvement also varies widely. Because English composition and other entry-level skill courses are often included in learning communities, teachers in these areas are overly represented. Many learning communities attract liberal arts faculty, but research and comprehensive university learning communities usually have substantial reach into professional programs as well, especially through general education courses. In a few professions, such as engineering, there has been substantial learning community program development involving full-time faculty members as a result of national reform initiatives funded by the National Science Foundation.

It is evident that the current profile of learning community teachers is problematic in several ways. First, many of the early leaders who gravitated to learning community teaching in the 1980s are nearing retirement without having mentored a new generation to succeed them. Second, many learning community programs do not include significant numbers of full-time faculty because full-time faculty tend not to teach freshman-level courses. This situation, especially prevalent at research universities, ensures that learning communities remain on the margin of the larger faculty culture. Another problem is that teachers frequently rotate in and out of learning community teaching, a pattern that requires enormous investments in recruitment and staff development of new teaching teams. Aware of these important issues, many institutions are now striving to use more full-time faculty members in learning communities, a strategy that holds the prospect of building more stable and vibrant communities of faculty. In addition, the intentional construction of cross-divisional teaching teams and the involvement of faculty with student affairs professionals, undergraduate peer mentors/advisers, and librarians are making learning communities a place where innovation can thrive and prosper. Living-learning communities, for example, are creating a new seamlessness between the curriculum and the co-curriculum and challenging traditional roles and approaches (Schoem, 2004). The use of undergraduate peer mentors is widespread and especially notable in light of the literature on the positive impact of the peer culture on student motivation and learning (Astin, 1993a, 1993b; Tinto, Goodsell-Love, and Russo, 1993, 1994; Tinto, 2002; Whitman, 1988; Light, 1992). Studies of the impact of undergraduate peer mentors at Iowa State, UCLA, Temple University, University of Washington, and the University of Missouri suggest that they are often the best teachers of other students, while they themselves also benefit by gaining leadership experience.

There are not only different groups teaching at colleges and universities, but also different cultures operating across these groups. In his classic book, *The Four Cultures of the Academy,* William Bergquist (1992) argues that we have four distinct cultures in the academy—the collegial, the managerial, the developmental, and the negotiating cultures—with different values, expectations, and work styles. The managerial and the collegial cultures are the oldest, dating back to the colonial era, whereas the developmental and negotiating culture are more recent. The collegial culture is characteristic of the faculty who find meaning in the academic disciplines, faculty teaching, research and scholarship, and a long tradition of autonomy and self-governance. The managerial culture is typified by the administration, which values organization, implementation, and evaluation. The developmental culture is emblematic of student affairs, where there is a commitment to creating programs and services that support student personal and professional development. The negotiating culture emerged when changing conditions in higher education created the "inability of the managerial culture to meet the personal and financial needs of faculty and staff" (Bergquist, 1992, p. 129). Collective bargaining and unionization are hallmarks of the negotiating culture, along with a belief that change takes place through confrontation and negotiation. Although these different cultural groups give our colleges and universities a useful complexity and diversity, their existence also produces misalignments and conflict because they all have different work styles, assumptions, communication approaches, and attitudes.

Learning community teams are challenged to cross boundaries and create a different type of culture characterized by mutuality, collegiality, and equality. Working in this way may require new skills for educators long accustomed to privacy, autonomy, and privilege, whether it be in their individual classrooms or in their offices in academic advising or residence life. The theoretical concept of a learning community requires practical application of fairness and equality and a commitment to build on everyone's ideas and participation, despite classic differences in role and status. Flexibility, patience, willingness to listen to others, and comfort with sharing the stage are important as these innovators become immersed in what is a new cultural milieu. Thus, the question of "who teaches in learning communities" must be answered at the cultural and systemic levels. Learning community teams need to see themselves as connectors, builders, and pioneers who are forging realignments of role, task, and culture in institutional environments that may be unsupportive.

Recruiting Teachers

In sum, learning communities prosper when capable and creative individuals become involved, when ownership of the task is shared, and when the work is seen as benefiting everyone's interests and needs. The challenge in recruiting faculty and other teachers to learning communities is twofold: at the outset, attracting appropriate teachers, and then as the initiative expands, reaching out and including others. Developing a critical mass of learning community teachers who will stay with the program and recruit successors is key to long-term viability. Looking at what attracts people to learning communities and listening to their feelings about them are good ways to begin thinking about how to recruit others.

Why Faculty Join Learning Communities

Faculty are drawn to learning communities for diverse reasons, and as we have noted, many different types of faculty members can teach in them successfully. The opportunity to learn and develop as teachers and connect with new colleagues is frequently the motivation. Faculty are often lonely in their departments, and learning communities literally open up the university as a community of learners. As one faculty member put it, "These communities gave me the opportunity in middle age to continue my undergraduate education in the humanities and the sciences." Another noted that there really is not any one *type* of teacher for learning communities, but there may well be a *time* when certain faculty members are ready to teach in them.

For these reasons, many senior faculty members are drawn to learning communities. William Bergquist's work, *In Our Fifties: Voices of Men and Women Reinventing Their Lives,* suggests that they are looking for new roles and different ways to leave a larger legacy (Bergquist and others, 1993). Teaching in a learning community can fulfill this need. These programs can also help build bridges between the generations of faculty (Smith, 1993b). In this regard, younger faculty often give homage to their senior faculty partners: as a colleague noted, "Teaching in learning communities taught me the importance of working collaboratively with other faculty members. In the past, when I taught classes by myself, I taught in accordance with how I learned. When I became involved with team teaching, I soon realized that the other instructors increased my level of teaching. They made me teach at a higher level of proficiency. What you learn from senior faculty is priceless. No seminar or three-day workshop can compare to being in the classroom for one full quarter."

Learning community teachers often discover new strengths as they collaborate with others. As a recently tenured teacher at a community colleges notes: "I am a different teacher when I teach in learning communities. I am more confident. I am more spontaneous, and my sense of humor surfaces more easily. The reasons for this additional 'surefootedness' are tied directly to the pedagogical and classroom environment."

Asked what sustained them over the long term, many of the fellows associated with the National Learning Community Project (2000 to 2004) pointed to the rewarding opportunity to build a supportive community of learning for students. As one noted, "I think going into a new and impersonal situation like my college, with its inhuman size and isolated freestanding classes, students need some social connections with other students and faculty. Learning communities are my vehicle for fostering community and encouraging deeper, more meaningful learning."

Another responded: "What sustains me? The opportunity to work closely with an extraordinary array of people deeply and passionately committed to improving undergraduate learning, people who are open to experimentation, innovation, and risk-taking in educational practice. Such a community is intellectually stimulating and a joy to be part of—and something often missing from our individual organizations."

Faculty join learning communities for many reasons, but ultimately they will join if they think it will add value to their professional lives. Because learning communities are a broad reform effort, connections can often be made to a variety of faculty interests. Interdisciplinary and discipline-based reforms, such as writing across the curriculum, internationalizing the curriculum, diversity, service learning, inquiry-based approaches to the sciences, and the scholarship of teaching and learning have high compatibility with learning communities. In addition, faculty members will join learning communities for practical reasons such as building enrollment for their department or offering a minor, or they might become involved because of an interest in teaching with a particular colleague, or designing and teaching interdisciplinary courses.

An Evolving Selection Process

The first faculty members teaching in learning communities are usually volunteers and they often set the tone, critically influencing how their colleagues perceive the program. Especially on small campuses, energetic, creative teachers are attracted because of the many opportunities to learn new things. Frequently at the forefront of change efforts, these people are called *early adopters* in the innovation literature. At the Seattle community colleges, for example, the early adopters included faculty members who had been leaders in writing across the curriculum as well as other interdisciplinary ventures. They were well-established teachers already practicing active learning in their classes. They had a record of being risk takers as well as faculty leaders. Their early involvement gave the learning community credibility and skilled teachers who could readily put the theory of interdisciplinary collaborative learning into practice.

Too often the selection process for teaching in learning communities is a combination of networking, invitation, and happenstance. Some people become engaged through informal conversations about a new opportunity on campus. Others may wonder what it is all about and why they have not been asked, and for others the process is often invisible and rumors and jealousy about "who gets to do it" may result. Because learning communities present the opportunity to address key alignment issues in the institution, it is important to develop a public and clearly articulated process for selecting teachers. Some institutions use a centralized "request for proposal" process, whereas others rely on departments, the student affairs division, or their relatively autonomous professional schools to recruit teachers. Learning community coordinators usually spend considerable time recruiting appropriate faculty and staff members. In the end, how people are invited to participate makes a big difference in establishing the learning community culture. In small institutions, face-to-face outreach to potential teachers is a good strategy, whereas in larger institutions a better strategy is to involve department chairs, who are crucial to the process of recruiting faculty to learning communities.

To build interest, many campuses hold annual retreats that serve as both a recruitment strategy and a faculty development event. These day-long or overnight outings provide an arena for community building, telling stories about learning community successes and difficulties, and orienting new faculty. They offer workshops on pedagogy and planning the curriculum. Who participates? In the best instances, all of the stake-holders and potential recruits: existing supporters, innovators the program hopes to recruit, key support people in advising, registration, and the library, students, and of course, key leadership people. Some campuses even invite those skeptical of the project, thereby creating a forum for dialogue about learning community purposes and possibilities. Recruiting faculty to learning communities needs to be continuous, not something relegated to the start-up phase. Often a learning community program founders when the originators move on. A sabbatical or a family illness can destabilize the whole program if other colleagues do not come forward to fill the gap. Many programs remain small and isolated because they have become too centered on an initial group of teaching faculty. A number of institutions with team-taught learning communities require that at least one member be new to the team. Others address the need for faculty rotation by requiring faculty to take turns teaching in learning communities. When thinking about whom to recruit, it is often useful to ask where you want the program to be in five or ten years to get a sense of how large the pool of interested faculty members must be to sustain the program. Learning community initiatives pass a huge milestone when the institution mentions interest in teaching in them in its job announcements for new faculty members.

At Skagit Valley College, which requires three learning communities as part of its general education program for transfer students, the learning community program has to involve large numbers of faculty on a continuous basis. Faculty recruitment strategies have evolved over time. They began with a grassroots initiative, with early participants simply finding each other through an informal process. Because the early learning communities were voluntary for the students and ran at enrollment levels typical of stand-alone courses, there were no substantial issues about recruiting faculty members or gaining administrative support. But when Skagit Valley established the learning community requirement for all its transfer students, it had to formalize recruitment strategies to attract the necessary numbers of teachers. The institution revised its negotiated union agreement to create incentives for faculty to participate. Recruitment activities introduced the learning community approach to a much wider spectrum of possible teachers. The learning community coordinator held mixers and brown-bag lunches and frequently brokered linkages among faculty members. As the learning community program matured, departments became more active in taking responsibility for matchmaking and made an effort to pair new faculty members with veteran learning community teachers. Language about collaborative interdisciplinary teaching was inserted into job descriptions and interest in it became an important factor in hiring at this institution. In all, Skagit Valley adopted an integrated systems approach to recruitment and retention of both faculty and students. Learning communities became the strategic lever for accomplishing institutional goals.

Listening to Faculty Concerns

Many faculty members *could* be interested in teaching in learning communities, but they want to do it well and may not understand what it involves. During faculty recruitment, the various concerns prospective teachers raise must be addressed. As learning community organizer Fred Ross put it, "It's the way people are that counts, not the way you'd like them to be" (1989, p. 13). Good recruitment of faculty relies on good listening and on a good partnership of the individual talents and experience with the needs of the learning community.

Practical concerns often surface, especially in institutions where the innovation is not (yet) incorporated into the existing reward system. Many faculty are concerned that innovation requires an extraordinary amount of time, time they cannot afford and for which they will not be rewarded. With good reason, they may ask, "Will teaching in learning communities help or hinder my prospects for promotion and tenure? Do the institution and the department really value this work? How will colleagues view me if I join a learning community? Will teaching in learning communities leave enough time to pursue my other goals and priorities?" As the studies mentioned earlier in this chapter reported, these are real issues for faculty members pressed by increasing expectations on all fronts—for research, teaching innovation, grant writing, and public service. Although reward systems appear to be moving toward more nuanced thinking about scholarship and teaching, this continues to be a great source of stress for many teachers.

Critics and skeptics should not be ignored either, because glossing over legitimate concerns can weaken the effort. In a provocative essay titled

"Methodological Doubting and Believing: Contraries in Inquiry," Peter Elbow (1986) points out that faculty are trained to be skeptical. So they ask often hard questions about new approaches. Does the approach work for all students and all disciplines? What are students really learning? Can students achieve learning outcomes in a learning community that are comparable to what they would achieve in discrete classes? These are all questions that learning community organizers should try to answer.

Faculty resistance may center on issues of turf and trust. As one pointed out, "Some of the scientists were reluctant to relinquish their territorial rights. . . . They were hesitant to give up their usual courses, fearing that they wouldn't get them back. Some divisions fought against the development of 'topics' courses that didn't have predefined content; there was a fear that their disciplines would be watered down. Other faculty felt a strong responsibility to the traditional delivery methods of content" (Dutcher, Mino, and Singh, 1999, p. 35).

At many four-year institutions, there is also faculty resistance to teaching first-year general education courses populated by younger students. Many teachers prefer upper-division courses or general education classes where a mix allows more mature students to acculturate the freshmen. However, at many of these institutions faculty members have student affairs partners as well as peer mentors to work with. These institutions have created excellent workshops and faculty development opportunities to help teaching teams develop learning community programs that successfully meet the needs and interests of freshman students.

Often the crucial unspoken questions are deeply personal: Can I successfully teach in learning communities? Will it require too much of a shift in my approach to teaching? What is it like to work with another faculty member, a librarian, or someone from residence life? Learning communities often ask us to reexamine our existing roles in ways that are both exciting and uncomfortable. Even faculty or staff members who endorse the idea may have questions about how to put the theory into practice. Although many learning communities are not team-taught, some are. Team teaching is the biggest leap for many because it requires extensive collaboration and can raise critical questions about autonomy and the ability to work with colleagues from other disciplines. At the same time, many report it is also the most satisfying type of teaching.

Some faculty concerns lie in deeply embedded roles and disciplinary expectations. As one colleague noted:

> As an English teacher, I find it difficult not to know the work each student is doing in response to the assignments: we divide the students into three groups, and although we rotate groups throughout the

quarter, I only end up seeing part of each student's work. Another problem for me is the nature of the science classroom, cavernous and inexorable in its seating arrangement, which makes it nearly impossible for students to work comfortably in small groups. The lack of daily focus on English is both a relief and a frustration. No course, translated to a learning community, can proceed in its usual format or structure, so a teacher feels sometimes that essential information fails to be conveyed, a sense that all teachers have from time to time in these programs, I think. [personal communication with the authors]

For this teacher, the experience of teaching in a learning community raised significant issues about status, roles, and long-established patterns of teaching well-honed courses. Still, she continues to teach enthusiastically in learning communities and lives with these tensions, a testimony to her personal growth as a teacher.

Depending on the institutional climate, the opportunity may also raise questions about the institution's motives. On many campuses, faculty have seen innovations come and go, with little follow-through or long-term impact. As another colleague notes:

Having taught at [this university] for fifteen years, I did not immediately jump at the chance of teaching in a learning community. I spend a great deal of time on teaching as it is, and I don't always feel that my efforts are appreciated by trustees, administrators, or students. Ambitious administrators have an interest in pedagogical change as a way of promoting their own careers. Faculty are often susceptible to calls for change because of the frustration involved in teaching. Often these changes fail to yield the desired results. Unfulfilled expectations lead to new initiatives with similar results. The only thing that remains constant is the general sense on the part of faculty that they could do better if only they tried harder. This dynamic has done much to contribute to the demoralization of college faculty across the country.

Another noted that involvement turned out to be a double-edged sword: "Clearly the most frustrating aspect of teaching in learning communities was the ripple effect in my institutional culture. Engaging in this curricular effort—really the first one of this sort in my institution—has exacerbated differences between me and the general cultural matrix in which I work. I did not imagine that the energy and effort to enhance first-year education would meet with a kind of suspicion by some colleagues and administrators, not all, but some important ones. I find it frustrating that a good model that serves students well can be stalled by these ripple effects. . . . It undermines my faith in education and educators."

Assessment information can be useful in addressing a common faculty concern about whether the learning community initiative benefits students. Information can be gathered on student retention, achievement, and satisfaction, for example, and disseminated through periodic reports, on Web sites, and at college meetings. Faculty and staff development opportunities, discussed later in this chapter, are also an important method for increasing the comfort level of newcomers with different pedagogies and new working relationships. Faculty concern about time issues often relate to the broader question of whether there will be financial support for their development and curriculum planning time. No teacher wants to fail at her work and especially in highly public collaborative planning and teaching arrangements. Support must be available to assist with curriculum planning, with coaching and advice provided by more experienced colleagues. Faculty members linking courses for the first time may be encouraged to develop some modest linkages initially and then gradually scale up to more fully integrated designs.

Many faculty concerns about teaching in learning communities can only be understood if you look at the institutional culture in a particular time and place. At some institutions, the president and provost may express support for learning communities while departments give short shrift to them in teaching assignments and in tenure and promotion decisions. Some tenure-track faculty in four-year institutions have become excited about learning communities, only to be discouraged by their chair or their mentors. At some institutions, faculty members who were heavily involved in learning community teaching were penalized because their loyalties were perceived as being displaced from their departments. In contrast, many other institutions have revised their policies on promotion and tenure to support their rhetoric about the scholarship of teaching and the importance of teaching in learning communities.

Because of institutional reward systems, some colleges and universities have chosen to involve only tenured faculty in learning communities. At other institutions where this is not an issue, untenured faculty are leading the effort and are rewarded for it. Some institutions promote innovation and risk taking by lowering the fear threshold; some formally agree to hold the teachers "harmless" by not administering course evaluations in pilot programs. Others find alternative ways to support participation through robust faculty development programs and various skill-building opportunities, discussed in the next section of this chapter.

What all this means is that despite many years of emphasizing the importance of teaching and undergraduate education, there remains a troubling misalignment in many institutions between the reward systems and the espoused goal of moving toward a more learning-centered environment. On many campuses, the rhetoric about making undergraduate education a priority is still way ahead of the reality. This dilemma remains unresolved and cuts across all issues having to do with the primacy of teaching and the support of innovation.

Learning to Teach in Learning Communities

Because teaching in a learning community may require new ways of taking up the teaching role and new opportunities to work with colleagues from different parts of the campus, faculty and staff development is essential. This is a substantial cultural change in our institutions, which have historically underinvested in faculty development, often defining it in terms of supporting the growth of individual teachers and their research agendas. As Robert Barr (1998) points out, "Colleges have a low-risk, low-feedback, process culture. . . . [They] have not developed an organizational capacity for self-reflection and systematic change [and they] devote precious few resources to developing new methods and redesigning their processes" (p. 23).

W. Norton Grubb and his colleagues note in their major study, *Honored But Invisible: An Inside Look at Teaching in Community Colleges,* that even our most student-centered institutions—community colleges—do not pay sufficient attention to supporting good teaching. They contend that "teaching should be viewed as a collective activity rather than the individual and idiosyncratic effort that it usually is" (Grubb and Associates, 1999, p. ix). Highly critical of the gap between the rhetoric of community colleges as teaching institutions and their actual practice, they argue that we need to step up to the challenge of being genuinely committed to teaching by investing in faculty and staff development. Citing team-taught learning communities as a rich arena for continuous staff development, they also point out that the learning community structure by no means guarantees the result: "Without both individual and institutional support, learning communities tend to collapse back to business as usual" (p. 269). In other words, institutions do not provide enough opportunities for teachers to learn about how best to teach. When we think about the additional challenges that learning communities present, the need for professional development activities becomes even more apparent.

Commonly cited teaching problems in learning community implementation include weak understanding of learning community goals and core practices on the part of teaching teams and the need for training and time for planning and collaboration. These problems often manifest themselves in inadequate assessment of and feedback on student work, poor integration of the content, and problems in teaching students to do collaborative work. Uneven quality is a particularly acute problem in large learning communities programs where there is high turnover among teachers and difficulty maintaining alignment around expectations and practices. Lack of leadership and accountability for faculty development is also an issue on many campuses. Often there is no convening authority to bring teaching teams together to discuss how the learning community is going. Nor is anyone assigned responsibility for gathering faculty teams at the term's conclusion to evaluate their experience and communicate what they learned to future teams.

The good news is that in the past two decades, many colleges and research universities have established teaching and learning centers with designated staff (*Reinventing Undergraduate Education*, 2001; Diamond, 2002; Sorcinelli, 2002). Mostly located in large research universities, many of these centers undertake the important work of orienting new faculty members and offer individual consultation on course development, assessment, and pedagogy (Alan Frantz, personal communication with the authors, October 2003). Many also regularly offer brown-bag lunch discussions and workshops on teaching issues and teaching approaches, or they create special interest groups to explore certain pedagogies. Some have assisted faculty members in writing major curriculum development or teaching reform grants. Many of these centers also have been given the enormous task of enabling teachers to become familiar with electronic technologies. Ironically, the biggest challenge these centers face is involving faculty members in their activities—because of the many reasons we have already cited (*Reinventing Undergraduate Education*, 2001; Beebe, 2003).

Unfortunately, many other campuses make only minimal investments in faculty and staff development. They have only a part-time faculty development person or a small committee of people; these individuals simply approve conference travel or put on a single annual event related to teaching and learning. At many community colleges, the entire faculty development activity is built into union contracts around designated staff development days and activities, often planned by a committee, the vice president of instruction, or a district office. Sometimes these events are geared to faculty only; at other times they are held for the entire campus staff. Although these are often worthwhile events, they can also engender cynicism when the "important new pedagogy" changes every year or when workshops are too generalized to be of immediate use. These types of faculty and staff development events seem random and ever-changing, and unrelated to institutional priorities or change initiatives. At four-year schools with teaching and learning centers, the agenda can come across like a smorgasbord, with one workshop after another on effective lecturing and grading and a variety of pedagogical techniques not connected to strategic goals or programmatic initiatives. This elective approach to staff development is designed to offer something for everyone, but it seldom yields the kind of sustained building of expertise that a large-scale reform such as learning communities requires.

Developing learning communities requires a different way of thinking about faculty development in at least *two* respects. First, it means creating longer-term relationships with groups of teachers than usually happens in single workshops or consultations. In some instances, it means creating these relationships with individuals who are drawn from different sectors of the campus (faculty, part-time or contract instructors, advising staff, residence life personnel, technology support staff, librarians, graduate students or undergraduates). Second, it requires thinking about faculty and staff development from a more systemic or comprehensive perspective, paying attention to faculty recruitment, orientation, curriculum planning, the introduction and support of new pedagogies, student development and adjustment issues, and different forms of assessment. If learning community faculty and staff development are not multifaceted and ongoing, learning communities usually fail to live up to their potential and the effort loses quality and momentum in just the way that Grubb describes. It is clear that careful planning and commitment to core practices, supported by ongoing opportunities for participants to reflect on their work, are crucial to learning community sustainability.

Faculty Development Approaches and Strategies

Learning community coordinators and campus teaching and learning centers can play critical roles in assessing and supporting faculty development needs. Connecting learning community faculty development to existing resources is always a good idea, and a few institutions have established close working relationships between learning communities and existing development programs and structures. Effective faculty development programs often begin by offering exploratory workshops designed to introduce prospective teachers to learning communities by providing an overview of the theory, models, and core practices underlying them. Many campuses use the "Design a Learning Community in an Hour Workshop," which is usually a creative and motivating experience. (See Exhibit 8.1.)

Once teaching teams are formed, pedagogical support is frequently offered on the core practices of active learning, diversity, curriculum integration, community building, and assessment. These workshops usually address both the theory behind these core practices and ways to implement them. Teaching teams are often asked to develop their own answers to the question "What are the sites for this core practice in our learning community?" There is an extensive literature behind each of these core practices that can usefully shape these workshops. As Exhibit 8.2 indicates, each of these core practices includes many approaches known under more specific names. Of course, the approaches chosen depend on the specific learning community goals and the curricular framework chosen. Many institutions focus their workshops on different strands as a result of polling the teaching teams about their needs and interests. Sometimes annual orientations and planning retreats for learning community teachers feature one or more of these practices as well.

After the introductory orientations to learning communities, other workshops follow to provide a deeper orientation and support curriculum planning. Many institutions hold daylong orientation retreats for faculty and staff teaching in learning communities, and an increasing number of institutions sponsor summer institutes for their faculty. A common model is a three- to five-day institute that includes substantial team planning time as well. The heuristic for learning community curriculum planning described in Chapter Seven (Exhibit 7.1) is a good tool for a workshop in which teaching teams identify learning outcomes and ways to promote deep learning.

If the learning community curricular structure is one in which teachers coordinate their syllabi or team-teach, ongoing conversation and reflection are crucial to sustaining the intellectual and social glue of the program, not to mention strengthening the communities of teaching practice on each team. Teaching team members should talk regularly throughout the quarter or semester, continuing to plan classroom and co-curricular activities and assessment and reflecting on their progress and the problems related to student learning and the overall state of community in the program. It does not matter who convenes these meetings, but some member of each learning community teaching team should be designated as convener, and these meetings should happen regularly throughout the term. If a system is not set up for regular meetings, an important opportunity is lost both for continued coordination of the intellectual and social

---

Exhibit 8.1. Designing a Learning Community in an Hour

The idea in this exercise is for your team to engage in some boundary-crossing curricular brainstorming. Often, planning conversations start with what students will learn, and these conversations are usually based in existing courses. The purpose of this exercise is to practice inventing a new curriculum around topics or ideas that bridge or meld disciplines (and to have some fun getting to know one another!).

Pretend that you have been asked to be a learning community teaching team for a group of beginning students at a college for an entire semester.

Assume for this exercise that *all* the administrative logistics have been successfully worked out, and your job is simply to design and deliver the academic experience for the students. Although it will be a challenge, try to stay on task with all the steps of this exercise and to keep your side conversations about each other's existing learning community programs or campus issues to a minimum.

For those of you who are faculty members, this requires you "to leave your syllabus at the door" (but not your disciplinary background!) and engage in some intellectual bridge-building with your colleagues.

Every group will be given some flip chart paper and a colored marker or two. Each team should appoint a timekeeper and an individual who will agree to be the scribe. Do not proceed with this process until you are sure you have these materials and individuals in place.

1. Getting Focused (about 5 minutes):

Begin with some quiet reflective time to read through these instructions and to do some thinking and "free writing" in response to the following task: If you had the opportunity to teach in some sort of learning community format, what theme or themes might intrigue you? *Ways to get started:* What larger meaningful interdisciplinary questions, issues, ideas or problems might be intriguing for you and for students to explore?

2. Introductions and Generation of Ideas for a Theme (10 minutes):

Your group's timekeeper needs to start keeping time with this task. Taking no more than three to five minutes per person (be disciplined about this) introduce yourself to the group, name (no need to elaborate on) what your work is at your college or university, and if you are a faculty member, what courses you usually teach or what your discipline is. Then, briefly describe the interests that grow out of your expertise and passions, interests that are intriguing to you and might be intriguing to students today.

3. Together Choose a Theme for Your Program (5 to 10 minutes):

Once your group has generated ideas for possible learning community themes, see if you can come to consensus on any common theme, question, or topic that could conceivably be the organizing idea for a learning community. If members of your group are widely divergent in your interests, simply take a leap of faith and settle on one of the themes with which everyone feels comfortable working in this exercise.

Exhibit 8.1. (*Continued*)

4. Flesh Out the Themes and Activities (about 25 minutes):

Given an imaginary quarter or semester in which your group is teaching collaboratively around this theme, what might you and your students do? Flesh out the substance of your program brainstorm-fashion—that is, generate particular subthemes, concepts, authors, or titles of texts (reading of primary sources is encouraged!), films, field experiences, dramatic performances, or research projects that might illustrate the theme. *No need to prioritize or to lock in a sequence at this stage.* In the interest of generating just as much as you can, use this brainstorming protocol:

- Generate as many ideas as you can. Don't get bogged down judging or discussing the merits or fine points of each suggestion; the idea is just to generate as much as you possibly can now. Sorting and refining might occur at a later date.
- Create a "group memory" as you work: record *every contribution* that is suggested (in large print) on your newsprint paper so all members of your group can see. To the degree that you can, keep the newsprint in full view of everyone so your group has a common sense of thinking.
- In the brainstorming process, repetition of earlier suggestions is okay.
- Resist the temptation to embark on side conversations about the logistics of learning community implementation; we will get to these questions later.

5. Make a Summary Poster of Your Work (last 10–15 minutes):

Now, distill and summarize some of the key ideas or activities in your learning community design that might underpin a real program. Make sure your poster includes at least some of the following:

- A title that portrays a theme (such as "New York, New York," "Of Mice and Matter," "The Aims of Education")
- Key learnings for students
- Major concepts and learning activities (ideas for possible projects, experiential learning, books or authors that are important)
- Possible embedded disciplines or courses

environment for students and for continued professional collaboration and support.

As Chapter Three described, many of the learning community programs in the Meiklejohn-Tussman-Evergreen tradition ask students to come together weekly for book seminars, in which students and their teachers work to understand the program's themes through discussion of readings or entire texts. A number of institutions also hold weekly faculty seminars as a strategy for faculty teaching teams to discuss the material before teaching the student seminars. The Arts One program at University of British Columbia, the Hutchins School at Sonoma State University,

Exhibit 8.2. Faculty Development Topics on Learning Community Core Practices

Core Practice	Examples of Faculty Development Topics and Approaches
Community	Strategies for inclusion and community building; structured controversy; group development–group dynamics; making conflict productive; community-based learning and service learning; development of effective teaching teams
Diversity	Student intellectual development; multicultural teaching strategies; learning styles; intergroup dialogue; theories of identity development
Integration	Curriculum design; integrative curricular strategies; problem-based learning; writing across the curriculum
Active learning	Active learning in lectures; collaborative and cooperative learning; discussions and seminars; project- and problem-based learning; service and civic learning; labs and field study; undergraduate research; varieties of assessment; working in groups; writing, speaking, and quantitative reasoning across the curriculum
Assessment and reflection	Classroom assessment techniques; small group instructional diagnosis; student self-assessment; portfolio development; academic journals; designing performance-authentic assessment

and the integrated studies program at the University of North Dakota all use this practice. Evergreen does too, and so do several learning community programs in community colleges. Faculty teaching teams find these conversations intensely stimulating and worthwhile and an important professional development feature of team teaching.

Supporting Graduate Teaching Assistants and Undergraduate Peer Mentors

As we have already noted, at larger colleges and universities most freshman learning communities involve either undergraduate peer mentors or graduate TAs. The undergraduates may convene freshman seminars on their own or in tandem with a faculty member or student affairs professional; sometimes they assist as peer mentors in courses in the disciplines, working with the faculty members of those classes. Other learning community models involve graduate instructors who usually teach fresh-man seminars or introductory writing, math, or speech communication classes in the learning community program.

The staff orientation and development needs are especially great here because these individuals (whether undergraduates or graduate students) are generally novice teachers, and they frequently teach for only one year. The learning community arrangement often asks them to serve on teaching teams with faculty members, with all the attendant differences in age, experience, and status.

In the best situation, the support program for undergraduate peer mentors is built around a predictable recruiting and training cycle. The peer mentors are recruited in fall and early winter for teaching in learning communities the following year. Orientation and training usually takes place in the spring semester or quarter, often in the form of a credit-bearing course in student leadership taught by a student affairs professional. There may be a retreat or orientation session for this group of students just before classes begin with meeting time allotted for learning community teaching teams as well as just for the peer mentor team. Furthermore, throughout the terms in which they are teaching in learning communities, peer mentors are supported with weekly debriefing meetings. Peer mentors may be compensated for their learning community teaching through work-study funds, special stipends, tuition waivers, or reduced residence hall fees, or they may receive undergraduate credit for teaching in these programs. In any event, learning community leaders' investment in the development and support of these students can reap significant rewards in creating an energetic and highly creative cadre of teachers and in building a community of practice in this group of emerging leaders and mentors.

The training of graduate teaching assistants in general varies considerably from place to place. In some institutions there is centralized responsibility for supporting graduate student teachers, often through a center for teaching and learning, but in most institutions this is a decentralized function placed in the academic departments. Most graduate student training programs focus solely on first-time teaching assistants, often through onetime workshops, even though becoming a capable teacher is a complex developmental process that extends over many years. Because of this variable tradition of supporting the education of graduate students as teachers, learning community support of teaching assistants is similarly quite variable. Although a few campuses have highly developed programs to support teaching assistants, on many other campuses teaching assistants are simply assigned (often at the last minute) to a learning community and receive very little orientation and training.

With graduate students, the cycles of recruitment and training are similar to those of undergraduate peer mentors, but a persistent problem involves course assignment patterns. Often graduate students (and adjunct faculty) are not assigned to actual sections of classes (such as English composition, speech communication, mathematics, or the freshman seminar) until very late in the summer. This means that they have little or no time to meet the other faculty members involved, much less do any meaningful planning. Therefore, learning community leaders generally develop their own training and support programs for graduate students serving as freshman seminar teachers, or they develop partnerships with the individuals who supervise composition or math or speech instructors. Some institutions, such as Texas A&M-Corpus Christi and California State University-Hayward, which enroll their entire entering classes in learning communities, have made institutional commitments to graduate students who teach in learning communities. Graduate students take required classes in college teaching and have a strong support system throughout the academic year.

With late assignments to teaching sections, many learning community programs hold learning community orientation and planning meetings just before classes begin in the fall to introduce the members of the teaching teams to one another, including faculty members, graduate students, part-time instructors, and student affairs professionals. An important emphasis of these gatherings is to name and bring out into the open the obvious differences in status and experience represented in the team's makeup. Paying attention to building the learning community team means recognizing the diversity, in age, experience, gender, race, and so on, that is included in the team.

Faculty Development as an Evolving Process

As a learning community program is developed over time, its leaders can create faculty and staff development activities that encourage broad involvement and respond to the evolving needs of the students and faculty. For newcomers to learning community teaching, some kind of firsthand, experiential exposure to actual learning community teaching can be extremely valuable. Many teachers gravitate to the learning community idea or have a sense of the rationale for these programs but still have difficulty putting theory into practice. Visiting institutions with established programs can be quite helpful, as can visiting ongoing communities on the campus. At some colleges and universities, release time or stipends are provided not only for learning community planning but for learning community visiting prior to teaching in a first learning community program.

The evolution of Temple University's faculty development work is typical of a long-established and large learning community program. In the beginning, Temple received significant external funding to initiate learning communities. The leaders made the conscious decision not to invest this money in release time for teaching because it might raise expectations and make the program unaffordable in the long run. Instead, they created a position of Faculty Fellow for Learning Communities (a professor drawn from the faculty to act as a faculty development leader for the initiative) and invested heavily in faculty development through workshops and summer planning meetings. Also, because Temple relies heavily on graduate teaching assistants to deliver certain freshman courses in the learning communities, the learning community leaders immediately recognized the need to orient and train these instructors continually.

In the ten years since the learning community initiative began at Temple, the faculty development effort has evolved in response to the changing context and goals of the program and to important information gleaned through an evolving assessment effort. At first, faculty development emphasized orienting faculty members and graduate teaching assistants to the definitions and purposes of learning communities—often involving external consultants to lead these workshops. This approach was valuable for recruiting the first generation of learning community teachers and for familiarizing the campus with the learning community approach. Later, more extensive faculty development workshops focused on key aspects of learning community pedagogy, such as writing across the curriculum, group dynamics, learning theory, and classroom assessment. The administrative decision to double the size of the learning community offerings called for new faculty development. Concerns about consistent program quality led not only to more extensive orientations but to various print materials to guide planning, including a curricular planning worksheet for faculty teams, and a faculty handbook for learning community teaching.

More recent assessments of the learning community program at Temple have led to additional modifications of the faculty development effort: a Web-based Blackboard Community for Faculty, summer planning meetings with an emphasis on curricular integration, a modified stipend plan for curricular planning, and a midsemester community report that functions as an informal assessment strategy. Looking back on how faculty support has evolved, Jodi Levine Laufgraben comments, "Over the past ten years, we have learned that faculty development decisions need to be integrated with ongoing program planning and assessment activities. Our advice: be flexible and willing to change the focus and content of faculty development. Listen to faculty and survey the learning community landscape to benefit from what has worked or not worked on other campuses. Faculty development should be not merely training but an important opportunity to create a learning community for faculty" (Levine Laufgraben, 2003, p. 37).

As we pointed out previously, Skagit Valley Community College requires students to enroll in three learning communities as part of its general education program. The stakes are high when a requirement is institutionalized because it necessarily involves a larger number of faculty. Thus, Skagit Valley invests heavily in ongoing faculty development and assessment, offering workshops, retreats, and other support. The learning community coordinator regularly assesses program impact, does exit interviews of teaching teams, and provides periodic reports on needed improvements, which she then tries to implement.

Here too, the approach to faculty development evolved over time. From the outset, Skagit Valley leaders recognized that building a faculty learning community was essential. An annual off-campus curriculum planning retreat has become a cornerstone. The retreat is intentionally designed to strengthen the faculty community as well as the courses in the community. All activities model integrative/collaborative strategies and showcase faculty collaborations. Food, fun, and learning are the recipe for success here. The day is divided between structured workshops on various topics and time for faculty teams to work together. The nature of the workshops has changed over time. In the early years, the focus was on the purpose and design of learning communities, overcoming the fear of teaching collaboratively, and strategies for helping students adjust to the new pedagogies. As the learning community program matured, faculty development activities have focused on deepening the pedagogical approaches.

At Skagit Valley, the written learning community proposal process itself fosters alignment around best practices. In their learning community proposal, each faculty team must explicitly indicate the program's theme or themes, how the structure and activities will encourage students to become active participants, and how the curriculum will be integrated. Johnson C. Smith, a historically black institution, uses a somewhat similar approach, with clear expectations at the front end as well as formal assessment practices at the conclusion. Surveys and faculty logs ascertain how and whether learning community programs include core practices. These exit assessment strategies provide essential information for shaping subsequent faculty development activities.

Seattle Central Community College, another institution with an extensive and long-standing commitment to learning communities, uses a variety of faculty development approaches, including faculty exchanges, summer institutes, course development stipends, workshops, and support to attend conferences. One early initiative was a yearlong "Alternative Pedagogies Institute" that covered a wide range of topics for anyone interested in improving their teaching. The course focused on student intellectual development, active and collaborative learning, effective syllabus design, and approaches to evaluation, including student self-evaluation. About a hundred learning community and non-learning-community faculty members participated over a three-year period. This institute was important in attracting vocational faculty into the learning community effort and in educating large numbers of faculty about learning community rationale and practices. Many community colleges like Seattle Central give salary credit for professional development activities such as these.

Team Teaching as Faculty Development

Coplanning and team teaching are themselves legitimate faculty development opportunities that can be supported through release time, stipends, summer workshops, and curriculum planning retreats. Indeed, many faculty involved in team teaching regard it as the most important form of faculty development they undertake because it is continuous, day-to-day, and executed in the context of real classrooms with real students.

At St. Lawrence University, the team teaching in the first-year program and the Cultural Encounters programs led to fundamental transformations in the faculty culture. As Grant Cornwell and Eve Stoddard point out:

> Since its inception, the program has been a laboratory for innovative pedagogy. . . . Pedagogical innovation is bound to occur when three faculty from different disciplines together work out how to teach a course. . . . The first growth spurt is when the team sets about in earnest to define collaboratively the thematic focus of the course. For example, it may happen that a biologist, a historian, and a philosopher agree that they have a shared interest in how humans construct their relationships with the natural world. . . . Constructing a syllabus with an interdisciplinary team tends to be an exercise in reining in enthusiasms. As faculty liberate themselves from the discipline of disciplines, there emerges a collective, creative energy, the products of which are a joy for the faculty. . . .

A significant number of participants have created new professional identities for themselves out of these efforts. . . . Faculty trained in Eurocentric fields have expanded their teaching and research to new areas, more global in scope and more self-reflective about the points of view being represented. The most significant change for those already trained in area studies has been increased cross-disciplinary theoretical development. Others have changed their pedagogies to include more self-reflection through writing. [Cornwell and Stoddard, 2001, pp. 165–172]

Whatever form it takes, team teaching introduces additional challenges and opportunities as faculty learn to navigate the unfamiliar waters of planning and teaching together, but their comfort with team teaching grows over time (Smith, 1994).

As one colleague notes, "Previously I was intimidated by faculty who had much more experience, by teaching where I wasn't an expert, by not being able to teach skills by tried-and-true methods, by having to risk inventions daily. . . . Now I have anxieties but they're not the same. I don't worry anymore about not knowing everything. How some daunting faculty person (and for a time anyone who observed me teaching was daunting) perceives me hardly concerns me now."

Each day is filled with surprises, as another teacher describes, and this is part of the ongoing learning that makes team teaching so rich and fulfilling. As a colleague recalls:

I remember one day while teaching in a team that included me (a historian), a geographer, and an Asian studies specialist. An eighteenth-century Chinese novel with a complicated plot had been assigned. When we came to class for the first discussion of the novel, the geographer slammed the book on the table and loudly protested: "I don't know why we chose to read this book. I couldn't keep the characters straight. I wanted to throw the book against the wall." I was academically embarrassed, almost scandalized, that a member of the faculty should voice the kind of anti-intellectual protest we often hear from self-righteous, inexperienced students. I was about to try to shush my colleague and have him postpone his critique to the safe haven of the faculty lounge when he completed his tirade with the statement, "Yes, I couldn't make sense of this book until I did this . . ." and unfolded a chart he'd made tracing the characters and their relationship. What a powerful teaching moment this was for students on how to read a book! They were exposed to a real-life snapshot of how an experienced learner dealt with a difficult text. The students were exposed to the faculty engaging in learning and the process of learning was itself demystified in an authentic way. They could relate to this faculty member as a learner as they saw how he overcame the barriers and was successful in what had seemed hopeless at first.

At the same time, it must be acknowledged that many learning communities fail to reach their potential in team teaching and the true integration of the content, becoming little more than take-turn teaching situations. Sometimes the administrative procedures for staffing a team exacerbate the situation, as one veteran English teacher describes:

> I've had two intensely frustrating experiences in collaborative courses. The first was with a new, young part-timer assigned at the last minute. It was not her newness and youth that created the problems. Instead it was her lack of understanding of learning theory, the ins and outs of collaboration, and the structural problems created by the necessity of collaborating with someone paid on a per-credit basis with no incentive for collaboration or learning about it. This colleague relied on the lecture method, delivered straight from the book. I was unfamiliar with her field (music history) and she was unable to help me understand how to create effective writing assignments that would underscore the learning. . . . As a result I was pretty much on my own. She would lecture for an hour and then leave. The students would start my class angry, bored, and frustrated. It was hard to persuade them that there was any value in continuing the course. During that quarter, I was really blessed with colleagues who helped me learn the value of humor and play. It's what I relied on to keep the students engaged. . . . The students and I survived. We learned a little about music. We learned a lot about learning. More importantly, I learned the importance of creating supportive institutional structures for part-time faculty as well as addressing how one teaches and how one collaborates right up front.

When done well, team teaching provides a rich venue for deep faculty development. Well-designed, single faculty development workshops or meetings can be valuable, but sustained approaches that include day-to-day teaching, modeling, and reflection have a transformative power. Nonetheless, team teaching requires continuous institutional support. Curriculum planning is usually *the* central issue. This is a faculty development issue in terms of learning to collaborate, learning how to create integrated syllabi, and learning to work across the boundaries of different disciplines and work styles. It is also a time issue. Institutional strategies for supporting curriculum planning time include stipends, summer institutes, and curriculum planning retreats. Many institutions have found that public planning retreats are much more effective than simply providing stipends to individual teams. Public planning retreats help develop a collective commitment to learning community core practices and set a standard for curriculum planning.

The Evergreen State College bases its entire curriculum on team-taught learning communities, and the faculty form new teams and redesign their coordinated studies programs each year. The ambitious scale of this approach requires substantial investment in faculty development. Although team teaching is itself seen as the most important form of faculty development, Evergreen also offers a variety of summer workshops and institutes for faculty on topics such as collaborative learning, curriculum design, the use of instructional technology, and diversity. In addition, most faculty teams attend a five-day summer curriculum planning institute. This not only provides time for individual teams to plan their programs but creates an important public venue for working with colleagues and sharing ideas. Student affairs staff members, called "core connectors," are each attached to individual freshman learning community programs. They also attend these summer institutes to ensure that they are part of the teaching teams. These faculty development activities are regarded as an opportunity for curriculum planning, team development, and skill building, and for finding new teaching partners as well.

Institutions using team teaching find that sufficient planning time is also an issue once the term begins. Here again, it is important to develop shared expectations among teammates. As the term unfolds, teachers often work together intensively and may have to limit their time or this constant planning becomes exhausting. This is especially true if the learning community teaching assignment is only part of an instructor's teaching load. Team-planned and team-taught learning communities should include agreements about when to meet and touch base, how to stay in touch—especially if student issues come up—and who is responsible for which program logistics. On some campuses, these understandings are written up in a set of agreements called a "faculty covenant," whose development is usually more a means of having a discussion about working together than of forming a prescriptive set of rules. Still, the development of a faculty covenant is often useful in building collaboration and reaching beyond teachers' traditional habits of going it alone.

Interinstitutional Faculty Development Strategies

As we indicated in Chapter Two, interinstitutional strategies and organizations have been important in building the learning community movement across the nation. Interinstitutional work has increased the rate of innovation and allowed campuses to learn quickly from one another without, as one put it, "reinventing too many flat tires." Interinstitutional work can give participants a sense that they are part of something larger while sharing approaches and gathering energy and validation from like-minded colleagues.

Much of the interinstitutional support for learning community faculty development has come through existing higher education organizations. National organizations such as the AAHE and the AAC&U have featured learning community sessions at their specialized and annual conferences for more than two decades and continue to do so. In addition, AAC&U offers a regional conference on learning communities each spring. Both AAHE and AAC&U also offer general purpose summer institutes for campus teams, which have been important venues for some campuses to do learning community planning in the company of others.

Regional meetings are providing another venue for interinstitutional faculty development in the form of open houses, periodic conferences, and curriculum retreats throughout the United States. These fill a real need for affordable ways to plan learning communities in the company of kindred spirits and learn more about what other institutions are doing.

The Evergreen State College's public service center, the Washington Center for Improving the Quality of Undergraduate Education, also provides ongoing support for learning communities through conferences, interinstitutional visitations, faculty exchanges, curriculum planning retreats, workshops, and publications. For more than twenty years, interinstitutional summer institutes and curriculum retreats sponsored by the center have brought campus teams together to plan learning community programs with the assistance of more experienced colleagues. This center continues to sponsor an annual residential summer institute for campus teams from across the United States interested in developing or strengthening learning communities. The Washington Center is the home of the National Learning Community Web site at http://learningcommons.evergreen.edu. (For accounts of the Washington Center work, see Smith, 1988, 2001b, 2003.)

Faculty exchanges have been a powerful interinstitutional vehicle for disseminating learning community practices, especially in Washington State where the Washington Center has acted as a statewide broker of faculty exchanges that ultimately involved hundreds of faculty. Faculty exchanges have stimulated learning community development at such schools as Brookhaven Community College, Spokane Falls Community College, Lower Columbia College, Seattle Central Community College, and the University of Hawaii.

During the most intensive start-up years for learning communities at community colleges in Washington, the Washington Center directors conducted end-of-quarter debriefing interviews with learning community teaching teams throughout the state. These interviews proved to be valuable for both assessment and faculty development. The center then circulated some feedback to these individuals through an informal newsletter, *Learning Community Gleanings,* which both shared bright ideas and discussed difficulties that many teachers and programs were encountering. Faculty members interviewed repeatedly commented that these conversations would never have happened without the presence of a supportive third party and that having the chance to reflect on their experience brought both broader perspectives and a sense of closure. End-of-term debriefing has been widely adopted on various campuses, with the learning community coordinator or the director of faculty development serving as the convener of the debriefing conversation.

Lessons About Recruiting and Supporting Learning Community Teachers

To expand and sustain learning communities, supportive structures and practices must be invented for those who do not have the intrinsic motivation of early adopters. It is important to create venues to learn new practices, develop supportive incentive systems, and build structures that encourage face-to-face relationships (Elmore, 1996). Nurturing a lively learning community of teachers is essential to the ongoing vitality of a learning community program. What are the other key lessons we have learned in recruiting and supporting learning community teachers over the past fifteen years?

o Building an ongoing inclusive learning community of teachers around issues that matter is an important goal of faculty development.

o Developing a critical mass of learning community teachers is necessary to ensure the long-term viability of a program.

o Identifying and utilizing existing resources, such as the teaching and learning center, the office of institutional research, and current faculty development funds are good strategies to build allies and find resources.

o Faculty and staff recruitment needs to be continuous, and someone must be clearly responsible for this task.

o Building faculty development activities around groups rather than individuals is an effective way simultaneously to build the larger campus learning community.

o Faculty development activities should be used to support current participants and to recruit future learning community teachers.

o Institutional roles and rewards need to support learning community participation or the effort will remain fragile.

o In addition to faculty, many people can be learning community teachers: student affairs professionals, librarians, undergraduate and graduate students, even members of the external community.

o Building faculty development activities around the core practices of learning communities—fostering community, diversity, active learning, curricular integration, reflection, and assessment—is a way to ensure that learning communities are based on educationally effective approaches.

o Investing in curriculum planning time is crucial, especially for learning communities that involve team planning or team teaching.

o Faculty development efforts change over time; it is important to recognize this.

o Building the faculty development program *with* the faculty and teaching staff is always desirable, as is continuing to assess what works and what is needed.

Finally, some timeless advice from others includes this: Honor those who come. Recognize and celebrate good work. Provide food, and make it fun.

9

INITIATING AND SUSTAINING
LEARNING COMMUNITIES

*In facing the challenges of profound change, there is no substi-
tute for collaboration—people coming together out of common
purpose and willing to support one another so all can advance.*

—Peter Senge

BOTH THE EARLY AND RECENT HISTORIES of learning community
implementation are instructive. Many of the early programs were attempts
at fundamental reform, but they failed to sustain themselves for more than
a few years. More recent efforts have more varied and limited aims, and
they have endured longer. The learning community effort is now so large-
scale that there are many different forms of learning communities in existence at various points of development. They offer a rich perspective on
what is required to become a viable and lasting institutional reform.

This chapter explores the process of initiating and sustaining learning
communities and the issues that must be addressed if they are to flourish.
In the wake of any substantial reform initiatives, political, cultural, and
structural challenges follow. Initiating any innovation is often a messy
and unpredictable process. As community organizer Fred Ross was fond
of putting it, the effort often revolves around forging ahead and working
on the details simultaneously. Waiting for everything to be perfectly in
place is unrealistic.

The process of implementing learning communities raises issues of
reforming the existing organization in various ways. In their attempts to

craft more communal and interdisciplinary teaching and learning environments, cross-disciplinary learning communities challenge the traditional academic culture of seeing the world through the disciplines. Indeed, it can be difficult to find a place for cross-disciplinary learning communities in an academy structured around departments and disciplines. Rearranging the existing geography and political relationships in the organization, adding or restructuring human resources, making new investments, and as learning communities grow, rethinking existing support services, hiring, and faculty and staff development processes may also be involved. Ultimately, the success of a learning community initiative depends on the institution's strategic understanding of why learning communities are important and its ability to support this vision. As Peter Senge points out, collaboration is fundamental to facing the challenges of change.

Learning communities face typical developmental challenges as they move from a bright idea to a new and struggling program on the ground to a well-established initiative. We begin this chapter with a description of the process of initiating learning communities and the complex tasks that must be accomplished during implementation. Building on Chapter Eight's discussion of recruiting and supporting learning community teachers, we then turn to the subjects of forming a collaborative leadership team, defining goals and choosing a learning community framework, student recruitment, marketing and promotion, advising and registration, financing learning communities, demonstrating cost-effectiveness, and assessment. The concluding section of the chapter discusses institutionalizing learning communities and what it means to turn an innovation into a genuine reform.

In *Leadership Without Easy Answers*, Ronald Heifetz (1994) points out that organizations face several types of challenges. Some are what he calls *technical challenges*. Though often complicated and requiring enormous attention to detail, technical challenges can be solved through routine and known procedures. Many of the initial issues a learning community faces are of this sort: How do we make our registration system work for the program? How do we promote the program? What should we provide in terms of faculty development? What will the program cost? How will we fund it? How should faculty load be configured? Technical challenges are important, and they need to be addressed for a program to succeed, but they can usually be resolved. Hundreds of colleges and universities have successfully solved these technical challenges already.

Sustaining learning communities over the long term and scaling them up to have a substantial impact on the institution often present a bigger set of challenges. But this test of time is critical if learning communities are to move from innovation to genuine reform. Reflecting on the experience of several dozen campuses in one of the few extensive studies of learning community implementation, Geri, Kuehn, and MacGregor (1999) note that genuine "reforms are associated with a process of structural change, political gamesmanship, and the reforming of working relationships that generate a huge amount of discomfort and disarray. . . . Institutionalizing learning community efforts means also confronting and overcoming these problems associated with reform" (MacGregor, 1999, p. 196). These are what Ronald Heifetz refers to as *adaptive challenges*.

As Heifetz points out, adaptive challenges cannot be easily resolved through existing procedures and practices. They are about bigger, long-term issues, often involving fundamental value conflicts. Heifetz cites the American civil rights movement as an example of an adaptive challenge of trying to close the gap between rhetoric about equality and practice. This adaptive challenge continues today. Committing to the academic success of all students is an adaptive challenge faced by the academy. Learning communities are one way to address this challenge. Because learning community initiatives are new and intersect so many structures, cultures, and systems on a campus, they face a host of both technical and adaptive challenges.

Initiating Learning Communities

The first step in initiating learning communities is, obviously, seeing the opportunity in the idea. This idea can be sparked in many different ways: faculty members or student affairs professionals may learn of a program at another school and see the potential for their institution; new administrators may see a unique opportunity to revisit the institution's agenda while also communicating their own values and ideas. Many learning community programs have been developed as a result of campus teams attending a conference. Spending a few days together provides an exceptional and rare opportunity to become a collaborative group mobilized around a common interest in educational improvement.

There are obviously many triggering opportunities, but the idea of the learning community finds fertile ground when it is matched with an institutional need, when someone decides it might address her own organization's agenda. In his work *Diffusion of Innovations,* Rogers refers (1995) to this as a process of "matching," where a new idea connects to an existing issue or need.

Prior conditions often play a role in shaping an institution's orientation to new ideas. Certain colleges and universities seem to be early adopters or bellwethers for change, and they often set the pace for others. Institutionally, some departments or units are more change-oriented than others. Although this does not mean that innovation *only* happens in change-oriented departments or institutions, predispositions for transformation do often shape institutional perspectives. Many of the early learning community programs began at institutions with a history of innovation. Their cultures were open to change, and they had many points of compatibility with the new ideas. These kinds of institutions tend to recruit and reward individuals who are similarly predisposed to new ideas and also provide opportunities for them to influence others.

The fit between an idea such as the learning community and an institutional goal or need can be relatively narrow or quite broad. Learning communities might be seen as a means of addressing "the retention problem" or more broadly as a vehicle for building a more collaborative culture. In addition, people's roles often shape their perceptions. As a result, faculty and administrators usually describe the benefits of learning communities in different terms. Faculty stress the intellectual and personal growth they experience, whereas administrators point to the value of building a better institutional climate, greater faculty inventiveness, and more engagement with students. Notions of the value of learning communities evolve and change over time. When the transformative power of these approaches becomes apparent, institutions often begin thinking about them in larger, more strategic ways.

Why do some institutions have limited notions about what learning communities can accomplish while others see them more broadly? And why do some remain limited in impact while others take off and expand their reach? The answer appears to lie in the different abilities of institutions to build, frame, and reframe their environment, which is strongly related to their internal capacity for team building, communication, and feedback. The process of institutional change is one of continuous learning, which healthy institutions promote through various structures and practices.

Establishing a Collaborative Leadership Team

Learning communities require leadership at many different levels. Establishing a collaborative leadership team is probably the single most important step in initiating and sustaining them. This has been the key finding from intensive work with nearly 150 colleges and universities involved in the National Learning Community Project carried out from 1996 to 2003. Institutions with learning community programs that failed to thrive invariably lacked a broad-based leadership group. When facing the large and often puzzling adaptive challenges that come in truly institutionalizing a program, having many individuals with different institutional perspectives and roles working together on these issues is extremely valuable.

There is no one "best" place to vest leadership for learning communities. Each institution has its own culture and context and therefore its own best place to establish and nurture an innovative enterprise. Sometimes the learning community effort is placed in a particular administrative area for political or personal reasons, often because there is a strong champion there for the effort. A key consideration may be that some offices provide a better platform for influencing the campus. Where a program is situated can make a difference. Here again, institutional goals should provide the desiderata. What is the long-term vision for the program? Who does the institution want to include in the learning community? Many campuses have faced the dilemma of having the reform begin in one part of the university or college and then getting stuck there. This has frequently been an issue with programs originating in student affairs when they try to connect with full-time faculty. At one college where the first learning communities were focused on developmental education, other faculty members thought that learning communities were a strategy only for underprepared students.

Most often a learning coordinator is appointed to be responsible for learning communities. With smaller programs, the responsibility may be added to the desk assignment of an existing administrator. At many community colleges, a faculty member is given partial release time to coordinate a learning community program. Many large research universities have full-time coordinators for their programs who are located in a college of undergraduate studies, a teaching and learning center, or the provost's office, but many also have part-time coordinators in the different schools and colleges. Several programs at large research universities have cochairs of learning community programs coming from academic affairs and student affairs, often residence life. Iowa State and the University of Missouri are notable in this respect. This leadership model sends an important message about collaboration between these two units and indicates that both elements of learning communities—academic and student life—are fundamentally important.

In addition to appointing a learning community coordinator, it is important to create a larger leadership team. This is often done through an advisory or steering committee. When deciding who should be on the steering committee, it is important to have a clear reporting line to the appropriate administrator and to consider the various functional support needs of the learning community program. Figure 9.1 describes these needs.

At Harper College, the faculty coordinator works with a steering committee that reviews program proposals, helps recruit and broker team formation, and offers general advice on the program. A similar committee has guided Bellevue Community College for a number of years and helped broaden ownership and ensure that the critical support people are involved. At Iowa State University, with a large and decentralized learning community program, the steering committee is critical in providing coherence and good communication. Iowa State has a very active advisory committee that includes several subcommittees, one focusing on assessment, another on curriculum enhancement and development. One of the most crucial initial actions in establishing a learning community program is to define goals and choose an appropriate curricular structure. A collaborative leadership group is an ideal locus for this discussion.

Figure 9.1. Learning Community Support Needs

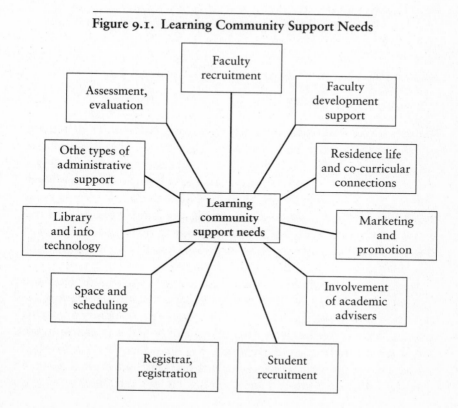

Defining Learning Community Goals

Innovations often start with a flurry of energy and optimism, through a planning process that might be described as "fire-ready-aim." Learning communities are not immune to this spontaneous process, often beginning with vague goals, unclear roles and responsibilities, and little broad institutional discussion and buy-in. Successful efforts eventually become more focused as planners define their aspirations more clearly and weigh different strategies for reaching their goals.

Reviewing institutional needs and goals is a good first step in the planning process because these goals will guide myriad decisions about the initiative. Exhibit 9.1 provides a summary of typical institutional goals that may develop from this process.

Many learning communities begin with goals for students, such as increasing retention and academic engagement, and improving student achievement and learning. As Chapter Seven suggested, learning community research and assessment are demonstrating that learning communities are indeed effective in promoting these goals. Institutions also embrace learning communities to enhance teaching practice and promote faculty vitality and creativity. Learning communities often build a more collaborative culture among the faculty or between faculty and student affairs staff. It is valuable to start with broadly understood goals and then keep revisiting them because they can and do change over time.

Choosing a Curricular Structure

Chapter Three described three major learning community structures, stressing the point that there is no single right or best one. In addition to institutional goals, a variety of institutional factors influence the choice of a structure, such as the size of the student cohort, student enrollment patterns, faculty availability, the shape of the existing academic programs, the faculty role and reward system, faculty teaching loads, and institutional readiness to embrace innovation. Once these goals have been defined and the target population identified, it is time to analyze which curricular frameworks will be most appropriate.

The typical teaching load of the faculty, the average credit load and course-taking patterns of the students, and departmental expectations are principal planning constraints. A full-time learning community organized into a block of fifteen or sixteen credits will not be viable in an institution in which most students enroll part-time. Nor would such a model work in a research institution in which the faculty teaching load is two courses a semester. Most institutions have complex student enrollment patterns

Exhibit 9.1. Frequently Cited Goals of Learning Communities

- *Goals for students:*   Improve retention, promote academic maturity, increase student learning and achievement, increase time on task, promote teamwork and active learning, develop student leadership, increase the success rate for underrepresented students in certain majors.

- *Goals for faculty:*   Increase experimentation within curriculum, broaden pedagogical repertoire of faculty, increase faculty engagement with one another, promote more interaction between faculty and students, promote interaction between junior and senior faculty.

- *Goals for curriculum:*   Increase coherence of general education program, make curriculum more interdisciplinary, promote diversity, infuse skills such as writing, speaking, and quantitative reasoning across the curriculum.

- *Goals for institution:*   Enhance the quality of undergraduate education, better serve underrepresented student populations, increase the sense of community in the institution, promote collaboration between faculty and staff, create entry points for study in the major, create coherent linkages for students in a minor.

- *Goals for community:*   Increase connection between the academy and the community by building learning communities with service or civic learning components.

- *Goals for parents:*   Enroll their son or daughter in an institution that promotes student success, active learning, and intellectual engagement.

and therefore employ different learning community structures for different student groups.

Another key decision concerns teaching teams. Will the teaching teams be made up of full-time or part-time faculty? Will they be faculty–student affairs partnerships? Will they include peer mentors? These decisions are also influenced by the existing culture, usual staffing patterns, and availability and interests of different people. Some institutions have a long-standing practice of involving librarians and counselors in the classroom; for others this would be an entirely new approach. At one institution, the initial vision was to build the teams around full-time tenured faculty members, but economics and faculty interest led the effort in an entirely different direction to adjunct faculty and teaching assistants. Another institution began a freshman interest group program with student affairs staff teaching the freshman seminar but hoped eventually to include regular faculty also, but then found, as have many others, that established staffing patterns are difficult to alter.

Scale is another issue that should be considered from the start. Do the founders envision a large program that reaches across the institution, or will the program be a small enterprise intended to provide an alternative pathway for a limited number of students? It has become clear that some approaches "scale up" more readily than others. For example, the freshman interest group approach has become popular in many large research institutions because it can be built around large enrollment classes taught in conventional lecture formats. It can also easily grow from a small pilot to a more pervasive initiative.

Resources also play an important role in the choice of curricular structure. Linked classes and FIGs can usually be offered with little change in existing resource allocation patterns. Team-taught learning communities, in contrast, usually require more complex support and organization as well as substantial changes in faculty teaching approaches.

The learning community approach needs to support the institution's goals, so implementation must be consistent with these goals. Thus, if faculty development is a key goal, some features of the model need to include faculty interaction through team teaching or team planning, and there must be structural arrangements to harvest and disseminate teaching and learning approaches. If the emphasis is primarily on student retention and creating a sense of community among the students, then a close link with student affairs is essential. If curricular coherence is a central goal, then strategies for curricular integration are important. If connecting to the external community is a goal, then the curriculum design may include service learning or community-based projects. If promoting collaboration rather than competition is a goal, then the pedagogy, evaluation, and grading systems need to take this into account. If the learning community effort is seen as a general incubator for ongoing reform in the institution, then there is good reason to keep the agenda and the goals somewhat open and to build a robust internal communication strategy. As these examples suggest, the goals are important in defining the major stakeholders who need to be included as well as the key pedagogical features of the initiative.

Recruiting Students

Once goals have been defined and a curricular framework has been chosen, planning for student recruitment is the next essential step. This is a complex task that involves many different offices in the institution. As a result, creating learning communities is often a community-building experience for a campus. Because learning communities are generally a completely new idea to students, the need to recruit continuously never really goes away. They are also a new idea for the campus, so it is important to involve campus leaders and key support staff to build their understanding and support.

Recruitment strategies need to be tailored to the specific learning community goals. Freshman interest group programs usually do not market themselves as fascinating curricular excursions into interdisciplinary education, but rather present themselves to students as a convenient way to get adjusted to college, register for a coherent package of needed courses, and make friends in the freshman year. Many community colleges market team-taught interdisciplinary programs as a convenient way to meet general education requirements or link required writing courses.

Learning communities are most effectively promoted when they are built around *real* student needs and enrollment patterns. What is usually paramount to students is a good schedule, the opportunity to make friends, the ready availability of courses that count toward their degree, and a coherent, high-quality educational experience. There is a persistent myth that a good faculty team and an interesting theme will attract students. As a result, faculty often make the mistake of offering course combinations that are interesting to them but esoteric from students' point of view. At one community college three faculty members had fascinating ideas about ways to link courses in contemporary fiction, sociology of deviance, and abnormal psychology. Unfortunately, there were not enough students who wanted and needed these 200-level courses, and the program failed to attract students. This scenario has been repeated on campuses all over the country.

Dan Thompkins and Jodi Levine at Temple University call this the "boutique approach" to building the learning community curriculum. As intellectually interesting as such offerings might be, they do not attract students. Commenting on Temple's belated recognition of this fact, Levine and Thompkins noted:

> At first, we either linked nonrequired courses that stimulated faculty but attracted too few students or used courses that did not draw significant numbers of first-year students. No amount of publicity about our exciting new program to improve student success increased enrollment. . . . After this experience, we sought more refined data about student course selection, and planned communities more deliberately. By fall 1994, we were able to offer learning communities that appealed

to a wide range of entering undergraduates. These courses meet our key requirements: they fill important core areas, have few or no prerequisites, and leave the students ahead of the pack in progress toward a degree." [Levine and Thompkins, 1996, p. 3]

Thompkins and Levine advocate building learning community programs like "shopping malls" around anchor stores that attract large numbers of shoppers, and not boutiques, which come and go. The anchor stores in learning community curricula are the basic distribution courses such as English composition and high-enrollment introductory general education courses. In most institutions, students aim for efficiency in choosing courses and will only enroll in those they need. Building learning communities around required courses is therefore one of the most effective ways to ensure enrollment. In fact, across American higher education, twenty-five key gateway courses carry more than half the student enrollment. Getting a critical mass of students in other areas is difficult, except in very large institutions or in majors with large enrollments. There are also pointed differences between first- and second-semester enrollment patterns that need to be taken into account during planning.

Most learning community programs are one quarter or one semester long. Generally speaking, it is difficult to hold enrollment beyond a single term. A number of community colleges have tried to build an associate of arts degree entirely through learning community offerings but have not succeeded, finding that students have too many other interests and requirements to enroll in a yearlong program, much less a two-year one. Even at The Evergreen State College, where much of the curriculum is organized around yearlong programs, students often change programs midyear, and enrollments by the third quarter of a yearlong program are low. The exception around the country has been multiquarter pre-professional programs in which students enroll as a cohort, in living-learning residential programs, and in multiquarter general education programs where the enrollment is sustained through requirements.

When learning communities offer attractive, compact schedules and a good array of needed courses, the effort contributes to improving student progression. Two five-year studies at North Seattle Community College demonstrated that students in learning communities made better progress in time-to-degree and were more likely to complete a degree (Wilkie, 1990). The most recent five-year study of students seeking the associate transfer degree at this campus found that 55 percent of the learning community students completed it compared with 13 percent of the non-learning-community students (Smith, 2003; Harnish, 2002).

Marketing and Promoting Learning Communities

Marketing and promotional efforts need to be closely linked to student recruitment activities. These two functions—marketing and student recruitment—are frequently located in different offices in an institution. To ensure that they are closely coordinated, many learning community steering committees include people from both enrollment services or student recruitment, and marketing or public relations.

Marketing is often narrowly equated with promotional strategies, but it is actually a much broader and more complex planning function. We define marketing here as the analysis, planning, and implementation of carefully formulated programs to inform students and other stakeholders about learning communities and recruit students into these programs. Marketing is a sequential planning process that moves from data gathering to analysis, to making decisions about product design, and to developing and enacting various promotional strategies. Marketing rests on what are called the four P's in the marketing literature: *product, place, price,* and *promotion.* As Sevier (1998) points out, "A true marketing effort involves creating a product that is valued, at a price that people will pay, in a place to which people will come. . . . Your product, price, and place must be brought to people's attention through promotion" (p. 37). Learning communities across the nation offer a wide spectrum of variations on these four dimensions.

As we have already indicated, learning communities are a highly flexible product: they vary widely in design and can be situated in almost any curricular area. In terms of place, they may be designed as on-campus or off-campus programs, as daytime offerings or evening-weekend programs. They may focus on commuter or residential students. These are all ways to appeal to students for whom place and schedule are important. There is generally less variation in price because most institutions have uniform practices for pricing their curricular offerings, but some living-learning communities do vary on this dimension as well, charging an extra fee to reside in a living-learning community that provides a rich array of additional benefits. A number of institutions are now using their learning communities as distinctive programs to attract students. In the years since learning communities have been featured in a number of college guides, this strategy has become more pervasive. The important point here is that the learning community must be aligned with the preferences of prospective students in order to attract them successfully. Therefore, it is critical to know student preferences and needs.

Research is the cornerstone of all effective marketing efforts because it tells us what students want and need, what they think about our programs, and what factors might make a difference in attracting them. Research can also help us understand the views of key stakeholders, including college advisers, administrators, and faculty. Many of these people are key communicators with students, and the success of the learning community program depends partly on their knowledge and support. With an empirical understanding of student and stakeholder views, an institution is in a better position to respond. Market research methods take many different forms, ranging from intensive interviews, to telephone and mail surveys, to focus groups. Market research also includes analysis of existing sources of information, such as registration patterns, studies of alumni, and so forth. (A more detailed description of learning community marketing and market research is available on the learning community Web site at http://learningcommons.evergreen.edu under the Frequently Asked Questions section.)

Promotional efforts need to recognize that most students are unfamiliar with learning communities. Because they are accustomed to choosing conventional courses from set curriculum lists, learning communities may seem like a detour from the path they believe they need to follow. Yet there are key times and places to publicize learning communities and attract students. It is important also to recognize that publicity is for everyone—not just students. It is about building understanding of the effort on the part of a wide segment of the college or university community.

When thinking about student recruitment, it is helpful to ask who the key communicators with students are in an organization, where students get information, and when the key communication moments occur. No single communication and promotional approach will suffice. Students learn about learning communities in many different ways: academic advisers, peer advisers, faculty, student organizations, Web sites, and print material often play a role. Furthermore, different approaches are needed to reach both new students and students who are already enrolled.

Colleges and universities with large enrollments usually have many ways to communicate with new students, through summer orientation sessions, special mailings, and required advising. Large programs such as the Freshman Interest Group programs at the University of Washington, the University of Oregon, California State University-Hayward, Arizona State University, Ball State, the University of Texas, the University of Missouri, and Temple have natural advantages simply because they are so large and visible. The University of Washington's Freshman Interest Group program, for example, now enrolls nearly 75 percent of all first-quarter freshmen. This program grew from a small effort that began with only two FIGs in 1987. Like most programs, it went through a period of experimenting to find the best approach. After attempting to offer winter and spring FIGs, the university quickly found that the program only attracted students in the fall quarter. It promotes the program through special mailings and highlights the effort during its mandatory summer orientation for parents and students. Over the years, the University of Washington has found that parents, especially those from rural communities, are concerned about sending their sons and daughters to such a large, urban institution. Many see the FIG program as an ideal opportunity for their children to meet others, get individual attention, and find a more coherent curriculum. As it has turned out, parents have helped recruit students into the program. The peer advisers have also become very effective in recruiting students. Many of the senior student peer advisers were in the FIG program as freshmen and speak compellingly about its advantages.

Smaller learning community programs at commuter schools and community colleges have more difficulty publicizing their programs simply because it is hard to reach new students. The student body is more transient, and there are few vehicles for sustained communication about new educational opportunities. Research at twelve Washington colleges suggested that most students learned about learning communities through personal contact—an adviser, a faculty member, or a friend. This insight directed marketing efforts to more personal contact as a key strategy in reaching students.

Web sites are an increasingly important communication vehicle, and many institutions now use Web-based registration. Unfortunately, few college Web sites do a good job of promoting learning communities and providing the kinds of information new students need. But there are some good models, including the Web sites of De Anza Community College, Lane Community College, New Century College at George Mason University, the University of Oregon, and UCLA. Essential features are ease of navigation, up-to-date information, content relevant to student questions, and course schedules and descriptions. Student photos and testimonials are also helpful.

Marketing materials need to be appealing to students and based on practical considerations. Prominently featuring the learning community program in the catalogue and the class schedule is important. A picture of typical students and student quotes is attractive to prospective students. Several campuses have found that including pictures of students of color in learning community materials did more to recruit minority students than all the words in the text. At many institutions, the learning community coordinators have made it their work not just to recruit students but to build consciousness and understanding among staff and faculty throughout the institution.

The language with which learning communities are promoted can make a difference in attracting students and give the program an ongoing identity to help establish it over the long run. Many learning community programs carry names other than "learning community" to communicate their intentions, such as freshman interest groups, integrated studies, interdisciplinary studies, linked courses, learning clusters, first-year initiative, and freshman year experience programs, to name just a few. Some institutions have invented completely new names: the Quanta program at Daytona Beach Community College, for example, developed its name precisely to avoid misinterpretations of overused words. Field testing names and titles of programs with students can be highly instructive.

Advising

Advisers and counselors are key players in learning communities. At a number of institutions, advisers teach the freshman experience course, help lead the FIG seminar, or teach a study skills link to a course in a discipline. Many learning community steering committees wisely include advisers and counselors because they are so crucial to planning. Advisers can help think through course choices, program titles, and recruitment strategies. A number of institutions have developed learning community handbooks for advisers in order to ensure accurate information and to cope with the high turnover that is common in advising positions.

Advisers are often the key first point of contact in recruiting or not recruiting students to learning communities. Uninformed or hostile advisers have sabotaged learning communities in a variety of ways:

o One institution discovered that students who had enrolled in a learning community were later persuaded by an adviser to drop it because he did not agree with the concept.

o At another institution, one adviser told students the learning community was "Mickey Mouse" while another told them it was an honors course, only appropriate for highly motivated students.

o At yet another institution, faculty heard that students were being advised out of learning communities because of the risk of a fifteen-credit block in which they could lose all their credit if they dropped any one part of the learning community.

On many campuses, though, learning communities have been embraced by advisers as an excellent student-centered opportunity. They have often created new relationships between advisers and faculty at the same time. One thing is certain: reaching out to advisers and working closely with them is absolutely essential.

Registration and Scheduling

In the same way that students must be continually recruited to learning communities, registration and space scheduling arrangements must be carefully watched each term. A memo to the registrar is not enough. Getting full administrative support requires patience, tact, and communication. Meetings with the people associated with the registration process are essential. At one campus two linked classes were scheduled back-to-back but at opposite ends of the large campus, so students found it impossible to get to the second class on time. This situation could have been avoided if there had been a meeting with the campus space schedulers. As a result of these consultations, classes are frequently rescheduled to fit learning community patterns better.

There are numerous reports of problems registering students into a block of linked or clustered courses. Initially, these problems were often solved through manual registration, a technical solution that does not work with large programs. As problems and issues involved in manual registration have been resolved, technology and automated registration have provided more challenges. However, even here the issues that were common at the outset are being resolved as registration software is becoming more flexible. Although telephone and Web-based registration that allows students to register without any advising can be an obstacle to recruiting students into special programs like learning communities, this depends largely on how the system is set up. At some institutions, on-line advising is required and it has actually helped students learn more about learning communities, but at others registration staff have been unwilling to promote individual programs on-line. This resistance is often the result of poor communication and inadequate understanding of the learning community approach.

Although students often register for a learning community program under a general theme-based title, learning community credits at the end of the program are usually added to transcripts by listing the embedded standard course titles and numbers rather than entering the credit as a block under the learning community title. Thus a sixteen-credit program titled "Paradox of Progress" would appear on a student's transcript as four standard course equivalencies, such as English Composition, Survey of American History I and II, and Sociology of Change. In some institutions, a prefix, such as an asterisk, is added to indicate that the program has a special feature—being writing-intensive, or meeting a diversity or a technology requirement, for example. Ironically, transcripting learning communities to ensure easy transfer may at the same time conceal the special interdisciplinary, writing-intensive, or high-challenge nature of these programs.

One of the biggest problems learning communities face is finding and negotiating for suitable classroom space, because these offerings often require special arrangements. Team-taught coordinated studies programs, often involving sixty to seventy-five students, require both large and small meeting spaces over extended periods of time. Most learning community teams prefer extended meeting times (often three hours) rather than conventional fifty-minute time blocks. On many campuses, large meeting spaces, especially ones with furniture for collaborative learning, are hard to come by. Because learning communities often become close-knit groups and students study together after class ends, it is ideal to have an additional space, such as a small lounge, dedicated to the group.

Assessment

Effective learning community programs routinely gather and use assessment information to evaluate their effectiveness and improve their programs. Innovative programs generally carry an extraordinary burden of proof in demonstrating their effectiveness, so pioneers would do well to include a robust process of documentation and evaluation from the start. This requires that assessment be built into the entire implementation process from the beginning, that there be a locus of assessment, that appropriate measures be developed, and that the results be used for improving the program and for communicating about it in the institution. (Chapter Seven discusses the assessment process in more detail.)

One of the best ways to think about assessment is to begin with the goals of the program and the multiple audiences that need to be informed through assessment information. Assessment usually serves many different masters and audiences, and the language and methods will vary depending on the audience and purposes. The first use of assessment should be to guide planning. Our previous discussion on marketing makes a strong case for a data-driven marketing process. Assessment is also used to demonstrate the program's effectiveness and improve the program. Different stakeholders may ask different questions. Institutional

leaders and legislators might ask how the program affects student retention and student progress toward degree. Deans might ask, "Is the
program cost-effective?" and "Does it better retain students than
conventional stand-alone courses? Does it lead to fewer withdrawals and
low grades?" Residence life staff and academic leaders might want to
know if the learning community affects campus climate. Faculty might
want to know other things about the innovation: Do the students learn
more? Are they better prepared in basic skills and disciplinary content?
Students might bring an entirely different set of criteria to bear when
assessing learning communities. Balancing all these multiple and sometimes competing stakeholder questions is a challenge. The learning community leadership and assessment team must develop a workable plan
that sets priorities and answers all in turn.

Financing Learning Communities

What Do Learning Communities Cost?

Learning communities need adequate financial support to be strong.
Securing funding and administrative support can be challenging when trying to mount ambitious, boundary-crossing initiatives, but in many cases
support can come from redeploying existing budgets. Exhibit 9.2 describes
typical expenses associated with learning communities.

In the start-up years, funds to orient staff and faculty to the new programs and to recruit students are especially critical. As we pointed out in
Chapter Eight, many schools invest in seminars or retreats to discuss different choices about curricular structures and to familiarize participants

---

Exhibit 9.2. Typical Budget Needs of Learning Communities

- Salaries and benefits for learning community teachers
- Peer mentor stipends
- Salaries and benefits for learning community program coordinators
- Clerical support
- Marketing support and promotional materials
- Student recruitment support
- Training events for graduate TAs
- Support for planning time for learning community teachers
- Learning community planning retreats
- Faculty development
- Goods and services and travel support for learning community program
  participants
- Assessment-evaluation support (staff time, assessment instruments)

with the approach. Once the program is under way, a small support budget for speakers, photocopying, out-of-class trips, and films can be immensely helpful. Because learning communities are cumulative experiences, activities that create new and different ways for students and faculty to work together add cohesiveness to the community. Mundane details such as promotional brochures, adequate classroom space, or a nearby copier may seem more like annoyances than important considerations, but these kinds of things are necessary to the good functioning of a learning community program.

Although some programs have identifiable budget lines, many live within institutional budgets. There is no easy formula for saying exactly what a learning community should cost. The actual cost depends on a number of factors, including the framework chosen, the program's enrollment, support costs, and the cost of the instructor or instructors. The principal cost is the latter, instructor salaries, which vary depending on whether the learning community is staffed with tenure-track faculty, part-time faculty, graduate students, or professional staff in student affairs. Generally speaking, learning community models that are built around large classes, such as freshman interest groups, are less expensive because the cost of the instructor is carried by a large number of students. The amount of time the instructors spend in the learning community classroom also influences the cost. Learning community programs with teaching teams often involve some differentiation of roles and time investment.

Instructional costs may also include faculty compensation for planning time. Policies and approaches to planning and release time vary widely. They depend on the wealth of the institution, the availability of external resources, and the extensiveness of the learning community effort. They also depend on the institutional culture and the reach that the innovation requires in terms of existing faculty capabilities and interests. Some institutions have a fairly long history with collaborative teaching and learning, whereas others are just starting. In some institutions, there is an expectation that faculty will be compensated for designing new courses, whereas in others this is considered a normal part of the faculty role.

Some campuses have created ongoing budget lines to support learning community faculty development and curriculum planning—a practice that we highly recommend. Support of part-time faculty and teaching assistants is especially important because these individuals are often new to this kind of teaching. Institutions may provide special incentives during the first term in which a new learning community is offered. However, many campuses use summer stipends for curriculum planning rather than release time, and this can become an unsustainable expectation for every learning community teaching team.

When learning communities are offered as an add-on to the existing curriculum, as they often are in the beginning, they are likely to raise few objections simply because they are so small that there is little competition for resources. But as they expand, these programs need to replace existing courses to be cost-effective; if not, institutions are simply adding cost by running duplicative courses. At this point, the competition for limited resources becomes more intense. Nonetheless, we know that learning communities can demonstrate their effectiveness in numerous ways. In many institutions, the curriculum is overextended as a result of the steady accretion of new courses over the years and the practice of offering many courses with small enrollments. Learning communities can become a means of offering a more efficient curriculum by combining small enrollment courses or eliminating the need to offer so many different courses. Instead of offering a series of courses to address learning outcomes in communications, diversity, or global understanding, for example, a learning community could address all of these outcomes at once.

What Are the Funding Sources for Learning Communities?

If learning communities are to be sustained, they need to be part of the regular college budget. Depending on where they are located administratively, they might be funded through departments, a college of undergraduate studies, or multiple budgets from academic and student affairs. One institution started a learning community for athletes with funding from the athletic department. Living-learning communities are often funded through housing fees. At the University of Wisconsin, for example, students pay an extra housing fee to live in the Chadbourne or Bradley learning communities. The students control some of the revenue from this fee, which is used to sponsor special cultural events and programs and support advising and special services based in the residence hall. A number of institutions, such as the University of Nebraska in its Goodrich program and St. John Fischer, use tuition waivers and scholarship funds to support their learning community students, a very attractive recruitment incentive. It is common in learning communities with strong peer mentor systems to use state and federal work-study funds to support the students, although some colleges give peer mentors credit instead.

Many learning community programs start with grant funding. In both two-year and four-year colleges, numerous learning communities have been initiated through federal funding through Department of Education Title III or Title V as part of an overall institutional initiative to improve undergraduate education, especially for students from underrepresented populations. A few learning community programs use federal money as an ongoing base of support because several of these grants (for example, TRIO programs) are renewable.

Federal and foundation funding priorities can make a big difference in generating learning communities. The substantial number of learning community programs in engineering, for example, is directly attributable to funding initiatives by the National Science Foundation. Grants can be an important source of funding for program start-up, lending visibility and credibility to a program, and they often allow for considerable faculty development. However, funding learning communities through grants can also be dangerous because grants are usually not an ongoing source of support. Institutions that rely extensively on grant funding for basic instructional costs often have difficulty making the transition to the college budget, especially if they provided lucrative stipends or extensive release time during the grant period.

Historical Funding and Staffing Patterns

Existing funding and staffing patterns provide an important context for learning community planning because they affect how faculty and administrators view these new approaches. As one teacher observed, "Some departments derive a benefit from donating someone to this program because it builds their numbers. For others it's costly. Departments with big majors believe they just have to have those courses taught and won't budge an inch, but we believe some of this is a matter of long-range planning, not money."

All institutions have an internal political economy in which some courses generate more student credit hours per faculty member than others. Therefore, certain curricular areas always subsidize others. Differential funding patterns are largely historical; at one time they were institutionalized in state higher education funding formulas that allocated a certain number of dollars to upper-division, lower-division, and graduate education and to various support functions such as administration, library, and facilities. Most states have long since abandoned strict formula funding and even where formulas are used to allocate money to institutions, institutions can usually decide how to distribute the funds internally.

Most baccalaureate colleges and universities, following time-honored habits, continue to use large lower-division lecture courses to subsidize small upper-division classes and faculty research. Many other factors also come into play in establishing norms about class size, such as pedagogical approach, room size, and equipment limitations. Student-faculty ratios in clinical programs and the studio arts, for example, are generally lower than in social science courses. Some vocational programs have lower student-faculty ratios than traditional liberal arts courses because of their applied components.

Although these staffing patterns are historical, they are often not rational from the standpoint of trying to foster success for larger numbers of students. We believe institutions need to think more strategically about where some of the "subsidies" (that is, smaller classes with opportunities for active learning and student engagement) need to be located. For example, the practice of running large lecture courses for freshmen is widely followed despite a huge attrition rate in the first year of college, and contrary to what we know about the importance of closer relationships between students and faculty in the first year. "Front loading" the curriculum by investing in smaller classes for first-term freshmen makes sense at many institutions, especially those with low retention rates. Developmental education is a good example of how federal and state financial aid programs can influence student enrollment patterns and curricula. This is an area where some of the most vulnerable student populations are taught in the largest classes by the most marginal faculty in the institutional hierarchy. These structural patterns are widely recognized as recipes for failure, but they are difficult to change when they are pervasive and institutionalized in union contracts and long-standing expectations.

Enrollment Expectations and Faculty Load

As noted, faculty salaries are the most significant expense associated with learning communities, so many questions are raised about this expense: What is the typical size of a learning community? What should the teaching load be? Are faculty teaching in learning communities carrying their load? Is the teaching equitably distributed? Should faculty be paid extra for planning new learning communities? How is teaching credit calculated for team-taught programs? How and by whom is all of this determined?

The accepted teaching load for faculty at a given institution generally operates as a constraint on innovation, but certain types of learning communities can tolerate load disparities (that is, deviations from the expected enrollment level or class size) more easily than others. FIGs and linked courses are fairly flexible and can conform to course-loading patterns typical of discrete classes. Linked writing classes, linked freshman year experience classes, and integrative seminars are common learning community approaches that can live within normal enrollment patterns and faculty loads, usually by attaching a small course to a large one.

In many institutions the fact that two linked courses have historically different enrollment levels can become a big issue in trying to build a common cohort in the two courses. Because of the way credit hours are counted and credited to different departments, these negotiations can be difficult. Sometimes a third party, like the dean or provost, or an incentive fund for improvements in retention, can help make up the difference, at least the first time, but eventually these differences need to be justified. Nonetheless, many institutions find that relatively small enrollment adjustments more than pay for themselves by yielding large gains in student retention. In learning community cluster models at places such as CUNY-Queens, the University of Northern Colorado, Texas A&M-Corpus Christi, and LaGuardia Community College, the faculty loads (in terms of total number of courses taught) do not usually change, but the size of the classes may be slightly altered. For example, usual enrollments might be sixty in history and twenty-five in English composition, but in a learning community there could be two sections of English tied to one section of history, with the history course enrollment reduced to fifty students to coincide with the English course enrollments. To promote further efficiencies from the standpoint of the instructor's load, both of the linked English classes might be taught by the same teacher.

Team-taught coordinated studies programs are more demanding when it comes to enrollment levels because these programs often constitute a full-time teaching load for two, three, or four faculty members. Many team-taught interdisciplinary courses in the 1960s were not viable because institutions offered one small interdisciplinary four-credit course with twenty students and two teachers. Contemporary learning communities succeed partly because they can operate at more viable enrollment levels. Curricular reconfiguration is the secret. Exhibit 9.3 describes how team-taught learning communities can be equivalent to teaching stand-alone courses if the enrollment level is carefully worked out. This example is based on typical class sizes and faculty teaching loads at public colleges and universities.

In a typical public institution, for example, each teacher in a team-taught program carries twenty to twenty-five students, *and* a larger proportion of the students' credit load is in the learning community. As a result, the faculty team's overall student credit-hour production is the same as that of their colleagues in conventional classes. If the enrollment is substantially lower, however, the cost of the learning community program increases.

When each learning community is initially planned, administrators and faculty should agree on faculty load and expected minimum enrollment levels. If those numbers are not met, there should be an agreed-upon contingency plan for whether the learning community will be canceled. Otherwise, serious misunderstandings can occur and much work, hope,

Exhibit 9.3. Faculty Credit Hours Produced in Team-Taught Programs Versus Stand-Alone Classes

	Section A	Section B
	Twenty-five students	Twenty-five students
9 A.M.	Sociology	English
10 A.M.	English	Sociology
	25 × 6 = 150 credits	25 × 6 = 150 credits

Stand-Alone Classes
The sociology teacher teaches two classes at three credits each with twenty-five students for 150 credit hours. The English teacher teaches two classes at three credits each with twenty-five students for 150 credit hours. The total is 300 credit hours.

Learning Community
The sociology and English teachers team teach both Sections A and B (the same fifty students between 9 and 11 A.M.). Multiply two teachers by six credits by fifty students for a total of 300 credit hours.

and energy can quickly dissipate if a learning community does not adequately enroll. Too many learning communities have been undone by an anxious chair or a dean who releases seats in the learning community courses and suddenly mixes the cohort, thereby undermining it. Most of these problems occur because agreements were not made at the outset about minimal enrollments or because the program was built around courses with insufficient enrollment pools to attract enough students. Some administrators will allow a new endeavor to proceed even without the required number of students, but most institutions have rigorous requirements in terms of faculty load. If the learning community does not conform to conventional definitions of faculty load or succeed in establishing new standards for load, there may be institutional resistance.

One institution reported what has become a common perception in many different types of colleges and universities: "We have realized that, in exploring ways to load and fund faculty teaching in learning communities, we are straddling two different systems: the old paradigm and the new. Trying to retrofit the work of LCs into the system of pay for courses taught, reassigned time, and so on, can create the impression that LCs are quite expensive. We would like to work toward a different understanding of faculty loading based on learning (both student and faculty) rather than courses taught. It may be that LCs can lead the way in the district in exploring other ways of loading and funding faculty" (Rings, Shovers,

Exhibit 9.4. Faculty Loading in Team-Taught Programs Converted to Traditional Course Equivalents

English 101 (Section 1) Teacher A:	9:00–10:15	Twenty students
English 101 (Section 2) Teacher A:	10:30–11:45	Twenty students
Bio 100 (Section 1) Teacher B:	9:00–10:15	Twenty students
Bio 100 (Section 2) Teacher B:	10:30–11:45	Twenty students

Source: Rings, Shovers, Skinner, and Siefer, 1999, p. 48.

Skinner, and Siefer, 1999, p. 48). In the meantime, this institution and many others have established ways to describe faculty load that look "normal." This institution's team-taught learning community has both instructors with the same forty students in class for two periods that are loaded for them. Students earn three credits in biology and English, but the official records appear as shown in Exhibit 9.4.

The credit base of an institution and its calendar system also make a difference. Because most colleges in Washington State are on the quarter system and most community college courses are five credits, it has been easy to assemble ten- and fifteen-credit learning communities that make up two-thirds or all of a teaching load for faculty members. In contrast, coordinating large teams in institutions on the semester system with three-credit courses is much more difficult. The most viable coordinated studies model in semester system schools seems to be nine-credit, three-member faculty teams. Chandler Gilbert College offers another good semester system model, where a two-member faculty team teaches two identical seven-credit learning communities with fifty students in each. This load is coherent for the faculty members because they are not distracted by teaching different discrete classes. All of their teaching load is in these two learning communities.

Union contracts also influence faculty load and compensation for planning new courses. At one West Coast community college the learning community is an eighteen-credit block for both students and faculty. Even though the teaching faculty wanted to teach eighteen credits in exchange for a smaller class size, this became the subject of a grievance with the union because the negotiated faculty load was fifteen hours. Ultimately, the involved faculty had to sit down with their union colleagues to get their support. At another institution, union contracts include elaborate ways of computing courseloads that differentiate writing-intensive classes and team-taught classes. Putting teaching teams and courses together across departments became extremely difficult, and the existing faculty load and assignment procedures became a structural barrier to innovation. Nonetheless, this institution too was able to work things out. It is hard to generalize about the obstacles or support that unions offer. In our experience, a practice that is anathema to one may be embraced by another union. This is truly a local situation that requires local solutions.

Faculty load issues are often resolved through a careful look at the data. An assessment study at North Seattle Community College dispelled many myths when it demonstrated that faculty who were team teaching in coordinated classes did not carry lighter teaching loads than their colleagues in traditional classes when teaching ratios were computed over a year. It also showed that retention and graduation rates were significantly higher for learning community students (Wilkie, 1990).

Issues of enrollment levels and faculty load are complex and deserve close attention at the outset. Some institutions think about loads in terms of the different stages of implementing an institutional change plan. In the early planning stages, administrators may be willing to provide more support in terms of faculty load, reductions in class size, and faculty development opportunities in order to ensure that the program gets off to a good start. Unfortunately, it is very difficult to step down from a richly supported start-up phase to a leaner level of ongoing support. A number of institutions have experienced faculty resistance and withdrawal when externally funded stipends were no longer available. The solution to this problem was to come to a new understanding of the issues and new agreements about what constituted adequate levels of support. For a program to survive it must eventually conform to established budget practice or provide a new model for configuring costs that has legitimacy and feels equitable. Otherwise, the program becomes a site of ongoing controversy and jealousy. Demonstrating the program's cost-effectiveness is an important way to build support for the program and quell myths that otherwise might arise. As resources become even more limited, these issues become increasingly important.

Demonstrating Cost-Effectiveness

There are numerous ways to describe learning community cost-effectiveness and demonstrate return on investment. Because innovations are often the first on the chopping block when budgets are cut, being able to describe the benefits is important (Ferren, 1997; Ferren and Slavings, 2000; Guskin, Marcy, and Smith, 2004). Many studies of cost-effectiveness focus on student retention because it is easily measured, and learning communities tend to have substantially higher student retention than traditional courses. At Iowa State University the learning community leadership team estimated that increased retention translated into increased revenue for the university of almost $2.5 million in tuition over three years (Huba, Ellertson, Cook, and Epperson, 2003). This information provided a compelling rationale for the institution to make a substantial, ongoing investment in learning communities. Indiana State and the University of Northern Colorado have also translated retention gains into dollars saved. At California State University-Hayward learning community students demonstrate higher pass rates on a rising junior exam, another way of describing cost-effectiveness. Many learning community programs for developmental students can demonstrate lowering the "W-D-F" rates (students withdrawing or earning nonpassing grades of D or F); this provides enormous cost savings when students move quickly into higher-level classes rather than repeating the developmental ones and is especially important now that we know that the odds of success are very low among students who do repeat.

Although much of the work on retention has focused on the freshman year, these gains have implications for the upper-division courses as well, especially in high-cost areas of the curriculum. A colleague of ours, an administrator at a research university, assessed his program's cost-effectiveness in the following terms:

> A four percentage point increase in retention of students into their junior year would result in an income increase of more than 10 percent for upper-level courses. Four percentage points isn't a lot of people. In science and engineering this is about twenty-five people. A four percentage point increase for us translates to a 10 percent increase in junior and senior students, since only about 40 percent of our students now make it into the junior year. There is an additional bump because the state funds junior- and senior-level courses at a higher rate. The current differential is 12 percent to 20 percent depending on the discipline. This turns out to be a bunch of money. For us, probably $2 million. So investing one-half million in improved undergraduate instruction would more than pay for itself.

There are other dimensions to look at in considering cost-effectiveness too, such as efficiencies gained from offering a more condensed and educationally effective set of offerings. Portland State University's more concentrated learning community program in general education has been shown to be more effective in terms of student learning and more cost-effective than the previous distribution system for general education

(Reardon and Ramaley, 1997). On a number of campuses investments in living-learning communities pay off in multiple ways: higher occupancy rates in campus housing and improved climate in the dorms, such as less drinking and fewer incident reports as well as improved academic performance (Brower, n.d.).

Sustaining and Strengthening Learning Communities

We have been making the case that the endurance of learning community efforts depends on the institution's strategic understanding of why they are important and its ability to support this vision structurally. This is an issue of institutional will and the ability to stay focused, but it is also about planning and setting up a supportive climate and good channels for communication and feedback. In some places, learning communities have been institutionalized in three or four years, but the process often takes much longer. Many learning community programs remain fragile for years. Even a seemingly well-established program can be destabilized by the retirement of several key teaching faculty or the departure of an administrative champion. Truthfully, having a broad base of support is the only way to weather the reality of a constantly changing institutional environment. Learning communities need both solid foundations and opportunities for dynamic evolution. Learning community leadership teams need to go through iterative processes of reflecting on their progress and setting new goals so that their program does not become ossified and out of touch with emerging needs.

Nonetheless, learning communities do go through predictable stages of development. In start-up, the typical challenges are to establish the program's focus, identity, and place in the institution, develop successful procedures to plan and implement the program, and address a variety of technical challenges including marketing, recruitment, funding, and securing administrative support and faculty involvement. Exhibit 9.5 provides a summary checklist of these implementation issues.

Many of the items on the checklist are technical challenges, but they may be adaptive challenges too in some institutions. The director of a teaching and learning center, for example, may want to support learning communities but have such a full plate with other priorities that she cannot figure out how to do it. Or a general education program may be so much in flux that the learning community program cannot figure out how to work with it. Some of these are important issues of timing that need to play themselves out, whereas others are issues of reframing the situation in fundamental ways.

Exhibit 9.5. Learning Community Implementation Checklist

1. *Goals:* What are your goals for the learning community initiative? Consider goals for students, faculty and staff, the curriculum, and the institution.

2. *Audience:* Who is the intended student audience for the LC offerings? How will you identify these students? Who can help you do this?

3. *Related campus initiatives:* What current initiatives are already under way on campus? How might learning communities fit with initiatives? Are any members of the LC effort connected to these other initiatives? Will the LC effort be seen as furthering these other initiatives?

4. *Curricular structure and themes:* What LC framework(s) are appropriate to your goals and sustainable over time? In what curricular areas? What curricular themes might be the foci for LC offerings?

5. *Recruiting and supporting teachers:* Which faculty members and student affairs professionals will be involved? How will broad involvement be encouraged? Are those involved representative of the leadership on the campus? What types of faculty and staff development or student training will support the LC?

6. *Leadership Group:* Who should be asked to join the LC leadership team at the outset? Who needs to be involved with LC implementation? Which senior administrators or other key communicators on campus need to be informed or involved?

7. *Assessment:* What kinds of feedback loops can be put in place so the LC effort is evaluated and improved over time? How can assessment information be disseminated to the campus and key decision makers?

8. *Resources:* What resources are needed to support the effort? What is a reasonable time frame if outside funding is needed for start-up? What resources are required to sustain and strengthen the LC effort over time?

9. *Marketing and recruitment:* How will the LC program be marketed to students and to others in the institution? What are the most appropriate media and timing for student recruitment? Who needs to be involved to help with this effort?

10. *Institutionalization:* How will the LC initiative be institutionalized over time? Who will lead the long-term effort? Where will LC leadership and coordination be situated on the campus? How will you recruit a critical mass of LC teachers to sustain the program? What will be the ongoing mechanisms for reflecting on and strengthening the program?

Second-stage challenges often include succession, transition, and leadership as early leaders depart and new people are brought into the effort. Maintaining high commitment and consistent quality often becomes a challenge as programs age. Periodic cycles of problems develop that test the program's boundaries and procedures. As a program matures, its vision may change, sometimes expanding to more ambitious notions of what the learning community effort can be or sometimes settling in and concluding that the work is done. How the learning community leaders and participants frame the effort strongly influences how it will develop. A critical issue over time is always about how to hold on to hard-won solutions while allowing flexibility for the program to remain open to new ideas.

Although many learning communities were established in the 1990s, a number of contemporary ones have a history that now spans two or three decades. The older, established programs have generally resolved the initial technical challenges, although all programs face ongoing technical challenges because of changing circumstances, especially in funding, technology, and personnel turnover. New programs are often up to their ears in technical challenges, and paying attention to the little things makes all the difference.

We now know what is critical in sustaining these programs, although the culture and history of specific institutions are always important. A study of two dozen institutions in a three-year FIPSE project (1996 to 1999) pointed to a number of critical factors that promote sustainable learning communities (MacGregor, 1999):

- *Institutional readiness.* There must be a critical mass of faculty interested in learning communities, a leadership group at the institution supporting the idea of learning communities and prepared to support implementation, and an opening in the curriculum where the learning community program can be focused—for example in general education or a first-year program.

- *A collaborative leadership group.* Successful programs require the building of strong collaborative leadership teams. Leadership needs to expand if the program is to be sustained. Working collaboratively across the lines of departments and status, academic and student affairs, often requires new skills and practices.

- *Faculty involvement and faculty support.* Broad faculty involvement is critical to these programs. Restructuring reward systems to support teaching and innovation is necessary to ensure long-term faculty involvement. Faculty development support is needed, especially for team-taught and team-planned programs. Many institutions are underinvesting in faculty development.

- *Funding and other resources.* Financial support is necessary to obtain administrative support, fund planning time, get the effort going, and eventually sustain the effort, but the scale of financial support varies enormously from institution to institution. The source of funding may include institutional budgets from a variety of places or grant funding. Eventually, though, grant funding needs to be replaced with institutional funding.

o *Assessment as a strategy for program development.* Assessment can be a powerful tool for learning community development, especially if it is used to improve practice. It needs to be a central element of all learning community programs.

o *Commitment.* Persistence, patience, and commitment to a long-term vision are crucial in sustaining learning communities. Resilience in the face of periodic setbacks helps maintain the emotional energy to stay with the effort. Personal passion and commitment are the key ingredients in most of these programs.

This significant study of learning community development at diverse institutions concluded that many of the learning community leaders saw their programs as an adaptive challenge. "Learning communities are educational efforts that are not 'achieved,' 'reached,' or 'accomplished.' There is no end state at which the learning community team can sit back, heave a sign of relief, and claim 'the work has been done'" (MacGregor, 1999, p. 202).

Indeed, as Peter Senge points out, "The search for definitive answers is the bane of innovation. There are no answers for creating the new. New practical knowledge develops only from engaging in the hard work of translating concept into capacity" (Senge, 2000, p. 297). Learning communities must ultimately be viewed as ongoing efforts to meet the fundamental challenges of improving student learning, creating vital communities of practice in our institutions, and creating a stronger academy.

PART FIVE

CONCLUSION

THE FUTURE OF LEARNING COMMUNITIES

If I care about teaching, I must care not only for my students and my subject but also for the conditions, inner and outer, that bear on the work teachers do. Finding a place in the movement for educational reform is one way to exercise that larger caring. . . . An authentic movement is not a play for power—it is teaching and learning writ large. Now the world becomes our classroom, and the potential to teach and learn is found everywhere.

—Parker Palmer

WHEN THEY ARE THOUGHTFULLY DESIGNED and implemented, learning communities can play an extraordinary role in deepening the ways that students *and* teachers learn, and their influence may extend past that one learning community to the way that an institution (or group of institutions) creates a diverse and meaningful learning organization. Our underlying purpose in writing this book has been to describe the process of creating learning communities by working together collaboratively and strategically with intelligence and passion. Our mental model is responsible social change, led by compassionate people, and effected with a commitment to thoughtful planning, core teaching practices, community-based action and reflection, and ongoing assessment. In asserting that we and our colleagues have created and are still in the process of creating a reform movement, we are also saying that learning communities have the potential to become a transformational force, not only on one campus but in higher education more broadly.

Learning Communities as Learning Organizations

Our first learning community book, *Learning Communities: Making Connections Among Students, Faculty, and Disciplines* (Gabelnick, MacGregor, Matthews, and Smith, 1990) was published more than ten years ago. At that time, the editor of the Jossey-Bass series New Directions for Teaching and Learning resisted using the term *learning community* because he did not think it was current in higher education. Coincidentally, in 1990 Peter Senge, at MIT, published a book called *The Fifth Discipline* that would also use a phrase not yet common in organizational theory: *learning organization*. Coming from seemingly very different perspectives and academic traditions, both of these books focused on what it means to learn with others and how an internally held series of ideas or mental models can guide our actions in organizations and in life, serving as both barriers and opportunities for change. By the end of the twentieth century, the fields of higher education and organizational systems theory would be linked through a common vision of leading and learning. What was revolutionary about Senge's first book and *The Fifth Discipline Fieldbook* (Senge and Kleiner, 1994), which was written subsequently to illustrate how the concepts could be used, was their ability to describe, through a series of "disciplines," how organizations can change when they link organizational competencies with what Senge calls personal mastery. Senge brought together research and inventive thinking from many academic disciplines, and most importantly, he linked the capabilities of individuals and teams with the processes of change: "Thus, the primary leverage for any organizational learning effort lies not in policies, budgets, or organizational charts, but in ourselves. . . . The disciplines of personal mastery, mental models, and systems thinking all help us to productively examine and change the way we think. . . . In the end, the premise that organizations are the product of our thinking and interacting is powerful and liberating. It suggests that individuals and teams *can* affect even the most daunting organizational barriers (Senge and Kleiner, 1994, p. 48).

As Senge and his colleagues have written and as Parker Palmer later echoed, the role of the leader or teacher is not simply to proclaim a vision but rather to be able to see the whole, to understand a piece of an organization as both containing that whole and being able to influence the whole, and to create change by passionately leading from within. This concept expands to a more collective vision in learning community teams. When teams or groups of teachers work well together, they bring more than their individual perspectives; they join forces to create a complex and dynamic view of learning, and as they continue to work together, they too can affect "even the most daunting organizational barriers."

When we wrote our first book, we focused on the more practical aspects of initiating and developing learning communities, and we gathered the words of the pioneering students, faculty, and administrators to describe the learning transformations occurring in themselves through their new experiences. We tried to capture the processes of change and acknowledge the key people, models, and pedagogies needed to implement this vision. Through these wonderful stories of risk takers and learning community adventurers, we were, in many ways, unintentionally illustrating the very concepts that Senge and his associates were developing. Since then, the vocabulary of educational reform and institutional transformation has expanded considerably. We now have the language and conceptual frameworks for describing how learning communities can function and flourish as vital learning organizations, especially when led by active, committed faculty, administrators, staff, and students who take time to develop a plan and a purpose.

We realized then, as we do today, however, that the challenge remains to assist our present and future colleagues in understanding how their local efforts might have an impact on broader institutional transformation. In the earlier history of learning communities, and even today, many were and are grassroots initiatives, begun by individuals seeing themselves not as revolutionaries or reformers but simply as passionate teachers trying to establish more effective and more connected ways of engaging with their students. They have worked in small cohorts, gathered at regional and national learning community conferences, and influenced the lives of many, many students. These pioneers have laid the groundwork for the future, and their successors must build on their vision and experience in order to realize the great opportunities that learning communities offer for addressing key issues in higher education.

This new volume provides a much larger vista for the learning community movement. It sets the work of many in the context and language of educational reform and institutional transformation that have been occurring over the past twenty-five years. And although we do not explicitly use the language of systems thinking, each chapter in this book presents an important piece of the learning community story while placing that piece in a larger "system" of change movements in various institutions, and ultimately, in higher education overall. Senge calls this gradual elaboration of the themes of an individual career or an institutional history a "purpose story." The purpose story of learning communities spans almost a century, and it is not yet concluded. It is marked by the passion and foresight of pioneers and scholars who have charted the course in thinking about how to create learning environments that help students work collaboratively, encourage teachers to work together across departments and divisions, and foster active and democratic learning.

We have claimed that the twenty-first century offers unprecedented opportunities for higher education to integrate new knowledge and perspectives on how people learn, how organizations change, and how institutional transformation can occur. In *The Courage to Teach* (1998), Parker Palmer writes that people who have a vision about their life's work often feel that they are at the margins of their communities and that in order for them to live "an undivided life," they must find "communities of congruence." To find such a community, one must "go public" (pp. 173–174). Writes Palmer: "The area of social change offers no safe harbor for the purity of thought and action so dear to intellectuals. . . . The life of the world is messy . . . and if we want to work for change, we must learn to live with the mess" (pp. 175–176).

When learning communities were first introduced by the dean of the Lee Honors College at Western Michigan University in 1988, faculty were skeptical, students were puzzled, and senior administrators waited for the "experiment" to run its course and fade away. Five years later, faculty "went public," talking with each other about teaching and learning in more complex ways, introducing in their other classes elements of active learning, transdisciplinary education, and community building, and demonstrating an overall commitment to learning about learning. The messiness of change was fully evident in an explosion of innovation—not necessarily replicating additional learning communities, but enacting a more general view that teaching changes dramatically when the diverse needs of the students and the ways these students learn become as important for the course design and process as for the course material. Importantly, a "community of congruence" came into place: the president created a sense of expectation for change, the academic vice president worked with all deans to collaborate with this innovation, and the dean of the Honors College created a plan and gradually built a community of faculty and staff from across the campus who began to realize that teaching in a learning community offered unexpected opportunities not only for their students but for themselves personally. In addition, the support services, such as the registrar and the housing office, were engaged in the project and publicly acknowledged as vital elements in the initiative. After the first year, most of the faculty who had been involved wanted to teach again and thus became ambassadors to help others join. They made friends with other faculty and discovered an approach to teaching and learning that strengthened and supported their professional identity. Eventually, many faculty wrote about their experiences, presented their ideas at regional and national conferences, and transferred many of their teaching strategies to their other classes. Throughout this book, we recount some version of this story, enacted at hundreds of colleges and universities in the United States. Taken at one level, it is a story of institutional transformation. But when we look at all the individual stories as a narrative, we see that they describe a movement of change—a purpose story—about the role of learning communities in higher education.

Learning Communities and Institutional Change

Although we have learned much about how to initiate educational innovations and can report many success stories, on the whole we continue to be challenged to effect long-term, large-scale changes. Learning communities have functioned and continue to function as learning laboratories, but their ability to effect transformational change on campuses and eventually throughout higher education remains an extraordinary, but not fully realized, opportunity.

Some very helpful insights about the process of scaling up a change effort are offered by Richard Elmore of the Harvard School of Education. Elmore frames his analysis of the difficulties of instituting these core changes in an article in the *Harvard Educational Review,* "Getting to Scale with Good Educational Practice" (1996). He defines these changes as "fundamental . . . in the way knowledge is constructed" (p. 3) and in the ways these changes are implemented. Writes Elmore: "I am interested in . . . why, when schools seem to be constantly changing, teaching practice changes so little, and on so small a scale" (pp. 3, 6). The same question could be posed about learning communities: If there are so many learning communities at hundreds of universities throughout the United States, why have they not become more pervasive and deeply institutionalized, and why have they not more deeply affected the ways people think about teaching and about their students' learning? This book presents relatively few examples of large-scale innovations that have truly resulted in a change in the way faculty, staff, and the administration think about and deliver education. Often learning communities, even successful learning communities, still remain encapsulated in a particular program or led by a small group of devoted learning community champions, some of whom become exhausted and burnt out or are or will be retiring.

Chapter Two, "Learning Community History: Education for What? Education for Whom?" provides important lessons from educational reformers who led with remarkable vision but were defeated by practice. Elmore underscores this important point—namely, that change is a function of *both* individual motivation, competence, and values *and* institutional vision and strategy. "Preserving the connection between big ideas and teaching practice, embodied in earlier reform strategies, is an essential element in tackling the problem of scale," he writes (1996, p. 18). He recommends four approaches to increase scale: the leaders of the change must connect the change to external benchmarks of effective teaching and learning, they must create personal and supportive environments for change, they must assist in the replication of these success stories, and they must guide the promulgation of a commonly held theory or position on learning. We agree with these principles and describe in Chapter Four the core practices that can serve as guides not only for developing learning communities but also for scaling up learning community programs.

As we say in Chapter One, the past two decades have been marked by an extraordinary amount of educational reform on campuses and also a tremendous amount of writing about the theory and practice of educational reform. Supporting this work with millions of grant dollars have been governmental agencies, such as the National Science Foundation and the U.S. Department of Education, as well as private foundations such as the Ford Foundation, Hewlett Foundation, Kellogg Foundation, and The Pew Charitable Trusts. Although many of these agencies and foundations supported specific programs at one institution or a group of institutions, the Kellogg Foundation provided funds in 1995 to the American Council on Education (ACE) so that it could study the ways institutions build on these reform programs to effect broader institutional transformation. ACE's Project on Leadership and Institutional Transformation tracked twenty-six institutions engaged in serious change over six years. The series of reports produced illustrate a number of lessons learned from the experience of these campuses and offer additional insights into the challenge of scaling up learning community initiatives on campuses.

One of the chief concepts presented in these reports is of change as a continuum. In institutions that have achieved significant change, even in Elmore's terms, the transformation has been gradual—a long, continuous process that addresses deep questions about the assumptions behind why the change is being proposed, what problems or issues the change attempts to address, and how the entire system needs to respond to the change. The ACE reports use the language of systems thinking and organizational transformation and echo Elmore's language about core change:

> Transformation does not entail fixing discrete problems or adjusting and refining current activities. The depth of transformation addresses those assumptions that tell organizations what to do, how to behave, and what to produce. In other words, transformation touches the *core* [emphasis added] of the institution. . . . It is pervasive; it is a collective, institutionwide movement, even though it can happen one unit (or one person) at a time. When enough people act differently or think in a new way, that new way becomes the norm. The institution becomes transformed because it has adopted a new institutional culture [Eckel, Green, and Hill, 2001, p. 6].

Elmore, the ACE reports, and many others emphasize that if institutions are to take advantage of the wonderful opportunities for transformation that are available on all campuses, then change must be effected by people at all levels who truly understand and embrace the idea of institutional transformation as a process. Most importantly, these writers and publications note that when change occurs *over time,* new norms and new cultures are created. Senge would say that the mental model of the organization shifts.

Our experience has shown that learning communities can be wonderful incubators for cultural change because they create a *place,* a community, for practicing and deepening understanding of *who* people are and *how* people learn. Etienne Wenger, who has written extensively on creating communities of practice, writes:

> Because learning transforms who we are and what we can do, it is an experience of identity. It is not just an accumulation of skills and information, but a process of becoming. . . . Viewed as an experience of identity, learning entails both a process and a place. It entails a process of transforming knowledge as well as a context in which to define an identity of participation. As a consequence, to support learning is not only to support the process of acquiring knowledge but also to offer a place where new ways of knowing can be realized in the form of such an identity. [Wenger, 1998, p. 215]

As we describe in Chapter Eight, the faculty, staff, and administrators who have stepped forward as learning community leaders have faced many challenges in order to support both the process of learning and its place in the academy. They have encountered *political challenges* of territory and competition for scarce resources, *structural challenges* of where to situate learning communities inside the institution, an array of *cultural challenges* ranging from the faculty and staff reward system to the great disparity in student preparedness, and *quality challenges* in faculty development, assessment, and strategic institutionalization. Yet throughout, most of these individuals persisted because they discovered that teaching in a learning community brought them closer to their core identity as teachers and created a safe space for experimentation. Their courage to teach, to wrestle with interminable "administrivia," faculty resistance, and institutional inertia, yielded a stronger inner identity, not simply an accumulation of skills and information. In turn, their students learned in a *place* that fostered active learning and mutual respect, helping them to mature as individuals. Learning communities give faculty and staff members a place to transform learning experiences for students, their relationships with each other, and their understanding of the teaching-learning process—all at once. Learning communities thus become a vehicle for transformation.

Scaling up the learning community program is, therefore, very complex because it must occur over time, in a special space, with individuals and teams who are pulled in many directions. In addition, the process of scaling up must be connected to a larger organizational strategic vision if real institutional transformation is to occur. If we are truly to reform higher education, we cannot simply focus on one program or a small group of dedicated individuals. We must have a more transformational view of the educational landscape.

Unfortunately, a common stance in higher education that endures as a barrier to getting to scale and expanding the promise of learning communities is a mental model of scarcity and efficiency. This view relies on the management of resources to maintain the status quo in order to survive. Most people do not like the messiness and uncertainty involved in risk and change, and more importantly, new ideas can cost money—a very scarce commodity in today's higher education world. That is why, in this book, we describe specific pathways, offer guidelines, and present examples from the field of learning community development and then connect those examples with important scholarship in higher education. We believe that learning communities can and do respond to the critical educational issues of enrollment management, student access and success, cross-disciplinary learning, developmental education, and general education. Many offer fine examples of assessment and institutional collaboration among faculty and staff. They provide safe and effective environments for difficult dialogues about diversity, community, and tough social and political issues; they genuinely increase student retention; they encourage cross-campus collaboration among faculty, student life personnel, and other campus support staff, such as librarians and IT staff. And if carefully designed and executed, they are efficient as well as effective.

Reforming Undergraduate Education: Challenges and Opportunities

Administrators and faculty are being and will continue to be challenged by extraordinary changes in the ways that education can be delivered and the cafeteria-style educational options that students expect. As we have noted throughout the book, public universities and community colleges are now flooded with tremendous numbers of students and new immigrants, all seeking the greatest asset the United States can offer: a college education. University administrators are overwhelmed by the need to provide not only access but also a high quality of education to many who are not fully prepared for study. This demand is occurring when state budgets for higher education are woefully inadequate, and faculty are being asked to do more and more with fewer rewards. It is not surprising that administrators look to educational models that seem to offer efficient and effective ways of providing a high-quality education. However, when campuses create learning communities under these circumstances and try to "solve" the problems of access, diversity, student persistence, and developmental education without thinking through the systemic implications and possibilities, they are simply moving around the institutional furniture. Learning communities thus become another "silver bullet" in an attempt to address persistent and complex issues. So although it may seem unrealistic or burdensome to insist on careful planning or to challenge institutions to make a deep commitment to learning communities as a transformational and strategic opportunity, we believe that they will have a future in higher education only if institutions do both.

After access and student persistence, the next big issue facing higher education is probably faculty succession. Throughout this book, we make the case that those who teach in learning communities play a special but often unrecognized role on their campuses as idea champions for learning communities. We have also noted that many of these leaders are retiring or will soon retire. Who will succeed those who have worked tirelessly to create and to teach in learning communities, and who will provide the administrative support for this next generation of innovation and implementation? These questions remain unanswered when it comes not only to learning community faculty but to all faculty in higher education. Chapter Eight offers important information about recruiting and retaining faculty and staff members who may teach in learning communities and provides key ideas for the support of those who take a risk to create or join an existing learning community on their campus. Clearly, the reward systems must change (and some are changing) to recognize the expanding field of the scholarship of teaching and learning and its applications to areas such as learning communities.

Finally, we have raised the bar for faculty and staff participation in learning communities. This is a blessing and a curse. Most of the faculty, staff members, and administrators who have taken on the challenge of learning communities are motivated not only by their personal drive for change but also by their core values and commitment to improving the quality of education for their students. Deep learning is ultimately a personally transforming experience, for both faculty and students, and it involves not only planning for learning but also deep reflection and assessment of that learning. All of this takes a tremendous amount of time and commitment, often in the face of a benign or even hostile teaching or administrative environment. Clearly, barriers abound for teachers who want to participate in learning communities, and not the least of them is that many teachers in learning communities, especially at large public institutions, are part-time faculty, graduate students, student life personnel, or even librarians. Although they are highly motivated and hardworking, their place in the academy is still perceived to be at the edges of the political and social power structures. It is hard to persist with the innovation when a campus remains committed to a very different perspective about teaching and learning and when it asks only its marginalized and less influential employees to teach in learning communities or even to become the principal teachers in them.

It is extraordinary, therefore, to be able to acknowledge the work of those individuals whose vision continues to embrace social change and generosity. As we note in earlier chapters, hundreds of people who have been associated with learning communities are adaptive leaders, attempting to align their own ethical values with their vision for theory and practice. In *Leadership Without Easy Answers,* Ronald Heifetz (1994, p. 35) describes the qualities of adaptive leaders:

> If we define problems by the disparity between values and circumstances, then an adaptive challenge is a particular kind of problem where the gap cannot be closed by the application of current technical know-how or routine behavior. To make progress, not only must invention and action change circumstances to align reality with values but the values themselves may also have to change. Leadership will

consist not only of answers or assured visions but also of taking action
to clarify values. It asks questions like: What are we missing here?
Are there values of competing groups that we suppress rather than
apply to our understanding of the problem at hand? Are there shared
values that might enable us to engage in competing views? Ongoing
adaptive capacity requires a rich and evolving mix of values to inform
a society's process of reality testing. It requires leadership to fire and
contain the forces of invention and change, and of the next step.

The examples presented in this book repeatedly illustrate the adaptive,
visionary force of those who have stepped forward to try to improve the
educational landscape and make it more hospitable and meaningful to our
students. And as we have shown, the barriers to change are enormous.
Still, we assert, like Heifetz, that the values themselves may also have to
change. If we seek only technical solutions to the challenges of implementing learning communities, then huge issues like faculty succession,
student persistence, and second-stage transformation will never be
addressed. In contrast, if learning communities can offer multitargeted
and richly layered responses to an array of adaptive challenges, then they
will realize their potential as a reform in higher education.

Many of the learning communities we have described in this book
attempt to do more than solve a particular problem or offer a technical
solution to the larger issues of enrollments, teaching and learning, faculty
development, and cross-disciplinary learning. In a variety of them, we
have found evidence that learning communities are and will remain agents
for change. However, they cannot easily accomplish this change if they
continue to be developed outside of larger institutional transformational
strategies. Therefore, when planning a learning community and choosing
a particular structure for it, intentionality is critical. In Chapter Four we
offer core practices that should be built into the developmental process.
We believe that all learning communities ought to embrace these core
practices—community, diversity, integration, active learning, reflection,
and assessment—because we have learned that they are fundamental to
building and sustaining learning communities. We have also seen that deep
learning can be achieved when a combination of these teaching practices
is employed. Both teachers and students benefit from a pedagogically
complex learning environment, and the quality of the learning environment is similarly improved through reflection and assessment. This is an
ambitious vision for higher education but one that resonates with many
educational reformers and a subject that was addressed most recently in
the work of Gardner, Csikszentmihalyi, and Damon (2001). As these

authors put it, "authentic alignment" is necessary for good work and for adaptive leaders to thrive. Authentic alignment is not easy to achieve or sustain, but it is crucial for the integrity of any educational innovation.

The Future of Learning Communities

Learning communities are designed for tomorrow's students, students who are multicultural, poorer than students in previous generations, more stressed by multiple responsibilities, and seeking an education that is delivered in a variety of formats and locations. Although institutions will struggle for many years with financial shortfalls and issues of succession and faculty workloads, the students will continue to demand that they be prepared for a rapidly changing world.

Learning communities provide what students are asking for. We know that students now actively construct their curriculum and value cross-disciplinary education, opportunities for service learning, research with a faculty member, and involvement in classroom learning. They are comfortable with technology both as a tool and as a vehicle for instruction, they use the library as a technology information commons, and in the case of older women students, who make up the majority population in higher education, they already bring an ability to work simultaneously on several tasks, manage diverse roles, and look at problems from different perspectives. When these students are given the opportunity to join and participate in a learning community, their positive reaction is strong and well-documented. Well-designed learning communities provide a structure that can be adapted throughout the academic term. They can become the needed glue for a fragmented college experience. Ultimately, the most important reason for incorporating learning communities into a college or university's curriculum is to provide a place where students can practice collaborative learning, problem definition, problem solving, leadership development, reflection, and self-assessment. We believe that these competencies and their inherent value are key to an undergraduate education that prepares people for work and service in the world today.

Faculty also want to be lifelong learners, and institutions have a responsibility for the educational nurturance of those who prepare our future citizens. Although the value of diverse learning strategies and community building among students is well-documented, sustaining those who teach in learning communities has received less attention and less resources have been provided for it. We believe that recruiting, supporting, and sustaining learning community teams in a variety of educational programs are vital to the future of the movement. Like students, teachers learn to work in teams, they develop relationships with colleagues in different areas of their institutions, they learn about different ways to teach, and they learn about themselves. Learning communities become places for them to learn from and support one another as they discuss the hard work of teaching diverse students, designing appropriate pedagogies, thinking in cross-disciplinary terms, and leading change. But teachers cannot labor alone; they need institutional support. When an institution makes a public commitment to teachers as learners, it becomes a transformational learning environment itself, and all can celebrate and appreciate both the complexity and the rewards of learning in community.

As we look to the future of learning communities, we acknowledge and salute the adaptive faculty, staff, *and* institutions that, in Parker Palmer's words, have "gone public" and been able to tolerate the messiness and the disappointments while sustaining the vision of educational reform. They have taken risks to envision and create an exhilarating movement that continues to challenge how we think about higher education, in general, and how we can purposely structure the curriculum, in particular, to put students on the pathway to a fully engaged and thoughtful life. The purpose story of learning communities is a story of vision, optimism, and risk.

As we have said from the beginning of this book, we stand at a crossroads in higher education, burdened with economic and financial pressures, more knowledgeable about learning than ever before, looking toward a great generational shift in our faculty and administrators. Our students invite change even as they demand new ways to earn their degrees, and our society seeks leaders who will ask the difficult questions and have the courage to identify good solutions for big problems. In learning communities, open inquiry and a desire for connection are nourished and taught. The future of learning communities is ours to construct.

REFERENCES

Adelman, C. *Answers in the Tool Box: Academic Intensity, Attendance Patterns, and Bachelor's Degree Attainment.* Washington, D.C.: U.S. Department of Education, 1999.

Adler, L. "Uncommon Sense: Liberal Education, Learning Communities and the Transformative Quest." In B. L. Smith and J. McCann (eds.), *Reinventing Ourselves.* Bolton, Mass.: Anker Press, 2001.

Advisory Committee on Student Financial Assistance. *Empty Promises: The Myth of College Access in America.* Washington D.C., Advisory Committee on Student Financial Assistance, 2002. [www.ed.gov/offices/ag/acsfa/access.html].

Alexander, C., and Associates. *A Pattern Language: Towns, Buildings, Construction.* New York: Oxford University Press, 1977.

Allen, J., and Bresciani, M. J. "Public Institutions, Public Challenges: On the Transparency of Assessment Results." *Change,* 2003, *34*(1), 20–23.

Alverno College Faculty. *Student Assessment-As-Learning at Alverno College.* Milwaukee, Wis.: Alverno Productions, 1994.

American Association of Community Colleges. *Building Community.* Washington, D.C.: American Association of Community Colleges, 1988.

American Association of Community Colleges. *The Knowledge Net: Connecting Communities, Learners, and Colleges.* Washington, D.C.: American Association of Community Colleges, 2000.

Anderson, J. "Developing a Learning-Teaching Style Assessment Model for Diverse Populations." In L. Suskie (ed.), *Assessment to Promote Deep Learning: Insights from AAHE's 2000 and 1999 Conferences.* Washington, D.C.: American Association of Higher Education, 2001.

Anderson, L. W., and Krathwohl, D. R. (eds.). *Taxonomy for Learning, Teaching, and Assessment: A Revision of Bloom's Taxonomy of Educational Objectives.* New York: Longman, 2001.

Angelo, T. A., and Cross, K. P. *Classroom Assessment Techniques: A Handbook for College Teachers* (2nd ed.). San Francisco: Jossey-Bass, 1993.

Argyris, C., Putnam, R., and Smith, D. M. *Action Science.* San Francisco: Jossey-Bass, 1985.

Argyris, C., and Schön, D. A. *Organizational Learning II: Theory, Method and Practice*. Reading, Mass.: Addison-Wesley, 1996.

Assessment in and of Collaborative Learning: A Handbook of Strategies. Olympia: The Evergreen State College, Washington Center for Improving the Quality of Undergraduate Education, 1995. [http://learningcommons.evergreen.edu/].

Association of American Colleges. *The Classroom Climate: A Chilly One for Women?* Washington, D.C.: Association of American Colleges, 1982.

Association of American Colleges. *Integrity in the Curriculum: A Report to the Academic Community*. Washington, D.C.: Association of American Colleges, 1985.

Association of American Colleges. *Liberal Learning and the Arts and Sciences Major*. Vol. 1: *The Challenge of Connected Learning*. Washington, D.C.: Association of American Colleges, 1990.

Association of American Colleges and Universities National Panel. *Greater Expectations: A New Vision for Learning as a Nation Goes to College*. Washington, D.C.: Association of American Colleges and Universities, 2002.

Astin, A. "What Really Matters in College: Provocative Findings from a National Survey of Student Outcomes." *Perspectives*, 1992, 22(1), 23–46.

Astin, A. "What Matters in College?" *Liberal Education*, 1993a, 79(4), 4–15.

Astin, A. *What Matters in College? Four Critical Years Revisited*. San Francisco: Jossey-Bass, 1993b.

Astin, A. W. *Assessment for Excellence: The Philosophy and Practice of Assessment and Evaluation in Higher Education*. New York: Macmillan, 1991.

Astin, A. W., Tsui, L., and Avaolos, J. *Degree Attainment Rates at American Colleges and Universities: Effects of Race, Gender, and Institutional Type*. Los Angeles: Higher Education Research Institute, University of California, 1996.

Avens, C., and Zelley, R. *A Report on the Intellectual Development of Students in the Quanta Learning Community at Daytona Beach Community College*. Daytona Beach, Fla.: Daytona Beach Community College, 1990.

Babbitt, M. "Making Writing Count in an ESL Learning Community." In I. Leki (ed.), *Academic Writing Programs*. Alexandria, Va.: Teachers of English to Speakers of Other Languages, Inc., 2001.

Barber, B. R. *An Aristocracy of Everyone: The Politics of Education and the Future of America*. New York: Oxford University Press, 1992.

Barefoot, B. (ed.). *Exploring the Evidence: Reporting Outcomes of Freshman Seminars*. Monograph No. 11. Columbia, S.C.: National Resource Center for the Freshman Year Experience, University of South Carolina, 1993.

Barefoot, B. O. *Second National Survey of First-Year Academic Practices, 2002.* Brevard, N.C.: Policy Center on the First Year of College, Brevard College, 2002. [http://brevard.edu/fyc/Survey/2002/].

Barr, R. "Obstacles to Implementing the Learning Paradigm." *About Campus,* Sept.-Oct. 1998, pp. 18–25.

Barr, R., and Tagg, J. "From Teaching to Learning—A New Paradigm for Undergraduate Education." *Change,* Nov.-Dec. 1995, 27(6), 13–25.

Bartlett, T. "Universities of Michigan and Texas Will Require Applicants to Take a Writing Exam." *Academe Today: The Chronicle of Higher Education's Daily Report for Subscribers,* Jan. 16, 2003. [http://chronicle.com/daily/2003/01/2003011602.htm]

Baxter Magolda, M. B. *Knowing and Reasoning in College: Gender-Related Patterns in Students' Intellectual Development.* San Francisco: Jossey-Bass, 1992.

Baxter Magolda, M. B. *Making Their Own Way: Narratives for Transforming Higher Education to Promote Self-Development.* Sterling, Va.: Stylus, 2001.

Beebe, S. "Best Teaching Practices and Learning Centers." Unpublished paper presented to the American Council on Education Fellows, Washington, D.C., June 2003.

Belenky, M., Clinchy, B., Goldberger, N., and Tarule, J. *Women's Ways of Knowing: The Development of Self, Voice, and Mind.* New York: Basic Books, 1986.

Bellah, R. N., and others. *Habits of the Heart: Individualism and Commitment in American Life.* New York: Harper and Row, 1986.

Bergquist, W. *The Four Cultures of the Academy.* San Francisco: Jossey-Bass, 1992.

Bergquist, W. H., Greenberg, E. M., and Klaum, G. A. *In Our Fifties: Voices of Men and Women Reinventing Their Lives.* San Francisco: Jossey-Bass, 1993.

Bland, C., and Bergquist, W. *The Vitality of Senior Faculty Members.* ASHE-ERIC Higher Education Report, no. 25. San Francisco: Jossey-Bass, 1997.

Bloom, B. S., and collaborators. *Taxonomy of Educational Objectives: The Classification of Educational Goals Handbook I: Cognitive Domain.* New York: David McKay, 1956.

Bonwell, C. C., and Eison, J. A. *Active Learning: Creating Excitement in the Classroom.* ASHE-ERIC Higher Education Report, no. 1. San Francisco: Jossey-Bass, 1991.

Boyer Commission on Educating Undergraduates in the Research University. *Reinventing Undergraduate Education: A Blueprint for America's Research Universities.* Princeton, N.J.: The Carnegie Foundation for the Advancement of Teaching, 1998.

Boyer, E. L. *College: The Undergraduate Experience in America.* New York: HarperCollins, 1987.

Boyer, E. L. *Scholarship Reconsidered: Priorities of the Professoriate.* Princeton, NJ: The Carnegie Foundation for the Advancement of Teaching, 1990.

Bransford, J. D., Brown, A. L., and Cocking, R. R. (eds.). *How People Learn: Brain, Mind, Experience, and School.* Washington, D.C.: National Research Council, Committee on Developments in the Science of Learning, National Academy Press, 1999.

Brookfield, S. D., and Preskill, S. *Discussion as a Way of Teaching: Tools and Techniques for Democratic Classrooms.* San Francisco: Jossey-Bass, 1999.

Brower, A. "Residential Learning Communities: A New Approach to Cleaning Up the Outcomes of Binge Drinking," n.d. [http://wiscinfor.doit.wisc.edu/teaching-academy/LearnignLink/ll.30].

Brown, B. "A Study of the Nature of Faculty Professional Development in Community College Learning Communities." Unpublished doctoral dissertation, University of Missouri-Columbia, 2003.

Brown, C. S. (ed.). *Alexander Meiklejohn: Teacher of Freedom.* Berkeley: Meiklejohn Civil Liberties Institute, 1981.

Brown, J. S. "Growing up Digital: How the Web Changes Work, Education, and the Ways People Learn." *Change,* 2000, *32*(2), 11–20.

Brown, J. S., Collins, A., and Duguid, P. *Cognitive Apprenticeship, Situated Cognition, and Social Interaction.* Institute for Research on Learning, Report No. IRL88–0008, June 1988.

Brown, J. S., Collins, A., and Duguid, P. "Situated Cognition and the Culture of Learning." *Educational Researcher,* 1989, *18*(1), 32–42.

Bruffee, K. *Collaborative Learning: Higher Education, Interdependence, and the Authority of Knowledge.* Baltimore, Md.: Johns Hopkins University Press, 1993.

Bruner, J. *Acts of Meaning.* Cambridge, Mass.: Harvard University Press, 1990.

Bureau of Guidance and Records. "Report of the Bureau of Guidance and Records on the Experimental College." Madison: University of Wisconsin, Feb. 1932.

Bystrom, V. A. "Post-Program Interviews." In *Assessment in and of Collaborative Learning: A Handbook of Strategies.* Olympia: The Evergreen State College, Washington Center for Improving the Quality of Undergraduate Education, 1995. [http://learningcommons.evergreen.edu/].

Bystrom, V. A. "Getting It Together: Learning Communities." In W. E. Campbell and K. A. Smith (eds.), *New Paradigms for College Teaching.* Edina, Minn.: Interaction Book Company, 1997.

Cadwallader, M. "A Manifesto: The Case for an Academic Counter Revolution." *Liberal Education,* 1982a, *68*(4), 403–420.

Cadwallader, M. "General, Liberal, or Political: A Theory of Citizen Education." *Liberal Education,* 1982b, *68*(3), 249–258.

Cadwallader, M. "The Destruction of the College and the Collapse of General Education." *Teachers College Record,* Summer 1983, *84*(4), 909–916.

Cadwallader, M. "Experiment at San Jose." In R. Jones. and B. L. Smith (eds.), *Against the Current.* Cambridge, Mass.: Schenkman Press, 1984a.

Cadwallader, M. "The Uses of Philosophy in an Academic Counterrevolution: Alexander Meiklejohn and John Dewey in the 1980s." *Liberal Education,* 1984b, *70*(4), 275–292.

Callan, P. M., and Finney, J. E. "Assessing Educational Capital: An Imperative for Policy." *Change,* 2002, *34*(4), 24–31.

Cambridge, B. L., Kahn, S., Tompkins, D. P., and Yancey, K. B. (eds.), *Electronic Portfolios: Emerging Practices in Student, Faculty, and Institutional Learning.* Washington, D.C.: American Association for Higher Education, 2001.

Candy, P. C. *Self-Direction for Lifelong Learning: A Comprehensive Guide to Theory and Practice.* San Francisco: Jossey-Bass, 1991.

Chickering, A. W., and Gamson, Z. F. "Seven Principles of Good Practice in Undergraduate Education." *AAHE Bulletin,* 1987, *39*(7), 3–7.

Chickering, A. W., and Reisser, L. *Education and Identity* (2nd ed.). San Francisco: Jossey-Bass, 1993.

Chilemsky, E., and Shadish, W. R. (eds.). *Evaluation for the 21st Century: A Handbook.* Thousand Oaks, Calif.: Sage, 1997.

Clark, D. J., and Bekey, J. "Use of Small Groups in Instructional Evaluation." *Professional and Organizational Development Quarterly,* 1979, *1,* 87–95.

Coleman, S. "Dangerous Outposts: Progressive Experiments in Higher Education in the 1920s and 1930s." In B. L. Smith and J. McCann (eds.), *Reinventing Ourselves.* Bolton, Mass: Anker Press, 2001.

Cook, T. D. "Lessons Learned in Evaluation Over the Past Twenty-Five Years." In E. Chimelsky and W. R. Shadish (eds.), *Evaluation for the 21st Century: A Handbook.* Thousand Oaks, Calif.: Sage, 1997.

Cooper, J. L. and Robinson, P. "Getting Started: Informal Small-Group Strategies in Large Classes." In J. MacGregor, J. L. Cooper, K. A. Smith, and P. Robinson (eds.), *Strategies for Energizing Large Classes: From Small Groups to Learning Communities.* New Directions for Teaching and Learning, no. 81. San Francisco: Jossey-Bass, 2000.

Coover, V., and others (eds.). *Resource Manual for a Living Revolution.* Philadelphia: New Society Press, 1978.

Cornwell, G. "Living/Learning Communities: The First Year Program at St. Lawrence University." *Washington Center News,* Fall 1996, *10*(2), 11–12.

Cornwell, G., and Stoddard, E. "Toward an Interdisciplinary Epistemology: Faculty Culture and Institutional Change." In B. L. Smith and J. McCann (eds.), *Reinventing Ourselves*. Bolton, Mass.: Anker Press, 2001.

Cornwell, G., and Stoddard, E. "St. Lawrence University: Experiential Learning Communities—Dialectics of Ideas and Experience." In K. Spear and others (eds.), *Learning Communities and Liberal Arts Colleges*. National Learning Communities Project Monograph Series. Olympia: Washington Center for Undergraduate Education, The Evergreen State College, and Washington, D.C.: American Association for Higher Education, 2003.

Council on Aid to Education. *Breaking the Social Contract: The Fiscal Crisis in Higher Education*. Washington, D.C.: Rand Corporation, 1997. [www.rand.org/publications/CAE/CAE100/index.html].

Cousins, J. B., and Earl, L. E. "The Case for Participatory Evaluation." *Educational Evaluation and Policy Analysis*, 1992, *14*(4), 397–418.

Cronon, E. D., and Jenkins, J. W. *The University of Wisconsin: A History, 1923–1945. Politics, Depression and War* (Vol. III). Madison: University of Wisconsin Press, 1994.

Cross, K. P. *Beyond the Open Door*. San Francisco: Jossey-Bass, 1971.

Cross, K. P. "Why Learning Communities? Why Now?" *About Campus,* July-Aug. 1998, *3*(3), 4–11.

Cross, K. P. *Learning Is About Making Connections*. The Cross Papers, no. 3. Mission Viejo, Calif.: League for Innovation in the Community College, 1999. [www.league.org].

Cross, K. P. "Portraits of Students: A Retrospective." *Planning for Higher Education,* Fall 2000, pp. 5–13.

Cross, K. P., and Angelo, T. A. *Classroom Assessment Techniques: A Handbook for Faculty*. Ann Arbor: National Center for Research to Improve Postsecondary Teaching and Learning, University of Michigan, 1988.

Cross, K. P., and Steadman, M. H. *Classroom Research: Implementing the Scholarship of Teaching*. San Francisco: Jossey-Bass, 1996.

Cuban, L. *How Scholars Trumped Teachers: Change Without Reform in University Curriculum, Teaching and Research, 1890–1990*. New York: Teachers College Press, 1999.

Cuban, L. "Teaching and Learning at the Research University." *Peer Review,* 2000, *2*(4), 15–19.

Davis, J. R. *Interdisciplinary Courses and Team Teaching: New Arrangements for Learning*. Phoenix: Oryx Press, 1995.

Della-Piana, C. K., Bader, J., Darnell, A., Romo, L., Rubio, N., Flores, B., Knaust, H., Brady, T., and Swift, A. "A Longitudinal Study of Student Persistence in Science, Technology, Engineering and Mathematics (STEM) at a Regional Urban University." *Proceedings of the American Society for Engineering Education Annual Conference and Exposition*, 2003.

Dewey, J. *How We Think*. Lexington, Mass.: Heath, 1933.

Dewey, J. *Experience and Education*. Old Tappan, N.Y.: Macmillan, 1938.

deWinstanley, P. A., and Bjork, R. A. "Successful Lecturing: Presenting Information in Ways that Engage Effective Processing. In D. F. Halpern and M. D. Hakel, (eds.), *Applying the Science of Learning to University Teaching and Beyond*. New Directions for Teaching and Learning, no. 89. San Francisco: Jossey-Bass, 2002.

Diamond, R. M. "Faculty, Instructional, and Organizational Development: Options and Choices." In K. H. Gillespie, L. R. Hilsen, and E. C. Wadsworth (eds.), *A Guide to Faculty Development: Practical Advice, Examples, and Resources*. Bolton, Mass.: Anker, 2002.

Dressel, J. P. "The Meaning and Significance of Integration." In N. Henry (ed.), *The Integration of Educational Experiences, The Fifty-seventh Yearbook of the National Society for the Study of Education*. Chicago: University of Chicago Press, 1958.

Dutcher, J., Mino, J., and Singh, R. "How Long Is the Coast of Holyoke Community College?" In J. MacGregor (ed.), *Strengthening Learning Communities: Case Studies from the National Learning Communities (FIPSE) Dissemination Project*. Olympia, Wash.: The Evergreen State College, 1999.

Dwyer, J. O. "A Historical Look at the Freshman Year Experience." In L. Upcraft, J. Gardner, and Associates (eds.), *The Freshman Year Experience*, San Francisco: Jossey-Bass, 1989.

Eaton, J. "General Education in the Community College: Developing Habits of Thought." In N. Raisman (ed.), *Directing General Education Outcomes*. New Directions for Community Colleges, no. 81. San Francisco: Jossey-Bass, 1993.

Eaton, M., MacGregor, J., and Schoem, D. "The Educational Promise of Service-Learning Communities." In J. MacGregor (ed.), *Integrating Learning Communities with Service Learning*. National Learning Communities Project Monograph Series. Olympia: The Evergreen State College, Washington Center for Improving the Quality of Undergraduate Education, with the American Association for Higher Education, 2003.

Eaton, M., and Patton, J. "Reflection, Civic Engagement, and Learning Communities." In J. MacGregor (ed.), *Integrating Learning Communities with Service Learning*. National Learning Communities Project Monograph Series. Olympia: The Evergreen State College, Washington Center for Improving the Quality of Undergraduate Education, with the American Association for Higher Education, 2003.

Eby, K. "Teaching and Learning from an Interdisciplinary Perspective." *Peer Review*, 2001, 3/4 (4/1), 28–31.

Eckel, P., Green, M., and Hill, B. *On Change V: Riding the Waves of Changes: Insights from Transforming Institutions.* Washington, D.C.: American Council on Education, 2001.

Edmonds, C. "General Education in Occupational Programs: The Barriers Can Be Surmounted." In N. Raisman (ed.), *Directing General Education Outcomes.* New Directions for Community Colleges, no. 81. San Francisco: Jossey-Bass, 1993.

Edmonds Community College. "Impact of Coordinated Studies on Student Outcomes in College Chemistry" 2001, p. 4. Internal document.

Educational Testing Service. *Towards Inequality: Disturbing Trends in Higher Education.* Princeton, NJ: Educational Testing Service, 1998.

Elbow, P. "Methodological Doubting and Believing: Contraries in Inquiry." In P. Elbow, *Embracing Contraries: Exploration in Learning and Teaching.* London: Oxford University Press, 1986.

El-Khawas, E. *Campus Trends, 1995.* Higher Education Panel Report No. 85. Washington, D.C.: American Council on Education, 1995.

Elmore, R. "Getting to Scale with Good Educational Practice." *Harvard Educational Review,* 1996, 66(1), 1–27.

Endicott, P., Suhr, D., McMorrow, S., and Doherty, P. "The Flexible First-Year Seminar as the Centerpiece of Five Learning Community Programs." In J. M. Henscheid (ed.), *The Role of First-Year Seminars in Learning Communities.* Columbia: University of South Carolina, National Resource Center for the First-year Experience and Students in Transition, 2004.

Entwistle, N. "Promoting Deep Learning Through Teaching and Assessment." In L. Suskie (ed.), *Assessment to Promote Deep Learning: Insights from AAHE's 2000 and 1999 Assessment Conferences.* Washington, D.C.: American Association for Higher Education, 2000.

Esperian, J., Hill, P., and MacGregor, J. "Bibliography on the Federated Learning Communities and Related Programs." Unpublished manuscript, The Evergreen State College, 1986.

Estrich, S. "It's Not Who Goes to College: It's Who Can Stay There." *USA Today,* May 12, 1998. [http://www.ncpa.org/pi/edu/May98d.html].

Ewell, P. "Organizing for Learning: A New Imperative." *AAHE Bulletin,* December 1997, pp. 3–6.

Ewell, P. "Major Trends in Higher Education: Implications for Accreditation." Paper presented to the Middle States Association Meeting, Baltimore, December 2001.

Ewell, P. "An Emerging Scholarship: A Brief History of Assessment." In T. Banta (ed.), *Building a Scholarship of Assessment.* San Francisco: Jossey-Bass, 2002a.

Ewell, P. "Grading Student Learning: You Have to Start Somewhere." In National Center for Public Policy and Higher Education's, *Measuring Up 2002: The State-by-State Report Card for Higher Education*. San Jose, Calif.: National Center for Public Policy and Higher Education, 2002b. [http://measuringup.highereducation.org/2002/articles/peterewell.htm]

Ewell, P. "Three Dialectics in Higher Education's Future." Project on the Future of Higher Education Working Paper. Seattle: Antioch University, 2002c.

The Experimental College of the University of Wisconsin, 1927–1932 (exhibit catalogue). Madison: University of Wisconsin, university archives in conjunction with the Meiklejohn Education Association, 1995.

Eyler, J., and Giles, D. E. *Where's the Learning in Service Learning?* San Francisco: Jossey-Bass, 1999.

Ferren, A. "Achieving Effectiveness and Efficiency." In J. Gaff, J. Ratcliff, and Associates (eds.), *Handbook of the Undergraduate Curriculum*. San Francisco: Jossey-Bass, 1997.

Ferren, A., and Slavings, R. *Investing in Quality: Tools for Improving Curricular Efficiency.* Washington, D.C.: Association of American Colleges and Universities, 2000.

Fink, L. D. *Creating Significant Experiences: An Integrated Approach to Designing College Courses.* San Francisco: Jossey-Bass, 2003.

Finkel, D. *Teaching with Your Mouth Shut.* Portsmouth, N.H.: Heinemann, 2000.

Finkel, D., and Monk, G. S. "Teaching and Learning Groups: Dissolution of the Atlas Complex." In G. Bouton and R. Garth (eds.), *Learning in Groups*. New Directions for Teaching and Learning, no. 14. San Francisco: Jossey-Bass, 1983.

Finkelstein, M. J., and LaCeller-Peterson, M. (eds.). *Developing Senior Faculty as Teachers*. New Directions for Teaching and Learning, no. 55. San Francisco: Jossey-Bass, 1993.

Finkelstein, M., and Schuster, J. "Assessing the Silent Revolution: How Changing Demographics are Reshaping the Academic Profession." *AAHE Bulletin,* 2001, *54*(2), 3–7.

Finkelstein, M. J., Seal, R., and Schuster, J. *The New Academic Generation: A Profession in Transformation,* Baltimore: Johns Hopkins Press, 1998.

Finley, N. J. "Meeting Expectations by Making New Connections: Curriculum Reform at Seattle Central." *Educational Record,* 1990, *71*(4), 50–53.

Flateby, T. L. "The Evolution of a Participatory Approach to Evaluate Learning Communities." In J. MacGregor (ed.), *Doing Learning Community Assessment: Five Campus Stories*. National Learning Communities Project Monograph Series. Olympia: The Evergreen State College, Washington Center for Improving the Quality of Undergraduate Education, with the American Association for Higher Education, 2003.

Fogarty, J., Dunlap, L., and others. *Learning Communities and Community Colleges*. National Learning Communities Project Monograph Series. Olympia: The Evergreen State College, Washington Center for Improving the Quality of Undergraduate Education, with the American Association for Higher Education, 2003.

Freire, P. *Pedagogy of the Oppressed*. New York: Seabury, 1970.

Fullilove, R. E., and Treisman, P. U. "Mathematics Achievement Among African American Undergraduates at the University of California, Berkeley: An Evaluation of the Mathematics Workshop Program." *Journal of Negro Education*, 1990, *59*(3), 463–478.

Gabelnick, F., MacGregor, J., Matthews, R., and Smith, B. *Learning Communities: Making Connections Among Students, Faculty, and Disciplines*. San Francisco: Jossey-Bass, 1990.

Gaff, J. "The Rhetoric and Reality of General Education Reform: An Overview." *Perspectives,* Fall 1992, *22*(1), 47–57.

Gaff, J. "Overcoming Barriers: Interdisciplinary Studies in Disciplinary Institutions." Keynote speech at the Association for Integrative Studies, Detroit, Michigan, Oct. 8, 1993.

Gaff, J. *General Education: The Changing Agenda*. Washington, D.C.: Association of American Colleges and Universities, 1999.

Gaff, J., and Associates. *The Cluster College*. San Francisco: Jossey-Bass, 1970.

Gallagher, W. *The Power of Place: How Our Surroundings Shape Our Thoughts, Emotions, and Actions*. New York: HarperCollins, 1994.

Gamson, Z., and Associates. *Liberating Education*. San Francisco: Jossey-Bass, 1984.

Gardiner, L. F. *Redesigning Higher Education: Producing Dramatic Gains in Student Learning*. ASHE-ERIC Higher Education Report, no. 7. San Francisco: Jossey-Bass, 1994.

Gardner, H., Csikszentmihalyi, M., and Damon, W. *Good Work: When Excellence and Ethics Meet*. New York: Basic Books, 2001.

Gladwell, M. *The Tipping Point: How Little Things Can Make a Big Difference*. Boston: Little, Brown, 2000.

Gleazer, E. J. "The Community College: Issues of the 1970s." *Educational Record,* 1970, *51,* 47–52.

Goodsell, A. "Freshman Interest Groups: Linking Social and Academic Experiences of First-Year Students." Unpublished doctoral dissertation, Syracuse University, New York, 1993.

Gordon, T., and others. "Connections: Freshman Learning Communities at Illinois State University: Where We've Been and Where We Are Going." In J. MacGregor (comp.), *Strengthening Learning Communities: Case Studies from the National Learning Communities Dissemination Project (FIPSE)*. Olympia: The Evergreen State College, Washington Center for Improving the Quality of Undergraduate Education, 1999.

Gordon, V. "Origins and Purpose of the Freshman Seminar." In L. Upcraft, J. Gardner, and Associates (eds.), *The Freshman Year Experience*. San Francisco: Jossey-Bass, 1989.

Grant, G., and Riesman, D. *The Perpetual Dream: Reform and Experiment in the American College*. Chicago: University of Chicago Press, 1978.

Greater Expectations: A New Vision for Learning as a Nation Goes to College. Washington, D.C.: Association of American Colleges and Universities National Panel, 2002.

Grubb, W. N., and Associates. *Honored But Invisible: An Inside Look at Teaching in Community Colleges*. New York: Routledge, 1999.

Guarasci, R. "Developing the Democratic Arts." *About Campus*, 2001, 5(6), 2001.

Guarasci, R. "The Wagner Plan for the Practical Liberal Arts: Deep Learning and Reflective Practice." In J. MacGregor (ed.), *Integrating Learning Communities with Service Learning*. National Learning Communities Project Monograph Series. Olympia: The Evergreen State College, Washington Center for Improving the Quality of Undergraduate Education, with the American Association for Higher Education, 2003a.

Guarasci, R. "Wagner College: Learning Communities for the Practical Liberal Arts." In K. Spear and others (eds.), *Learning Communities and Liberal Arts Colleges*. National Learning Communities Project Monograph Series. Olympia: Washington Center for Undergraduate Education, The Evergreen State College, with American Association for Higher Education, 2003b.

Guarasci, R., Cornwell, G., and Associates. *Democratic Education in an Age of Difference: Redefining Citizenship in Higher Education*. San Francisco: Jossey-Bass, 1997.

Guba, E., and Lincoln, Y. *Effective Evaluation: Improving the Usefulness of Evaluation Results through Responsive and Naturalistic Approaches*. San Francisco: Jossey-Bass, 1981.

Guskin, A., and Marcy, M. "Facing the Future: Faculty Work, Student Learning and Fundamental Reform." Working Paper 1, Project on the Future of Higher Education. Seattle: Antioch University, 2001.

Guskin, A., and Marcy, M. "Dealing with the Future Now: Principles for Creating a Vital Campus in a Climate of Restricted Resources," *Change*, 2003, 35(4), 10–21.

Guskin, A., Marcy, M., and Smith, B. *Learning Communities and Fiscal Reality: Optimizing Learning in a Time of Limited Resources*. National Learning Communities Project Monograph Series. Olympia: The Evergreen State College, Washington Center for Improving the Quality of Undergraduate Education, with the American Association for Higher Education, 2004.

Guskin, A. E. "Restructuring the Role of Faculty Part I." *Change*, July-Aug. 1994a, 4(4), 22–30.

Guskin, A. E. "Restructuring the Role of Faculty Part II." *Change,* Sept.-Oct. 1994b, *5*(5), 16–25.

Guskin, A. E. "Facing the Future: The Change Process in Restructuring Universities." *Change,* July-August 1996, *4*(4), 27–37.

Halliburton, D. "A Voice That Still Speaks to Us." *Change,* Jan.-Feb. 1997, *29*(1), 24–29.

Halpern, D., and Hakel, M. "Applying the Science of Learning to the University and Beyond: Teaching for Long-Term Retention and Transfer." *Change,* 2003, *35*(4), 36–41.

Hansen, E. "Essential Demographics of Today's College Students." American Association for Higher Education *Bulletin,* Nov. 1998, *51*(3), 1–7.

Harnish, J. "Impact of Coordinated Studies Programs at North Seattle Community College." Unpublished study, Seattle, Wash.: North Seattle Community College, 2002.

Harris, J., and Sansom, D. "Discerning Is More Than Counting." Occasional Papers in Liberal Education, No. 3. Washington, D.C.: American Academy for Liberal Education, 2001.

Hebel, S. "New York Regents Approve CUNY's Remediation Plan After 3 Years of Monitoring." *Academe Today: The Chronicle of Higher Education's Daily Report for Subscribers,* Dec. 13, 2002a. [http://chronicle.com/daily/2002/12/2002121301n.htm]

Hebel, S. "A New Look for CUNY." *Academe Today: The Chronicle of Higher Education's Daily Report for Subscribers,* Mar. 1, 2002b. [http://chronicle.com/weekly/v48/i25/25a02001.htm]

Hebel, S. "Cal State Sees Reduced Need for Remediation, but Finds English Skills Lacking." *Academe Today: The Chronicle of Higher Education's Daily Report for Subscribers,* Jan. 29, 2003. [http://chronicle.com/daily/2003/01/2003012901.htm]

Heifetz, R. *Leadership Without Easy Answers.* Cambridge, Mass.: Belknap Press, 1994.

Helling, J. *Law and Diversity Program Annual Report.* Bellingham: Fairhaven College, Western Washington University, 2003.

Henscheid, J. M. *Washington State University Freshman Seminar Program Research Findings.* Pullman: Washington State University Student Advising and Learning Center Report, 1999.

Henscheid, J. M. (ed.). *The Integrative Role of First-Year Seminars in Learning Communities.* National Resource Center for the First-Year Experience and Students in Transition. Columbia: University of South Carolina, 2004.

Hesse, M., and Mason, M. "Teaching the Theme of Community." In J. MacGregor (ed.), *Integrating Learning Communities with Service Learning.* National Learning Communities Project Monograph Series.

Olympia: The Evergreen State College, Washington Center for Improving the Quality of Undergraduate Education, with the American Association for Higher Education, 2003.

Higher Education Research Institute (HERI). *2001 CIRP Press Release. Cooperative Institutional Research Program (CIRP) Freshman Survey.* Los Angeles: University of California-Los Angeles Graduate School of Education and Information Studies, 2001.

Hill, P. "The Incomplete Revolution." *Cross Currents,* 1975, *24*(4), 423–443.

Hill, P. "Communities of Learners: Curriculum as the Infrastructure of Academic Communities." In J. Hall and B. Keveles (eds.), *In Opposition to Core Curriculum.* Westport, Conn.: Greenwood Press, 1982.

Hill, P. "A Deweyan Perspective on Higher Education." *Liberal Education,* 1984a, *70*(4), 307–314.

Hill, P. "Intergenerational Communities: Partnerships in Discovery." In R. Jones, and B. L. Smith (eds.), *Against the Current.* Cambridge, Mass.: Schenkman Press, 1984b.

Hill, P. "The Rationale for Learning Communities." Paper presented by Provost Patrick Hill at the Inaugural Conference on Learning Communities of the Washington Center for Undergraduate Education, The Evergreen State College, Olympia, Washington, Oct. 22, 1985.

Hill, P. "Multiculturalism: The Crucial Philosophical and Organizational Issues." *Change,* July-Aug. 1991, *4*(4), 38–47.

Hoffman, N. "Increasing College Attainment Rates for Underrepresented Students." *Change,* 2003, *35*(4), 42–48.

Holyer, R. "The Oriel Common Room: General Education and Faculty Culture." *Liberal Education,* 2002, *88*(1), 36–41.

Huba, M., Ellertson, S., Cook, M. D., and Epperson, D. L. "Assessment's Role in Transforming a Grass-Roots Initiative into an Institutionalized Program: Evaluating and Shaping Learning Communities at Iowa State University." In J. MacGregor (ed.), *Doing Learning Community Assessment: Five Campus Stories.* National Learning Community Project Monograph Series. Olympia: The Evergreen State College, Washington Center for Improving the Quality of Undergraduate Education, with the American Association for Higher Education, 2003.

Huba, M. E., and Freed, J. E. *Learner-Centered Assessment on Campuses: Shifting the Focus from Teaching to Learning.* Needham Heights, Mass.: Allyn & Bacon, 2000.

Huber, M. T. *Community College Faculty Attitudes and Trends, 1997.* Stanford, Calif.: National Center for Postsecondary Improvement, Stanford University, 1998.

Hutchings, P., and Shulman, L. S. "The Scholarship of Teaching: New Elaborations, New Developments." *Change,* 1999, *31*(5), 11–15.

Ibarra, R. *Beyond Affirmative Action: Reframing the Context of Higher Educa-tion.* Madison: University of Wisconsin Press, 2001.

Indiana University Purdue University-Indianapolis. *Restructuring for Urban Student Success: IUPUI Self-Study Report.* Indianapolis: Indiana University Purdue University-Indianapolis, 1999.

Jacobs, J. "Vocational Education and General Education: New Relationship or Shotgun Marriage." In N. Raisman (ed.), *Directing General Education Outcomes.* New Directions for Community Colleges, no. 81. San Francisco: Jossey-Bass, 1993.

Jacoby, B., and Associates. *Service Learning in Higher Education: Concepts and Practices.* San Francisco: Jossey-Bass, 1996.

Johnson, D. W., and Johnson, R. T. *Creative Controversy: Intellectual Chal-lenge in the Classroom.* Edina, Minn.: Interaction Book Company, 1995.

Johnson, D. W., Johnson, R. T., and Smith, K. A. *Active Learning: Cooperation in the College Classroom.* Edina, Minn.: Interaction Book Company, 1998.

Johnson, W. C. *Freshman Interest Groups (FIGs) Versus Non-FIGs on Scales and Items from Fall, 1997 House Environment Survey.* Columbia: Univer-sity of Missouri Residence Life Internal Document, 1998.

Jones, R. *Experiment at Evergreen.* Cambridge, Mass.: Schenkman, 1981.

Jones, R. "What Employers Expect of Education." *Liberal Education,* 2003, *89*(2), 41–43.

Jones, R., and Smith, B. L. (eds.). *Against the Current: Reform and Experimen-tation in Higher Education.* Cambridge, Mass.: Schenkman, 1984.

Kanter, S., Gamson, Z., and London, H. *Revitalizing General Education in a Time of Scarcity.* Needham Heights, Mass.: Allyn & Bacon, 1997.

Kazis, R., Vargas, J., and Hoffman, N. (eds.). *Doubling the Numbers: State Policies to Promote Postsecondary Attainment for Underrepresented Youth.* Cambridge, Mass.: Harvard Publishing Group, 2004.

Kegan, R. *The Evolving Self: Problem and Process in Human Development.* Cambridge, Mass.: Harvard University Press, 1982.

Kegan, R. *In Over Our Heads: The Mental Demands of Modern Life.* Cambridge, Mass.: Harvard University Press, 1994.

Kellogg Commission on the Future of State and Land-Grant Universities. *Returning to Our Roots: Executive Summaries of the Reports of the Kellogg Commission on the Future of State and Land-Grant Universities.* Washington, D.C.: National Association of State and Land-Grant Universities, 2001.

Kellogg Commission on the Future of State and Land-Grant Universities. *Returning to Our Roots: Six Reports, 1999–2000.* Washington, D.C. National Association of State and Land-Grant Universities.

Kerr, C. "Higher Education Cannot Escape History: The 1990s." In L. Jones and F. Nowotny (eds.), *An Agenda for the New Decade.* New Directions for Higher Education, no. 70. San Francisco: Jossey-Bass, 1990.

Kimball, B. *A History of the Idea of Liberal Education.* New York: Teachers College Press, 1986.

Kimball, B. "Toward Pragmatic Liberal Education." In R. Orrill (ed.), *The Condition of American Liberal Education.* New York: College Board, 1995a.

Kimball, B. *Orators and Philosophers: A History of the Idea of Liberal Education.* New York: College Entrance Board, 1995b.

Koolsbergen, W. "Approaching Diversity: Some Classroom Strategies for Learning Communities." *Peer Review,* 2001, 3(4), 25–27.

Kuh, G., Schuh, J. H., Whitt, E. J., and others. *Involving Colleges: Successful Approaches to Fostering Student Development and Learning Outside the Classroom.* San Francisco: Jossey-Bass, 1991.

Kunstler, J. H. *Home from Nowhere: Remaking Our Everyday World for the 21st Century.* New York: Simon & Schuster, 1996.

Kupiec, T. Y. (ed.). *Rethinking Tradition: Integrating Service with Academic Study on College Campuses.* Providence, R.I.: Campus Compact, Education Commission of the States, 1993.

Lane, J. C. "The Rollins Conference 1931 and the Search for a Progressive Liberal Education: Mirror or Prism." *Liberal Education,* Winter 1984, 70(4), 297–305.

Lardner, E. *Approaching Diversity Through Learning Communities.* Occasional Paper No. 2. Olympia: Washington Center for Undergraduate Education, The Evergreen State College, 2002.

Lave, J., and Wenger, E. *Situated Learning: Legitimate Peripheral Participation.* Cambridge, England: Cambridge University Press, 1991.

Lavin, D. E., and Hyllegard, D. *Changing the Odds: Open Admissions and the Life Chances of the Disadvantaged.* New Haven: Yale University Press, 1996.

Lazerson, M., Wagener, U., and Shumanis, N. "What Makes a Revolution: Teaching and Learning in Higher Education, 1980–2000." *Change,* May-June 2000, 3(3), 12–19.

Lederman, M. J. "Launching a Remedial Reading, Writing, Speech Program: Titanic or Good Ship Lollypop?" *Contemporary Education,* 1974, 46(1), 34–37.

Lenning, O. T., and Ebbers, L. H. *The Powerful Potential of Learning Communities: Improving Education for the Future.* ASHE-ERIC Higher Education Report, vol. 26, no. 6. San Francisco: Jossey-Bass, 1999.

Levine, J., and Thompkins, D. "Making Learning Communities Work: Seven Lessons from Temple" *AAHE Bulletin,* 1996, 48(10), 3–6.

Levine Laufgraben, J. "Faculty Development: Growing, Reflecting, Learning, and Changing." In J. O'Connor and others. *Learning Communities in Research Universities*. National Learning Communities Project Monograph Series. Olympia: The Evergreen State College, Washington Center for Improving the Quality of Undergraduate Education, with the American Association for Higher Education, 2003.

Levine Laufgraben, J., and Shapiro, N. S. (eds.). *Sustaining and Improving Learning*. San Francisco: Jossey-Bass, 2004.

Levine Laufgraben, J., Ayers, H. W., Evenbeck, S., Hoffman, N., Jackson, B., and Patton, J. *Learning and Changing Through Programmatic Self-Study and Peer Review: Solving Problems and Improving Practice Collaboratively*. Washington, D.C.: American Association for Higher Education, 2004b.

Light, R. J. *The Harvard Assessment Seminars: Explorations with Students and Faculty About Teaching, Learning, and Student Life* (1st report). Cambridge, Mass.: Harvard University Graduate School of Education, 1990.

Light, R. J. *The Harvard Assessment Seminars: Explorations with Students and Faculty About Teaching, Learning, and Student Life* (2nd report). Cambridge, Mass.: Harvard University Graduate School of Education and Kennedy School of Government, 1992.

Light, R. J. *Making the Most of College: Student Speak their Minds*. Cambridge, Mass.: Harvard University Press, 2001.

Loacker, G. (ed.). *Self-Assessment at Alverno College*. Milwaukee, Wis.: Alverno College, 2000.

Locke, L. "General Education: In Search of Facts: Still Scarce, But More on the Way." *Change*, July-Aug. 1989, *21*(4), 21–23.

Loevy, R. *Colorado College: A Place of Learning 1984–1999*. Colorado Springs: Colorado College, 1999.

Love, A. G., and Tokuno, K. A. "Learning Community Models." In J. H. Levine (ed.), *Learning Communities: New Structures, New Partnerships for Learning*. Monograph No. 26. Columbia: National Resource Center for the First Year Experience and Students in Transition, University of South Carolina, 1999.

Lowell, N. *Freshman Interest Groups, Autumn 1996: Faculty Survey*. Seattle: Office of Educational Assessment, University of Washington, 1997.

Lowell, N., Jundt, M., and Johnson, J. *1998 FIG/Freshman Survey*. Seattle: Office of Educational Assessment, 1999.

MacGregor, J. *Intellectual Development of Students in Learning Community Programs 1986–87*. Occasional Paper No. 1. Olympia: Washington Center for Improving the Quality of Undergraduate Education, 1987.

MacGregor, J. "Collaborative Learning: Shared Inquiry as a Process of Reform." In M. Svinicki (ed.), *The Changing Face of College Teaching*.

New Directions for Teaching and Learning, no. 42. San Francisco: Jossey-Bass, 1990.

MacGregor, J. "Learning Self-Evaluation: Challenges for Students." In J. MacGregor (ed.), *Student Self-Evaluation: Fostering Reflective Learning.* New Directions for Teaching and Learning, no. 56. San Francisco: Jossey-Bass, 1993.

MacGregor, J. *Strengthening Learning Communities: Case Studies from the National Learning Communities (FIPSE) Dissemination Project.* Olympia, Wash.: The Evergreen State College, 1999.

MacGregor, J. (ed.). *Integrating Learning Communities with Service Learning.* National Learning Communities Project Monograph Series. Olympia: The Evergreen State College, Washington Center for Improving the Quality of Undergraduate Education, with the American Association for Higher Education, 2003.

Maki, P. "Developing an Assessment Plan to Learn about Student Learning." *Journal of Academic Librarianship,* 2002, *28*(1/2), 8–13.

Malcom, S. "Making Mathematics the Great Equalizer." In L. A. Steen (ed.), *Why Numbers Count: Quantitative Literacy for Tomorrow's America.* New York: College Board, 1997.

Malnarich, G., and Lardner, E. D. *Designing Integrated Learning for Students: A Heuristic for Teaching, Assessment and Curriculum Design.* Occasional Paper No. 1. Olympia: Washington Center for Improving the Quality of Undergraduate Education, The Evergreen State College, 2002.

Marchese, T. "The New Conversations About Learning: Insights from Neuroscience and Anthropology, Cognitive Science and Work-Place Studies." In *Assessing Impact: Evidence and Action.* Washington, D.C.: American Association for Higher Education, 1997.

Marcy, M. "Diversity, Demographics, and Dollars: Challenges for Higher Education." Working Paper No. 3, Project on the Future of Higher Education, Seattle: Antioch University, 2002.

Massy, W., and Wilger, A. "It's Time to Redefine Quality." Paper presented at the AAHE Annual Conference on Faculty Roles and Rewards, Atlanta, Feb. 1996.

Massy, W. F. *Honoring the Trust: Quality and Cost Containment in Higher Education.* Bolton, Mass.: Anker Press, 2003.

Matthews, R. "Learning Communities in the Community College." *AACJC: Community, Technical and Junior College Journal,* 1986, *57*(2), 44–47.

Matthews, R. "Enriching Teaching and Learning Through Learning Communities." In T. O'Banion (ed.), *Teaching and Learning in the Community College.* Washington, D.C.: Community College Press, 1994.

Matthews, R. S., Cooper, J., Davidson, N., and Hawkes, P. "Bridging the Gap Between Cooperative and Collaborative Learning," *Change,* July-Aug. 1995, *28*(40), 35–39.

Matthews, R. S., and Lynch, D. J. "Learning Communities: Collaborative Approaches to Engaging Differences." In R. Guarasci, G. Cornwell, and others. (eds.), *Democratic Education in an Age of Difference: Redefining Citizenship in Higher Education.* San Francisco: Jossey-Bass, 1997.

Matthews, R. S., Smith, B. L., MacGregor, J., Gabelnick, F. "Creating Learning Communities." In J. Gaff, J. Ratcliff, and Associates, *Handbook of the Undergraduate Curriculum.* San Francisco: Jossey-Bass, 1997.

Mazur, E. *Peer Instruction: A User's Manual.* Englewood Cliffs, N.J.: Prentice Hall, 1997.

McCabe, R. *No One to Waste: A Report to Public Decision Makers and Community College Leaders.* Washington, D.C.: Community College Press, 2000.

McKeachie, W. J., Pintrich, P. R., Yi-Guang, L., and Smith, D.A.F. *Teaching and Learning in the College Classroom: A Review of the Research Literature.* Ann Arbor: Regents of the University of Michigan, 1986.

Mehan, H. *Learning Lessons: Social Organization in the Classroom.* Cambridge, Mass.: Harvard University Press, 1979.

Meiklejohn, A. "A New College: Notes on a Next Step in Higher Education." *Century Magazine,* Jan. 1925, pp. 312–320.

Meiklejohn, A. *The Experimental College.* Bulletin of the University of Wisconsin. Madison: University of Wisconsin, 1927.

Meiklejohn, A. *The Experimental College.* Madison: University of Wisconsin Press, 2000. (Originally published 1932.)

Mellow, G., van Slyck, P., and Eynon, G. "The Face of the Future: Engaging in Diversity at LaGuardia Community College." *Change,* Mar./Apr. 2003, *35*(2), 10–17.

Menand, L. *The Metaphysical Club: A Story of Ideas in America.* New York: Farrar, Straus and Giroux, 2001.

Mentkowski, M., and Associates. *Learning That Lasts: Integrating Learning, Development and Performance in College and Beyond.* San Francisco: Jossey-Bass, 2000.

Miller, G. *The Meaning of General Education.* New York: Teachers College Press, 1988.

Millis, B. J., and Cottell, P. G., Jr. *Cooperative Learning for Higher Education Faculty.* American Council on Education Series on Higher Education. Phoenix: Oryx Press, 1998.

Moore, D. M., and Kerlin, S. T. "Research Report: Examining the Effectiveness of Coordinated Studies, 1990–1994." Unpublished report, North Seattle Community College, 1994.

Moore, L. H. *A Mixed Method Approach to Evaluating Learning Communities for Underprepared Community College Students: The Integrated Studies Communities at Parkland College.* Unpublished doctoral dissertation, University of Illinois at Urbana-Champaign, 2000.

Moore, W. S., and Hunter, S. "Beyond 'Mildly Interesting Facts': Student Self-Evaluations and Outcomes Assessment." In J. MacGregor (ed.), *Student Self-Evaluation: Fostering Reflective Learning.* New Directions for Teaching and Learning, no. 56. San Francisco: Jossey-Bass, 1993.

Morante, E. *Report on the Character and Effectiveness of Remedial Programs in New Jersey Public Colleges and Universities in Fall 1981.* New Jersey: Basic Skills Council, 1982.

Morante, E. *Report on the Character and Effectiveness of Remedial Programs in New Jersey Public Colleges and Universities in Fall 1982.* New Jersey: Basic Skills Council, 1983.

Morgan, J. J., and others. "Can Systemic Change Really Help Engineering Students from Underrepresented Groups?" *Proceedings of the International Conference on Engineering Education,* 2002, Manchester, United Kingdom.

Musil, C. M. "Educating for Citizenship." *Peer Review,* 2003, *5*(3), 5–8.

Musil, C. M., and Associates. *To Form a More Perfect Union: Campus Diversity Initiatives.* Washington, D.C.: Association of American Colleges and Universities, 1999.

National Center for Education Statistics. "Remedial Education at Higher Education Institutions in Fall 1995." (NCS 97–584) Washington, D.C.: U.S. Department of Education, National Center for Education Statistics, October 1996.

National Center for Postsecondary Improvement. "Gauging the Impact of Institutional Student-Assessment Strategies: Revolution or Evolution?" *Change,* 1999, *31*(5), 53–56.

National Center for Public Policy and Higher Education. *College Affordability in Jeopardy. Special Supplement.* San Jose, Calif.: National Center for Public Policy and Higher Education, 2002a.

National Center for Public Policy and Higher Education. *Measuring Up 2002: The State-by-State Report Card for Higher Education.* San Jose, Calif.: National Center for Public Policy and Higher Education, 2002b.

National Center for Public Policy and Higher Education. *Losing Ground: A National Status Report on the Affordability of American Higher Education.* San Jose, Calif.: National Center for Public Policy and Higher Education, 2002c.

National Institute of Education, Study Group on the Conditions of Excellence in American Higher Education. *Involvement in Learning: Realizing the Potential of American Higher Education.* Washington, D.C.: U.S. Government Printing Office, 1984.

National Research Council. *Transforming Undergraduate Education in Science, Mathematics, Engineering and Technology.* Washington, D.C.: National Academy Press, 1999.

National Resource Center for the First-Year Experience and Students in Transition. *National Survey of First-Year Seminar Programming,* n.d. [http://www.sc.edu/fye].

National Survey of Student Engagement. Bloomington: Indiana University, 2001.

Nelson, A. *Education and Democracy: The Meaning of Alexander Meiklejohn, 1872–1964.* Madison: University of Wisconsin Press, 2001.

Nelson, L. "On and Off Campus: Learning in the Context of Democracy and Discomfort." In J. MacGregor (ed.), *Integrating Learning Communities and Service Learning.* National Learning Communities Project Monograph Series. Olympia, Wash.: The Evergreen State College, Washington Center for Improving the Quality of Undergraduate Education, in cooperation with the American Association for Higher Education, 2003.

Newcomb, T. M., and Wilson, E. K. (eds.). *College Peer Groups: Problems and Possibilities.* Hawthorne, N.Y.: Aldine de Gruyter, 1996.

Newell, W. H. "The Promise of Integrative Learning." *About Campus,* 1999, 4(2), 17–23.

Newell, W. H. Powerful Pedagogies." In B. L. Smith and J. McCann (eds.), *Reinventing Ourselves: Interdisciplinary Education, Collaborative Learning, and Experimentation in Higher Education.* Bolton, Mass.: Anker Press, 2001.

Newton, F. B. "The New Student." *About Campus,* Nov.-Dec. 2000, 5(5), 8–15.

O'Connor, J., and others. *Learning Communities in Research Universities.* National Learning Communities Project Monograph Series. Olympia: The Evergreen State College, Washington Center for Improving the Quality of Undergraduate Education, with the American Association for Higher Education, 2003.

O'Meara, K., and Rice, R. E. (eds.). *Encouraging Multiple Forms of Scholarship: Voices from the Field.* Washington, D.C.: American Association for Higher Education, 2004.

Oates, K. "Integration and Assessment of Service Learning in Learning Communities" In B. L. Smith and J. McCann (eds.), *Reinventing Ourselves.* Bolton, Mass.: Anker Press, 2001.

Oates, K., and Leavitt, L. *Service-Learning and Learning Communities: Tools for Integration and Assessment.* Washington, D.C.: Association of American Colleges and Universities, 2003.

Office of Institutional Research and Planning. "Project Success: An Examination of a Collaborative Effort in English Coursework." San Diego, Calif.: Office of Institutional Research and Planning, Grossmont College, 1995.

Olson, W. *The Origins and Birth of the Hutchins School of Liberal Studies.* Unpublished manuscript, Sonoma State University, n.d.

Orrill, R. (ed.). *The Condition of American Liberal Education: Pragmatism and a Changing Tradition.* New York: College Board, 1995.

Orrill, R. (ed.). *Education and Democracy: Reimagining Liberal Learning in America.* New York: College Board, 1997.

Ory, J. C., and Braskamp, L. A. "Involvement and Growth of Students in Three Academic Programs." *Research in Higher Education,* 1988, *28,* 116–129.

Outcalt, C. *Community College Faculty: Characteristics, Practices, Challenges.* New Directions in Community Colleges, no. 118. San Francisco: Jossey-Bass, 2002.

Palmer, P. J. *The Courage to Teach: Exploring the Inner Landscape of a Teacher's Life.* San Francisco: Jossey-Bass, 1998.

Parks, S. D. *Big Questions, Worthy Dreams: Mentoring Young Adults in Their Search for Meaning, Purpose, and Faith.* San Francisco: Jossey-Bass, 2000.

Pascarella, E. T. "Cognitive Growth in College." *Change,* 2001, *33*(6), 21–22.

Pascarella, E. T., and Terenzini, P. T. *How College Affects Students: Finding and Insights from Twenty Years of Research.* San Francisco: Jossey-Bass, 1991.

Patton, J., Jenks, P., and Labissiere, Y. "Student Learning as Program Evaluation: Student Portfolio Assessment in University Studies at Portland State University." In J. MacGregor (ed.), *Doing Learning Community Assessment: Five Campus Stories.* National Learning Communities Project Monograph Series. Olympia: The Evergreen State College, Washington Center for Improving the Quality of Undergraduate Education, with the American Association for Higher Education, 2003.

Patton, M. Q. *Utilization-Focused Evaluation.* Thousand Oaks, Calif.: Sage Publications, 1997.

Pelligrino, J., Chudowsky, N., and Glaser, R. (eds.). *Knowing What Students Know: The Science and Design of Educational Assessment.* Washington, D.C.: National Academy Press, 2001.

Perkins, D. *Outsmarting IQ: The Emerging Science of Learnable Intelligence.* New York: Free Press, 1995.

Perkins, D. "What is Understanding?" In M. S. Wiske (ed.), *Teaching for Understanding: Linking Research with Practice.* San Francisco: Jossey-Bass, 1998.

Perry, W. G., Jr. *Forms of Intellectual and Ethical Development in the College Years: A Scheme.* Austin, Tex.: Holt, Rinehart and Winston, 1970.

Pike, G. R. "A Student Success Story: Freshman Interest Groups at the University of Missouri-Columbia." Columbia, Mo.: Student Life Studies Abstracts, *1*, 1996.

Policy Center on the First Year of College. *Second National Survey of First-Year Academic Practices, 2002*. Brevard, N.C.: Brevard College, 2002. [http://www.brevard.edu/fyc/Survey2002/index.htem].

Project Kaleidoscope. *Report on the Reports—Recommendations for Action in Support of Undergraduate Science, Technology, Engineering, and Mathematics*. Washington, D.C.: Project Kaleidoscope, 2002.

Project on Strong Foundations for General Education. *Strong Foundations: Twelve Principles for Effective General Education Program*. Washington, D.C.: Association of American Colleges and Universities, 1994.

Putnam, R. D. *Bowling Alone: The Collapse and Revival of American Community*. New York: Simon and Schuster, 2000.

Quartz, S., and Sejnowski, T. *Liars, Lovers, and Heroes: What the New Brain Science Tells Us About How We Become Who We Are*. New York: William Morrow, 2002.

Raftery, S., and Van Wagoner, R. "Learning Abstract: Using Learning Communities to Develop Basic Skills." League for Innovation in the Community College, 2002. [http://www.league.org/publication/abstracts/learning/lelabs0902.htm].

Raisman, N. "Creating Philosopher-Bricklayers: Redefining General Education and the Liberal Arts." *Community, Technical and Junior College Journal*, 1991–92, *62*(3), 16–20.

Raisman, N. (ed.). *Directing General Education Outcomes*. New Directions for Community Colleges, no. 81. San Francisco: Jossey-Bass, 1993a.

Raisman, N. "The *de facto* State of General Education." In N. Raisman (ed.), *Directing General Education Outcomes*. New Directions for Community Colleges, no. 81. San Francisco: Jossey-Bass, 1993b.

Ramsden, P. *Learning to Teach in Higher Education*. New York: Routledge, 1992.

Ratcliff, J., and Associates. *Realizing the Potential: Improving Postsecondary Teaching, Learning and Assessment*. University Park, Pa.: National Center on Postsecondary Teaching, Learning, and Assessment, 1996.

Ratcliff, J., Johnson, D. K., La Nassa, S., and Gaff, J. *The Status of General Education in the Year 2000: Summary of a National Survey*. Washington, D.C.: Association of American Colleges and Universities, 2001.

Reardon, M., and Ramaley, J. "Building Community While Containing Costs." In J. Gaff, J. Ratcliff, and Associates (eds.), *Handbook of the Undergraduate Curriculum*. San Francisco: Jossey-Bass, 1997.

Reinventing Undergraduate Education: Three Years After the Boyer Report. Stony Brook: Reinvention Center, State University of New York, 2001.

Reitano, J. "CUNY's Community Colleges: Democratic Education on Trial." In R. C. Bowen and G. H. Muller (eds.), *Gateways to Democracy: Six Urban Community College Systems.* New Directions for Community Colleges, no. 107, San Francisco: Jossey-Bass, 1999.

Rendón, L. I. "Validating Culturally Diverse Students: Toward a New Model of Learning and Student Development." *Innovative Higher Education,* 1994, *1,* 34.

Rendón, L. I. "Facilitating Retention and Transfer for First Generation Students in Community Colleges." Paper presented at the New Mexico Institute Rural Community College Initiative, Espanola, New Mexico, Mar. 1, 1995. (ERIC 383 369)

Rendón, L. I., and Hope, R. O. "An Educational System in Crisis." In L. A. Rendón and R. O. Hope (eds.), *Educating a New Majority: Transforming America's Educational System for Diversity.* San Francisco: Jossey-Bass, 1996.

Renner, K. E. "Racial Equity and Higher Education," *Academe,* Jan.-Feb. 2003, *89*(1), 38–43.

Rings, S., Shovers, B., Skinner, E., and Siefer, N. "Learning Communities in the Maricopa Community Colleges: A Faculty-Driven Initiative Moving Toward District Impact." In J. MacGregor (ed.), *Strengthening Learning Communities: Case Studies from the National Learning Communities (FIPSE) Dissemination Project.* Olympia, Wash.: The Evergreen State College, 1999.

Rogers, E. M. *Diffusion of Innovations* (4th ed.). New York: Free Press, 1995.

Ross, F., Sr., *Axioms for Organizers.* San Francisco: Neighbor to Neighbor Education Fund, 1989.

Roueche, J. E., and Roueche, S. D. *High Stakes, High Performance: Making Remedial Education Work.* Washington, D.C.: Community College Press, 1999.

Ruhl, K. L., Hughes, C. A., and Schloss, P. J. "Using the Pause Procedure to Enhance Lecture Recall." *Teacher Education and Special Education,* 1987, *10*(1), 14–18.

Russ-Eft, D., and Preskill, H. *Evaluation in Organizations: A Systematic Approach to Enhancing Learning, Performance and Change.* Cambridge, Mass.: Basic Books/Perseus Publishing, 2001.

Rye, A. "The Impact of Teaching in Coordinated Studies Programs on Personal, Social and Professional Development of Community College Faculty." Unpublished doctoral dissertation, Oregon State University, 1997.

Sanderson, A., Phau, V. C., and Herda, D. *The American Faculty Poll*. Chicago: National Opinion Research Center, 2000.

Sax, L. J., and others. *Designing an Assessment of the First College Year: Results from the 1999–2000 Pilot Study*. Brevard, N.C.: Brevard College, Policy Center on the First Year of College, 2000.

SCANS Commission (Secretary's Commission on Achieving Necessary Skills), U.S. Department of Labor. *Learning a Living: A Blueprint for High Performance*. Baltimore: The Johns Hopkins Institute for Policy Studies, 2000, and Washington, D.C.: U.S. Government Printing Office, 1991.

Schilling, K., and Schilling, K. "Increasing Expectations for Student Effort." *About Campus*, May-June 1999, *4*(2), 4–10.

Schneider, C. G., and Shoenberg, R. "Habits Hard to Break: How Persistent Features of Campus Life Frustrate Curricular Reform." *Change*, 1999, *31*(2), 30–35.

Schoem, D. "Sustaining Living Learning Programs." In J. L. Laufgraben and N. Shapiro (eds.), *Learning Communities in Context: A Practical Guide to Sustaining Change, Expanding Support, and Improving Programs*. San Francisco: Jossey-Bass, 2004.

Schoem, D., Frankel, L., Zuniga, X., and Lewis, E. A. (eds.), *Multicultural Teaching in the University*. Westport, Conn.: Praeger, 1993.

Schoem, D., and Hurtado, S. *Intergroup Dialogue: Deliberative Democracy in School, College Community and Workplace*. Ann Arbor: University of Michigan Press, 2001.

Schoem, D., and Pasque, P. A. "Learning for the Common Good: A Diverse Learning Community Lives and Learns Together in the Michigan Community Scholars Program." In C. Schroeder and G. Kuh, "How Are We Doing at Engaging Students?" *About Campus*, 2003, *8*(1), 9–16.

Schön, D. *The Reflective Practitioner: How Professionals Think in Action*. London: Temple Smith, 1983.

Schön, D. *Educating the Reflective Practitioner: Toward a New Design for Teaching and Learning in the Professions*. San Francisco: Jossey-Bass, 1987.

Schroeder, C. C., and Hurst, J. C. "Designing Learning Environments that Integrate Curricular and Co-curricular Experiences." *Journal of College Student Development*, 1996, *37*(2), 174–181.

Schuster, J., and Finkelstein, M. *The American Faculty*. Baltimore: Johns Hopkins Press, forthcoming.

Schwartz, D. L., and Bransford, J. D. "A Time for Telling." *Cognition and Instruction*, 1998, *16*(4), 475–522.

Scriven, M. "Types of Evaluation and Types of Evaluator." *Evaluation Practice*, 1996, *17*(2), 151–162.

Selingo, J. "States Seek to Stiffen Their Admissions Standards." *Academe Today: The Chronicle of Education's Daily Report for Subscribers,* Jan. 25, 2002. [http://chronicle.com/weekly/48/i20/20a02201.htm]

Senge, P. *The Fifth Discipline.* New York: Doubleday, 1990.

Senge, P. "The Academy as Learning Community: Contradictions in Terms of Realizable Future?" In A. Lucas (ed.), *Leading Academic Change.* San Francisco: Jossey-Bass, 2000.

Senge, P. M., and Kleiner, A. (eds.), *The Fifth Discipline Fieldbook.* New York: Doubleday, 1994.

Sevier, R. A. *Integrated Marketing for College, Universities, and Schools.* Washington, D.C.: Council for the Advancement and Support of Education, 1998.

Seymour, E. "Tracking the Process of Change in U.S. Undergraduate Education in Science, Mathematics, Engineering, and Technology." *Science Education,* 2001, *86,* 79–105.

Seymour, E., and Hewitt, N. M. *Talking About Leaving: Why Undergraduates Leave the Sciences.* Boulder, Colo.: Westview Press, 1997.

Shapiro, N. S., and Levine, J. *Creating Learning Communities.* San Francisco: Jossey-Bass, 1999.

Shavelson, R. J., and Huang, L. "Responding Responsibly to the Frenzy to Assess Learning in Higher Education." *Change,* 2003, *34*(1), 10–19.

Shepard, L. A. "The Role of Assessment in a Learning Culture." *Educational Researcher,* 2000, *29*(7), 4–14.

Sherman, J., and others. *Comparative Indicators of Education in the United State and Other G9 Countries: 2002* (NCES 2003–026). Washington, D.C.: U.S. Department of Education, National Center for Education Statistics, 2003.

Shoenberg, R., and others. *General Education in an Age of Student Mobility.* Washington, D.C.: Association of American Colleges and Universities, 2001.

Shulman, L. S. "Teaching as Community Property: Putting an End to Pedagogical Solitude." *Change,* 1993, *26*(6), 6–7.

Shulman, L. S. "Making Differences: A Table of Learning." *Change,* 2002, *34*(6), 36–45.

Smilkstein, R. "Ask Them: Assessing What Students Already Know." In *Assessment in and of Collaborative Learning: A Handbook of Strategies.* Olympia: The Evergreen State College, Washington Center for Improving the Quality of Undergraduate Education, 1995. [http://learningcommons.evergreen.edu/]

Smith, B. L. "The Washington Center: A Grassroots Approach to Faculty Development and Curriculum Reform." *To Improve the Academy,* 1988, *7,* 165–177.

Smith, B. L. "Revitalizing Senior Faculty through Statewide Initiatives." In M. J. Finkelstein and M. LaCeller-Peterson (eds.), *Developing Senior Faculty as Teachers.* New Directions for Teaching and Learning, no. 55. San Francisco: Jossey-Bass, 1993.

Smith, B. L. "Team Teaching Methods." In K. Prichard and R. M. Sawyer (eds.), *Handbook of College Teaching.* Westport, Conn.: Greenwood Press, 1994.

Smith, B. L. "The Challenge of Learning Communities as a Growing National Movement." *Peer Review,* 2001a, 3/4(4/1), 4–8.

Smith, B. L. "Learning Communities: Creating a Convergence Zone for Education Reform." In B. L. Smith and J. McCann (eds.), *Reinventing Ourselves: Interdisciplinary Education, Collaborative Learning and Experimentation in Higher Education.* Bolton, Mass.: Anker Press, 2001b.

Smith, B. L. "Learning Communities and Liberal Education." *Academe,* 2003, 89(1), 14–18.

Smith, B. L. "Beyond the Revolving Door: Learning Communities and Changes in the First Two Years of College." In R. Kazis, J. Vargas, and N. Hoffman (eds.), *Doubling the Numbers: State Policies to Promote Postsecondary Attainment for Underrepresented Youth.* Cambridge, Mass.: Harvard Publishing Group, 2004.

Smith, B. L., and MacGregor, J. "Reflective Interviews with Learning Community Teaching Teams: Strengthening Dialogue About Teaching and Learning." *Washington Center News,* 1991, 6(1), 26–28.

Smith, B. L., and MacGregor, J. "What Is Collaborative Learning?" In A. S. Goodsell, A. M. Maher, and V. Tinto (eds.), *Collaborative Learning: A Sourcebook for Higher Education.* University Park: The Pennsylvania State University: National Center on Postsecondary Teaching, Learning, and Assessment, 1992.

Smith, B. L., and McCann, J. (eds.). *Reinventing Ourselves.* Bolton, Mass.: Anker Press, 2001.

Smith, D., and Associates. *Diversity Works: The Emerging Picture of How Students Benefit.* Washington, D.C.: Association of American Colleges and Universities, 1997.

Smith, D., and Associates. *A Diversity Research Agenda.* Washington, D.C.: Association of American Colleges and Universities, 2000.

Smith, R. "Changing the Institutional Culture for First-Year Students and Those Who Teach Them." *About Campus,* 2003, 8(1), 3–8.

Sorcinelli, M. D. "Ten Principles of Good Practice in Creating and Sustaining Teaching and Learning Centers." In K. H. Gillespie, L. R. Hilsen, and E. C. Wadsworth (eds.), *A Guide to Faculty Development: Practical Advice, Examples, and Resources.* Bolton, Mass.: Anker, 2002.

Spear, K., and others. *Learning Communities and Liberal Arts Colleges.* National Learning Communities Project Monograph Series. Olympia: The Evergreen State College, Washington Center for Improving the Quality of Undergraduate Education in cooperation with the American Association for Higher Education, 2003.

Spencer, M. "Triads at Texas A&M University-Corpus Christi: A Core Curriculum Commitment to Freshmen." In J. MacGregor (comp.), *Strengthening Learning Communities: Case Studies from the National Learning Communities Dissemination Project (FIPSE).* Olympia: The Evergreen State College, Washington Center for Improving the Quality of Undergraduate Education, 1999.

Stake, R. *The Art of Case Research.* Thousand Oaks, Calif.: Sage Publications, 1995.

Stassen, M.L.A. "Student Outcomes: The Impact of Varying Living-Learning Community Models." *Research in Higher Education,* 2003, 44(5), 561–613.

Stearns, P. "General Education: Revisited, Again." *Liberal Education,* 2002, 88(1), 42–47.

Steen, L. A. (ed.). *Why Numbers Count: Quantitative Literacy for Tomorrow's America.* Washington, D.C.: The College Board, 1997.

Study Group on the Conditions of Excellence in Higher Education, *Involvement in Learning: Realizing the Potential of Higher Education.* Washington, D.C.: National Institute of Education, 1984.

Sullivan, W. M. "The University as Citizen: Institutional Identity and Social Responsibility." Washington, D.C.: Council on Public Policy Education, n.d. [http://www.publicpolicy-educouncil.org/publications_program/iisr.html]

Tagg, J. *The Learning Paradigm College.* Bolton, Mass.: Anker Press, 2003.

Taylor, K., Moore, W. S., MacGregor, J., and Lindblad, J. *Learning Community Research and Assessment: What We Know Now.* National Learning Communities Project Monograph Series. Olympia: The Evergreen State College, Washington Center for Improving the Quality of Under-graduate Education in cooperation with the American Association for Higher Education, 2003.

Taylor, M. *Colorado College: Memories and Reflections.* Colorado Springs, Colo.: Colorado College, 1999.

"Teach a Person to Fish: Spokane Falls Community College's Paired Biology and Study Skills Class." *Washington Center News,* 1994, 8(2), 8–10.

Terenzini, P. T. "Collaboration: The Key to Visible and Credible Assessment Efforts." In R. L. Swing (ed.), *Proving and Improving: Strategies for Assessing the First College Year.* Monograph No. 33. Columbia: National Resource Center for the First-Year Experience and Students in Transition, University of South Carolina, 2001.

Terenzini, P. T., and Pascarella, E. T. " Living with Myths: Undergraduate Education in America." *Change*, 1994, *26*(1), 28–32.

Tierney, W. G. "The College Experience of Native Americans: A Critical Analysis." In L. Weis and M. Fine (eds.), *Beyond Silenced Voices: Class, Race and Gender in United States Schools*. Albany: State University of New York Press, 1993.

Tierney, W. G. "Overcoming Obstacles to Reform." *About Campus*, 2001, *6*(2), 20–24.

Tierney, W. G., Colyar, J. E., and Corwin, Z. B. *Preparing for College: Building Expectations, Changing Realities*. Los Angeles: Center for Higher Education Policy Analysis, University of Southern California, 2003.

Tinto, V. *Leaving College: Rethinking the Causes and Cures for Student Attrition*. Chicago: University of Chicago Press, 1987.

Tinto, V. "Classrooms as Communities: Exploring the Educational Character of Student Persistence." *Journal of Higher Education*, 1997, *68*(6), 599–623.

Tinto, V. "Learning Communities and the Reconstruction of Remedial Education in Higher Education." Keynote speech at the Conference on Replacing Remediation in Higher Education, jointly sponsored by the Ford Foundation and the United States Department of Education, Stanford University, Stanford, Calif., 1998.

Tinto, V. "Taking Retention Seriously: Rethinking the First Year of College." *NACADA Journal*, 2000, *19*(2), 5–10.

Tinto, V. *Learning Better Together: The Impact of Learning Communities on Student Success*. Syracuse, N.Y.: Higher Education Program, Syracuse University, 2002. [http://soeweb.syr.edu/faculty/Vtinto/index.html].

Tinto, V., and Goodsell, A. *A Longitudinal Study of Freshman Interest Groups at the University of Washington*. University Park, Pa.: National Center on Postsecondary Teaching, Learning, and Assessment, 1993a.

Tinto, V., and Goodsell, A. *Freshman Interest Groups and the First Year Experience: Constructing Student Communities in a Large University*. (ED 358 778). University Park, Pa.: National Center on Postsecondary Teaching, Learning, and Assessment, 1993b.

Tinto, V., Goodsell, A., and Russo, P. *Building Learning Communities for New College Students*. University Park: National Center on Postsecondary Teaching, Learning, and Assessment, The Pennsylvania State University, 1994.

Tinto, V., Goodsell-Love, A., and Russo, P. "Building Community." *Liberal Education*, Fall 1993, *79*(4), 16–21.

Tokuno, K. "Long-Term and Recent Student Outcomes of the Freshman Interest Group Program." *Journal of the Freshman Year Experience*, 1993, *5*(2), 7–28.

Tokuno, K., and Campbell, F. "The Freshman Interest Group Program at the University of Washington: Effects on Retention and Scholarship." *Journal of the Freshman Year Experience,* 1992, 4(1), 7–22.

Tollefson, G. "Collaborative Learning Communities in Washington Community Colleges." Unpublished doctoral dissertation, Seattle University, 1990.

Tommerup, P. "Adhocratic Traditions, Experience Narratives, and Personal Transformation: An Ethnographic Study of the Organizational Culture and Folklore of The Evergreen State College, an Innovative Liberal Arts College." Unpublished doctoral dissertation, University of California, Los Angeles, 1993.

Treisman, U. "Studying Students Studying Calculus: A Look at the Lives of Minority Mathematics Students in College." *College Mathematics Journal,* 1992, 23(5), 362–372.

Trow, K. "The Experimental College Program in Retrospect: An Exploratory Study." Unpublished manuscript, July 1987.

Trow, K. *Habits of Mind: The Experimental College Program at Berkeley.* Berkeley: Institute of Governmental Studies Press, University of California, 1998.

Tussman, J. *Experiment at Berkeley.* London: Oxford University Press, 1969.

Tussman, J. *The Beleaguered College.* Berkeley: Institute of Governmental Studies Press, University of California, 1997.

Twigg, C. "Improving Learning and Reducing Costs: Redesigning Large-Enrollment Courses." [www.center.rpi.edu/PewSymp/mono.html]. n.d.

Twigg, C. "Improving Quality and Reducing Cost." *Change,* 2003, 35(4), 22–29.

United States Department of Education, National Commission on Excellence in Education. *A Nation at Risk: The Imperative for Educational Reform.* Washington, D.C.: U.S. Government Printing Office, 1983.

Upcraft, M. L., Gardner, J., and Associates. *The Freshman Year Experience.* San Francisco: Jossey-Bass, 1989.

Upcraft, M. L., and Schuh, J. H. "Assessment Versus Research: Why We Should Care About the Difference." *About Campus,* 2002, 7(1), 16–20.

Van Gennep, A. *The Rites of Passage.* (M. Viedon and G. Caffee, trans.). Chicago: University of Chicago Press, 1960.

Van Slyck, P. "Repositioning Ourselves in the Contact Zone." *College English,* 1997, 59(2), 149–170.

Vygotsky, L. S. *Mind in Society: The Development of Higher Psychological Processes.* Cambridge, Mass.: Harvard University Press, 1978.

Waluconis, C. "Student Self-Evaluation: Outcomes as Learning." Unpublished paper, Seattle Central Community College, 1993.

Walvoord, B. E., and Anderson, V. J. *Effective Grading: A Tool for Learning and Assessment.* San Francisco: Jossey-Bass, 1998.

Wellman, J. V. *Weathering the Double Whammy: How Governing Boards Can Negotiate a Volatile Economy and Shifting Enrollments.* Washington, D.C.: Association of Governing Boards, 2003.

Wenger, E. *Communities of Practice: Learning, Meaning, and Identity.* Cambridge, England: Cambridge University Press, 1998.

Wenger, E., McDermott, R., and Snyder, W. M. *Cultivating Communities of Practice.* Cambridge, Mass.: Harvard Business School Press, 2002.

White, K. "Midcourse Adjustments: Using Small Group Instructional Diagnosis to Improve Teaching and Learning." *Washington Center News,* 1991, 6(1), 20–22.

Whitehead, A. N. *The Aims of Education and Other Essays.* New York: Mentor Books, 1949. (Originally published in 1929.)

Whitman, N. A. *Peer Teaching: To Teach Is to Learn Twice.* ASHE-ERIC Higher Education Reports, no. 4. San Francisco: Jossey-Bass, 1988.

Whyte, W. F. (ed.). *Participatory Action Research.* Thousand Oaks, Calif.: Sage Publications, 1991.

Wiggins, G. *Educative Assessment: Designing Assessments to Inform and Improve Student Performance.* San Francisco: Jossey-Bass, 1998.

Wiggins, G., and McTighe, J. *Understanding by Design.* Englewood Cliffs, N.J.: Merrill/Prentice-Hall, 1998.

Wilkie, G. *North Seattle Community College Learning Community Enrollment Study.* 1986–1990. Seattle: North Seattle Community College, 1990.

Wiske, M. S. (ed.), *Teaching for Understanding: Linking Research with Practice.* San Francisco: Jossey-Bass, 1998.

Wlodkowski, R. J., and Ginsberg, M. B. *Diversity and Motivation: Culturally Responsive Teaching.* San Francisco: Jossey-Bass, 1995.

Wyche-Smith, S. "Everything You Wanted to Know About Your Students' Response to Class, But Were Afraid to Ask—Inkshedding." In *Assessment in and of Collaborative Learning: A Handbook of Strategies.* Olympia: The Evergreen State College, Washington Center for Improving the Quality of Undergraduate Education, 1995.

Zlotkowski, E. "A New Voice at the Table? Linking Service Learning and the Academy." *Change,* 1996, 28(1), 20–27.

Zlotkowski, E. (ed.). *Successful Service-Learning Programs: New Models of Excellence in Higher Education.* Bolton, Mass.: Anker Press, 1998.

Zlotkowski, E., and Williams, D. "The Faculty Role in Civic Engagement." *Peer Review,* 2003, 5(3), 9–11.

Zull, J. E. *The Art of Changing the Brain: Enriching the Practice of Teaching by Exploring the Biology of Learning.* Sterling, Va.: Stylus, 2002.

NOTES

CHAPTER TWO

1. We are grateful to Robert Frase, Harold November, and Emanuel Lerner for their comments on an early draft of this chapter. These Meiklejohn alumni provided valuable insights into the lived experience of being students in the Experimental College.

2. Adam Nelson, in *Education and Democracy: The Meaning of Alexander Meiklejohn, 1872–1964* (2001), provides an excellent intellectual biography.

3. In *Education and Democracy,* Nelson describes new ventures at Reed, Swarthmore, Sarah Lawrence, Rollins College, Deep Springs, the Claremont Colleges, Bennington, Black Mountain, and the all-black Atlanta Consortium. See also Steven Coleman's chapter, "Dangerous Outposts," in *Reinventing Ourselves* (2001). Many of these innovations involved honors students or special populations, but Meiklejohn's interests were in serving a cross section of the student body. Freshman seminars also emerged in this era as a response to residence life.

4. For an account of their disputes see Nelson, *Education and Democracy.*

5. See Alexander Meiklejohn, "A New College: Notes on a Next Step in Higher Education" (1925), which called for an integrated general education program. This program closely resembled what would become the Experimental College.

6. See Cronon and Jenkins (1994) and Nelson (2001) for excellent histories of the Experimental College. The reprinted version (2000) of Meiklejohn's 1932 synopsis of the Experimental College remains the authoritative source on its rationale and how it was organized. Unfortunately, no one has yet done a detailed study of the educational approach by looking at the original work of the students, which is available in the University of Wisconsin archives.

7. Technically not a learning community in the sense of linked courses over a single semester, the integrated liberal studies program offers a horizontal learning community through a sequence of related courses. ILS was established in 1948, in part because of the efforts of Experimental College

faculty member William Agard. It was not set up as a separate unit, instead relying on senior tenured faculty borrowed from departments. This administrative arrangement helped it avoid many of the conflicts that had plagued the Experimental College. The ILS program fell on hard times in the 1970s but was reborn in the early 1980s. It now offers popular interdisciplinary courses on Western thought from its classic origins to contemporary times to literally thousands of university students, as well as a certificate program for a small number of students who wish to complete twenty-one prescribed credits and a senior integrating seminar (Robert Fowler, personal communication with the authors, 2001).

8. For an account of the Colorado program see Robert Loevy, *Colorado College: A Place of Learning* (1999), and Maxwell F. Taylor, *Colorado College: Memories and Reflection* (1999).

9. There is an ongoing two-year program at Malaspina College in British Columbia, Canada, and the first year program called Arts One at the University of British Columbia. Both Canadian programs are more than twenty-five years old and thriving today. Arts One grew out of dissatisfaction with the undergraduate curriculum. It was initiated in 1967 by Robert Rowan, a student of Tussman and a political philosopher. The program adopted the coordinated studies format of team teaching, using primary texts, and seminars. Tussman came to UBC a number of times to visit the program in its early years.

10. For a detailed account of the founding of the Hutchins School, see Adler, 2001, and Olson, n.d.

11. See Esperian, Hill, and MacGregor, 1986, for a comprehensive unpublished bibliography on the federated learning community model.

12. Hill, 1975, is the most developed argument of this point.

CHAPTER THREE

1. We should note that in our first book on learning communities (Gabelnick, MacGregor, Matthews, and Smith, 1990), we presented five different models for learning communities, which reflected the most common structures in use at that time. For the sake of simplification here, we have collapsed the five into three.

2. Other scholars involved with learning communities have invented different typologies altogether. Noted community college researcher Norton Grubb (Grubb and Associates, 1999) categorizes learning communities according to their overall intentions: (1) learning communities that attempt to

address a problem (such as the high rate of failure in a basic biology course); (2) learning communities that create multidisciplinary approaches to general education; and (3) learning communities designed to meet the needs of a particular group of students (such as evening programs for older, working adults). In her research on the benefits of living-learning programs at University of Massachusetts-Amherst, Martha Stassen offers another way to categorize learning communities that expands on an earlier framework offered by Anne Love and Kenneth Tokuno (1999). Stassen (2003) uses six dimensions that learning communities aim to foster—student collaboration, faculty collaboration, curricular coordination, a shared setting, group identity, and interactive pedagogy—and indicates that these dimensions are developed to varying degrees "from low to high focus" in any learning community program.

CHAPTER FOUR

1. An excellent discussion of teacher and student roles in collaborative learn-ing settings can be found in Donald Finkel and Stephen Monk's article "Teachers and Learning Groups: Dissolution of the Atlas Complex" (1983).

2. Several useful texts on pedagogical practices that support diverse learners include Robert Ibarra's *Beyond Affirmative Action: Reframing the Context of Higher Education* (2001), Raymond Wlodkowski and Margery Ginsberg's *Diversity and Motivation: Culturally Responsive Teaching* (1995), and *Multicultural Teaching in the University,* edited by D. Schoem, L. Frankel, X. Zuniga, and E. A. Lewis (1993).

CHAPTER SIX

1. Gail Bakst-Jarrett, Director of Financial Aid at LaGuardia Community Col-lege, and Sherwood Johnson, Director of Financial Aid at Brooklyn College, provided information and resources for this section of the chapter.

2. Such programs include the federally funded TRIO (which funds, among others, Upward Bound and Student Success programs for students who meet one or more of several "at-risk factors," such as being a first-generation college student and coming from a family whose income is below the poverty line), Educational Opportunity Programs (EOP), and Higher Education Opportunity Programs (HEOP). At CUNY, programs include Search for Education, Elevation, and Knowledge (SEEK) and College Discovery (CD).

3. This material was adapted from "Learning Communities: Collaborative Approaches to Engaging Differences" (Matthews and Lynch, 1997).

4. In 2002 the Lumina Foundation for Education awarded Vince Tinto and his colleagues in the higher education program at the School of Education at Syracuse University a multi-year grant to study learning communities for underprepared students in two- and four-year colleges. The Learning Community Project will study twenty campuses, ten two-year and ten four-year, and develop case studies of four or five. As the announcement of the project pointed out, an important outcome from both an educational and policy perspective will be "its ability to provide convincing evidence to a national audience about programs that work in addressing the needs of at-risk students in higher education."

CHAPTER SEVEN

1. For informative discussions of student understanding, see Perkins, 1998, and Wiggins and McTighe, 1998.

2. In learning community programs, the nationally available questionnaires that have been most widely used are the following:

National Survey of Student Engagement (NSSE) [http://www.indiana.edu/~nsse/] and its counterpart, the Community College Survey of Student Engagement (CCSSE) [http://www.ccsse.org/]

College Student Experiences Questionnaire (CSEQ) and the College Student Experiences Questionnaire (CSXQ) [http://www.indiana.edu/~cseq/] and their counterpart, the Community College Student Experiences Questionnaire (CCSEQ) [http://www.people.memphis.edu/~coe_cshe]

Student Satisfaction Inventory—a variety of versions are available from the consulting firm, Noel Levitz [http://www.noellevitz.com/]

Your First College Year [http://www.gseis.ucla.edu/heri/yfcy/]

College Student Survey associated with the Cooperative Institutional Research Program (CIRP) [http://www.gseis.ucla.edu/heri/css.html]

NAME INDEX

A

Adelman, C., 6, 139, 181, 201
Adler, L., 169
Alexander, C., 67, 69
Allen, J., 222
Alverno College Faculty, 124, 224
American Association of Community
    Colleges, 11
Anderson, J., 110
Anderson, L. W., 114
Anderson, V. J., 124
Angelo, T. A., 14, 224, 239
Anthony, S., 237
Argyris, C., 223, 229
Association of American Colleges and
    Universities, 11, 57, 110–111, 115
Astin, A., 48, 58, 99, 131, 141, 171,
    172, 224, 251, 273
Avens, C., 258

B

Babbitt, M., 207, 208, 209
Barber, R. N., 103
Barefoot, B. O., 94
Barr, R., 12, 282
Barrett, K., 238
Bartlett, T., 188
Baxter Magolda, M. B., 224
Bekey, J., 241
Belenky, M., 27, 111, 121, 223
Bellah, R. N., 103
Bennett, J., 148
Bergquist, W., 273, 275
Bjork, R. A., 121
Bloom, L., 114

Bonwell, C. C., 120
Boyer, E., 115, 225
Bransford, J. D., 27, 113, 118, 121,
    125, 223
Bresciani, M. J., 222
Brookfield, S. D., 102
Brower, A., 327
Brown, A. L., 27, 113, 118, 125, 223
Brown, B., 89
Brown, C. S., 31
Brown, J. S., 13, 119
Bruffee, K., 20, 100–102, 119, 223
Bruner, J., 223
Bystrom, V. A., 89, 266

C

Cadwallader, M., 28, 36, 43, 45
Callan, P. M., 22
Campbell, F., 151
Candy, P. C., 223
Cedarblom, J., 164
Chickering, A., 117, 224
Chilemsky, E., 223
Chudowsky, N., 126
Clark, D. J., 241
Clinchy, B., 27, 111, 121
Cocking, R. R., 23, 27, 113, 118, 223
Cole, R. S., 237
Collins, A., 13, 119
Colyar, J. E., 111
Cook, M. D., 227, 264, 326
Cooper, J. L., 102, 120
Coover, V., 242
Cornwell, G., 89, 90, 116, 128, 168,
    264, 293

Cornwell, R., 90
Corwin, Z. B., 111
Cottell, P. G., Jr., 102
Council on Aid to Education, 17
Cousins, J. B., 229
Cronon, E. D., 29
Cross, K. P., 14, 20–21, 175, 177, 178, 224, 225, 239
Csikszentmihalyi, M., 268, 343
Cuban, L., 62

D

Damon, W., 268, 343
Davidson, N., 102
Davis, J. R., 116
de Winstanley, P. A., 121
Della-Piana, C. K., 110, 205
Dewey, J., 24, 25–26
Doherty, P., 160, 161
Downing, S., 177
Dressel, P., 112
Duguid, P., 13, 119
Dutcher, J., 279
Dwyer, T., 144, 145

E

Earl, L. E., 229
Eaton, M., 90, 154, 243
Ebbers, L., 91
Eby, K., 89
Eckel, P., 339
Edgerton, B., 161
Edmonds, C., 154
Educational Testing Service, 17
Eison, J. A., 120
Elbow, P., 279
El-Khawas, E., 221
Ellertson, S., 227, 264, 326
Elmore, R., 94, 298, 337–338
Endicott, P., 160, 161, 264
Entwistle, N., 113–114, 223
Epperson, D. L., 227, 264, 326

Estrich, S., 176
Ewell, P., 6, 14, 15, 16, 17, 23, 139, 221, 222
Eyler, J., 103
Eynon, G., 112

F

Ferren, A., 17–18, 325
Fink, L. D., 232, 235
Finkel, D., 27, 102, 121
Finkelstein, M. J., 8, 120, 270, 271
Finlay, N. J., 89
Finney, J. E., 222
Flateby, T. L., 227
Fogarty, J., 154, 156
Frase, R., 30
Freed, J. E., 124, 224, 232, 235
Freire, P., 26
Fullilove, R. E., 109

G

Gabelnick, F., 334
Gaff, J., 34, 116, 134, 135, 136, 137, 164, 172
Gamson, Z., 49, 50, 117, 136
Gardiner, L. F., 13, 27, 58–59, 120, 141, 224
Gardner, H., 268, 343
Giles, D. E., 103
Gladwell, M., 62
Glaser, R., 126
Goldberger, N., 27, 111, 121, 223
Goodsell, A., 57, 150, 151, 194
Goodsell-Love, A., 273
Gordon, J. O., 144
Gordon, T., 151
Grant, G., 36
Greater Expectations, 6, 115, 133, 139, 175, 176, 215
Green, M., 339
Grubb, W. N., 106, 213–214, 282
Guarasci, R., 167

R

S

T

SUBJECT INDEX

A

Academic culture: authentic alignment in, 268–269; types of, 273–274

Academic disciplines, reforms based on, 14

Academic majors, and general education programs, 115, 136, 138–139

Academic restructuring: and academic appointments, 8; and faculty roles, 268–272

Access: and democratic ethos, 178; and educational resources, 17; to learning community programs, 60, 61; for underserved/underprepared students, 4, 107, 175–178

Accountability, and high-stakes testing, 220

Accreditation associations: and accountability, 221–222; and assessment arenas, 237

Active learning, 30, 117–123; assessment and, 124; context and issues in, 119; in lecture-centered classes, 120–121; across multiple classes, 118–119; rationale for, 117; students' new roles in, 122–123

Advisers, learning community role of, 304–305, 314–315

American Association for Higher Education (AAHE), 14, 297; Engaged Campus for a Diverse Democracy initiative of, 103; survey of chief academic officers, 271

American Association of State Colleges and Universities (AASCU), democracy project of, 103

Anza College, learning community project of, 60–61

Assessment: accountability and, 221–222; campus context of, 225–227; as core practice, 123–127; and critical self-reflection, 265–267; cycle, 227–229; design, 221, 229, 230–232; and educational reform, 14; embedded, 249–260, 316; of "enduring understanding," 232–234; and feedback, 230, 238–244, 263–265; formative in-class, 238–244, 257–258; and general education goals, 138; and higher education assessment, 219–220; inputs-environment-outputs (I-E-O) framework for, 251–253; institutional, 226; as learning, 123–124; in learning community programs, 168, 235–238, 244–267; mandates, 226; measures and instruments, 241–242, 253–259, 262–263; national standards for, 222; planning, 229–235; and process evaluation, 242; process and strategies, 229, 240–241, 253–260; and program evaluation concept, 223; reports, 261–263; research and, 224–225, 245–249; resources, 220, 221; results, sharing and

CREDITS

Chapter One, p. 3: Epigraph from William M. Sullivan, "The University as Citizen: Institutional Identity and Social Responsibility." Washington, D.C.: Council on Public Policy Education, n.d. [http://www.publicpolicy-educouncil.org/publications_program/iisr.html]. Used by permission.

Chapter Two, p. 24: Epigraph from Alexander Meiklejohn in C. S. Brown, (ed.), *Alexander Meiklejohn: Teacher of Freedom*. Berkeley: Meiklejohn Civil Liberties Institute, 1981, p. 20. Used by permission.

Chapter Two, pp. 37, 38, 41–42: Quotes from Joseph Tussman, *The Beleaguered College*. Berkeley: Institute of Governmental Studies Press, University of California, 1997.

Chapter Three, p. 67: Epigraph from Christopher Alexander and Associates, *A Pattern Language: Towns, Buildings, Construction*. New York: Oxford University Press, 1977, p. xiii.

Chapter Five, p. 131: Epigraph from Alexander Astin, "What Really Matters in College: Provocative Findings from a National Survey of Student Outcomes," *Perspectives*, 1992, 22(1), 23–46. Used by permission.

Chapter Five, pp. 136–137: List from Jerry Gaff, *General Education: The Changing Agenda*. Washington, D.C.: Association of American Colleges and Universities, 1999. Used by permission.

Chapter Six, pp. 175: Epigraph from *Greater Expectations: A New Vision for Learning as a Nation Goes to College*. Washington, D.C.: Association of American Colleges and Universities National Panel, 2002.

Chapter Six, pp. 208, 209: Material from M. Babbitt, "Making Writing Count in an ESL Learning Community." In I. Leki (ed.), *Academic Writing Programs*. Alexandria, Va.: Teachers of English to Speakers of Other

Languages, Inc., 2001. Used by permission. Permission conveyed through Copyright Clearance Center, Inc.

Chapter Six: Section on LaGuardia Community College's New Student House: A Model Basic Skills Learning Community adapted from R. S. Matthews and D. J. Lynch, "Learning Communities: Collaborative Approaches to Engaging Differences." In R. Guarasci, G. Cornwell, and others. (eds.), *Democratic Education in an Age of Difference: Redefining Citizenship in Higher Education*. San Francisco: Jossey-Bass, 1997. Copyright © 1997 by John Wiley & Sons, Inc. This material is used by permission of John Wiley & Sons, Inc.

Chapter Six: Material and list (p. 189) from J. E. Roueche and S. D. Roueche, *High Stakes, High Performance: Making Remedial Education Work*. Washington, D.C.: Community College Press, 1999. Used by permission.

Chapter Seven, pp. 219: Epigraph from Lorrie Shepard, "The Role of Assessment in a Learning Culture." *Educational Researcher*, 2000, 29(7), p. 10. Copyright © 2000 by the American Educational Research Association. Used by permission.

Chapter Seven, pp. 219: Epigraph from D. Halpern and M. Hakel, "Applying the Science of Learning to the University and Beyond: Teaching for Long-Term Retention and Transfer." *Change*, 2003, 35(4), 36–41.

Chapter Eight, pp. 268: Epigraph from John Tagg, *The Learning Paradigm College*. Bolton, Mass.: Anker Press, 2003. Used by permission.

Chapter Nine, pp. 300: Epigraph from Peter Senge, "The Academy as Learning Community: Contradictions in Terms of Realizable Future?" In A. Lucas (ed.), *Leading Academic Change*. San Francisco: Jossey-Bass, 2000. Copyright © 2000 by John Wiley & Sons, Inc. This material is used by permission of John Wiley & Sons, Inc.

Chapter Ten, pp. 333: Epigraph from Parker Palmer, *The Courage to Teach: Exploring the Inner Landscape of a Teacher's Life*. San Francisco: Jossey-Bass, 1998. Copyright © 1998 by John Wiley & Sons, Inc. This material is used by permission of John Wiley & Sons, Inc.